Quest for Identity

This book lays bare the reality of being an *adivasi* in India today and, beyond that, a woman in a globalising world, building commonalities with the author's own personal experiences and life trajectory. The lived experiences of Santal women and men are unfolded here along with the political and economic changes that took place after the creation of the Jharkhand state. Using ethnographic methods, the book weaves a multidimensional and multi-relational mosaic of lives and livelihoods, struggles for resources, gender identities and new narratives of citizenship. Ordinary people's everyday struggles for survival with dignity and respect form the core of the analysis. Rich in field insights, the gender lens adopted gives a fresh perspective to understanding issues of land and labour, indigenous identity, political aspirations and state relations. It contributes significantly to the slim literature on *adivasi* development in Jharkhand and fills a gap in knowledge on gender relations.

Nitya Rao is Professor of Gender and Development at the University of East Anglia, Norwich, and Director of the Norwich Institute for Sustainable Development. Her areas of interest are women's rights and gender justice, with a particular focus on food, nutrition, health and livelihood security. She has served on the Global Advisory Committee of the United Nations Girls' Education Initiative for over a decade. She is currently a member of the High Level Panel of Experts on Food Security and Nutrition to the Committee on World Food Security and of the Scientific Advisory Committee to the United Nations Food Systems Coordination Hub. She is the author of *'Good Women Do Not Inherit Land': Politics of Land and Gender in India* (2012).

Quest for Identity

Gender, Land and Migration
in Contemporary Jharkhand

Nitya Rao

Shaftesbury Road, Cambridge CB2 8EA, United Kingdom

One Liberty Plaza, 20th Floor, New York, NY 10006, USA

477 Williamstown Road, Port Melbourne, VIC 3207, Australia

314–321, 3rd Floor, Plot 3, Splendor Forum, Jasola District Centre, New Delhi – 110025, India

103 Penang Road, #05–06/07, Visioncrest Commercial, Singapore 238467

Cambridge University Press is part of Cambridge University Press & Assessment, a department of the University of Cambridge.

We share the University's mission to contribute to society through the pursuit of education, learning and research at the highest international levels of excellence.

www.cambridge.org
Information on this title: www.cambridge.org/9781009358002

First published 2023

Printed in India by Avantika Printers Pvt. Ltd.

A catalogue record for this publication is available from the British Library

ISBN 978-1-009-35800-2 Hardback

To Mina and M. S. Swaminathan, my parents,
who inspired me to speak for the voiceless

Contents

Part IV   Livelihoods and Well-Being

Part V   Policy and Politics

Part VI   Conclusion

Figures

Tables

Acknowledgements

This book recounts the everyday struggles and agency of poor women and men to lead dignified lives. Despite the multiple crises they confront, they seek not just welfare, but a renegotiation and even a redefinition of power and knowledge hierarchies across institutions of the state and society. Portrayed as voiceless, and in need of help, they want recognition and respect as individuals and to not be labelled as categories.

My personal and research journey over the past three decades is reflected in this book. Many have traversed this path with me, challenged me, inspired me and shaped my thinking along the way. More than all it is the women and men of the Santal Parganas, Jharkhand, who shared their lives and stories with me, who made me look at issues, from the perspective of their everyday struggles and relationships. Rather than research subjects, many of them are friends, equals, we respect each other's perspectives, despite differences in class and social position.

The chapters in this book were written at different periods over the last two decades. Numerous people and institutions have contributed to this research: the Friedrich Ebert Stiftung (Friedrich Ebert Foundation) and the non-governmental organisation (NGO) Adithi in the 1990s; the School of International Development at the University of East Anglia, which funded my PhD research; the Ministry of Rural Development and the NGO PRADAN (Professional Assistance for Development Action) for work on the legal frameworks in relation to land, water and forests in the newly created Jharkhand; the British Academy and the Department for International Development, United Kingdom (UK), in the 2000s; and, more recently, the UK government's Global Challenges Research Fund (GCRF). I am not able to thank each one of them individually here, but this cumulative support from a range of funding and research institutions with whom I have worked over the years has been invaluable in the making of this book.

I specifically wish to thank Anwesha Rana of Cambridge University Press for discussing the idea of this book with me several years ago. I started the work prior to the COVID-19 pandemic and was unable to progress during the pandemic due to both emotional and physical stress at work and home. I am grateful for her patience and understanding in keeping the project alive. Various people at the Press have been extremely helpful in the process of the book's production, and in particular I wish to thank Priyanka Das and Saniya Puri. I also thank all the journals, publishers and book editors for granting permission to republish articles in this book.

Over the past few years, I have been working with PRADAN in the Santal Parganas. The numerous young professionals working on the ground gave me inspiration to document this journey. I wish to thank Nivedita Narain for this partnership, Arundhita Bhanjdeo, Shuvojit Chakrabarty and many others for their enthusiasm, and the youth in the Santal Parganas looking to drive change, in terms of both research and carrying it forward into ground-level transformations.

Last but not least, I would like to thank Amit Mitra for visually documenting the processes of change in the Santal Parganas over the last two decades and for co-authoring two of the chapters in this book. I also thank Arundhita for sharing more contemporary photographs from the field and for research assistance for the final chapter. I am grateful to my family for being a source of strength and support during this period.

May 2023　　　　　　　　　　　　　　　　　　　　　　　Nitya Rao

Part I

Introduction

1

A Crisis of Reproduction

Gender, Land and Migration in Contemporary Jharkhand

This book collates papers I have written over the past twenty-five years based on intensive long-term engagement with the *adivasi* (mainly Santal) population of the Santal Parganas region of Jharkhand state. The main arguments presented in this book, while located within particular historical and political moments in the region, have global relevance across multiple disciplines, like development and gender studies and explorations of indigeneity and ecological change. The chapters in this book contribute to the production of knowledge in three broad areas.

First, they contribute to an improved understanding of gender as contextual, relational and dynamic, moving beyond the socially constructed roles and relationships between men and women. Such an understanding generates the need for reflexive methodologies that provide possibilities for studying relationships across space, time and institutional settings. Second, they seek to deepen our understanding of *adivasi* societies in relation to their ecological environment, especially their conceptualizations of land and labour, and how these ideologies feed into shaping unequal power relationships amongst themselves and with other groups. Third, they help us realise the importance of locating these dynamic relationships, whether at the level of the household or the community, and the interlocking of personal or individual, community and ecological needs and aspirations, within the changing political and economic context.

On 2 August 2000, the parliament approved the Bill for the reorganisation of Jharkhand as a separate state. Much has been written about the politics and governance of the newly established Jharkhand state and the continuities and changes in livelihoods. But analyses of gender roles and relations, and how these are affected by resource relations, livelihood transitions and the new narratives of citizenship, are missing from the discourse. This provided me the space to focus on the opportunities and the contradictions that have emerged in the new state, as aspirations of the state and its *adivasi* populations diverge – the former focusing on capitalist growth and the latter on the control over natural resources.

Methodologically, my approach combines historical and ethnographic methods from a feminist epistemological lens. I combine early insights on gender, indigeneity and ecology from colonial archival records like the land revenue settlement records of the early twentieth century with life history narratives from the post-independence years to the present. The land records largely exclude women in line with colonial constructions of the man as the 'head of household'. I triangulate and challenge such narratives through ethnographic fieldwork, focusing particularly on the perspectives of Santal women on their own life-course transitions, combined with a study of court records, interviews with village leaders, lawyers, politicians, missionaries and civil society activists (see Chapter 2).

The chapters reflect a temporality of my own research over the past two decades. As the political, economic and social contexts changed, so did women's experiences and the choices and crises they confronted. Sheila, a teenager when I first met her in a remote, hilly village of the district, eloped with Prakash, a mason working on the road being constructed nearby. She sought love, security and a better life in the plains. Confronted, however, with drunkenness and violence, hard work remained central to her existence. She negotiated with Prakash to move from the village to the district headquarters, Dumka, where she found work as a cook in a government school. She also started gardening on a plot of land near their home, using her farming skills and intelligence to support her children and reproduce her household. Chronology here is critical for telling the story of gendered change and the workings of power and agency over time.

My broader quest for gender and wider social equality and justice, emerging from my involvement with communities, especially women amongst them, their everyday lives and well-being, as a researcher, advocate and friend over the past three decades has shaped the scope and structure of the book. A deep understanding of the mutual relationships between land and labour – the primary means of production – analysing them within a relational framework, rather than as discrete themes, has contributed to the evolution of my own personal, intellectual and methodological journey. While the Santals are the largest *adivasi* group in Jharkhand today, they are by no means the majority, even in the Santal Parganas. My primary focus in this book, however, remains the experiences of the Santals, and their strategies for survival and securing a life of dignity, as this provides an opportunity to examine in depth how gender and ethnicity play out in the lives of people.

Taking this explicit position helps bring to the fore the mechanisms, both material and symbolic, through which a range of unequal power relations operate – between individual women and men, the *adivasis* and non-*adivasi*s, and institutions of the state and civil society. While individuals may invest in their lives, strive for justice and struggle to move out of material poverty, existing institutional systems, operating at multiple scales, may often fail to provide them access to valuable skills and basic productive resources. Structural inequalities then pose a barrier to mobility (see Chapter 7). Unpacking the role of macro-policies and the political context in shaping opportunities and choices helped me contextualise these very local insights within a wider global context. Further, each of these groups and scales is heterogenous and internally divided – hence generalised assumptions are unable to identify the sticky points that inhibit equality. It is these interfaces and nuances which this book highlights.

In this introductory chapter, I set out the broad contours of my journey, starting in 1994, its underlying philosophies and conceptual underpinnings. During this period, Jharkhand has not just become a separate state, but has also made great strides in development indicators, including literacy rates and the expansion of basic infrastructure (see Chapter 14). My own positionality, too, has changed from being an activist and development practitioner to a full-time academic. I draw on anecdotes to reflect on my journey, pointing at the same time to key social and political changes that Jharkhand has witnessed over this period.

I then turn to a brief discussion of four critical changes which inform the organisation of the book: (*a*) the sharpening of ethnic, class and gender divides, (*b*) the nexus between land, labour and migration, (*c*) the rise in modern education and its implications for both changing aspirations and highlighting contradictions, including those of gender, and (*d*) the double bind of state policies, especially those relating to land, water, agriculture and food security, as spaces for the simultaneous practice of equality and subordination. The focus on mining, for instance, while generating incomes, can threaten food security and sustainability in the medium to longer term. Collectively, these shifts point to a growing crisis of social reproduction, a key concept underpinning the book. Apart from limiting material improvements, this crisis of social reproduction has enhanced conflict across institutions, from the household to the state, with implications for gender justice. I draw on Fraser (1989) to frame gender justice as marking the intersection of socio-cultural (recognition), economic (redistribution) and political (representation) rights, grounded in the everyday lives and struggles of Santal women.

My Personal Journey

My first encounter with Santal women was in 1994 through a women's empowerment project run by a feminist non-governmental organisation (NGO). A training programme had been scheduled in Jarmundi block of Dumka district, then still a district of Bihar state, but the 'trainer' from the capital city, Patna, failed to turn up. The place was seen as too 'remote, backward and unsafe' for an educated woman from Bihar. Along with the head of the NGO, I conducted the training, but became acutely aware of the inequality and sense of difference, even amongst women of the same state. Clearly ethnicity mattered, as did education. I was confronted with stereotypes of the 'simple Santal woman', hard-working, exploited sexually, a voiceless victim subject to all sorts of crimes including witch-hunting. She was denied agency by NGOs and the state, as a strategy for raising donor funding for her 'empowerment'. This kind of representation, of *adivasi* exploitation at the hands of external settlers and contractors, and their 'victimhood', gave strength to the discourse of 'internal colonialism' propagated by *adivasi* leaders in pushing the case for a separate state of Jharkhand (Munda, 1988; Corbridge, 1988). In my interactions over the next few years, I found Santal women to be strong and articulate, in the face of huge odds – economic exploitation, social marginalisation and political exclusion. They wanted to be heard, but this was not always easy, as a majority of women were monolingual in Santali (Census of India, 2001). I decided therefore to conduct deeper research to explore some of the puzzles I was confronted with.

The second moment of my engagement was between 1998 and 2000, when I lived in Santal villages for an extended period of time and explored questions of power, agency and rights as part of my doctoral research (Rao, 2008). To capture the diversity of resource relationships within the community, I divided my time between two villages – one in the plains, close to Dumka, and the second in a remote hilly forested terrain. Several questions were in my mind. Who were the Santal women killed as witches? Were they really voiceless or were they women who challenged stereotypes and, more importantly, exercised claims to land and property? Did the law support the claims of these women? Or, in the absence of state support, did they negotiate and perhaps compromise with community-level, traditional institutions in order to secure their livelihoods? What was driving resistance to women's land claims, despite notions of relative gender equality within *adivasi* communities like the Santals? How was the larger political economy shaping the construction of adivasi identity on the eve of the formation of Jharkhand as a separate state?

The Hindu nationalist Bharatiya Janata Party (BJP) and its allies formed the first government of Jharkhand in November 2000, rather than the coalition of political parties that had fought for statehood under the umbrella of the Jharkhand movement. The *Vision 2010* document, launched in February 2003, outlined some of the policy directions and emphases of the new state. These included commercialisation, export orientation and market development, both in the agricultural and industrial sectors. Dealing with food insecurity, inequities in resource distribution and control, and destitution did not appear as priorities (see Chapter 11). One of the first steps taken by the new government was to set up an all-party committee to review the existing land legislation and suggest amendments, as the non-transferability of land (Section 20 of the Santal Pargana Tenancy Act [SPTA], 1949) was seen as a major obstacle to economic growth and development. A Santal headman in one of the villages I visited in 2004 said:

> The Chief Minister of Jharkhand [from 2000–03] has the body of an *adivasi*, but the head and mind of a Marwari [a trading group]. He does not care about our land and is trying to give it to big industries. Buses have been given to cooperatives of ten tribal youth. But their school certificates have been retained, so they cannot apply for any other job, probably till such time as the loan component (70,000 rupees) is repaid, if ever. Second, schools have been built, but new teachers have not been appointed, and the existing teachers are overloaded with other work – hence hardly any teaching takes place. On top of that, liquor sales have been legalised. The policy seems to be to keep the *adivasi*s drunk and uneducated.

My next phase of fieldwork in the Santal Parganas was between 2003–06. The priorities of the state and the *adivasi*s had already begun to diverge: to the latter land was more than a productive resource; it was a key element of their social and cultural identity, giving them public visibility, bargaining power and enhanced status. In fact, *jal, jangal, jameen* (water, forests, land) was the foundation of their struggle for a separate state, with the recent Pathalgadi movement adding two more dimensions – *jan* (people) and *janwar* (animal) (Xaxa, 2019). For the government, however, land (both private and common property) was now a commodity that could be used to achieve economic growth through private sector investments. In such a context of uncertainty, women's rights to land were no longer a priority (See Chapter 13).

In 2006, while walking to the remote village where I was staying, a policeman, the head of the local *thana* (police station), accosted me. He was visiting the village to talk to the *parganait* (leader of a group of villages) about the tense situation in the area. There were press reports on the growing activities of Maoist (left-wing extremist) groups in the region, which, he said, were led by 'civil elements from outside'. Training in the use of firearms was being organised, and an atmosphere of violence prevailed in this otherwise peaceful region. I soon realised that he was talking about the neighbouring *panchayat* (elected village council) of Pachwara in Pakur district, which was witnessing strong resistance to a coal mining project. I was told that compensation had been paid out in cash and the resistance broken. Work was in full swing on the project, and it was 'only a few people with vested interests who were creating problems, and they would be arrested at the earliest'. One of these ostensible 'troublemakers', a Catholic nun, earlier the principal of a missionary girls' school in the area, was sadly killed in 2011 (*Matters India*, 2015). He gave me a 'lift to the village' in his police jeep, checking out my credentials as we drove.

This brief encounter raised several troubling issues: How had the state managed to acquire land and get an agreement on cash compensation from the local *adivasi* people? Was any dialogue ever held or was this agreement one-sided? Was this solution not in contradiction to the existing protective land policies, including SPTA? And was it not a gross violation of the Supreme Court's Samatha judgment of 1997 that prioritised the decision of the local village *panchayat*s on issues of land use? On a more personal note, this was the first time in over a decade of my visiting the Santal Parganas that I sensed fear and insecurity and a lack of trust – a breaking down of the sense of community. The bogey of Maoist violence meant that people were afraid to help each other, unsure of the consequences.

My next visit was after nearly a decade, in 2015. This was a personal visit to meet my Santal friends, women and men, who had welcomed me into their homes and who continue to inspire my academic journey. In the plains' village, the Santal teacher with whom I had stayed between 1999–2000 was now the *sarpanch* (elected head of the village council) and had worked hard to implement the development programmes allocated to the *panchayat*, claiming rights wherever possible. She had streamlined the public distribution system (PDS), ensuring food security, as well as other public works programmes (Figure 1.1). This seemed like a big step forward.

In the forest village, however, my experience was depressing. The road had broken down, and while school buildings existed, there were hardly a handful of children present. The health centre was locked up. The area was officially under 'Maoist control'. Some of the little boys who had stayed with me, now in their twenties, were missing from the village. Rumours had it that they

Figure 1.1 The woman *sarpanch* showing her accomplishments

Source: Photograph by the author.

were in jail, seen as threats to local peace and security. Several young people asked me why the only work available to them, provided by the Mahatma Gandhi National Rural Employment Guarantee Act (MNREGA), 2005 – the largest social protection scheme in the world – was manual and unskilled? With some education and no jobs, they were frustrated, challenging the development trajectory and the nature of opportunities available to them (see Chapter 7). Older men, like the village leader with whom I had stayed, had now started migrating to Delhi to work in factories, a sign of sheer desperation for survival. The breakdown of the social fabric appeared to have worsened – from cultivators, with pride in their land, a majority of Santals had been converted into 'footloose labour' (Breman, 1996).

In 2016, the Jharkhand government, led for the first time by a non-*adivasi*, to hasten the process of acquiring agricultural land for non-agricultural, so called 'developmental' purposes, tried to amend the SPTA by stealth (see Chapter 14). There was an explicit emphasis on a modernist, neo-liberal growth model, with little attention to culture, identity or social structure. In Polanyi's (2001 [1944]) terms, the modern market economy, which seeks to commodify land, labour and money, and transform people's economic mentalities from one of reciprocity and redistribution to utility maximisation and growth, is untenable in the long run, as the economy is ultimately embedded in social relations. People's behaviour is informed not just by the satisfaction of material wants but also notions of social recognition and status. The move towards economic liberalism over the last two decades, following the creation of Jharkhand state, has led to a growing alienation from land, a loss of status and recognition, and increasing social inequalities, all contributing to the rise in violent opposition.

My last encounter is one of hope. In February 2020, just prior to the national lockdown due to the COVID-19 pandemic, I visited the Santal Parganas for initiating an action research project with youth and women's groups on the theme of sustainable food systems. This experience led me towards a closer engagement with participatory action research methodologies in my praxis, entailing reflection on enduring and emergent issues, challenges and aspirations of local communities and informing action for transformation and change (see Chapter 14). The shift in methodology also reflects a shift from an impersonal to a more personal approach, one that is 'political' in recognising our shared interests and aspirations. Overcoming the social distance between the Santal women and myself, the researched and the researcher, has contributed to building an inclusive analytical framework, enabling the exploration of critical points when change happens, and the mechanisms through which research becomes relevant to the local context.

In the 2019 state elections, Hemant Soren of the Jharkhand Mukti Morcha (JMM), a Santal, was elected to the post of Chief Minister. His father, Shibu Soren, had been the face of the Jharkhand movement, leading the fight for social justice and against land alienation in the 1960s and the 1970s (Rao, 2008). While reversing trends may not be easy, his government appears mindful of *adivasi* interests, seeking to create inclusive institutions and equitable policies that can restore their dignity and enable communities to have some say over their local environments. Providing a democratic space for articulation and contestation of needs and priorities is perhaps the only way out of the impasse created by a combination of socially exclusive development, migration for securing livelihoods and anti-state violence. I reflect further on the future in the final chapter of this book but now turn to a discussion of the key themes reflecting a crisis of reproduction.

What Underlies the Crisis of Reproduction?

From Friedrich Engel's (1972 [1884]) observation about the confinement of women to the domestic domain and the devaluation of the 'domestic' to the 'productive' as societies settled and became dependent on market exchange to the present, there has been a lot of debate around the production–reproduction divide and its implications for gender equality. The 1970s and the 1980s witnessed the 'domestic labour' debate, which led to feminist demands for the valuation of domestic work and providing notional 'wages for housework'. They sought to ensure women's autonomy not by redistributing 'unpaid domestic and care work', as suggested by the Sustainable Development Goal 5 on gender equality, but by emphasising 'difference' and seeking recognition for domestic work as a legitimate economic activity (Federici, 1975).

This debate made it imperative to analytically distinguish between the various dimensions of reproduction – biological, daily household maintenance and social reproduction – though all inter-related (Edholm, Harris and Young, 1978). Social reproduction covers not just everyday tasks and activities necessary to reproduce households and families, but also the realm of care and reproduction of society more broadly, its social institutions, culture and the productive economy (Locke, Seeley and Rao, 2013), spanning both human and environmental dimensions. Social reproduction includes but goes beyond accounting for the time and labour spent on unpaid care and domestic work by including the motivation and meaning of caring labour and the dynamic relationship between labour and the environment. There is an emotional and relational dimension to care work. However, caring for others (people and nature) does not necessarily imply the lack of self-interest, but could be mediated by expectations of reciprocity or ethics of responsibility (Folbre, 1995). While responsibility or obligation, being socially constructed values, can be coercive, there are constant attempts to enhance mutuality, albeit asymmetric (Nelson, 2016), seeking to redefine the very meanings of power.

During my doctoral research, I found several women in polygynous relationships. I reacted negatively, seeing this practice as an affront to gender justice. As I got to know the women better, I realised that both the *badki* (senior wife) and the *chutki* (junior wife) had limited choices (Chapters 3 and 4). Mahani, Jeevan Soren's daughter, was criticised for entering a new relationship as a *chutki*, abandoning her daughter. But for her, confronted with hunger, a stable relationship was the only way to ensure both food security with dignity and bring some stability into her life (Rao, 2008: 221–22). While raising a dilemma regarding the framing of struggles against the cultural and social devaluation of women's work, this example points to the multi-planarity of women's lives and work. Mahani's exercise of agency is both an expression of strength and a sign of weakness. It questions the dualisms of power and powerlessness, production and reproduction, to recognise the simultaneous importance of material well-being and the recognition of women's identities, knowledges and agency.

Should the focus of our larger struggles then be on 'prioritizing equality with men' through market processes, 'revaluing the ways that women are different from men' (Folbre, 1995: 84), or problematising the gendered world itself and challenging the male norm (Verloo and Lombardo, 2007)? The choice is between reducing, maintaining or challenging the meaning of women's caring labour. It is a question of how citizenship is constructed for women: is it as workers, commanding equal wages to men in the labour markets, or as wives and mothers, with states providing welfare or needs-based entitlements, or by recognising interdependence in human relationships, well-being, and work–care balance (Fraser, 1997)? While human attachments are critical, we cannot forget the gendered nature of institutions such as labour markets, which, while creating an illusion of freedom and independence – for migrant domestic workers, for example – also control their emotions and relationships (Chapter 5).

Migration raises the issue of spatiality and its impacts on people's lives and value systems and on gender relations more broadly. What are the meanings of work at home and away? Does the nature of work or its precarity matter for caring labour? Can education and social capital override the effects of being an Adivasi woman or man (Chapters 5–7)? In what ways can traditional or modern institutions be used to negotiate both the present and the future? Recent feminist work on new materialisms challenges the persistent binaries of male–female, nature–culture, structure–agency, material–discursive, as setting up hierarchical relations of value and power, and overlooking the gendered meanings of livelihood resources and agency as relational and dynamic. Such a view of agency not as an attribute but as an 'enactment of iterative changes to particular practices' (Barad, 2003: 827) opens up the possibility of reconfiguring boundaries and exclusions across space and time. Even a single woman's interests and claims can change as she progresses through life (Rao, 2014) and also as the world around her changes. With most younger men now migrating out of the region to secure household livelihoods, gender relationships are changing, from those of everyday cooperation, support, or conflict to monetary remittances and individualised forms of struggle and hardship.

In such a formulation, nature (land, water or forests) and gender (women, men or children) are not oppositional entities, but part of a larger social, political, economic, ecological and theological environment (Haraway, 1992). Situated within a temporal and spatial context, people make sense of the world through the relationships in which they are embedded. The political-economic and governance systems are also not linear or predictable in the ways in which the 'material dimensions of regulatory practices' influence the distribution of power and resources between people (Jagger, 2015). This, in turn, shapes emergent mechanisms for coping with change.

Most of the chapters in this book point to a gradual undermining of the processes of social reproduction, of the mutuality within and across households and communities with the acceleration of the 'development' agenda of Jharkhand state. The forces of the state and economy have laid emphasis on growth and markets, ignoring their embeddedness in society and sociality. In different ways and across different spheres, the chapters demonstrate the untenability of this pathway. A range of everyday resistances point to an assertion of identity, of seeking dignity and respectability, and not just the fulfilment of material needs. Reproduction here emerges in terms of two core values: the resistance to hierarchies and the attempt to build alternate definitions of power and agency.

The Sharpening of Ethnic, Class and Gender Divides

The past two decades have undoubtedly witnessed a decline in extreme poverty and hunger. Between 2005–06 and 2019–20, the multi-dimensional poverty index (MPI), which captures 12 indicators dealing with education, health and standard of living, declined from an incidence of 75 per cent to 42 per cent in Jharkhand state, though still much higher than the national MPI of 25 per cent in 2019–20. During my first and second encounters in the 1990s, children in remote villages were only eating palm fruits during the lean summer months, when stocks of grain were exhausted, and the maize was yet to be harvested. Almost all the Santal villagers at that time were poor, differentiation amongst them was minimal, and solidarity remained strong.

With the implementation of the universal PDS and Midday Meal Scheme in schools, following the passage of the National Food Security Act, 2013, such hunger is rarely seen. Major improvements have also occurred in education and sanitation, following the Sarva Shiksha Abhiyaan (Education for All Campaign), 2001–02, and the Swachh Bharat Abhiyan (Clean India Campaign), 2014, and yet nutrition, maternal health, quality of housing and access to drinking water and cooking fuel leave much to be desired. The *adivasi*-dominated districts of the Santal Parganas do much worse than Jharkhand state as a whole, with Dumka district having an MPI of 53 per cent and neighbouring Pakur 61 per cent in 2019–20. Rural poverty at 51 per cent is much worse than urban poverty at 15 per cent (NITI Aayog, 2021).

With improvements in education and communications, the aspirations of Santal youth are rising; they are also more critical of the discrimination they confront in their everyday lives. Santal youth often spoke to me about their frustrations, their inability to secure formal jobs, despite their best efforts (Chapters 5 and 7) in contrast to young people of other castes and social groups. The choices they have remain limited: continuing with subsistence agricultural production, barely sufficient to provide food for four to six months, migrating for seasonal work in agriculture or industries in better developed parts of India (Rao et al., 2020), or, for young women, engaging in domestic work, paid and unpaid.

Domination within patron–client relations was earlier perpetrated within facades of caring, a moral economy wherein the patron never allowed the client to die; rather, exploitation on a daily basis was accompanied with gifts and support in times of crisis (Scott, 1977). Recognising local frustrations resulting from growing inequality, a result at least in part of the alienation from nature and natural resources, such facades are now being created and recreated through state expressions of benevolence and justice. Examples include *garibi hatao* (removal of poverty, a slogan provided by Prime Minister Indira Gandhi in 1975), an attack on the rich and corrupt (the rationale behind the demonetisation implemented by Prime Minister Narendra Modi in 2016), or blaming the ruthlessness of the Maoists for the current state of affairs. It is true that the Maoist resistance in Dumka's villages does not seem to have a clear goal or ideology; rather, it signals a ruthlessness emerging from the lack of satisfactory livelihoods.

In the face of sharpening ethnic and class divides, Santal youth are creating cultural spaces for the articulation of their identities, rather than being seen either as marginalised groups or as violent anti-nationalists. Young Santal writers are publishing bold stories about the exploitation and discrimination that persist against them, apart from restoring their heritage (Hansda, 2015). Hansda (2017), a doctor by training, was dismissed by the Jharkhand state's health department for writing about the plight of *adivasi* frontline health workers in the state. Developing an alternate vocabulary that is affirmative rather than divisive or dismissive is central to re-establishing the social fabric and community ethic, based on principles of reciprocity and redistribution, rather than the commodification of both nature and people (Polanyi, 2001 [1944]). It is not repression, but a constructive dialogue and action-agenda that is needed to address real-life problems with sensitivity and dignity.

Within the discourse of indigeneity and marginalisation in India, gender has not been a major axis of analysis. While women may be excluded from authority within patriarchal structures, particularly in terms of resource control, they do exercise other forms of productive power to ensure reciprocal relations in daily practice. Power does not just come from those in authority: it manifests itself in many different ways and from many different points at once (Foucault, 1978). In fact, this is reflected in Jharkhand's slightly better gender-related development indices compared to those of Bihar (29 versus 35) (Government of India, 2009). At the same time, not all men necessarily have authority in the public sphere, and the collective marginality of the *adivasi*s might have intensified opposition to women's claims, especially to landed property.

This became obvious during my doctoral research. In response to two writ petitions – *Madhu Kishwar v. State of Bihar*, 1982, and *Juliana Lakra v.*

State of Bihar, 1986, filed on behalf of two women – the Supreme Court of India (in May 1996), while clarifying in its judgment that it had no intention of interfering with customary law, granted the concerned women rights to land in keeping with the fundamental right to life guaranteed to all citizens, irrespective of sex, creed or caste, by the Indian Constitution. *Adivasi* leaders in Jharkhand condemned the judgment. They felt that initiating a discussion on individual rights, counter to their claims to 'community' rights, based on the principles of mutuality and responsibility, was an attempt to create divisions in *adivasi* society. They pointed to *adivasi* women's greater autonomy and that the issue of rights could not be examined in isolation from their overall social context and cultural practices (Abhiyaan, 1999). They feared that women would become the channel for the intergenerational transfer of land to wealthy *diku*s (outsider-traders). The discourse of 'community' was used to deny women access to land as 'individuals'.

This position was also supported by several Adivasi women leaders, many of them aligned to the Jharkhand Mahila Mukti Morcha (JMMM), a network of local women's organizations. They found it strategic to negotiate their rights within marriages and the community. By supporting the discourse of 'community', they exerted moral pressure on village leaders, obliging them to support women's claims as a means of establishing their own credibility as guardians of community rights – the normative basis of the movement (Rao, 2008).

Today, the debate is beyond women's rights to 'private land' and its social acceptability in a context where *adivasi*s as a group are fast losing control over their natural resources – both private and community. *Adivasi* identity as reflecting a collective ownership of the ecosystem is no longer prioritised in the construction of Jharkhand as a modern state. This is seen in several recent moves – the appointment of a non-tribal Chief Minister, Raghubar Das, in 2014, or ordinances to amend the Santal Parganas and Chhota Nagpur Tenancy Acts to allow for the commercial use of *adivasi* land in 2016 (which had to be withdrawn following widespread protests). Gender relations are directed towards survival and reproduction of the household in a context where their access to resources is declining, both in quantity and its quality.

The Nexus between Land, Labour and Migration

It is important to recall that while the very premise for the formation of Jharkhand state was the control of land, water and forests by the *adivasi* communities as central to their identities and livelihoods, this vision was quickly replaced by one of 'modernity' and 'urbanisation'. The first BJP government appointed an *adivasi* leader as the Chief Minister to ensure acceptance from the people of the state. Its main support base being largely non-*adivasi*, located amongst traders and petty businesspeople, there was no pressure to prioritise the equitable distribution of resources or its control by the *adivasis* (Chapter 11). Most schemes for the development of *adivasi* youth focused on diversification out of farming and natural-resource dependence rather than strengthening and developing their resource base. Given the competition from better-placed and better-educated groups, and bureaucratic red tape, these schemes were hardly successful. Greater wealth replaced social equity as a goal of the state, leading gradually to an alienation of the *adivasis* from their land and labour. This has been accompanied by cultural alienation, the promotion of 'Hindutva' social norms that constrain women's mobility, voice and choices. This Hindutva stance has also aggravated social tensions, the lack of trust between communities, especially Christian and non-Christian *adivasis*, and fuelled a rise in violent extremism. Six districts of Jharkhand were affected by Maoist violence in 2000, but this soon spread to the entire state, taking almost a decade for it to come under control.

These broader trends emerging from the failure of state policy to protect the land rights of the *adivasis*, instead encouraging alienation, point to the changing relations between land and labour both physically and ideologically. Are the Santals being converted from cultivators to 'footloose labour', to use Breman's (1996) term? Meillasoux (1981: 115), theorising the relationship between persistent low wages and migration patterns of rural labour, notes that the implication of permanent migration for capitalism would be the need to pay for both the immediate labour time of the worker and the costs of biological and social reproduction of the labour force. Circular migrants can be exploited by drawing their labour during the long duration when they have no work at home, in a context of monocropping, and yet have the backup of their domestic production to meet the costs of family maintenance and reproduction. Such rotating migration establishes a double-labour market, where the labour is divided between self-production at home and production for the employer, while also supporting a discriminatory ideology based on notions of skills, ethnicity and poverty.

Globally, land is key to the identities of indigenous people. Many of their struggles for recognition begin with land. More than a material resource, it becomes a metaphor for their culture, language, social and community norms, and identity. Rimani, a Santal woman I knew in the plains' village, refused her husband a share of the household land, even though the land title was in his name, when he wanted to bring a second wife. Despite his threats and harassment, she did not give in. Her strategy in this case was carefully chosen – faithfulness to her husband and responsibility towards her children gave her the moral high ground to retain control over her husband's landed property. She was pointing to the unity between the productive, reproductive and symbolic values of land. She turned the tables on the community leaders, who were earlier inclined to partition the land between husband and wife. She could demonstrate that she had lived up to the image of the 'good woman' and 'good wife' (Rao, 2008). Thus, while grounded in and informed by the material politics of everyday life, her discursive strategies, the way she presented her case, comprised a central site of contestation.

She raised very strongly the issue of identity and the need to assert it, to claim one's rights. A woman is not just a mother or a homemaker or even a cultivator; she is all of these, and more. It is this coexistence of multiple identities that is seen in the differential use of the terms *orahor* (homemaker), *chasahor* (cultivator) and *gogohor* (woman). In the use of these terms, the Santals acknowledge and recognise that women have role-based identities, but also identities beyond these roles, just as women. It is also men's identities as *chasahor* that shapes both their resistance to women's land claims and their choice or not of particular forms of labour.

Rimani's strategy found support in the larger political context wherein women's rights to land are now centrally located in the national policy agenda. While the original demand for equal property rights lay in the discourse around gender equality, this is now seen functionally as a key strategy to enhance food production and food security, in a situation when men are often absent from the rural areas (Rao, 2006). The translation, however, of such policy statements into practice remains weak, precisely due to the underlying assumptions which link it to the performance of particular roles, largely materialist, rather than seeing them as being socially embedded and networked. Women hitherto labelled as homemakers are now categorised as producers. Yet women refuse such labels in seeking reciprocity, increasingly important in a context of declining male roles in joint production and the domestic economy.

A reciprocal economy has the potential of ensuring food security, alongside a security of identity, as the social valuation of labour is high and contributions to the household economy are recognised. For women, this recognition enables them to negotiate and 'bargain' with patriarchy (Kandiyoti, 1988). When working as footloose labour, detached from their land, the market values labour, though differentiating value by social identity, be it of gender or ethnicity. While undoubtedly earning incomes, such work does not add up to a holistic identity entailing elements of production and reproduction. This raises a fundamental question of how land should be positioned within the larger context, not just of gender equality but also of labour relations within a globalised economy. Dominated by money, the lack of state investments in the rural agricultural sector, and limited recognition of the productivity of the entire ecosystem, not just specific crops, patriarchy and women's spaces for negotiation too adapt to contextual variations and shifts over time.

New forms of labour and land alienation are now visible. A good example comes from the contracting of stone quarries. The existence of the SPTA and its non-transferability clause, while posing restrictions on the official transfer of land, has led to the creation of ambiguous 'agreements', in terms of time period and value of the land, with *adivasi* 'owner-contractors'. Lacking capital and struggling to meet their consumption needs, a majority of these so-called contractors are fronts for non-*adivasi* owners of capital. The stone quarries have raised a range of issues. Minimum wages have been bypassed and mining rules on health and safety ignored (Chapter 13). The use of common property, including sacred groves and grazing lands, have been lost, and the social character of the community challenged. The loss of land, while negatively impacting their diets, nutrition and household food security, has also been a blow to their identities, as converted from landowners into landless labour, there are few remaining platforms for their voices to be heard.

Economic Survey 2017–18 found 5 million working-age people migrating from Jharkhand each year, the highest amongst Indian states (Government of India, 2018). West Bengal receives the highest number of migrants followed by Bihar and Uttar Pradesh (UP). Female migration has almost doubled in the decade following the formation of Jharkhand, mainly to cities for domestic work. Stereotypes of *adivasi* women as honest, obedient and hardworking, easier to control than their non-*adivasi* counterparts, drive a preference for them as live-in domestic workers (Chapter 5). Seasonal migration to West Bengal for transplanting and harvesting paddy is also dominated by women, as men, priding themselves as *chasabor*, cultivators of their own land, prefer not to engage in agricultural wage work, especially near their homes. While some educated men get jobs as teachers or are recruited into the armed forces and police services, a majority engage with construction and roadbuilding in border areas, factory work in the more developed states of western and southern India, or contract labour for agriculture in the Green Revolution areas of western UP. Incomes are predictable; hence, despite involving hard manual work, this is a secure option for meeting immediate food, health and educational needs.

The nature of labour regimes and relations provide limited scope for upward mobility, but also have implications for wider notions of production and reproduction, at home and at the destination. Anil Murmu, aged twenty-two, educated to grade ten, also owns some land. His skills and knowledge are recognised at home; yet he was unable to command the same authority at the destination, despite possessing demonstrable symbols of wealth such as a bank account and mobile phone (Chapter 6). Santals like Anil strive to create relations of reciprocity and redistribution in their quest for social parity and dignity; yet the exchanges at the destination reinforce hierarchies based on ethnicity and language rather than education or even capital, giving credence to Meillasoux's (1981) contention that identity is crucial to any transaction.

Deshingkar and Farrington's (2009) postulate that knowledge and experience gained over time may allow a migrant to move up the ladder from survival to accumulation clearly does not hold true in this instance. Migration enables survival, but it has not contributed to improving migrants' lives substantially. Earnings and savings vary by ethnic group, gender, occupation, wage rates, living costs, contracting arrangements and debts. Strategies of domination and control over the labour, life and social processes of the migrant workers are clearly visible. They include filling the time of the worker completely through over-exploitation of their labour, close supervision to avoid possibility of socialisation with co-workers, feet-dragging or other forms of resistance, using the language of kinship to co-opt workers into employer's households, and a control over their sexuality. While not necessarily consenting to this treatment, the workers tend to conform to ensure that full wages are received, and an element of dignity maintained. At home, however, they are able to express their feelings; they are clear that this is not something they can do on a regular basis as the work is too strenuous. Their short-time horizons vis-à-vis such migration contribute to a higher rate of time preference, making them accept lower wages and difficult working conditions for the immediate security and benefits it provides. Migration, especially from the remote, hilly parts of the state, was infrequent in 2000;

male migration is now near universal, though it is still not the preferred option. It is the only response to the status quo, heavily stacked against them.

While migration is hard for both men and women, employed as they are at the lowest rungs of the labour market, receiving low wages and subject to harassment, the choices available to women, especially as domestic workers, tend to further bind them emotionally and physically. Expectations of gift-giving by women as domestic workers, for instance, are central to processes of social reproduction, while the same is not the expectation of migrant men, seen as household providers. Women's remittances are high but not viewed in the same way as men's. Growing frustrations with their 'choices' has led to resistances of different kinds – some violent, as reflected in the rapid spread of the Maoist movement through Jharkhand after its formation in 2000; others political, to protect their land and forests; and still others cultural, through efforts to either escape or reassert their language and identity.

Status, dignity and self-esteem are central to migrant representations of their work and lives. As Scott (1990) notes, dignity is both a private and a public attribute, to be particularly preserved and built in one's closest circle of family and friends. While the migrants do not mention the rigours of their work, 'spatial distanciation', a term used by Giddens (1984) to discuss the stretching of social systems across time and space, helps challenge structures of authority within the village, whether hierarchies of age or gender. Talamai and Sunil, who got married without parental approval, were hence disinherited; they migrated to save some money, lease in land and establish a home (Chapter 6). Dorothy, a domestic worker for many years, built a respectable persona in the village through her gift-giving rituals over the years (Chapter 5). Current trends in terms of land loss are, however, likely to have serious implications for their dignity and status.

Modern Education and Prospects for a Better Life

Modern education has expanded rapidly as visible in the rising literacy levels in the state. While education remains an aspiration, for people residing in remote geographies, a key deciding factor in the pursuit of higher education is the physical access to upper primary schools and colleges. According to the 2011 census, children from over 14 per cent of villages in Jharkhand still have to travel 5–10 kilometres for upper primary school, and the distance to the nearest college for 78 per cent of villages was more than 10 kilometres. Eleven out of twenty-four districts in Jharkhand do not have a single women's college

(*Business Standard*, 2016). In attempts to connect the remote areas of the state
to the 'centres' of education, and especially to improve the gross enrolment
ratio (GER) of women in higher education, the state government launched
a free bus service for women. But the scheme never saw the light of day. The
difference between male and female literacy rates was 28 percentage points in
2001, declining to 21.5 percentage points in 2011.

The politics of identity continues to play a part in augmenting educational
exclusion for the *adivasi* children of the state, especially the Santals.
There exists a wide gap between Scheduled Tribes (STs) (57 per cent), the
classification used in state records, and the non-ST population (72 per cent),
of over 15 percentage points (Census of India, 2011) (Table 1.1).[1] Inequalities
in the local land and market dynamics have played an important role in
restricting *adivasi*s and other poor communities from accessing education
(Rana and Das, 2004). Ranchi district (the capital city) still leads the literacy
rate at 68 per cent, while the Santal Parganas districts of Sahibganj (40 per
cent) and Pakur (42 per cent) fall at the bottom of this ladder. Despite the
inclusion of Santali as a national language in Schedule 8 of the Constitution
through the ninety-second amendment in 2003, Hindi remains the medium
of instruction, essentially a foreign language never used at home by *adivasi*
children, constraining learning outcomes.

The quality of schooling is poor. Many children leave the village to study
in residential mission schools; yet few of the graduates have secured regular
employment. In the absence of money to pay bribes and social contacts in
the bureaucracy, they find schooling unhelpful in gaining jobs (*cf.* Jeffrey,
Jeffrey and Jeffrey, 2008). As Samuel, aged thirty-two, of Mahari village,
who graduated in 2001, told me, 'I was appointed only as a helper in this
school on a ten-year contract, with a monthly salary of 2,000 rupees. This
is totally insufficient to support my family, but without money to pay bribes,

Table 1.1   Gaps in literacy rates based on social and gender profile (per cent)

	Total literacy rate		Male literacy rate		Female literacy rate	
	2011	2001	2011	2001	2011	2001
India	74	65	82	76	65	54
Jharkhand	66	54	77	68	55	39
Scheduled Tribes (STs) in Jharkhand	57	41	68	54	46	27

Source: Census of India (2001, 2011).

I am unable to get a job' (Chapter 7). Educated youth are unwilling to become footloose labour, but without a clear agenda for action, it has resulted in rising frustrations and violence.

For girls, segmented labour markets have meant fewer job opportunities, with the only exceptions being the 'volunteer-based' and contractual jobs such as those of the Accredited Social Health Activist (ASHA), or health worker, and Anganwadi, or child-care worker, in the locality. While this does give them the confidence to negotiate new contexts and institutions, it is clearly insufficient in their quest for justice. My research assistant and companion during my PhD research, an educated young woman, unable to fulfil her aspiration of securing a teaching job, is today a migrant factory worker in north India. Her husband is a volunteer teacher in their home village. While both of them are educated and share similar social contacts, and are not amongst the poorest, the outcomes for them have been different. During the COVID-19 pandemic, when schools were closed, her husband was not paid his salary, resulting in both of them engaging in migrant work to make ends meet. Paying fees for the tertiary education of their two daughters is a major expense for them, so she continues to work as a migrant, while her husband has returned to his teaching post. The stereotype of gender and ethnicity and the combination of capitalism and patriarchy have limited the range of opportunities open to her, while creating the illusion of freedom and choice. Yet education remains the only hope for the future.

But critical to note here is that rather than modern education per se, it is educational thresholds – in this case, tertiary education – that have the potential to shape migration outcomes and life chances more broadly. It is not necessarily education as 'credentials' but rather its role in shaping agency, opportunities and identity – and, in particular, the capacity to fight stereotypes of the *adivasi* – that have a transformative potential. While less educated men engage with manual labouring tasks, often for low wages, this young woman works in a factory, securing at least a minimum wage. If her children move for work, she hopes this will be for professional jobs, be it in hospitals or educational institutions, in large cities, offering better services and mobility options for future generations.

The Double Bind of State Policies

Jharkhand state was formed at a time when India had already witnessed a decade of neo-liberal economic reforms. Fewer restrictions on enterprises with the reform of the 'permit raj'[2] enhanced wealth amongst the middle classes, beyond the traditional elite. States started competing with each other to attract investments, promising an expansion of employment opportunities and livelihood security. As a first step, they focused on infrastructure development, but this required the acquisition of land. In Jharkhand, the stringent land tenure laws, which prevented transfer of land from the *adivasis* to other communities, came to be seen as the major bottleneck in the path of 'development'. Several attempts have been made to liberalise these laws, allow the transfer and sale of land and privatise natural resources (Chapter 13), but each one has been thwarted by protests, communities fearing a vicious cycle of indebtedness and precarious livelihoods following the loss of land.

Capital investments and capital formation do not work in the same way across contexts, particularly in remote rural areas and those inhabited by indigenous communities. In Jharkhand, we find two trends: first, the entry of large corporations mainly in the mining sector and, second, a more small-scale and insidious process of capital formation on the ground. Due to the high levels of awareness and mobilisation created by the Jharkhand movement, outright dispossession and the handing over of resources to large corporations has been less easy to push through. While private land has indeed been alienated in the name of 'development' – diverted to the construction of schools, hospitals or other public institutions – it has not been possible to handover land to private corporations as in many other parts of the country. This is more so in the Santal Parganas, which have seen a much smaller influx of large corporations compared to Chota Nagpur, the centre of mining and industry in the state.

While I have therefore not addressed the issue of large corporations in this book, several chapters discuss instances of small-scale privatization from a range of perspectives. For instance, with the construction of roads even in the remote and hilly parts of the state, petty traders and contractors are now purchasing forest products in bulk from the villages, often on a contractual basis, rather than the local markets. The price is fixed in advance, so despite improved connectivity, the women sellers do not necessarily benefit from a better yield (Chapter 9). Chapter 13 discusses the transfer of common property to small companies and contractors for stone quarrying and the implications of this for resource degradation and loss, livelihoods and, indeed, health. Such capital formation has led to the decline in community responsibility for the management of their local ecology, contributing in turn to a weakening of reciprocal social relationships. The focus on individual wealth and property as a symbol of modernity is, however, also used by women, especially those who are most vulnerable, to secure their rights (Chapter 4).

While wealth has undoubtedly been created in Jharkhand over the past two decades, it has not been equally distributed, with the *adivasis* lagging behind other social groups. This is visible across development indicators – incomes, educational achievements, health and nutrition, as further discussed in Chapter 14 – and raises questions about the meanings of citizenship itself. How are entitlements determined? Are these based on 'need' (means-tested) or 'deserts' (linked to employment) or are they universal? While one can argue for needs-based entitlements in terms of being redistributive, they can stigmatise the needy, but, worse, given the biases and inefficiencies in implementation, can also miss those most vulnerable. Clear patterns of patronage and corruption are visible, based on an underlying subtext of 'dependence' (Fraser, 1997), or what Breman (1996) called the 'undeserving poor'. Seen as a negative moral trait (an individual, often psychological problem) rather than a structural problem in recent years, the poor are blamed for their poverty, and the commitment to redistribution amongst the field-level bureaucracy appears low. In Dumka, I was often told by the generally upper-caste Hindu bureaucrats that *adivasi* (Santal) men are lazy, often drunk and do not work hard and that is why they continue to live in such poverty. The issues, however, being both structural and ideological, struggles are required with the state and the economic system, not only for welfare services but also over norms and meanings of work.

The second basis for entitlement is more exclusionary, often defined and implemented in relation to public employment, including pensions, paid leave, maternity benefits, and so on, and hence limited in scope. Even public employment is increasingly informalised, with ASHAs and Anganwadi workers, and even teachers, now seen as 'volunteers', who receive an honorarium rather than wage in compensation. While there have been demands for mandatory social insurance for informal sector workers in India, current provisioning continues to be voluntary (Mehrotra and Parida, 2020).

In contexts where needs and work-related entitlements are failing, the provision of public services, including education and healthcare services to all citizens, and social security and support become critical for ensuring a degree of stability in lives and livelihoods (Drèze and Sen, 1995). The National Food Security Act, 2013, taking a life-course perspective, emphasised maternity benefits for ensuring the rights of the young child, as part of the food security agenda. While distributing basic grains to 80 per cent of the population, budgetary provisions for maternity benefits are inadequate, the amount payable too reduced. The proper functioning of public health and education services is key to equality, in terms of both gender and ethnicity. However, in line with the policies of liberalisation, there is a trend towards privatisation, with visibly negative consequences for *adivasi* children. Parents struggle to enrol them into private, fee-paying schools, often residential; yet stereotypes of *adivasis* as good agricultural workers persist, and despite investments in education or their landowning status, they are over-represented in manual, 'unskilled' work.

Political contestation then seems critical for securing both one's material needs and social identities. It is a struggle over cultural meanings, over modes of subjectification – positioning people as specific sorts of people with specific capacities and needs – and over the power to construct both authoritative definitions of social situations and legitimate interpretations of social needs (Fraser, 1989: 107). The importance of a new vocabulary, a re-description of social life, is crucial to this process, especially as it has consequences for garnering access to material resources. To quote Thompson (1978: 231), '... every contradiction is a conflict of value as well as a conflict of interest ... every class struggle is at the same time a struggle over values'.

Social Justice and the Crisis of Reproduction

The idea of justice as a core element of social reproduction underpins the chapters in this book. Repeated struggles for land and against alienation, exploitation and indebtedness have continued, with people no longer afraid to use courts if needed in their struggles for justice. Exploitative land relations have taken new forms with the rise in market capitalism. Migration and opportunities for wage labour provide women, in particular, visibility for their work and control over money; yet these relationships too are by no means equitable.

Oppositional movements in Jharkhand can only shift the current development trajectory by articulating an alternate model, a new vocabulary, based on the sustainable use of land and natural resources, which can ensure social and livelihood security to a majority and arrest the rapid rise of social inequalities. The ideational work to create a collective ideology of identity and recognition, fundamental elements of justice, are based on several premises. These include:

1. Living in harmony with nature to ensure long-term sustainability rather than living off nature and exploiting natural resources for short-term benefits.
2. Struggles for justice at multiple levels, from the everyday to the more institutional–structural ones. They reflect the exercise of agency essential to survival, for challenging social norms and building an alternate definition of power as productive rather than dominating.
3. Frameworks that are dynamic rather than static, where roles and relationships change over time and space, responding to contexts, both internal and external. Yet this very dynamism implies that outcomes remain unpredictable – an educated woman may be obliged to migrate to work in a factory to fulfil her obligations towards her children and their educational aspirations, while another woman may need to leave her young daughter under the care of her parents in search of stability in her own life.
4. Empowerment is not only about assertion and action, but reflects efforts to resist subordination through negotiating relationships, especially those at the intersection of land and labour. Where women's labour contributions to production and reproduction are not socially valued, the withdrawal of labour from these activities helps negotiate patriarchy and contribute to more just relationships.
5. While the role of modern education appears ambiguous at first, threshold levels of education, especially tertiary education, do contribute to shifts in roles, responsibilities, expectations and aspirations. They are generative of new forms of expression, articulation and struggle. *Adivasi* youth, as discussed in Chapter 14, are using the skills provided by modern education to document and analyse traditional knowledges and cultures, finding solutions for development problems that lie in their control.
6. At a global level, international conventions on indigenous peoples provide frameworks for self-determination and cultural identity. These larger struggles provide a supportive context for local struggles for change and transformation. They point to shared values around solidarity and collective contributions to ensure social reproduction.

While emerging from *adivasi* perspectives, the aforementioned premises of justice apply to other contexts too. They challenge existing notions of social reproduction, by questioning the concepts of power and agency and underlining the unity between materiality and social relations, seen often as binaries operating at different scales. They highlight the importance of 'patiency' and listening to others alongside reciprocity in relation to both individual and collective interests (Reader, 2007), moving away from the two poles of alienation or integration towards an understanding of mutual embeddedness. Land and labour are not apart from each other nor from their social meanings, so notions of justice, too, move beyond the dualisms of men and women, dominant and subordinate, winners and losers. Economic valuations of the human enterprise cannot be disengaged from their social or cultural underpinnings, bringing into question the comparisons of equivalence often made between male earnings and women's emotional or caring labour. Such an *adivasi* critique of power points out that the security of identity and recognition of diverse knowledges are as critical to conceptions of justice as material equality.

Organisation of the Book

The book is structured along four main themes: gender and land (Part II), migration and identity (Part III), livelihoods and well-being (Part IV), and policy and politics (Part V). The first theme, on gender and land, has three chapters which present a historical account of women's struggles for land as reflecting not just claims to a material resource, but rather struggles over recognition of their identities as producers and reproducers and a search for justice as equal members of society. These chapters make at least three significant contributions: First, the chapters argue for a more nuanced account of gender itself, moving away from considering women as a homogenous group with unified interests. They highlight the difference between women's interests and gender interests, based on the social and kinship position of women. Second, they bring out the socially embedded nature of land claims by pointing to the close links of land to identity – more than its potential for production itself, land signals one's social and symbolic position within the community. While women's land rights can be legally claimed, for many women, social negotiation is often the preferred option, as they face a trade-off between material poverty and social alienation, including the loss of social support. Third, and related to the aforementioned points, the chapters bring out the complex nature of land rights as a 'bundle of rights', differentiated and negotiable in a range of arenas, from community institutions to the legal courts. These arenas have their own pros and cons for women but, importantly, open up spaces for negotiation and conversation, leading to a form of hybridity in practice, drawing on rules and norms which are most likely to be followed.

The second theme, on migration and identity, explores the unequal power relations embedded in processes of labour migration. It is not just the social distance between the labour contractors and the workers which is at stake, but equally between women and men, calling into question the construction of gender identities in Santal society. Two chapters in this part focus on issues of respectability and representation of migrant workers. By examining labour and social relations at home and the workplace, they highlight how spatial distanciation provides opportunities to the workers to challenge structures of authority, both of age and gender, within the rural context, while submitting to exploitative conditions of work at the destination. The third chapter focuses on an important dimension shaping labour opportunities – namely, access to good quality education. It discusses migration for education and the aspirations this raises amongst *adivasi* youth. Yet social structure – in this case, the stereotypes around their identity – contribute to limiting opportunities and thwarting these aspirations.

The chapters under the third theme examine the links between livelihoods and well-being from the perspectives of communities and households. At the community level, the gendered meanings of displacement are explored over time, the potential alleviating effects of compensation payments, alongside the new risks that confront displaced communities. This is more so when unmet state promises are compounded by the failure of individual initiatives such as educational investment to make a substantial difference to people's lives. At a more micro-level, two of the chapters under this theme explore relationships between genders and generations in the context of divisions of labour and access to assets. The responsiveness, or not, of state policies in mediating these relationships is also examined. For instance, much of women's work revolves around the fields, forests and local markets; yet transport provision to assist with these tasks is minimal. Transport policy focuses narrowly on the 'economic domain', understood as formal markets, rather than supporting the range of tasks and spaces which constitute productive, economic activity.

Where state policy is more distant, if not absent, as in the case of women's rights to land, the relationships across generations could often be conflictual, with notions of fairness being compromised.

The final theme consists of two reflective chapters on different dimensions of policymaking and a more detailed analysis of land laws and policies. These were all written in the first few years of the formation of Jharkhand state, when the aspirations of *adivasi*s and their expectations from the new state were high. Yet disappointment and disillusionment set in rapidly, as it became clear that the priorities of the new state were aligned more towards 'modern developmental imaginations' rather than fulfilling the needs and priorities emerging from the ground. The first chapter under the theme of policy and politics is a brief reflection on the *Vision 2010* document of the newly constituted Jharkhand state, which highlights the failure to address questions related to basic needs – of food security, freedom from hunger, as well as assured employment. The second chapter uses agricultural extension as an example to reflect on the social construction of *adivasi*s as 'lazy' and 'backward' by the state machinery. Their non-participation in agricultural extension activities is interpreted as a lack of interest rather than emerging from the structural inequalities they confront, including time and money poverty in the case of women. The final chapter engages in a fine-grained analysis of land laws and policies, pointing to the loopholes and contradictions that have led to a growing alienation of *adivasi* land despite legal provisions to prevent this from happening. It also reflects briefly on the trend of viewing protesters as anti-social and anti-national, even though these terms were not as common in the public narrative then as they are today.

The concluding chapter briefly recaps the development trajectory of the state since its formation, critically questioning policy assumptions and narratives but also identifying potential opportunities for change. It concludes on a note of hope, with youth building collectives on principles of equality rather than chauvinism to reclaim their traditional knowledges and identities. Hansda's '*adivasi* will not dance' (2015) seems to be playing out in real time, with the youth resisting directives from above, yet collectively seeking to build a just and equal future.

While celebrating the everyday agency of poor women, and indeed men, in the Santal Parganas, the chapters in this book point to a crisis of social reproduction. This is much broader than material poverty or low productivity; it reflects the gradual wearing down of cultural and social norms of reciprocity and sharing, of balancing individual and communal needs and interests, and, most of all, a degree of gender equality. Girls were as valued as boys in Santal society, but today there is a growing incidence of child marriage and an emergence of dowry in place of bride price. Land was seen as sacred, and a symbiotic relationship was maintained between people and their ecological environment; yet today land enclosures are visible for commercial plantation and appropriation. The growing alienation from land (including forested land) has resulted in young men routinely migrating for work to distant locations, uncommon two decades ago. Women are left behind to manage the land and the home, and while perhaps enhancing their agency, they miss the mutuality and reciprocity they had been accustomed to, in both production and reproduction.

The chapters reflect my research journey, with my position also changing in response to changes in the environment, whether political or economic. Good science is reflexive of these changes and engages constructively with new evidence as they emerge. It is time now to take action before these trends become irreversible.

Notes

1. The GER in higher education is 18 per cent as compared to the national average of 26.3 per cent. From 2010–11 figures, this percentage has increased by 10 per cent for the total population and doubled for the ST population, but it stands at a meagre 12.5 per cent for STs, with GER for women slightly lagging at 17.6 per cent (Ministry for Education, 2018).
2. The 'permit raj', or 'licence raj' (*raj* meaning 'rule' in Hindi), was the system of licences, regulations and accompanying red tape that hindered the setting up and running of businesses in India prior to 1991, when the government of India initiated liberalisation policies.

References

Abhiyaan. 1999. *Jharkhandi Mahilaon Ki Davedari, Satta Mein Aadhi Bhagedari* (Hindi). Madhupur.

Barad, K. 2003. 'Posthumanist Performativity: Toward an Understanding of How Matter Comes to Matter'. *Signs: Journal of Women in Culture and Society* 28(3): 801–31.

Breman, J, 1996. *Footloose Labour: Working in India's Informal Economy*. Cambridge, UK: Cambridge University Press.

Census of India. 2001. *Primary Census Abstracts*. New Delhi: Ministry of Home Affairs, Government of India.

———. 2011. *Primary Census Abstracts*. New Delhi: Ministry of Home Affairs, Government of India.

Corbridge, S. 1988. 'The Ideology of Tribal Economy and Society: Politics in the Jharkhand, 1950–1980'. *Modern Asian Studies* 22(1): 1–42.

Deshingkar, P., and J, Farrington (eds). 2009. *Circular Migration and Multilocal Livelihood Strategies in Rural India*. New Delhi: Oxford University Press.

Drèze, J., and A. Sen. 1995. *India: Economic Development and Social Opportunity*. Oxford: Clarendon Press.

Edholm, F., O. Harris and K. Young. 1978. 'Conceptualising Women'. *Critique of Anthropology* 3(9–10): 101–30.

Engels, F. 1972 (1884). *The Origin of the Family, Private Property, and the State*. New York: Pathfinder Press.

Federici, S. 1975. *Wages against Housework*. Bristol: Power of Women Collective.

Folbre, N. 1995. '"Holding Hands at Midnight": The Paradox of Caring Labor'. *Feminist Economics* 1(1): 73–92.

Foucault, M. 1978. *History of Sexuality*, vol. 1. London: Penguin Classics.

Fraser, N. 1989. *Unruly Practices*. Cambridge, UK: Polity Press.

———. 1997. *Justice Interruptus: Critical Reflections on the 'Postsocialist' Condition*. New York: Routledge.

Giddens, A. 1984. *The Constitution of Society: Outline of a Theory of Structuration*. Berkeley and Los Angeles: University of California Press.

Government of India. 2009. *Gendering Human Development Indices*. http://ngocc. org.zm/wp-content/uploads/2020/10/gendering_human_development_ indices.pdf. Accessed on 26 March 2023.

———. 2018. *Economic Survey 2017–18*. New Delhi: Ministry of Finance. https:// mofapp.nic.in/economicsurvey/economicsurvey/index.html. Accessed on 24 March 2023.

Hansda, S. S. 2015. *The Adivasi Will Not Dance*. New Delhi: Speaking Tiger.

———. 2017. '"I Am a Santhal, and My Opinion Too Should Matter": In Conversation with Sujit Prasad'. *Antiserious*, 16 August.

Haraway, D. 1992. 'Otherworldly Conversations; Terran Topics; Local Terms'. *Science as Culture* 3(1): 64–98.

Business Standard. 2016. 'Jharkhand Plans to Improve Its Education System'. 26 May.

Jagger, G. 2015. 'The New Materialism and Sexual Difference'. *Signs: Journal of Women in Culture and Society* 40(2): 321–42.

Jeffrey, C., P. Jeffery and R. Jeffery. 2008. *Degrees without Freedom? Education, Masculinities, and Unemployment in North India*. Redwood City, CA: Stanford University Press.

Kandiyoti, D. 1988. 'Bargaining with Patriarchy'. *Gender and Society* 2(3): 274–90.

Locke, C., J. Seeley and N. Rao. 2013. 'Migration and Social Reproduction at Critical Junctures in Family Life Course'. *Third World Quarterly* 34(10): 1881–95.

Matters India. 2015. 'Story of Sister Valsa John', 17 October. https://mattersindia.com/2015/10/story-of-sister-valsa-john. Accessed on 1 November 2022.

Mehrotra, S., and J. K. Parida. 2020. 'Social Security for All of India's Informal Workers Is Possible: Here's How'. *The Wire*, 10 February. https://thewire.in/economy/social-security-informal-workers-code-welfare. Accessed on 1 November 2022.

Meillasoux, C., 1981. *Maidens, Meal and Money: Capitalism and the Domestic Community*. Cambridge, UK: Cambridge University Press.

Ministry of Education. 2018. *All India Survey on Higher Education: AISHE (2017–18)*. Government of India. New Delhi: Ministry of Education, Government of India. https://epsiindia.org/wp-content/uploads/2019/02/AISHE-2017-18.pdf. Accessed on 25 October 2022.

Munda, R. D. 1988. 'The Jharkhand Movement: Retrospect and Prospect'. *Social Change* 48(2): 28–58.

Nelson, J. A. 2016. 'Husbandry: A (Feminist) Reclamation of Masculine Responsibility for Care'. *Cambridge Journal of Economics* 40: 1–15.

NITI Aayog. 2021. *National Multidimensional Poverty Index: Baseline Report*. New Delhi: NITI Aayog, Government of India.

Polanyi, K. 2001 (1944). *Great Transformation: The Political and Economic Origins of Our Time*. Boston, MA: Beacon Press.

Rana, K., and S. Das. 2004. 'Primary Education in Jharkhand'. *Economic and Political Weekly* 39(11): 13–19.

Rao, N. 2006. 'Land Rights, Gender Equality and Household Food Security: Exploring the Conceptual Links in the Case of India'. *Food Policy* 31: 180–93.

———. 2008. *'Good Women Do Not Inherit Land': Politics of Land and Gender in India*. New Delhi: Social Science Press and Orient Blackswan.

———. 2014. 'Caste, Kinship and Life-Course: Rethinking Women's Work and Agency in Rural South India'. *Feminist Economics* 20(4): 78–102.

Rao, N., N. Narain, S. Chakraborty, A. Bhanjdeo and A. Pattnaik. 2020. 'Destinations Matter: Social Policy and Migrant Workers in the Times of Covid'. *European Journal of Development Research* 32(5): 1639–61.

Reader, C. S. 2007. 'The Other Side of Agency'. *Philosophy* 82: 579–604.

Scott, J. C. 1977. *Moral Economy of the Peasant: Rebellion and Subsistence in Southeast Asia*. New Haven, CT: Yale University Press.

———. 1990. *Domination and the Arts of Resistance: Hidden Transcripts*. New Haven, CT: Yale University Press.

Thompson, E. P. 1978. *The Poverty of Theory*. New York: Monthly Review Press.

Verloo, M., and E. Lombardo. 2007. 'Contested Gender Equality and Policy Variety in Europe: Introducing a Critical Frame Analysis Approach'. In *Multiple Meanings of Gender Equality: A Critical Frame Analysis of Gender Policies in Europe*, edited by M. Verloo, 21–50. Budapest: Central European University Press.

Xaxa, V. 2019. 'Is the Pathalgadi Movement in Tribal Areas Anti-Constitutional?'. *Economic and Political Weekly* 54(1): 10–12.

Part II

Gender and Land

2

Kinship Matters

Women's Land Claims in the Santal Parganas*

Introduction: Land, Kinship and Identity

This chapter discusses the processes by which kinship relations, particularly patrilineages, are being strengthened amongst the Santal community in a village, called here Chuapara,[1] in Dumka district, Jharkhand (see Figure 2.1). The rise of a democratic state, accepting the notion of equal rights for all citizens, alongside the creation of market institutions (wage labour and land markets, for instance) to meet production requirements, is expected to lead to an erosion of men's base of power in terms of both caste- and kinship-based control over land. However, writings in the field of anthropology have demonstrated the continuing importance of kinship in determining property rights and gendered access to resources, social rights and obligations, and in organising power and authority.[2] Rather than withering away, social structures of kinship and caste have been re-fashioned, with the upper-caste elite diversifying and dominating non-agricultural assets, not just land. Women, who face disadvantages in terms of education, capital and mobility while continuing to be held responsible for household maintenance, are further marginalised in this diversification process (Epstein, Suryanarayana and Thimmegowda, 1998; Harriss-White and Janakarajan, 2004). Sacks notes that

---

*This chapter was originally published as an article in the *Journal of the Royal Anthropological Institute* © Royal Anthropological Institute 2005. All rights reserved. Reproduced with the permission of the copyright holder and the publisher, John Wiley and Sons, Hoboken, New Jersey. The chapter is based on fieldwork carried out between 1998 and 2000 in the Santal Parganas, Jharkhand, as part of my PhD research.

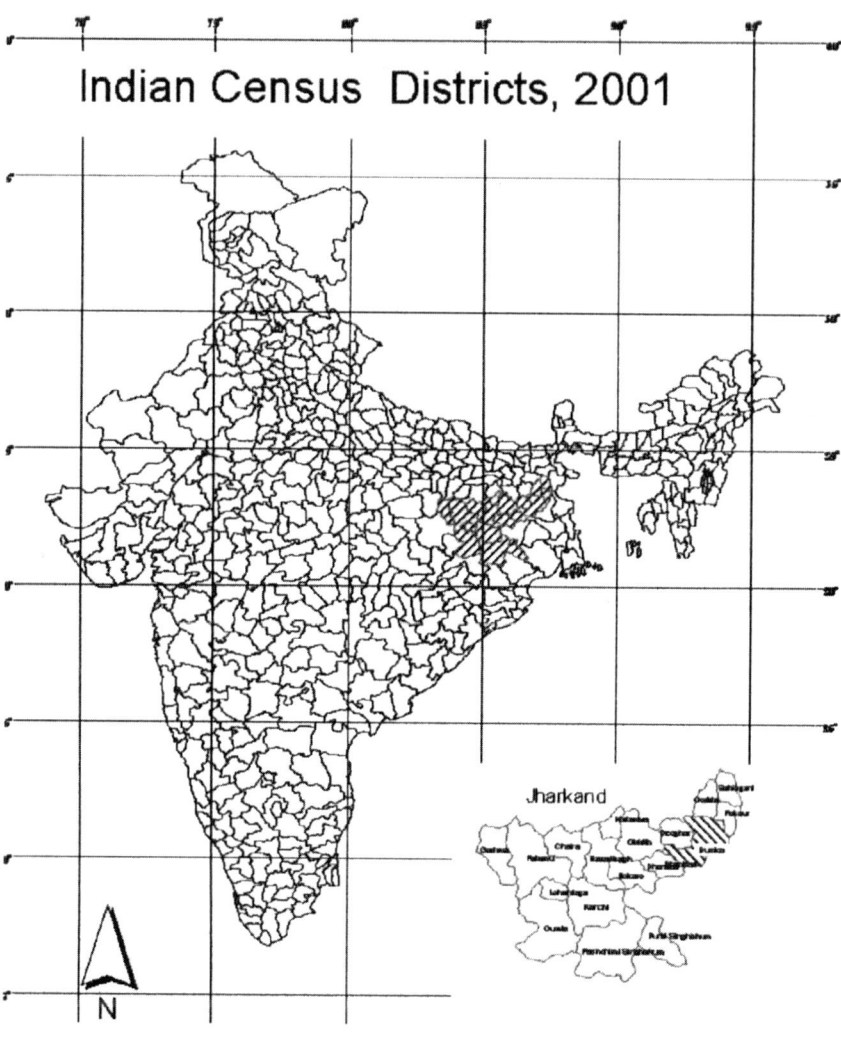

Figure 2.1 Location of Dumka district, Jharkhand

Source: Map prepared by the author based on data from Census of India, 2001.

Note: Map not to scale and does not represent authentic international boundaries.

the other side of that process is that kin corporations were not totally destroyed over-night. Rather they have been and continue to be slowly subverted, transformed, and overcome – only to struggle toward rebirth repeatedly as a defense against ruling-class attacks, as a means of spreading the risks of existence, or as a way of holding one's own against poverty. Women as sisters, mothers, and wives, have been the central actors in these struggles. This history has yet to be written. (1979: 7)

In this chapter, I examine the ways in which kinship relations are being reformulated and their implications for gender in a context where the struggle for a separate state of Jharkhand emphasises not just a class or proletarian identity but also a tribal, or *adivasi*, identity. There has been considerable debate on the use of different terms when representing the tribes, as these have varying political connotations. Hardiman notes that the term *adivasi* is preferable in the Indian context – with over 400 such communities representing close to 8 per cent of the total population – as it relates to 'a particular historical development: that of subjugation' (1987: 15) by traders, moneylenders and landlords[3] who established themselves under the protection of colonial authorities. 'This experience generated a spirit of resistance which incorporated a consciousness of "the *adivasi*" against "the outsider"' (1987: 15). There are different *adivasi* groups resident in the study village – the Santals, Kols and Paharias. The colonial heritage (leading to the loss of land and resources) and the impact of growing materialism and individualism, particularly in relation to market integration (Nathan and Kelkar, 2003), have, however, led many of these groups to mobilise across local and regional borders to assert a shared identity.

Though the *adivasi*s constitute only a quarter of the total population of present-day Jharkhand, one of the justifications for the creation of the new state in 2000 was the marginalisation and poverty of the region's populations, particularly the *adivasi*s, within the larger state of Bihar (Sengupta, 1982).[4] In terms of most development indicators – whether employment, income levels or literacy[5] – the tribes tend to be worse off than other populations in the region. The focus on *adivasi* identity as part of the Jharkhand movement had a clear political motivation in terms of gaining control over resources, particularly land and forests, viewed as an inalienable part of that identity. Yet, as Singh (1983) points out, the movement has gone through several phases. In its initial years, from the 1920s to the 1960s, it was a radical, sectarian movement focusing on strengthening *adivasi* identity through a mini-renaissance involving the development of a script, a literature, festivals (Parkin, 2000) and quotas in post-independence education and exployment[6]. By the early 1970s, with a decline in the percentage of *adivasi*s in the population due to a heavy influx of labour migrants from other parts of north India seeking work in the mines and factories (Corbridge, 1988), the only way the movement could sustain itself was by allying with other subordinated groups. A.K. Roy, trade union leader and convenor of the Marxist Coordination Committee, commented, in an interview in Dhanbad on 10 December 2000, that

> the movement for Jharkhand State gained strength after Shibu Soren and the Jharkhand Mukti Morcha [JMM] gave this demand a socio-economic basis. Till then it was a movement based on *adivasi* identity. With socio-economic issues in the forefront, poor people got interested and supported the demand for Jharkhand.

Despite this shift, the focus on *adivasi* identity has remained strong, as exemplified by the demand from all political groups that the chief minister of the newly formed state be an *adivasi*, and preferably a Santal, the largest *adivasi* group in the state. This emphasis on a 'community' identity, however, focuses on men, and solidarity in many ways is achieved by denying women, valued as economic actors, both agency and identity in the socio-political realm (Baviskar, 1995). Thus, the JMM, the major political party representing the *adivasi*s, offered women inheritance rights in marital rather than natal property on conditions of strict monogamy, restricted divorce and marriage within the tribe, effectively restricting their marital and sexual choice. 'Women are simple and get exploited by *diku* [a term used for outsiders; literally, those who give trouble] men, who marry them for the sake of their land,' says Shibu Soren, the leader of the JMM, in an interview in New Delhi on 2 August 2000. He clearly links alienation of land from *adivasi*s to non-*adivasi*s to women's marital choice.[7] This puts *adivasi* women, active in the movement, in a contradictory position, denying, rather than enhancing, both their political voice and their rights to resources. In the 2004 Lok Sabha elections, for instance, the JMM contested in nine out of fourteen seats in Jharkhand but put forward only one woman candidate, who lost. Interestingly, of the thirteen women candidates who fought this election, six were independents (Election Commission of India, 2004: 188–89). Skaria notes in the case of the Dangs, an *adivasi* group in western India, that implicit within such politics of *adivasi* identity are notions of accentuated masculinity, an exclusionary relationship with land and ethnic purity (1999: 299).

In Jharkhand, the demand for universal land rights for women was first raised through two public interest litigations filed in the Supreme Court of India in 1982 and 1986, respectively, on behalf of two *adivasi* women.[8] The judgments, both pronounced in 1996, went in favour of the concerned women. Following this, a meeting of *adivasi* leaders in Ranchi, the present state capital, rejected the judgments as interfering with their customary law. This was supported by several women activists, who argued for a more contextualised view of land, seeing support to their own men as more beneficial in terms of expanding their longer-term, strategic interests in a context of the marginality of the entire group.[9] In order to operationalise their rights and secure support for ploughing – an act traditionally forbidden to women (Dube, 1986) – it is critical that women have social sanction and legitimacy, which can derive from negotiations within kinship and clan structures. A gendered analysis of election results by Deshpande (2004) illustrates that low-caste, poor, *adivasi* and *dalit* women themselves tend to prioritise their community identities over their gender identities. Women are then caught between upholding their rights to land against the members of their own lineages through reliance on a progressive national framework[10] and supporting traditional institutions, representing an identity distinct from that of the state, as a legitimate basis for claiming resources both from the community and the federal state.

While the state in India sees itself as a welfare state, it does not have adequate resources to meet the basic needs of all people, let alone provide adequate social security.[11] Even if resources exist, weaknesses in implementation mechanisms, coupled with the unequal social relations of caste, class, ethnicity and gender, prevent all groups from equally accessing them. In such a situation, people have only kin and community to fall back on in emergencies as well as for reciprocal support on a daily basis. If a person is ill and needs to be taken to the hospital, local support is clearly needed: physical help in carrying the sick person, financial help to pay doctor's fees and domestic help with taking care of children as well as perhaps planting or weeding fields.

There is a further issue here in terms of the priorities and workings of the post-colonial state. The region is rich in mineral deposits, and after independence the state's major development investments have gone into extracting and industrially refining those resources. After its creation the government of Jharkhand, too, has emphasised this prioritisation in, for instance, its *Vision 2010* document (see Chapter 11),[12] even though over 80 per cent of the population continues to be rural and dependent on agriculture. The main source of economic security and in turn social mobility and political power is through diversification into non-agricultural sectors. There has been hardly any investment in improving agricultural productivity either through infrastructure development or through the provision of credit, inputs and other agricultural services. Claiming land titles in such a context, where land, while crucial to male status and identity, is unable to meet livelihood needs, could be a risky strategy for women in terms of future security.

There is perhaps a lesson to be learned from the ethnography of Stivens, Ng and Jomo (1994), which found a growing feminisation of landed property relations in rural Malaysia. With the modern state's focus on industrial investment, there was a massive out-migration from the rural sector, which was mostly male insofar as women were disadvantaged in the labour market. In parallel with this general decline in the rural economy, religious revivalism contributed to the cultural valuation of women as 'conservers' of the rural sector. In line with such a representation, as well as the growing feminisation of the rural workforce, matrilineal kinship systems were reworked. Younger women, however, preferred to look for socially valued work in the industrial sector rather than to stay on in the villages and tend the land.

The political context thus seems crucial in reconstructing local social systems. Among the Santals, patrilineal kinship ties appear to have grown stronger as mediators of entitlements, whether food cards, health care, information or access to strategic resources. This has occurred in response to the poverty and marginalisation of the *adivasi*s vis-à-vis other social groups in the region. It has manifested itself in several ways. The first involves the presentation of a united face in negotiations with the outside world. The second is a more subversive form of resistance to outside pressures, of representing the legitimacy of alternative cultures, institutions and ways of life, drawing its justification from the struggle for political autonomy. The third involves taking on the rituals and status symbols of the higher strata, especially as these pertain to controlling women's sexuality, in an attempt to defend communal honour while retaining official identity as a Scheduled Tribe so as to access state benefits and resources (Parry, 1979). All these strands are achieved through an emphasis on group boundedness (Das, 1976; Strathern, 1987).

Whatever the meaning, kinship operates in gendered ways in distributing resources and organising work, time and space (Dube, 1997). At the micro level, a strengthening of patrilineal kinship ties could work against women's interests by opposing their land claims (Agarwal, 1994) and excluding them from the more public, decision-making bodies of the village and at higher levels. There are several examples of women being denied their share of land, often with threats, and being then forced to either leave the village or live as subordinates to their brothers or other kinsmen. The idea of personal autonomy, in this case represented through women's claims to land, is linked to the idiom of detachment from the kin group and thus opposed. In Strathern's terms, gender becomes a 'vehicle for conceptualising differences in the quality of kinship attachments' (1987: 274). While women contribute to the expansion of the male clan through biological reproduction, their land claims pose a dangerous penetration into the hegemony of clans and patrikin. Women, however, do attempt to push back boundaries, often seeking alternate forms of legitimacy for their claims through state jural institutions – the courts, police and local government.

This points to an often overlooked issue, namely the interpenetration of models of kinship and polity and models of gender domains (Yanagisako, 1987). A brief review of the land settlement process in the next section provides insights into the role of the state in opening up the space for social negotiation by recording individual rights. Women, through their claims and contestations, have in fact contributed to a process of reconstructing and transforming patrilineal kinship. Despite opposition to the claims of individual women, lineage heads, often also the village elders, have supported women's claims to land in state arenas, with a view to enhancing their own legitimacy in a context of declining power and authority vis-à-vis the state. Nicholas's insight that the distribution of power and authority is reflected not only in relative command over material resources and benefits but also in interpersonal command (1968: 244) helps us to understand this renegotiation of kinship and gender relations.

History of Land Settlements in the Santal Parganas

The first land settlement in the Santal Parganas, constituted as a separate district in 1855 following the *hul* (rebellion) against economic and political oppression, was conducted between 1873 and 1879. It demarcated village boundaries, identified forest, irrigation and grazing rights, assessed the number of houses and ploughs and fixed rents for the whole village. The task of distributing the land amongst the *raiyat*s (cultivators) and collecting the rent from them was, however, left to the headman, who, in return for his services, received a 1 per cent commission from the rent collected or an allocation of land (O'Malley, 1984 [1910]). Given the fixity of rent, and the limit put on interests on loans at the same time, land became valuable in the period that followed and, in return for loans given to the Santals, moneylenders and traders rapidly took over a large part of the cultivable land (MacDougall, 1985: 110). The dispossessed Santals could file a case against the alienation of their land in the revenue court through the headman, but this rarely happened, due to the economic strength of the creditors, who could easily bribe headmen into silence. Furthermore, as non-tribals, these traders and lenders were also not accountable to the Santal village council. Subsequently the McPherson settlement (1898–1908) not only classified land and fixed individual rents but also set up alternative institutions for dispute resolution. This began the process of eroding the power of kinship-based authorities, including the councils of village elders, by cutting the material bases of their power despite leaving with them the rights to bring new land (forests, commons and wastelands) into cultivation.

During this time (from 1901 until 1907–08), C. H. Bompas, Indian Civil Service (ICS), Deputy Commissioner of the Santal Parganas (later Commissioner), prepared a comprehensive note, compiling case law on the subject of partition, inheritance and marriage, which formed the basis for the formulation of the settlement rules. He noted that daughters did not inherit a share of land, even though H. McPherson, his Settlement Officer, found many women in cultivating possession of land (McPherson, 1909: 123).

Given the potential undermining of their authority by the establishment of the settlement courts and the attempt by the government to interpret their custom in relation to land inheritance, the *parganait*s, *desmanjhi*s, *sardars*[13] and other community leaders organised a meeting in Dumka on 15 February 1916 to discuss these issues. The leaders felt that if a man had only daughters, they would be his heirs when married. When a man had sons and daughters and the sons died without having children, the girls would become the heirs. A widow, they argued, had a life interest in her husband's property (Bodding, Skresfrud and Konow 1994 [1942]: 198).

This articulation can be interpreted as a reassertion of customary rights and authority by the male leadership, defining itself as the protector of all members of the community – men and women – in the face of colonial domination. It also redefined women's rights in opposition to state-sponsored individual titling that tended to exclude women, thus reflecting simultaneous openness to change as well as the rootedness and strength of kinship and clan ties.

The Gantzer settlement (1924–29) followed, deleting names of tenants and legitimising land transfers, even though these may in fact have entailed the alienation of lands of poorer *adivasi*s to both *diku*s and the better off amongst the Santals. It carried forward Bompas's views on female inheritance while recognising *gharjamai* rights (Gantzer, 1936). This term, literally meaning a resident son-in-law, refers to a situation where after marriage a girl stays in her natal home with her husband and inherits natal property. The only subsequent settlement operation, started in 1978, has not yet been published, though the record for Chuapara was finalized in 1996.

The Santal Pargana Tenancy Act (SPTA), passed soon after independence in 1949, forms the basis for governing land relations and transactions in the Santal Parganas. Given a history of land alienation, the Act (through Section 20) has sought to protect *adivasi* rights by making all land in the region non-transferable. Yet there are a few exceptions to this clause, primarily in relation to women's rights. These include:

1. Gift to daughter or sister, with previous written permission of the DC [Deputy Commissioner];
2. Grant of not more than half of the area of his holding to his widowed mother or wife for her maintenance after his death with the previous written permission of the DC;
3. Transfer in favour of *gharjamai* or *ghardijamai*; and
4. Lease for the purpose of an excise shop for not more than one year, with the previous written permission of the DC. (Prasad, 1997: 30)

Interestingly, except in the case of the *gharjamai*, which is viewed as a right by the SPTA, the claims of widows, daughters and sisters, though articulated in custom, as documented by Archer (1984 [1946])[14], are presented as gifts or grants rather than rights. While a daughter generally does not inherit land, she can do so according to Santal customary law if she is married to a *gharjamai*, if a gift is made by her father and if her marriage fails. The wife has full access to her husband's property even though her rights are not legally recorded. If her husband takes a second wife, she gets an equal share of the property, and if she then decides to return to her natal village, she can claim a share there, locally called *taben jom*. Santal widows again have a number of rights, differentiated by their age and by the age and sex of their children. Given the legal status of the SPTA, these customary rights are now, however, demoted to social obligations or moral entitlements rather than legal rights. Further, such a statutory code, supported by the setting up of legal bureaucracies in each district, has led to a further decline in the real authority of kinship groups, in terms of their ability to mediate land inheritance and management. Nevertheless, the SPTA has ensured that all (male) *adivasis* retain some land on the records and thus, compared to other regions, landlessness is minimal amongst them.

There has been much discussion in recent years about the relative benefits of statutory and customary law in terms of women's rights. Customary systems of tenure are seen to be riven with inequalities based on gender, status and lineage, especially in patrilineal settings, and hence feminist lawyers, academics and activists (Agarwal, 1994; Dhagamwar, 2003) strongly argue in favour of statutory law. Scott, however, notes that despite the hierarchies and inequities involved, customs are also strongly local, particular and hence adaptable (1998: 35). States, too, are not monolithic entities; state norms and rules are interpreted by individual bureaucrats according to their own ideologies and positions as social actors (Goetz, 1997). Moore argues that state and community institutions are not autonomous spheres but shape each other within the same web of social relations (2001: 107). While the choice between statutory and customary law, available to the Santals to resolve disputes, can lead to some ambiguity, it also provides room for manoeuvre. Whether subject to statutory or customary law, it is important to recognise that women's land claims have always been different from those of men. This is because of the different positions of women and men in marriage and kinship systems, which continue to be in large part responsible for organising access to land.

Chuapara: Changes in Land and Society

I discuss the data from Chuapara in two sections. The first looks at changes in relationships based on tribe, clan and kin identity, while the second specifically explores the changes in gender relationships, discussing how various constructions of gender are related to propositions about group attachment and boundedness. In terms of methodology, the study of land records provided information on resource allocation in the village at particular moments of time. Yet ethnographic research in a context of multi-layered power struggles helped reveal 'the importance of de facto rather than de jure interpretations of local land tenure systems' (Nicholas, 1968: 266) in enhancing social status and interpersonal command locally and in asserting the superiority of the 'community' in a regional context. I therefore combine an analysis of the land records historically with an ethnographic study, conducted over a period of eighteen months during 1999–2000, to reflect on text in relation to context.

Strengthening Single Group Control: Shifting Ethnic Composition

Chuapara, 74 kilometres from the district headquarters of Dumka, is located 17 kilometres away from the nearest roadhead, within the Damin-i-koh, or 'skirt of hills', as the British colonisers named this tribal heartland. Surrounded by hills and forests, its name is derived from the stream that runs through it, *chuin sudo* in Santali.

Chuapara today continues to be home to an entirely *adivasi* population, with forty Santal, eleven Kol and two Paharia households. All the Santals and most of the Kols own 1–2 acres of paddy land and perceive themselves as farmers, even though a considerable proportion of their household income derives from the collection and sale of forest produce. While the Santal tribe includes twelve patrilineal clans, or *paris*, seven major and five minor, only five of the major clans are represented in Chuapara. At present, the Marandis account for twenty-two of the fifty-three households, with the rest made up of nine Murmu households, five Tudus, two Hansdaks and two Sorens. The settlement consists of three hamlets, or *tolas*. *Latar tola*, or the lower hamlet, has eighteen houses of the non-dominant Santal clans. A path leads south to *tala tola*, with twenty households, most belonging to the dominant Marandi clan, said to be the founders of the village. The Marandis collectively control the largest proportion of village land and also dominate positions of authority. Two of their men – the *parganait* Samli (leader of a group of villages; in this case 23) and his son Theo – have completed their matriculation, and a few others have been educated up to middle school. Only one woman – Mariam, the wife of Manas, Samli's younger brother – has completed primary school and serves as an assistant at the *anganwadi* (childcare) centre that runs in the house of Manas's father's brother's son. Five of the households in this *tola* have converted to Christianity. The Kol and Paharia households inhabit *chetan tola*, or the upper hamlet, which also has two Santal houses.

In the mid-nineteenth century there was in the village an almost equal demographic balance between the Kols (another tribe) and the Santals. By the turn of the twentieth century, there was a dramatic decline in the number of Kol households (by 50 per cent), while the Mahlis, or basket-makers, disappeared, and the Santals became predominant (Table 2.1). Their land ownership sustains the hegemony of the Santals; while accounting for 63 per cent of the *jamabandi* (JB)[15] households, they own 79 per cent of the village land. Although there is no apparent hostility between the Santals and the Kols, the dominant culture of the village is defined by the Santals, and the Kols accord them with this hegemony as they do not consider themselves strong enough to form a separate faction. They have their own language but use Santali in the course of daily life.

In addition to the two Paharia households in the village, there are a few more scattered on the hilltops around Chuapara, which are not included in its land records. The Santals interact with them, paying them a small amount of money to cultivate crops – maize and black-eye beans – on the hill slopes. While there is clearly a hierarchy amongst the *adivasi*s, with the Paharias at the bottom and the Santals (themselves ranked) at the top, all the tribes are marginal vis-à-vis other groups – Hindus and Muslims – who dominate the bureaucracy, trade and professions.

The process by which the Santals gained dominance can be illustrated through tracking changes in the land ownership of one sample household, that of Manas Marandi (JB 20). As the 'original settlers' of the village, his forefathers had 21.55 acres of land during the first settlement. Between 1872 and 1880, ten of the twenty-eight households in the village migrated to Assam, having been enticed to work on the tea plantations by both British administrators and missionaries. According to the records their lands were

Table 2.1 Distribution of households and land by ethnic communities across settlements

Ethnicity	Wood (1879)		McPherson (1908)		Gantzer (1936)		Current (1997)	
	No.	Acres	No.	Acres	No.	Acres	No.	Acres
Kol	12	51.52	6	34.99	6	38.15	6	38.21
Mahli	2	1.52	0	0	0	0	0	0
Paharia	0	0	1	1.80	1	2.31	1	2.31
Santal	14	109.87	13	94.69	12	152.14	14	152.00
Total*	29	162.91	21	131.48	20	192.6	22	192.52

Source: District Record Room (n.d.).

Note: *The total includes *pradhani jote*.

leased out for five years, but they were given the impression that they had lost their land in the village and were thus persuaded to stay on in Assam. Meanwhile, at home, the land was resettled to others, most of whom were the headman's clansmen and distant kin. This increased his personal authority while creating a support group of his own kinsmen in the village.

With the McPherson settlement most of the previous informal transfers were formalised. When the headman gave the land of Dasu Kol and Getha Santal to the ancestors of Manas, he increased the Marandi holding to 23.54 acres. They also appropriated the 9.65 acres of *pradhani jote*,[16] or headman's fields, getting it recorded in their own name. This holding, now less than an acre, is perceived as being too small a recompense for performing the administrative duties assigned to the headman. These involve not just the collection of rents, but also updating records, performing basic police functions and servicing the petty bureaucracy, including provision of meals during their visits to the village. In the mid-1950s, after the death of the previous *pradhan*, Chuapara became a *khas* village – that is, directly under state revenue administration. Yet, in the event of a dispute, the village first consults a group of elderly men, mostly Marandi but including one Tudu and one Murmu, who it considers as 'big men' due to their kinship affiliations and economic stature.

At the beginning of the twentieth century, out-migration to Assam stopped. Manas' ancestors, in lieu of taking over the fields of those who had left the village, now increased their holdings by clearing jungles and making new fields for which new revenue *patta*s (title deeds) were secured. The current settlement shows a stagnation in the quantum of landholdings, though in reality most of the families constituting this larger kin group had cleared and registered 1–2 acres of land (a total of about 25 acres of land) between 1992 and 1993. This was possible under the state provision to regularise and register land reclaimed for cultivation by marginal farmers (those owning less than 5 acres of land).

Discussing the granting of *patta*s by the government to eighteen households in the village, Chibu Murmu remarked, 'Manas took the leadership in getting this grant of *patta*s, but he only did so for his own kin. Our land, too, is shared by ten households, and each of us cultivate only a small portion, yet we did not get land.' While he is not entirely correct, as five households from his kin group also received *patta*s, his interpretation echoes that of most residents in seeing kinship and patronage as closely related to access to land resources.

Potential benefits from kinship ties is one factor that has prevented many junior men and women from getting their rights to land recorded in the current settlement. While in terms of cooking, living and income-sharing there are fifty-three household units in the village, there are only twenty-one recorded in the land settlement.[17] In many cases the land continues to be listed in the name of the father, often dead for several years. In the case of JB 20, which includes sixteen households, the name of Manas' elder brother Samli has replaced that of his father. A correction was made in the record; yet none of the households got their titles recorded separately even though each conjugal unit carries out the daily management of land and work on clearly demarcated plots of land. While partition of families has been viewed as a normal phase in the development cycle of a household, clearly choice and timing can be constrained by a range of factors, material and ideological (Parry, 1979), such as demographic changes, economic mobility or status considerations (Gould, 1968: 414).

In this particular case, though the senior-most male is now seen to control family property, this is more 'in a representative rather than a proprietory character', with the family expanding over generations to become a self-regulating 'brotherhood of relatives', the so-called 'village community' (Uberoi, 1993: 9). As among the Sikh Jats, in Chuapara, family power is also dependent on the 'concentration of the family [read brothers] in one place, in combination with the possession of a large land-holding and a wide network of linkages outside the village' (Pettigrew, 1975: 55).

The current land record is perhaps an attempt to project an image of a close-knit, self-regulating community to the outside world (Orans, 1965) and to reiterate the supremacy of community institutions in a context where clearly this authority is declining. While not controlling day-to-day land management decisions, the title holders retain a patriarchal hierarchy and a gate-keeping role in terms of external interactions, while at the same time ensuring some collectivity in decision-making on land (including cattle management, which is essential for double cropping). The kin elders, particularly the Marandis, have been able to secure land deeds and develop an irrigation infrastructure benefitting the larger group, thus maintaining their dominance in village affairs. Kinship seems to subsume both the material and ideological aspects of life in terms of links with the production system and property as well as with decision-making, entitlements to resources and social support (Dube, 1997).

This is visible also in the mediating role that the Santals have been playing in a land dispute between the Paharias and the Kols. With increasing state control and declining access to forest resources, following the Forest Conservation Act, 1980, the Paharias have realised the need for settled cultivation. Samu Grihi, a Paharia residing on the hill slopes, had cleared a few plots of land for cultivation within the boundaries of Chuapara. The Kols, led by Titu and Dinu, threatened him and staked claim to that land in mid-1997. Samu filed a complaint in the court of the Sub-Divisional Magistrate (SDM), but hearings have been few and far between. In July 1998, under the chairmanship of a Santal *parganait* of a neighbouring cluster of villages, a community hearing was held, wherein Samu was awarded full rights over the forest land, and the Kols over the *raiyati* lands (those settled for cultivation). This agreement was signed by all of them with witnesses from the village.

The quantum of land itself is not much – 0.62 acre in all – yet a dispute such as this not only impinges on the social relationships and interaction between the two communities in the village, but also provides some insights into the nature of power relationships. While the Kols are marginal in relation to the Santals, they are able to exert some authority over the Paharias. Clearly, here the power is seen to derive from their landholding status. The Santals, negotiating the settlement, have in the process asserted the superiority of their own traditional institutions, as well as indicating their clout as 'settlers of the land' to the other groups, namely the Kols and Paharias, as well as state structures and the bureaucracy.

This is in fact a paradox. In a context of state control over law and order as well as land revenue management, along with growing diversification into non-land activities for survival, one would expect to see people identify more with others in similar socio-economic positions, to be better able to claim their rights, rather than kinship (Pasternak, Ember and Ember, 1997: 263). But as Harriss has noted in his study of capitalism and peasant farming in northern Tamil Nadu, the process of differentiation is blocked by the character of the economy (which continues to work on the basis of patronage) and the ideological structures of caste and kinship (1979: 13). These, however, now play different roles, such as accessing new technologies, information, state resources, and so on.[18] In Chuapara, too, one finds the strengthening of community ties, based predominantly on kinship links within the different Santal clans, particularly the dominant Marandis, though also support to (often patronage of) other clans and tribes within the village. This appears as a resistance strategy to an increase in state controls, an assertion of their own authority in the sphere of land distribution and management and a survival strategy in terms of both retaining their distinct identity and maintaining a social security mechanism, in a context where state provision is seriously lacking. This has meant gains for certain kin groups, clans and tribes, and exclusions for others, as the aforementioned examples have illustrated. This becomes clearer as one interrogates the gender subtexts of these relations.

Gendered Changes in Land Ownership

Gough (1981), in her analysis of the land records of two villages in Thanjavur district, Tamil Nadu, has shown that while no women were recorded in 1827, eleven out of ninety registered owners (12.2 per cent) were women in 1897, increasing to 27 out of 139 (19.4 per cent) in 1952. Gough claims that due to the breakdown of the commune and the extended family system, which led to land becoming personal property, daughters got shares in land as their dowry. Widows got life interests in land on the deaths of their husbands, and several took to managing their own property. It appears from this that a decline in kin-group control is beneficial for women in terms of both access to productive property and control over sexuality, marriage partner, and so on. Yet there could be losses, too, as decline in kin networks could reflect a shrinking of safety nets for women. As Walker notes in the case of South Africa, 'while the patriarchal household may be a site of oppression for women, it is also a source of identity and support, providing membership in a social network that is often the only effective resource poor women have' (2003: 47).

While the legal recognition of women's rights and the decline in kin-group control are no doubt important factors for the growing presence of women in the land records, in this section I focus on the intense process of social negotiation around land rights in which women constantly seek ways to push back the boundaries of kinship norms without renouncing kinship relations altogether. There are many more women in possession of land than are recorded, and in some instances not recording their rights is a conscious strategy to best utilise social claims on their kin group.

As already mentioned, women do not inherit land as a right but are entitled to it in certain special circumstances. The goal of every woman is supposed to be marriage. Amongst the Santals, seven different forms of marriage are recognised, ranging from an arranged, first marriage to an elopement. In most forms of marriage the woman moves to her husband's village, given the preference for village exogamy. Unlike in clan exogamy, this is not, however, essential, especially in the event of some of the more informal marriages, particularly those relating to secondary alliances. After marriage, women share and cultivate their husbands' fields and have almost total control over the use of *bari*, or homestead plots, which, in Chuapara, constitute just over 70 per cent of recorded land (135 out of 189 acres).

Here I consider the *gharjamai* form of marriage (recognised by the SPTA), wherein, at the time of the marriage, the son-in-law formally gives up claims on the property of his own father as long as he stays in the marriage. The girl then inherits the land on which the couple live. Archer (1984 [1946]) gives several reasons why a *gharjamai* is brought; these include the need for an extra man to look after the land, the parents' desire to fill the house with children and guard against the loneliness of old age, their love for particular daughters, the daughter being disabled or having an illegitimate child, and the family's desire to keep the land in the immediate family rather than letting it pass on to more distant kin. Goody (1976) has pointed out that in contexts of intensive plough cultivation as well as individual titling linked to the commoditisation of property, the desire to transmit one's property to one's direct descendants becomes strong. In the case of a failure to produce a son, alternate strategies can be used depending on when decisions are made in the man's life cycle. These include allowing the daughter to inherit by gift (*taben jom*), appointing her as a social male through the formal adoption of a son-in-law (*gharjamai*) or taking more wives. While Archer's explanation offers a much broader view based on emotional and social bonds, it is interesting to note that Goody's emphasis on descent has in fact become the major justification for challenging, rather than supporting, *gharjamai* because of intensifying intra-kin competition for property in recent years.

At present, the only woman listed in the landholding records is Baha Marandi (JB 12) (see Table 2.2). Baha's father was a member of the dominant clan and kin group in the village – the Marandis. An only child, Baha was married to a *gharjamai*, Jadu Kisku of Badhniya village (about 10 miles away in 1981), when she was eleven years old. Her father had to secure the permission of the kin elders for such an alliance through a formal process of application and acceptance, sealed over several cups of rice beer (*handia*). Her father died in 1984. She and her husband cultivated their two acres of land, had three children and were well settled. In August 1995, Baha's mother died. That year she and her husband completed their cultivation, but then her father's brother's sons, Cheenu and Pappu, started demanding that they leave the land to them, under threats of death, so the couple moved to her husband's village (Figure 2.2). There is little land there, and they have to depend on wage labour for survival.

Table 2.2 Gendered changes in ownership patterns

	McPherson (1908)			Current (1997)		
Caste	No. of women	F. acre	M. acre	No. of women	F. acre	M. acre
Santal	0	0	94.69	1	2.94	149.06
Kol	2	4.47	30.52	0	0	38.21
Total*	2	4.47	127.01	1	2.94	189.58
Percent	9.5	3.4	96.6	4.5	1.5	98.5

Source: District Record Room (n.d.).

Note: *The total includes *pradhani jote*.

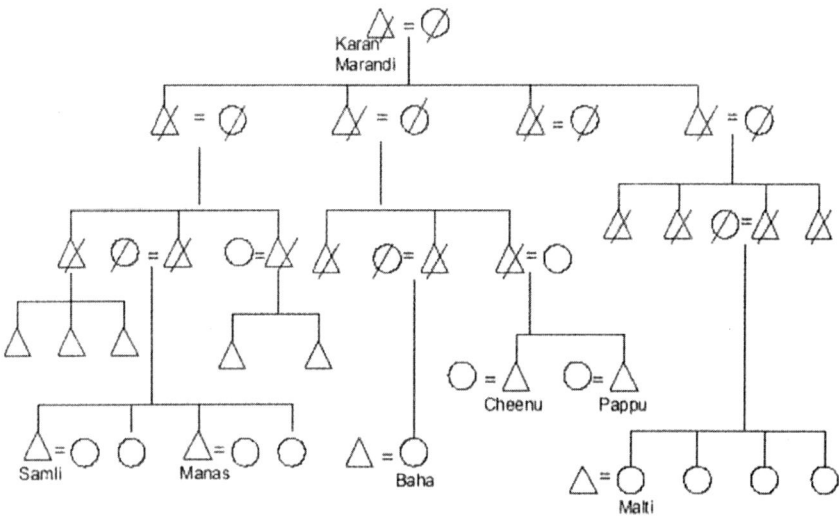

Figure 2.2 The Marandi family tree

Source: Prepared by the author.

Cheenu and Pappu based their resistance on the claim that the land had been for the lifetime maintenance of her mother rather than an inheritance for Baha. As they had performed the funeral rights of both her parents, they were the rightful claimants of the land. Further, if Baha inherited the land, it would then go to her sons. In line with patrilineal kinship descent, they would take the name of their father, a Kisku. As the Santals practise clan exogamy in marriage, the land would henceforth be transferred to another clan. Believing that it is their clan that has cleared and settled the land, they argue against the descendants of another clan enjoying the fruits of 'their' labour.

In 1996, Baha returned to Chuapara to ask for her share. Cheenu said, 'Nothing has been cultivated on the land, so what share can I give?' The following year, too, Cheenu refused to allow Baha and Jadu to plough the fields. A village hearing was held, but no consensus could be reached. There were several reasons for this. First, in the absence of a recognised *pradhan*, the group of leaders is not fixed, and hence Cheenu and Pappu were able to mobilize support for themselves especially among the younger generation of leaders. Fearing a potential scarcity of land, especially in successive generations, many of them were keen to establish more rigid boundaries in order to protect their own future interests. Yet a few, such as Manas and Samli, who had participated in Baha's wedding and were party to the *gharjamai* deed, supported her claim. But finding themselves challenged, they advised her to file a case in the sub-divisional court in the district headquarters and offered to accompany her there when required. Fighting the case has been expensive, entailing travelling all the way to Dumka several times a year as well as paying lawyer's fees. Although the case is still ongoing, it is likely to go in Baha's favour given that, in the absence of codified Santal civil rules or a codified customary law, *gharjamai* rights are recognised by the only source of legal guidance to the courts, the SPTA.

In the meanwhile, in January 1998, there was a second village hearing, following the listing of Baha's name in the new village land record. She has been officially paying the rent since 1996–97,[19] and hence Cheenu and Pappu agreed to take back their claim on the share of land belonging to her. Yet they continue to threaten her and do not allow her to cultivate the land. Cheenu and Pappu currently have less than 1.5 acres of paddy land and about 2 acres of *bari* each and are amongst the poorest of the villagers. Acquiring Baha's share of 2.1 acres of paddy land would, apart from improving their living conditions and allowing them to better perform their 'provider' roles (Jackson, 2000), also enhance their social status, enabling them eventually to join the 'big men' of the village.

There is a tension here between affinal ties and group rights, with Baha's claim (as a *gharjamai*) stressing spousal/conjugal relations over relations with siblings – in this case her male cousins (see also Sacks, 1979). Gould (1968), Parry (1979) and several other anthropologists have noted that solidarity is weaker among siblings than among parents and children. Among the Santals, too, both clan and village exogamy imply that women, though critical to the social reproduction of the patriliny, have to ensure their security by manipulating conjugal ties.

What seems also to be implicated here is a struggle for survival on limited resources (land cannot be purchased or sold according to the SPTA). With each partition, the quantum of landholding shrinks. Clearly, not everybody can have enough, and over the generations selections must be made among claimants. Kinship ideologies are increasingly called into play to do this. In the face of competition, people are likely to call first on the familiar notion of unilineal kinship (that is, descent and inheritance from the father) and only to forge cross-kin associations (developing networks on the mother's side as well) when the former proves insufficient to manage the property. This is clear in the case of Chuapara, where, in the previous generation, women's brothers and fathers allocated several women land even when they were not married in the *gharjamai* form. The rights of such women, however, are now being challenged (Figure 2.3), and one of them has been asked by her brother to

Figure 2.3 A widowed woman in Chuapara planting paddy to ensure her stakes in the land

Source: Photograph by Amit Mitra.

give up her property claims. Having lived in Chuapara for over twenty years, she is unhappy about moving to her husband's village, so at present they lease other lands for cultivation from those who may either have a surplus or are unable to cultivate due to sickness. In a patrilineal society, where women move between clans and kin groups at marriage, their claims are thus the first to be excluded.

Yet one also finds a woman such as Malti Marandi (JB 20) effectively exercising her rights to the land. A Marandi and a member of the dominant kin group in the village, Malti, the eldest of four sisters, was married to a *gharjamai*, Dhena Murmu, twenty years ago (see Figure 2.2). They have one seventeen-year-old daughter. Even though the kin group is now large, consisting of sixteen male descendants, its members decided to give Malti an equal share of 1.75 acres of paddy land, which she has been cultivating without any challenges to her control. This is recognised as an inheritance insofar as her marriage to a *gharjamai* had been approved by the kin elders (the Santals normally follow a system of bride price rather than dowry in terms of marriage exchange). In fact, her husband, who has knowledge of herbal medicine, is the accepted *ojha* (medicine man) of the village and is called upon both for herbal healing and for ritual incantations. When asked if they would bring a *gharjamai* for their daughter, however, the couple's reply was in the negative. Having witnessed Baha's case, they were afraid of trouble from Malti's patrikin if they did so. While not averse to the idea of getting their daughter married to a *gharjamai*, they are considering the possibility of doing so in Dhena's village.

Apart from the growing challenge to women's land claims, an interesting issue in terms of gender relationships is the differential treatment accorded to men and women in their claims on land. When women are deserted by their husband or leave their marriage and go back to their natal home, they are not automatically given a share of land. When men like Dhena or Baha's husband, Jadu, go back to their village, they are confident of getting a share of land despite having given up their claims formally at the time of their wedding as *gharjamai*. The problem for women seems to come from the disjuncture between inheritance of land and inheritance of the lineage name.

Kinship thus transmits both identity (in terms of name) and resources. It is those who do not benefit much from kinship who are less likely to be bound by kinship rules and norms and more likely to subvert them. Such persons try to seize opportunities within the local structures to transform the rules (Maynes et al., 1996), as in the case of Baha. While filing a case in court, she has not given up local negotiation. It needs to be reiterated that operationalising land claims requires local social support and recognition, and without this even a legal victory cannot realise the right. Women's first call in terms of making claims therefore remains the local kin group and village council, and if no consensus is reached here, then the district courts are used. The courts are none the less dependent on the woman securing some kin support as they call village leaders as witnesses and respondents for any case filed in them.

What emerges then is not only the growing contestation of women's rights to inherit land, but also the interpenetration of this struggle with the struggle for kin and community control of both resources and decision-making. The kin elders have held several village meetings to discuss Baha's case, and yet, unable to enforce their decision, they have themselves advised her to go to the legal courts for justice. While a positive order from the court would be an admission of their institutional failure, it would nonetheless be a recognition of their judgment and would enhance their legitimacy.

Conclusion

While the primary objective of land revenue settlements is the fixation and collection of rents and the recording of individual titles to avoid future disputes, an analysis of changes in settlement records over a period of time provides insights into changes in social relations as well. One finds a process of growing differentiation within different social groups, depending not only on their landholdings, but also on their levels of literacy, their access to government benefits, and so on. Despite this apparent expansion in the sources of power and wealth, those aspiring to retain a high status also attempt to expand their landholdings, as is shown by patterns of leasing and mortgaging in Chuapara.[20] Property is considered not just a commodity or material resource; there seems, in fact, to be an overall lack of capital accumulation in land. Property is also a cultural and symbolic resource (Peters, 2002: 160), which is essential to social identity and positioning as well as to the achievement of a political voice. It continues to be mediated by kin networks. The growing competition for land is thus kept in check through enhancing the power of patrilineal kinship so that it becomes more significant than other forms of social alliances. In fact, given the poor provision of state services in the area, kin groups also serve as the major social support network, and this cannot but enhance further the importance of these ties.

Nonetheless, there appears to be a growing assertion by women of their claims to land despite the strengthening of patriarchal strategies to deny these rights. Women negotiate with their extended households, kin groups and village leadership in different ways. They often manipulate patriarchal institutions by registering land in their father's name, engaging kin elders in their support or temporarily leasing land to their kin till their sons grow up. While many have been successful in staking their claims, economic and political marginalisation of the tribe as a whole is enhancing challenges to women's claims on grounds of threats to an essentially masculine lineage identity. The trade-off appears to be between inheritance and marital choice and mobility.

While kin groups are still important in legitimising access to land and ensuring social agreement, the declining ability of community institutions (largely representing the kin-elders) to protect their rights has led more women to engage with external state sources of legitimacy. In this engagement they have been supported by kin and community leaders, who are interested themselves in thus re-establishing their legitimacy and authority in land matters. Insofar as state policies have generally seemed to be pro-women, especially since the 1980s, village leaders and kin elders support such women in order to boost their own legitimacy.

There is an effort in villages such as Chuapara to strengthen kinship links, or at least to portray them as strengthened, as a strategy to resist growing state control and the marginalisation of local authority. What would seem naturally to accompany this is suppression of individual rights, particularly women's rights, and an increase in social inequity. Yet challenges from women have helped reformulate the terms on which kinship is practised, particularly in the context of complex interactions with institutions of the state and with markets. Such challenges, and community responses to them, break the illusion of *adivasi* community as a homogenous society, isolated from the outside world, while at the same time pointing to the importance of taking note of the complexities of kinship relations in formulating development policies.

Notes

1. All names of places and respondents in the chapter have been changed.
2. See, for instance, Berry (1993), Collier and Yanagisako (1987), Dube (1997), Hirschon (1984), Uberoi (1993), Whitehead (1984) and several others.

3. The Santals refer to them as *diku*s, or troublemakers. Belonging to the *teli* and *bania* castes, they have historically been the 'exploiters'.

4. Meenakshi, Ray, and Gupta (2000) show a head count ratio of poverty for Bihar as 62.4 per cent, but 75.7 per cent for the Scheduled Tribes.

5. Total literacy rate for the Scheduled Tribes of Dumka district was 29.3 per cent, with males 40.7 per cent and females at 17.85 per cent, according to the Census of India, 2001. This is about 10 percentage points below the general average for the district at 39.26 per cent – a worsening of the gap from a decade earlier despite a general improvement in literacy rates (Census of India, 2001).

6. This followed the designation of these communities as Scheduled Tribes in the Constitution of India, entitling them to special protection and privileges.

7. This view has been boosted by official recognition of illegal methods of alienation through collusive title suits, de facto possession, transfers in fake name and marriage to an *adivasi* woman. Land reforms commissioner I. N. Thakur (1977), however, does say that it is the former methods that are more common. There is no evidence of the extent of alienation due to marriage, and yet this has become a major argument for opposing women's rights today.

8. *Madhu Kishwar v. State of India*, 1982, and *Juliana Lakra v. State of Bihar*, 1986.

9. Personal interviews with Dayamani Barla, Pramodini Hansdak and several others.

10. The Sixth Plan document (1980–85) was the first public document to recognise the importance of land to women in India (Government of India, 1980).

11. The discussion by Chatterjee (1999) on the concept of 'political society' and the importance of political voice for securing resource allocation is useful.

12. The main focus of the document is commercialisation, export orientation and market development, both in the agricultural and industrial sectors, though the simultaneous articulation of the New Industrial Policy appears to prioritise the industrial sector.

13. *Parganait* refers to the head of a cluster of villages, *desmanjhi* his assistant in the cluster and *sardar* a village headman, known also as *manjhi*.

14. Archer considered his inquiry into and documentation of Santal law as reference material to be used by the civil courts. The information was collected and checked in twenty centres across the Santal portions of

the district. Submitted in 1946, the report was, however, filed and never published. It was finally published with the support of the Indian Council of Social Science Research (ICSSR) and the Anthropological Survey of India (ASI) in 1984.

15. This refers to the number allocated in the record of rights.

16. This is the rent-free land that is officially allocated to the *pradhan* of the village in lieu of his services to the government.

17. Yngstrom finds in Mzula village, Dodoma, Tanzania, that 425 household units had registered land while 1451 were cultivating land. She notes, '[T]he figures from the land register can be used to establish the importance of lineage as an indicator of land-holdings' (1999: 223).

18. See also Brass (1999) and Harriss-White (2003) on this point.

19. The new land record for the village was finalized in 1996, with her name on it, and hence the rent receipts began to be issued in her name. Earlier they were in the name of her father.

20. In Chuapara we find that while the Paharias are only leasing out land, amongst the Kols and Santals there are an equal number of households leasing out and leasing in land. Even a person with a little surplus cash or grain, seeks to lease in land (Rao, 2002).

References

Agarwal, B. 1994. *A Field of One's Own: Gender and Land Rights in South Asia.* Cambridge, UK: Cambridge University Press.

Archer, W. G. 1984 [1946]. *Tribal Law and Justice: A Report on the Santal.* New Delhi: Concept Publishing Company.

Baviskar, A. 1995. *In the Belly of the River: Tribal Conflicts over Development in the Narmada Valley.* New Delhi: Oxford University Press.

Berry, S. 1993. *No Condition Is Permanent: The Social Dynamics of Agrarian Change in Sub-Saharan Africa.* Wisconsin: University of Wisconsin Press.

Bodding, P. O., L. O. Skresfrud and S. Konow. 1994 [1942]. *Traditions and Institutions of the Santals.* New Delhi: Bahumukhi Prakashan.

Brass, T. 1999. *Towards a Comparative Political Economy of Unfree Labour.* London: Frank Cass.

Census of India. 2001. 'Primary Census Abstract', vol. 13. Data product no. 00-73-2002-Cen-CD. New Delhi: Office of the Registrar General and Census Commissioner of India, Government of India.

Chatterjee, P. 1999. 'Modernity, Democracy and a Political Negotiation of Death'. *South Asia Research* 19(1): 103–19.

Collier, J. F., and S. J. Yanagisako (eds.). 1987. *Gender and Kinship: Essays towards a Unified Analysis*. Redwood City, CA: Stanford University Press.

Corbridge, S. 1988. 'The Ideology of Tribal Economy and Society: Politics in the Jharkhand, 1950–1980'. *Modern Asian Studies* 22(1): 1–42.

Das, V. 1976. 'Masks and Faces: An Essay on Punjabi Kinship'. *Contributions to Indian Sociology* 10(1): 1–30.

Deshpande, R. 2004. 'How Gendered Was Women's Participation in Election 2004?' *Economic and Political Weekly* 39(50): 5431–36.

Dhagamwar, V. 2003. 'Invasion of Criminal Law by Religion, Custom and Family Law'. *Economic and Political Weekly* 38(15): 1483–92.

District Record Room. n.d. 'Village Record of Rights, Transfer Lists and Dispute Lists for Chuapara and Bagdiha over the Four Settlement Periods'. Dumka.

Dube, L. 1986. 'Seed and Earth: The Symbolism of Biological Reproduction and Sexual Relations of Production'. *In Visibility and Power: Essays on Women in Society and Development*, edited by L. Dube, E. Leacock and S. Ardener, 22–53. Delhi: Oxford University Press.

———. 1997. *Women and Kinship: Comparative Perspectives on Gender in South and South-East Asia*. Tokyo: United Nations University Press.

Election Commission of India. 2004. *Statistical Report on General Elections, 2004, to the 14th Lok Sabha*. New Delhi: Election Commission of India.

Epstein, T. S, A. P. Suryanarayana and T. Thimmegowda. 1998. *Village Voices: Forty Years of Rural Transformation in South India*. New Delhi: SAGE Publications.

Gantzer, J. F. 1936. *Final Report on the Revision Survey and Settlement Operations in the District of Santal Parganas, 1922-35*. Patna: Superintendent, Government Printing.

Goetz, A. M. 1997. 'Local Heroes: Patterns of Fieldworker Discretion in Implementing GAD Policy in Bangladesh'. In *Getting Institutions Right for Women in Development*, edited by A. M. Goetz, 176–95. London: Zed Books.

Goody, J. 1976. *Production and Reproduction: A Comparative Study of the Domestic Domain*. Cambridge, UK: Cambridge University Press.

Gough, K. 1981. *Rural Society in Southeast India*. Cambridge, UK: Cambridge University Press.

Gould, H. A. 1968. 'Time-Dimension and Structural Change in an Indian Kinship System: A Problem of Conceptual Refinement'. In *Structure and*

Change in Indian Society, edited by M. Singer and B. S. Cohn, 413–22. Chicago: Aldine Publishing Company.

Government Of India. 1980. *Sixth Five Year Plan*. New Delhi: Planning Commission.

Hardiman, D. 1987. *The Coming of the Devi*. Oxford: Oxford University Press.

Harriss, J. 1979. *Capitalism and Peasant Farming: A Study of Agricultural Change and Agrarian Structure in Northern Tamil Nadu* (Monographs in Development Studies). Norwich: University of East Anglia.

Harriss-White, B. 2003. *India Working: Essays on Society and Economy*. Cambridge, UK: Cambridge University Press.

Harriss-White, B., and S. Janakarajan (eds.). 2004. *Rural India Facing the 21st Century: Essays on Long-Term Village Change and Recent Development Policy*. London: Anthem Press.

Hirschon, R. (ed.). 1984. *Women and Property – Women as Property*. London: Croom Helm.

Jackson, C. 2000. 'Men at Work'. *European Journal of Development Research* 12(2): 1–22.

MacDougall, J. 1985. *Land of Religion? The Sardar and Kherwar Movements in Bihar, 1858–95*. New Delhi: Manohar.

McPherson, H. 1909. *Final Report on Survey and Settlement Operation in District Santal Parganas*. Calcutta: Government of Bengal Press.

Maynes, M. J., A. Waltner, B. Soland, and U. Strasser. 1996. *Gender, Kinship, Power: A Comparative and Interdisciplinary History*. New York: Routledge.

Meenakshi, J. V., R. Ray and S. Gupta. 2000. 'Estimates of Poverty for SC, ST and Female-Headed Households'. *Economic and Political Weekly* 35: 2748–54.

Moore, S. F. 2001. 'Certainties Undone: Fifty Turbulent Years of Legal Anthropology, 1949–1999'. *Journal of the Royal Anthropological Institute* 7: 95–116.

Nathan, D., and G. Kelkar. 2003. 'Civilisational Change: Markets and Privatisation among Indigenous Peoples'. *Economic and Political Weekly* 38(20): 1955–68.

Nicholas, R. W. 1968. 'Structures of Politics in the Villages of Southern Asia'. In *Structure and Change in Indian Society*, edited by M. Singer and B. S. Cohn, 243–84. Chicago: Aldine Publishing Company.

O'Malley, L. S. S. 1984 [1910]. *Bengal District Gazetteers: Santal Parganas*. Delhi: B. R. Publishing Corporation.

Orans, M. 1965. *The Santal: A Tribe in Search of a Great Tradition*. Detroit: Wayne State University Press.

Parkin, R. 2000. 'Proving "Indigenity", Exploiting Modernity: Modalities of Identity Construction in Middle India'. *Anthropos* 95: 49–63.

Parry, J. P. 1979. *Caste and Kinship in Kangra*. London: Routledge.

Pasternak, B., C. R. Ember and M. Ember. 1997. *Sex, Gender and Kinship: A Cross-Cultural Perspective*. Englewood Cliffs, NJ: Prentice Hall.

Peters, P. 2002. 'Bewitching the Land: The Role of Land Disputes in Converting Kin to Strangers and in Class Formation in Malawi'. *Journal of South African Studies* 28(1): 155–78.

Pettigrew, J. 1975. *Robber Noblemen: A Study of the Political System of the Sikh Jats*. London: Routledge & Kegal Paul.

Prasad, B. M. 1997. *Santal Parganas Tenancy Manual*. Patna: Malhotra Bros.

Rao, N. 2002. 'Standing One's Ground: Gender, Land and Livelihoods in the Santal Parganas, Jharkhand, India'. PhD thesis, School of Development Studies, University of East Anglia, Norwich.

Sacks, K. 1979. *Sisters and Wives: The Past and Future of Sexual Equality*. Westport, CT: Greenwood Press.

Scott, J. C. 1998. *Seeing Like a State: How Certain Schemes to Improve the Human Condition Have Failed*. New Haven, CT: Yale University Press.

Sengupta, N. 1982. *Fourth World Dynamics: Jharkhand*. Delhi: Authors Guild Publications.

Singh, K. S. (ed.). 1983. *Tribal Movements in India*, vol. 2. New Delhi: Manohar.

Skaria, A. 1999. *Hybrid Histories: Forests, Frontiers and Wildness in Western India*. Delhi: Oxford University Press.

Stivens, M., C. Ng and K. S. Jomo. 1994. *Malay Peasant Women and the Land*. London and New Jersey: Zed Books.

Strathern, M. 1987. 'Producing Difference: Connections and Disconnections in Two New Guinea Highland Kinship Systems'. In *Gender and Kinship: Essays towards a Unified Analysis*, edited by J. F. Collier and S. J. Yanagisako, 271–300. Redwood City, CA: Stanford University Press.

Thakur, I. N. 1977. 'Bihar'. In *Land Alienation and Restoration in Tribal Communities in India*, edited by S. N. Dubey and R. Murdia, 153–79. Bombay: Himalaya Publishing House.

Uberoi, P. (ed.).1993. *Family, Kinship and Marriage in India*. New Delhi: Oxford University Press.

Walker, C. 2003. 'Piety in the Sky? Gender Policy and Land Reform in South Africa'. *Journal of Agrarian Change* 3(1–2): 113–48.

Whitehead, A. 1984. 'Women and Men, Kinship and Property: Some General Issues'. In *Women and Property – Women as Property*, edited by R. Hirschon, 176–92. London: Croom Helm.

Yanagisako, S. J. 1987. 'Mixed Metaphors: Native and Anthropological Models of Gender and Kinship Domains'. In *Gender and Kinship: Essays towards a Unified Analysis*, edited by J. F. Collier and S. J. Yanagisako, 86–118. Redwood City, CA: Stanford University Press.

Yngstrom, I. 1999. 'Gender, Land and Development in Tanzania: Rural Dodoma 1920–1996'. DPhil thesis. University of Oxford.

3

Questioning Women's Solidarity

The Case of Land Rights in the Santal Parganas*

Introduction

The historic United Nations (UN) statement of the mid-1980s that women, comprising 50 per cent of the world's population, own just 1 per cent of its property, generated considerable research and policy interest in property and land rights, particularly in rural, agrarian societies. Women's land rights now constitute the magic potion for poverty reduction, agricultural growth and women's empowerment. The shift, partly due to feminist advocacy (Agarwal, 1994, 1998), has conflated gender inequality with inequality in resource allocation, particularly land. Other critical constraints that women face are disregarded (Razavi, 2003).

Women's land rights are seen as particularly important in the context of demographic changes in occupational patterns, with more and more men

*This chapter was originally published as an article in the *Journal of Development Studies* © Taylor & Francis Group Ltd 2005. All rights reserved. Reproduced with the permission of the copyright holder and the publisher, Taylor & Francis, Milton Park, Oxfordshire. The fieldwork for the chapter was conducted as part of my PhD research in Dumka district, Jharkhand, and I am grateful to the many men and women who provided deep insights into the issue of women's land rights. I would like to thank Cecile Jackson and Ben Rogaly for their comments. An earlier version was presented at the workshop 'Feminist Fables and Gender Myths: Repositioning "Gender" in Development Policy and Practice' at the Institute of Development Studies, University of Sussex, 2–4 July 2003. I would like to thank several of the workshop participants and two anonymous referees at the *Journal of Development Studies* for their feedback and comments on the work.

migrating to urban areas or looking for non-farm work in rural areas. In India, for instance, Visaria (1996) analyses National Sample Survey (NSS) data to show that while the proportion of rural male workers in agriculture declined from 83.7 per cent to 74 per cent from 1961 to 1993–94, the proportion of women dropped only marginally from 89.7 per cent to 86.1 per cent during this period. Given that the relative share of women in the agricultural labour force is higher than that of men, lack of women's land rights is seen as a major bottleneck in improving agricultural production.[1]

The International Fund for Agricultural Development (IFAD)'s *Rural Poverty Report* argues that 'the strength of custom and male power make it difficult to identify practical changes to land systems that will improve women's land rights' [2001: 87], consequently enhance production and lead to a reduction in poverty. Within this framework, the problem of land distribution is presented as a struggle for control between men and women, or between modern and customary law. Such oppositional positioning and dichotomisation between genders or legal frameworks, each presented as internally united and homogenous, ignores the mutuality and interdependence between men and women, as well as between the state and community institutions. These are not autonomous individuals or spheres, but constantly adapting in relation to each other (S. F. Moore, 1978), when seen from a historical perspective.

Acknowledging that women are likely to face resistance at multiple levels in securing land rights, Agarwal has argued that women's land claims can become effective through processes of collective struggle (1994, 2003). She claims that

> village women's strength derives not merely from the number of women seeking a change in rules and norms, but also from their willingness to act collectively in their common gender interest, over and above the possible divisiveness of caste or class. (2001: 1642)

Gender disadvantage potentially creates a commonality of interests for women to organise, reflected clearly, for instance, in movements against violence or sexual harassment, recognition of work and the payment of minimum wages. I argue in this chapter that the socially embedded nature of land as a resource – its value not just as a material resource, but as a symbolic resource conferring status and identity – makes collective organisation of women around land a difficult task. In the case of Brazil, which had active rural unions of women workers, land rights seemed to disappear as issues in relation to social security benefits or recognition as workers (Deere, 2003).

> Since attaining effective social security rights was an issue that united most rural women (whether temporary or permanent wage workers, landless or in the family farming regime) it is not surprising that these rights would constitute the most important arena of struggle for the rural women's movement in subsequent years, to the detriment of the struggle for women's land rights. (Deere, 2003: 267–68)

Secondly, even material production by women requires the support of male labour and networks. Giving too little attention to bonds of interdependence in conjugal relations in the domain of agricultural production leads to a 'methodological individualism which begins with women's interests, rather than with the ways in which different gender interests are socially and historically shaped' (O'Laughlin, 1995: 76). Such a view would help understand why women as a category have not organised around demand for land rights in India or elsewhere.

It is these two questions relating, first, to separation of male and female interests in relation to land and, second, to the willingness of women to act collectively in their common gender interest, which I examine in this chapter. While the opposition set up in the IFAD report between customary law and state law, and referred to by Agarwal (1994), is also problematic, it is not discussed here. I use examples of the struggles of Santal women for land in Dumka district to discuss both the aforementioned propositions. The data were collected through extensive fieldwork, conducted in two villages in the district – one remote, forested and relatively homogenous, which I call Chuapara,[2] and the other well-connected, partially urbanised and mixed caste, close to the district headquarters Dumka, which I call Bagdiha – over a period of eighteen months in 1999–2000.

In the next section, I examine the notion of women's interests and gender interests in the context of land. While class differences shaped by the quantum of landholding, as well as the quality and type of land held, are important,[3] this case study involves households that own some land. There is a relative homogeneity in terms of landholding status in the study villages. Assuming a similarity in wealth status,[4] I argue then that more than gender identities, it is other cross-cutting identities of kinship relations and marital status, ethnicity and education that both motivate women to stake their claims to land as well as oppose the claims of other women (and men). This entails disaggregating the category 'women' by their particular position in relation to marriage and kinship structures, such as being a daughter, wife, sister or widow, examining the legitimacy of land claims and the struggles of women in these different subject positions.[5] Further, the attitudes of women in relation to parental and marital property also vary. I thus argue that in representing collective interests, it is women in similar subject positions who are likely to support each other rather than women as a general category.

In the third section, I discuss the role and importance of solidarity and collective action in ensuring greater social and gender equity. While collective action may often be required to secure land rights, as I illustrate, this need not be only and exclusively a women's struggle. In fact, more strategic alliances with influential men, whether community leaders, lawyers or political leaders, might serve women's interests better. Further, 'collective investment and collective cultivation by women' (Agarwal, 2003: 206) need not necessarily be the solution. In Peru, Chile and Cuba, following the land redistribution programme, cooperatives or groups were used for strengthening access to agricultural inputs as well as consumer goods, rather than joint cultivation (Palmer, 1985).[6]

Women's Interests and Gender Interests

Several scholars have attempted to understand households and intra-household relations, the differential access to and control over resources, and the causes and processes of women's subordination (Dwyer and Bruce, 1988). Sen (1990) has conceptualised intra-household bargaining on the basis of perceived vis-a-vis actual interests and contributions of men and women within the household. Perceptions of interests, while not guides to objective notions of well-being, do make women partners in sustaining traditional inequalities, by supporting a false consciousness in relation to their relative contribution to the household. This, he argues, has a major impact on actual states and outcomes. He therefore calls for greater visibility to women's contribution through paid employment, either public or private, in order to improve their bargaining position.

Critiquing Sen, Agarwal (1994) has emphasised that women do know their self-interest, and yet they are unable to act on their understanding because of external constraints. In a similar vein, Folbre (1997) discusses the role of strongly gendered extra-household environmental parameters in negotiations of social norms and intra-household gender relations. The intra-household bargaining complex is thus defined by multiple factors such as the control over economic assets including land, access to communal resources, external economic and social support systems, social and legal recognition of claims, and support from state and non-governmental organisations (NGOs).

These structures of state and society not only set the parameters for intra-household bargaining, but, in a sense, the inequalities between genders built into these structures clearly point towards distinct areas of women's and men's interests. The near universal devaluation of domestic work, for instance, was the target of feminist campaigns such as 'wages for housework' in the 1970s and 1980s (Young, Wolkowitz and McCullagh, 1981). Struggles to change legal inequities, such as in the differential inheritance rights of men and women to land, can similarly be seen to be in women's interest.

However, the perspective shifts somewhat if women's interests are considered from a truly relational gender stance. There are several reasons why this may be so. First, the production–reproduction divide of tasks between men and women is less clear in agricultural societies. In a rice-producing area such as Dumka, even though men own land, production is critically dependent on women's labour. This is acknowledged in conversation by men in the villages, irrespective of the political discourse that renders women's contributions to production invisible. More importantly, in practical terms, to support women's labour contributions, men often provide substantial support in domestic activities, particularly visible during the transplanting season in July and August. Collecting water for household use, helping pound paddy in the *dheki* (hand pounder), taking care of young children and feeding the cattle are but some examples of such support. The failure to do so, or the taking of unilateral decisions on land use by men, can evoke sharp responses from women, including complete withdrawal. Apart from their own 6 acres of land in Bagdiha, Nirmala's husband, Sushil, leased in an additional 8 acres for paddy production during the summer of 2000. Even though labour was hired for cultivation, Nirmala was expected to cook and supply food twice a day to the wage labourers. She argued with Sushil that the additional workload was beyond her capacity, and yet when he still did not listen to her and went ahead with his plans, she simply left the village for her natal home during the few critical weeks of paddy transplantation. Thus, even in what appear to be restrictive, patriarchal structures, women do exercise agency, reflected not only in activity and resistance, but also in passivity and withdrawal (Scott, 1985; Wolf, 1992).

Sharma (1980), in her study of land and work in north-west India, found that in reality, women exercised considerable control over land, especially in situations of male out-migration. Though the ideology of a 'good wife' or a 'good sister' made them dependent on their relations with men for control over land, rather than feeling excluded, women continued to see land as a joint resource, with their contribution leading to male prestige and in turn their own. Investment of time in enhancing family prestige is seen as a legitimate activity for women, what Papanek (1989) labels 'status-production work'. Ideologies here seemed to reinforce male control over productive resources more in order to sustain male prestige rather than the desire to restrict land within the kin group or to exclude women. Women could thus negotiate informal access more easily than registered ownership. Strathern (1988) corroborates this from her study of the Hagen in Papua New Guinea, noting that property is not considered as an individual and absolute person–thing relationship, but it is seen to reflect multiple interests and mutual interdependence. Yet the links of property to male prestige, both individual and collective, provide some insights into why men challenge women's land claims. This may be the result of a struggle between groups of men for prestige in a context of resource scarcity rather than targeted at women per se.

While Sharma's settings are in a strongly patriarchal, heterogeneous, caste-based society, where the subordination of women is assumed, Strathern studies a relatively more homogenous people, similar to the Santals. Yet the importance of mutuality and interdependence between men and women is pointed to in both studies, as by others like O'Laughlin in Chad and Goebel in Zimbabwe.[7]

In this chapter, I use my case material to argue for the dynamic nature and variability of conjugal relations as well as intra-household relations more broadly, as men and women move through different positions in their lives and relationships. This case study is drawn from a tribal society that is assumed to be both homogenous and gender equitable and is hence an exception in the Indian context of what is otherwise seen as a highly heterogenous, caste-ridden society. I use examples of conflicts over land, in contexts involving women in different subject positions, to identify sources of support as well as opposition to these claims. The complexity of the issues emerging from just two villages questions the myth of common interests of women in land and the simplicity of assumptions behind the IFAD statement (2001: 87).

Women's Interests in Parental Property

Santal customary law does not guarantee women generalised inheritance rights in their parental property. They are expected to get married and share in their husband's property, whether as wives or widows. They do, however, have contingent rights to inheritance as daughters and sisters, depending upon the circumstances. So, for instance, a common practice was to gift a married woman some land in her natal village as *taben jom*, or maintenance, by her father, brother or other male agnates, for a temporary period of time. Not more than 10 *bighas*[8], this gift was generally made out of affection and as an insurance against a bad marriage. *Taben jom* for the Santals performs a similar normative role of distress insurance as *streedhan* (women's wealth)[9] amongst caste Hindus and hence brings out similarities in women's rights across tribal and non-tribal societies. Unlike *streedhan*, however, on her death, the control of the property would remain with the patriliny. Despite social recognition, with growing scarcity of land and the inability to acquire additional land due to the absence of a land market in the Santal Parganas,[10] implementing *taben jom* rights has become increasingly difficult in practice.

The accepted right, recognised in the Santal Pargana Tenancy Act (SPTA), 1949, is that of *gharjawae*,[11] wherein due to the absence of appropriate male heirs, the daughter inherits her father's land. During the marriage ceremony, there is a formal declaration to this effect, with the husband agreeing to live with and cultivate on his wife's land and give up claims on his paternal property as long as the marriage lasts. Local forms of opposition are visible to *gharjawae*, yet it is still considered legitimate for women as daughters to struggle for land in this way. And in most instances, they are able to secure the support of male community leaders as well as other women in this struggle. A few examples illustrate this.

Thirty-three-year-old Baha Marandi of Chuapara had a *gharjawae* marriage in 1981, when she was eleven years old. Her father died in 1984. She and her husband cultivated their land, almost 9 *bighas*, had three children and were well settled. In August 1995, Baha's mother died. That year she and her husband completed their cultivation and collected the output. Then her male kin threatened to kill them, so they moved 10 miles away to her husband's village. With little land there, they had to depend on wage labour for survival.

In 1996, Baha returned to Chuapara to claim her share. A village meeting was held. Cheenu, her male cousin said, 'Nothing has been cultivated on the land, so what share can I give?' In June 1997, she again came here to cultivate, but Cheenu did not allow her to plough. Thereafter, she instituted legal proceedings, supported by the village leaders, one of whom accompanied her to Dumka for this purpose. Having endorsed her marriage as being to a *gharjawae*, they had in fact recognised her entitlement to her father's property many years ago. Cheenu deposed her claim as invalid arguing that she never had a *gharjawae* marriage. In her rejoinder, she stated that being the only child, she was married in *gharjawae* form to Jadu Kisku on 9 May 1981. The leaders of both villages testified to this in writing. During the present survey and settlement operations, all lands in the Record of Rights of the village (under Record No. 12/9) were recorded in her name as the legal heir.

From 1997 to 1999, Baha went to the court in Dumka, but it was both expensive and time-consuming. Though the case is still ongoing, the court has prepared a provisional statement after a full enquiry, noting that women married in *gharjawae* form are eligible to inherit land. Meanwhile, in January 1998, there was yet another village hearing on this dispute. Cheenu agreed to give her a share of the land. Though Baha has been paying the land revenue since 1996–97, she is still unable to cultivate the land.

While Baha's case is still ongoing, one of the male village leaders in Chuapara, Samli Marandi, said, on 1 July 2000, 'She has already got an order in her favour from the court. Her kin cannot now oppose for long.' This is not the case, yet the very distance of the court and its formal language adds to the power it can wield in terms of influencing local discourse. In this case, their authority being openly thwarted by Cheenu, the male leadership in the village support her claims, not just for the sake of upholding local norms and practice, but in order to strengthen their own social position by using the court directives to boost the legitimacy of their own decision and hence authority. While several women are sympathetic to Baha, they prefer not to interfere in this dispute. The wives of Baha's male cousins, however, support their husband's rights and feel that Baha is unjustified in her claim.

A second example of claim to *gharjawae* rights, which had a violent ending, comes from Bagdiha. Munni was married in *gharjawae* form. She had three sons and two daughters. After her death in 1990, her father's brother's sons started harassing her sons to drive them away from the village. The main point of dispute was once again whether her marriage was to a *gharjawae* or not and whether Munni and her husband were in cultivating possession of the land after the death of her father. They tried to prove that her husband was a recorded tenant in his own village of Jaipahari. The Deed of Declaration, 1960, confirmed her marriage to a *gharjawae*, and the police spot report and receipts of revenue assessment confirmed their residence in the village.

For a while, Munni'ss sons had police protection at least during the planting and harvesting seasons. In January 1999, when her eldest son was returning from the *haat* (market), Munni's father's brother's sons murdered him. A police case was registered, and the male kin are all in jail. The women of the household face a difficult time now. They have sold their cattle and mortgaged their land to fight the case and secure bail for their husbands. The younger women have to migrate to West Bengal to earn some money to feed the children. Yet Phulmuni, the wife of one of the accused, said:

> They knew they would be allowed to eat from this land only as long as their mother lived; after that they wouldn't be allowed. We have many sons, and we are the descendants from the male line, while they are the daughter's sons. So why should we let them stay here? They may be winning on paper, but we will still drive them out.

A murder was the final straw. It showed the weaknesses of the state in providing protection at the village level and pushed the onus back on to the community. After the murder, the entire village gathered, men from all the *tolas* (hamlets), and the murderers' household was outcasted – no one could interact with them or share their *dheki* (a wooden device used for hand-pounding rice). The *gudit* (village messenger) would not collect contributions from them for *sohrai* (harvest) or other festivals. If anybody came forward to bail them out, they would be fined 3,000 rupees by the village. Even the female teacher said:

> The women helped their men, handed them the swords and knives and joined in the looting. They have small children and are having a difficult time now, but they didn't try to stop their men. They took advantage of the physical weakness and poverty of Munni's sons.

In this case, the wives of the male kin had no sympathy for Munni or her sons, but rather were strong advocates for exclusive male inheritance rights, on account of their own contextual positioning at that moment in time. Their marital as well as material interest lies in supporting their husbands to promote the potential well-being of their children.

Given this challenge to *gharjawae* rights, women married to *gharjawae*s in Bagdiha, supported by their husbands and community leaders, have increasingly got their land registered in the recent land survey and settlement. Alliances were also built with revenue officials – the *amin*s (assessors of revenue) and other petty bureaucrats – in this process.

Indeed, as some women intensify struggles for women's rights, others intensify struggles for men's rights. As the contestation becomes more intense, women too see themselves not merely as women, but rather within the larger social relations of a kin network in an increasingly competitive society. Apart from women in similar positions, there are men in the village who support women's land claims. The *majhi*s, or village headmen, in both the villages, due to their own positions (one of them is a *gharjawae* himself) and the need for authority, give full support to the rights of women married to *gharjawae*s. So also do other men married as *gharjawae*. It is in their interests to support their wives' claims and more so the claims of other women married to *gharjawae*s. If this becomes commonplace, then there is more likelihood of it being accepted and not challenged: in the *tola* where I lived, out of forty households, ten were *gharjawae* households, and there was little opposition to any of them.

Using the theme of sexuality as an example, Hollway (1984) has illustrated how men and women consciously take up differentiated positions within existing discourses as an investment in exercising power. H. Moore (1994) takes this discussion further in showing how this positioning changes with experience, circumstance and over time. There is no one defining difference, but markers like gender, race and ethnicity are adopted in response to particular contexts and discourses.[12] These competing discourses are not just ideas but have social and material force, with the hierarchical ordering of identities contributing to economic and political domination of some over others. Women, as 'good wives' or 'dutiful daughters', do often take forward projects of masculinity in furthering the material interest and prestige of their own household unit. But men, too, as 'responsible husbands' or the 'impartial elder', support the claims of their wives or of destitute women in general, when they see in such a position either symbolic or material gains or both.

As Hossain and Moore (1999) point out, in discussing poverty and development, the development discourse often highlights elite resistance as being more intense than it necessarily is in many sectors. They argue that it is possible to mobilise elite support for poverty reduction, if presented in contextualised ways, as notions of moral responsibility as well as respectability do also persist. The same would probably hold for gender struggles, as not all men resist women's land claims. They adopt different positions based on their own life experiences and contexts, including commitments within conjugal ties, and it is often only with male support that women's land claims can become effective. The village leaders, while discursively legitimising her claims, advise Baha to go to the court, and even accompany her, as they are unable to protect her physically. Struggles for land then involve alliances often across both gender and kinship lines.

One way to understand this phenomenon is to see gender, ethnicity and political status as mutually embedded. As Tsing (1993) demonstrates in the case of the Meratus Dayaks of Indonesia, there are creative intersections with the marginal extending not always towards the centre but to other marginalities. The struggles of women and the village leaders, who are also Santals and members of a marginalised group, for instance, may be different. Yet there are points of intersection where the two struggles can support and legitimise each other in the larger context of power and discourse.

Marriage: A Site of Shared and Separate Interests

I turn now to look at women as wives, highlighting the importance of reciprocity in conjugal relations in terms of negotiating claims to marital property. In situations of restricted mobility, leading to restricted choices, as in large parts of India, women may prefer to abide by the rules and regulations of marriage, as survival and protection is better assured by doing so.[13] With shared responsibilities for working on the land, shared rights are taken for granted in daily practice and rarely questioned as long as the marriage is stable. Love and caring, mutuality and trust, and the commitment they foster could indeed lead to the giving up of options, yet as Jonasdottir (1988: 51) points out, they can potentially open new possibilities. Standardised frameworks of women's subordination do not take into account the contextual differences that might restrict solidarity and collective action. Conflicts in interest could arise around notions of subjectivity and objectivity, public and private, material and abstract, as well as female and male interests versus role-based interests (Jonasdottir, 1988).

This is in contradiction to Agarwal's view that

> joint titles and family-based cultivation have several disadvantages for women. Women often find it difficult to gain control over the produce,

to bequeath the land as they want, and to claim their share in the case of marital conflict or violence … Wives may also have different land use priorities from husbands which they would be less able to exercise with joint titles. [1997: 1377]

The point about marital conflict and violence is correct, as property does become an issue for women when the marriage is precarious or breaks down. In other instances, however, in most farming families, particularly in rice production systems that are dependent on women's labour, women do have ways of influencing land use and crop choice.

A pertinent point here is the multiple classifications of land and the differing nature of rights and controls these entail. In the case of the Santals, while *dhani*, or paddy plot, is equivalent to household food producing land to which all members are expected to contribute, *baris*, or homestead plots, are considered as women's plots. *Kurram*, or shifting cultivation plots on hill slopes, once again are primarily women's plots (Figure 3.1). While women and men both work in the *dhani* plots during the monsoon to produce their staple food crop for the year, there is much more negotiation over the winter crop.

Figure 3.1   Mother and children in women's *kurram* fields
Source: Photograph by Amit Mitra.

In the *dhani* plots, after the paddy harvest, it is often the 'male' crops of wheat or potato that are grown. While used partly for household consumption, men also sell them for cash that they then control.

The reactions of women as wives in the two villages are different. Yet in both they assert the value of their own labour. In Chuapara, women are willing to contribute to 'male' winter crops, along with cultivating their own forest plots. Men are expected to provide support in clearing the forest land and guarding the crops from animal attacks as they ripen. This provides a source of income for women. Mutuality in labour contribution ensures that both men and women have a winter crop that is used partly for consumption and partly for sale (Figure 3.2). In Bagdiha, where such forest plots are not available, women clearly prefer to migrate for seasonal wage labour rather than contributing to men's winter crops. In a context where land is in short supply, competition between kin is intense and there is a growing tendency to follow rigid patriarchal practices for the sake of upward social mobility, women clearly prioritise their wage incomes from migration as contributing to their security and voice in marriage.[14] Often this income is used for making

Figure 3.2 Cooperation after harvest, essential to securing the annual food stock

Source: Photograph by Amit Mitra.

investments in cultivation, leasing in land, improving the house or paying off debts. The relationships and choices depend not just on the amount of land, but on its quality, as well as the structure of the household and the number of working hands available.

Coming back to the issue of marriage, this is considered as the beginning of a new partnership between husband and wife. 'In the short run, it is reasonable to assume that the members of any particular household are bound together by ties of mutual interest that surpass the possibilities for sharing and support available in alternative living arrangements' (Bruce and Lloyd, 1997: 214). In marriage, however, a Santal woman is subjected to certain new controls and rules of conduct, particularly on her sexuality. While pre-marital virginity is not a necessary condition for marriage in Santal society, any sexual relationship outside marriage would now be considered grounds for divorce.

However, women, too, exercise agency in the case of separation. Their grievances range from 'he was a stingy man', 'they were very poor' and 'he used to drink a lot' to 'he didn't care for me' and 'he didn't get me treated when I was sick'. However, flexibility and choice for women alters with stage in the life cycle. While it is relatively easy for women to exit a marriage in the first few years, once they have children, it becomes more difficult. If she takes her children with her, a son may eventually be able to claim his father's land, but a daughter gets nothing.

The situation gets more complex in the event of polygyny. Usually the man attempts to seek the consent of his *badki* (first wife) for the second marriage, in return for which she is allotted sufficient land for her maintenance, as in the case of Badku's household in Bagdiha. He has divided his 3 *bigha*s of land equally between his two wives. If the first wife were to resist the entry of the *chutki* (second or younger wife), however, she is often thrown out of the house or humiliated to the point when she leaves. Twenty-eight-year-old Thakrin said, in an interview on 18 August 1999, 'When he brought the second wife, he gave me my things and asked me to go. Later he said I too could stay, but I refused. I have now brought back all my things.'

If the situation of the *badki* is fragile, so is that of the *chutki*. Where the *badki*s are articulate and have a voice, the conflict intensifies. Their pride and self-respect have been hurt, and as their sexuality is no longer able to hold the man, they then resist the entry of the *chutki*. Thirty-five-year-old Rani said, in an interview on 19 August 1999, 'She has come with her eyes open. Why should I give her place to stay or a share of the land? He is looking for fields here and there; when he gets fed up of going to Bengal to earn, he will come home.'

The *badki*s blame the *chutki*s rather than their husbands. In their resistance, they seek the support of the village leaders. Rani managed to secure that support to keep the land, though her husband continues to harass her by clandestinely harvesting a part of the crop or not allowing other men to work for her. The leaders therefore suggest sharing of property between Rani and her husband, as is common in such cases. Yet she refuses, using her Christian identity and morality to strengthen her view of commitment of husband and wife to each other.

Despite increased hardship, women such as Thakrin and Rani make this choice to retain their social dignity, asserting in the process that mutuality is necessary between husband and wife to make a marriage work. Subordination is not unilaterally accepted.

Men entering polygynous relationships generally accept their responsibility towards the first wife. The problem for them has intensified because of multiplying claims over limited resources. Denying women a share of the land must be seen in the context of shrinking landholdings in each successive generation and the absence of any possibility of purchasing more land. While the patrilineal inheritance structure clearly gives men greater power than women in exercising their choices, this should not be an excuse to deny women a share of their marital property.

Widows: The Legitimate Claimants?

Customary law provides Santal widows a number of rights, differentiated by their age and by the sex and age of their children. If a childless widow remarries, she severs her connection with her dead husband – his family, land and movables – and can only keep her own personal property. If a widow has children, and then remarries, the situation is more complex. If there are no other male kin, then she herself will hold the property for her sons to inherit. If there are brothers or other kin with stronger claims, they will be the custodians of the property, till her sons can claim their share, and will also then be responsible for the provisioning and marriage of her daughters. This is irrespective of whether they continue to live in the village or elsewhere with their mother. Drèze (1990) shows that while a third of widows remarry, this does not necessarily reflect freedom to remarry as most of these are levirate unions imposed upon them. Amongst the Santals, while levirate is not necessarily imposed,[15] there is considerable pressure on younger widows to remarry and give up their property claims.

For a widow who does not remarry,

> She is virtually a substitute for her husband. She steps into his place, acts as his representative and exercises almost all his rights and duties … [P]rovided the community agrees, it is immaterial whether her husband's agnates approve or object. (Archer, 1984 [1946]: 171–73)

If she has sons, she will act as the head of the family, till her eldest son takes over. When her sons marry, they can demand partition, but she can keep sufficient land to maintain herself. One example is sixty-five-year-old Malati Kisku in Bagdiha. After her husband's death, the land was partitioned between her and her five sons. Her eldest son, Badku, ploughs the field for her, and then she employs labour to help her cultivate. The produce is sufficient for her consumption. She receives a widow's pension of 100 rupees per month from the state, which she uses to pay for the labour and for her additional expenses.

Younger widows, and particularly those without sons, face the greater challenges. While ensured a lifetime interest in land on conditions of residence in the village and no remarriage, the kin here try different strategies – convincing a young widow to get remarried, refusing to provide her plough labour, harassing her by calling her a witch – to make her leave the village.

Jhumri Murmu, married at the age of twenty years, widowed at thirty-two, has two daughters aged ten and six years. After her husband's death, she moved to her parent's place in a nearby village. She used to go for labour to earn money to be able to cultivate her share of 2 *bigha*s of land. When she came to cultivate in Bagdiha, however, she found that her land had been ploughed over by her husband's brother and father. On being questioned, they denied her claims as she had only daughters, while her husband's brother had a son, and there was a dispute. The *panchayat* (village council) decided in her favour. She has started cultivating the land. Ever since then, her male marital kin do not talk to her. Though she is prepared to pay the full wage for ploughing her land, they ask other men in the *tola* not to plough for her. This being a founding family of the village, still relatively powerful in the social hierarchy, other men do not want to risk breaking that relationship for a small monetary gain.

Another strategy used for thwarting widows' claims to land is to brand them as witches, or *dains* (Kelkar and Nathan, 1991). Such charges often emerge from other women within households due to jealousies of different sorts and are then pursued by their male kin in the more public domain. This once again seems to be a unifier in terms of resistance to women's claims to an independent livelihood in both caste and tribal societies. In Bagdiha, for instance, women charged with being *dains* included Santal women such as Sonamani Tudu, aged forty years, determined to hold on to her land till her son grew up, or a Hindu woman Mukta Gorain, aged fifty-five years, who dared expose and resist the illegal activities of her powerful male kin.

During the hearing on Jhumri's land claim, the headman asked her to get remarried, as she was still young. She, however, expressed doubt that a second husband would be prepared to keep her children, as he might have other children, which could lead to conflict. If the second marriage did not work out, she would be property-less, as she would lose her rights to land in this village, so she did not want to take that chance. She needed the property to bring up her children. Jhumri seems determined to fight, if necessary, as she sees her marital property as the only resource for her survival.

This case reveals that women themselves treat marital and parental property differently. While fighting for her marital property, Jhumri has not considered staking a claim to her parental property. Customary law does provide for a plot of land to women in the natal home in the event of marital breakdown (*taben jom*). This is, however, seen more as a bargaining tool to strengthen the fallback position of a woman within her marriage rather than as an inheritance. Marriage being a defining institution as far as property rights are concerned, women like Jhumri consider it appropriate to stake a claim to their marital property as long as they abide by the social rules for doing so. She does not equate widowhood with marital breakdown, where she needs to leave the village.

Interestingly, once married, unless in *gharjawae* form and hence with a socially legitimate claim on parental property, women largely prefer to stake claims to marital property. Cordial natal links are seen as critical for status as well as a fallback in the case of marital crisis. Shelter and security are seen as more important at such moments in life than a plot of land. In most instances, with support from both the natal kin and the village leadership in their marital village, widows are able to negotiate their land claims in the village, as these are seen as legitimate.

In a patriarchal framework, rights in marital property, however, imply managing the land only until a woman's sons can take over and support her. For instance, Bahamani of Chuapara, now aged thirty-five years, was widowed when still quite young. She has two children, a son aged fifteen years and a daughter who is thirteen. She is very protective of her children, and so are they vis-à-vis their mother. She has used the support of her niece's husband to cultivate her land for the past few years. Now her son ploughs the fields. Yet as she thinks of his marriage in the next few years, she is also clear that she will retain a plot of land for herself and continue to cultivate it independently, perhaps with his help, rather than jointly with him.

An important issue now arises. It is critical to note that agency, while demarcated by gender, is not exercised in a vacuum. It involves mutuality and interdependence, as much as domination and subordination. How a society constructs an acting subject, and how individual subjects creatively manipulate the identities and norms available to them, in relation to varying notions of power and control, located within kinship and family structures,[16] is then a useful way of understanding the theme of gender and landed property. However, it is equally important to note that these meanings change over time, with changes in women's agency as they move from one subject position to another through their life course. The relationship of a woman or widow with her minor son is likely to be different from that with her son, once he has entered adulthood.

As Molyneux (1985) has pointed out, women have different sets of interests, and one cannot assume that 'certain common interests by virtue of their gender' will always be prioritised. 'A theory of interests … must begin by recognising difference rather than assuming homogeneity.' These differences arise from their multiple identities and the interests these carry. They are not only used selectively at particular moments in time but also change with time.

I will now briefly examine the scope for women's collective interests in land leading to collective action.

Women's Solidarity and Collective Action

The role of collective action in the process of women's empowerment, both in terms of pushing for major structural changes at the policy level to meet their strategic interests, as well as in raising practical needs relating to basic survival issues, has been articulated by the Development Alternatives with

Women for a New Era (DAWN) (Sen and Grown, 1987). *Shramshakti: Report of the National Commission on Self Employed Women and Women in the Informal Sector*, too, recognised the need to organise women to claim their rights, stating

> the lack of organisation is the root cause of the exploitation of women workers ... Individually women are not in a position to fight against low and discriminatory wages and exploitative working conditions as they lack bargaining power. Laws will not be so flagrantly violated if workers are organised. (Government of India, 1988: 294)

The importance of collective action for mutual support and enhancing bargaining power is now almost universally recognised. Yet even the Self-Employed Women's Association (SEWA), one of the prime movers behind the aforementioned report in India, organises women around particular trades to ensure common interests in their struggles for better wages and working conditions. Literature on group organisation reveals the importance of homogeneity in social composition of the group to ensure long-term sustainability. Agarwal, too, notes in the context of forest protection and regeneration through collective action that success stories emerged from 'communities which were more or less economically and socially homogenous, and which have been able to ensure relative equity in benefit-sharing between households' (1997: 1374). Where differences do exist, due to religion, caste or class, for instance, as in most parts of India, strategies to build group solidarity are based often on non-conflictual group projects, clearly in women's interests, such as insurance schemes, childcare, housing projects and other social security benefits (Rao, 1996) (Figure 3.3).

If one acknowledges the importance of social legitimacy in making rights to land effective, then grassroots women often seek the support of men, especially influential men, to provide their claims greater legitimacy. This emerges from Agarwal's own example of the Bodhgaya struggle in India, for instance, when the petty bureaucracy only agreed to give the land titles in the names of women after the 'firm refusal by the villagers [both men and women] to take land in male names' (1994: 449). So while there was indeed a collective struggle for women's land rights, it could not have succeeded without the support and solidarity shown by the village men.[17] Similar conclusions emerge from my own data presented earlier.[18]

Figure 3.3 Informal groups in action during the process of transplanting paddy
Source: Photograph by Amit Mitra.

Finally, Agarwal's strong argument for women's collective land management notwithstanding (1997, 2003), such practices are likely to be successful only if supported by a gender-progressive NGO, and if dealing with groups of relatively homogenous women, say, from landless households. Analyses of cooperative farming interventions do suggest that these have often not been successful, due to conflicts over both input- and output-sharing arrangements. An analysis of a women's collective farming intervention with Santal women in Dumka supported by a gender-progressive NGO revealed that the enterprise was able to break even only by undervaluing women's work and with subsidies from the NGO concerned. Production was low, in many ways signifying that it was the NGO which was seen as responsible for the cultivation, rather than the women members. There were constant tensions in the group over labour contributions, as these again varied with women's household positions and responsibilities.

Sensitivity to socio-cultural factors that shape local relations of production are key to understanding the failure of group farming and lead to a questioning of the assumption that 'women prefer cooperative production to individual production' (Davison, 1995: 181).[19]

There is also not much evidence to suggest that such collective farming is necessarily better than working on family farms, as even without formal group arrangements, one does find certain labour- and asset-sharing practices in existence such as in cattle management, irrigation and pest management. It may be better perhaps to use the group to access supportive resources to enhance individual production and strengthen cooperation in different activities, including distribution, rather than engaging in collective farming itself.

Further, while land for such collective farming is accessed through either the state or market, it cannot be forgotten that the bulk of land in India is accessed through family inheritance, and for a majority of small farm households, production contributes directly to household consumption. Production in such instances is seen as a joint enterprise by both men and women for survival. Secondly, based on fieldwork in the Coimbatore district of Tamil Nadu, Heyer (1989) demonstrates that landless households tend to prioritise their own labour mobility and enhancing its quality through investments in education, housing and marriage instead of prioritising land acquisition.[20]

Conclusion

The discussion in this chapter highlights the existence of land claims by women in their parental and marital property, depending on their particular subject positions. Yet to varying degrees in different contexts, these claims are being contested, both by male agnatic and cognatic kin.

Two points need to be highlighted here. First, in individualised contexts such as Bagdiha, where land extension is not legally possible, but there is pressure on men to acquire land for status enhancement, there is an atmosphere of intense competition for land. If a woman insists on a share of land, it is interpreted as a challenge to particular men and opposed. The marginality of Santal men in the public domain vis-à-vis other caste groups, leads to an assertion of their authority in the private domain. To assuage their own male identities and position of authority, they would prefer their women to be dependent on them than to make a living independently.

Second, not all men resist. Many men support women's claims due to their own particular subject locations at that particular time, their life experiences or the need to reassert the legitimacy of their authority and position in the public domain. Similarly, 'women's unity and cohesion on gender issues cannot be assumed' (Molyneux, 1985: 285) as resistance comes from women too, who internalise their subject positions as wives and mothers. As long as the marriage is satisfactory, they do not consider male mediation of resources as necessarily oppressive but rather share in male prestige.

While it is clear that land does form a legitimate need-claim for most rural women, the evidence presented in this chapter reveals that the meaning of land for women changes according to the particular context and location in which they find themselves at different stages in their life cycle. While it may imply security against absolute poverty when they are widowed, it may also mean the ability to challenge domestic violence[21] or improve the intra-household distribution of resources within marriage. While the importance of women having land in their own names is clear, the understanding of difference amongst women provides an insight into how this might be operationalised in socially acceptable and contextualised ways. Further, one cannot afford to forget that the household is not just a site of separate interests but also shared ones.

From this perspective, too, several policy options emerge. The first policy response could be the inclusion of women in land titling and land reform programmes, particularly in relation to their marital property. Despite policy prescriptions since the early 1980s in India, there are not many instances of the inclusion of women as joint owners in the titling process. Little or no thought has been given to demarcating particular qualities of land, such as *bari*, for instance, perceived locally as women's plots, in women's names. It is important to ensure that both secondary rights as well as differentiated rights to different plots of land are recorded in the detailed record of rights, if there is to be a genuine attempt to strengthen women's position, both materially and socially. While there have been some attempts at land reform in terms of the distribution of wastelands, their reach and impact have been limited.

Second, land claims represent a 'need' not just for land but a bundle of related support. Agricultural inputs, technology and credit need to be better coordinated in their delivery. And this is where collective action can play a role in terms of enhancing women's political voice vis-à-vis these needs and facilitate access to a range of resources.

While law and legal reform do provide women leverage in bargaining, they are difficult to enforce in practice. This is not so much due to the resistance from customary law or institutions, but because of the difficulty of enforcing a new set of social relations, even conjugal relations, across a range of different cultural contexts. Given that customary law is often flexible, socially negotiated and hence more practicable, it may be worthwhile to legitimise socially recognised rights in state policy. A starting point could be the clarification of *gharjawae* rights and inclusion of *taben jom* rights in legislation such as the SPTA, 1949, in the case of the specific example discussed in this chapter. This is likely to have more positive outcomes for Santal women than a generalised land right.

Finally, the differences in terms of resource relations and gendered livelihood trajectories from an in-depth study of two villages in different agro-ecological contexts within Dumka district highlight the problems of clubbing together all Santals as a homogenous cultural category of 'forest people' in both research and policy, with implications for the nature of interventions and support. Caution is needed in generalising for bigger population categories, as a nation, across time and space, as the lives and social relations of people are embedded within their resource context and change with changes in that context.

Notes

1. In a historical analysis of labour relations in Andhra Pradesh, de Corta and Venkateshwarlu (1999) illustrate the processes by which men tried to become owners of assets and engage in freer, better-paid, non-agricultural wage labour, often migrating out for non-farm employment. This, however, depended on the stability provided by women, who remained largely unfree, lower-paid, tied agricultural labour.

2. All names of places and respondents in the chapter have been changed.

3. See Jackson (2003) on the cross-cutting nature of class and gender interests, and the differences in reactions between women in landed and landless households. Agarwal (1988) in her analysis of the impact of the Green Revolution has also identified differential impacts on different groups of women based on their class position.

4. Village landholding data reveal that 80 per cent of the households are small and marginal farmers and less than 5 per cent large farmers in both the study villages.

5. See Whitehead (1984a) on divisions among women.

6. See also Harrison (1997) on the use of women's groups to different women. O'Laughlin (1995: 84–85) points out that 'the different strata in the cooperatives were not united by their collective production, but rather by the access that the cooperatives gave them to other resources', whether special quotas of consumer goods or midday meals.

7. Interviews by Goebel of both men and women in a resettlement area in Zimbabwe evoked a similar response: '[H]ere it is our land, the two of us' (1999: 83), even though the permits were issued in the names of men.

8. Three *bigha*s make 1 acre of land.

9. It includes non-landed assets, and only occasionally landed property, though the control is supposed to remain with the woman.

10. The Santal Parganas Tenancy Act (SPTA), 1949, prohibits any form of land transfer in the Santal Parganas. This legislation was made with a view to protecting the land of tribals from alienation to non-tribals, as had been the historical experience.

11. It refers to a husband who is resident in his wife's home.

12. Arendt (1958) points out that affirming a particular identity, especially of a marginalised group or a group under attack, is a political act, emerging from political realities at that historical moment. However, such identities are not fixed, as we may adopt a different identity in a different context. Beteille (1991) makes a similar point in the case of India, wherein people prioritise one of their multiple identities in a particular context. See also Sen (1999) and Chatterjee (1999).

13. Several examples from the New Guinea Highlands point to the immediate interest of a woman to help her husband become a 'big man' rather than sink towards the position of a 'rubbish man', and hence contribute towards the production of gifts for exchange – a source of male prestige (Leacock, 1986). See also Jackson (2000) on this point.

14. Davison, in her study in Zomba district of Southern Malawi, noted for its matrilineal system of land inheritance and high male out-migration, points out in a similar vein that

> the lack of security in land for out-marrying males, as well as increasing land scarcity, means that men are less willing to make a labour investment to *banja* production, preferring wage labour as a more secure means of generating income and maintaining control over its distribution. (1995: 189–90)

15. I found only one case of levirate. The first wife, however, who was then not treated well, could not accept this polygynous arrangement and left the marriage.

16. Dube (1997) in her cross-cultural analysis of eight countries in South and South-East Asia demonstrates that kinship systems account for some critical differences among societies in the way in which gender operates. The bargaining power of women is linked to available choices, and these are often built into the social structure through the organisation of work, space and time, modes of punishment, distribution of resources, denial of information, withholding of love, and absence of opportunities to develop self-worth. See also Whitehead (1984b) on this point.

17. Despite the recognition of the importance of male support, Agarwal (1994: 449), analysing the variables responsible for this success, highlights women's participation in the struggle, growing solidarity among women and the involvement of some middle-class feminist women activists.

18. See also Kabeer's discussion of cross-gender solidarity as a conscious strategy by Nijera Kori, an NGO in Bangladesh, around various forms of collective action including struggles for land. Where male support appears weaker on gender issues is in cases of domestic violence (2002: 35–36).

19. Davison (1995) has reported the existence of tensions between female relatives over land, particularly in contexts of scarcity, in Southern Malawi, and their refusal to engage in cooperative production.

20. Using panel data from the rural Philippines, Estudillo, Quisumbing and Otsuka (2001) demonstrate that land inheritance decisions are made in accordance with the importance of land to each child in terms of their potential to earn from it. With better opportunities for girls in the non-farm sector and with rice cultivation becoming increasingly male in nature, parents show a preference towards sons in land inheritance but daughters in schooling investments, with a view to equalising their lifetime incomes.

21. This is reflected in the Bodhgaya struggle in Bihar (Manimala, 1984).

References

Agarwal, B. 1988. 'Neither Sustenance nor Sustainability: Agricultural Strategies, Ecological Degradation and Indian Women in Poverty'. In *Structures of Patriarchy: State, Community and Household in Modernising Asia*, edited by B. Agarwal, 83–120. New Delhi: Kali for Women.

————. 1994. *A Field of One's Own: Gender and Land Rights in South Asia.* Cambridge, UK: Cambridge University Press.

————. 1997. 'Editorial: Resounding the Alert: Gender, Resources and Community Action'. *World Development* 25(9): 1373–80.

————. 1998. 'Disinherited Peasants, Disadvantaged Workers: A Gender Perspective on Land and Livelihood'. *Economic and Political Weekly* 33(13): A2–14.

————. 2001. 'Participatory Exclusions, Community Forestry, and Gender: An Analysis for South Asia and a Conceptual Framework'. *World Development* 29(10): 1623–48.

————. 2003. 'Gender and Land Rights Revisited: Exploring New Prospects via the State, Family and Market'. *Journal of Agrarian Change* 3(1–2): 184–224.

Archer, W. G. 1984 (1946). *Tribal Law and Justice: A Report on the Santal.* New Delhi: Concept Publishing Company.

Arendt, H. 1958. *The Human Condition.* Chicago: University of Chicago Press.

Beteille, A. 1991. *Society and Politics in India: Essays in a Comparative Perspective.* London: Athlone Press.

Bruce, J., and C. B. Lloyd. 1997. 'Finding the Ties That Bind: Beyond Headship and Household'. In *Intra-Household Resource Allocation in Developing Countries*, edited by L. Haddad, J. Hoddinott and H. Alderman, 213–28. Baltimore: John Hopkins University Press.

Chatterjee, P. 1999. 'Modernity, Democracy and a Political Negotiation of Death'. *South Asia Research* 19(1): 103–19.

Davison, J. 1995. 'Must Women Work Together? Development Agency Assumptions versus Changing Relations of Production in Southern Malawi Households'. In *Women Wielding the Hoe: Lessons from Rural Africa for Feminist Theory and Development Practice*, edited by D. F. Bryceson, 181–99. Oxford: Berg Publishers.

da Corta, L., and D. Venkateshwarlu. 1999. 'Unfree Relations and the Feminisation of Agricultural Labour in Andhra Pradesh, 1970–95'. In *Rural Labour Relations in India*, edited by T. J. Byres, K. Kapadia and J. Lerche, 71–139. London: Frank Cass.

Deere, C. D. 2003. 'Women's Land Rights and Rural Social Movements in the Brazilian Agrarian Reform'. *Journal of Agrarian Change* 3(1–2): 257–88.

Drèze, J. 1990. 'Widows in Rural India'. Discussion Paper No. 26, Development Economics Research Programme, London School of Economics.

Dube, L. 1997. *Women and Kinship: Comparative Perspectives on Gender in South and South-East Asia.* Tokyo: United Nations University Press.

Dwyer, D., and J. Bruce (eds.). 1988. *A Home Divided: Women and Income in the Third World*. Redwood City, CA: Stanford University Press.

Estudillo, J. P., A. Quisumbing and K. Otsuka. 2001. 'Gender Differences in Land Inheritance, Schooling and Lifetime Income: Evidence from the Rural Philippines'. *Journal of Development Studies* 37(4): 23–48.

Folbre, N. 1997. 'Gender Coalitions: Extrafamily Influences on Intra-Family Inequality'. In *Intra-household Resource Allocation in Developing Countries: Models, Methods and Policies*, edited by L. Haddad, J. Hoddinott and H. Alderman, 263–74. Baltimore: Johns Hopkins University Press.

Goebel, A. 1999. 'Here It Is Our Land, the Two of Us: Women, Men and Land in a Zimbabwean Resettlement Area'. *Journal of Contemporary African Studies* 17(1): 75–96.

Government of India. 1988. *Shramshakti: Report of the National Commission on Self-Employed Women and Women in the Informal Sector*. New Delhi: Department of Women and Child Development, Government of India.

Harrison, E. 1997. 'Men in Women's Groups: Interlopers or Allies?' *IDS Bulletin* 28(3): 122–32.

Heyer, J. 1989. 'Landless Agricultural Labourers' Asset Strategies'. *IDS Bulletin* 20(2): 33–40.

Hollway, W. 1984. 'Gender Difference and the Production of Subjectivity'. In J*Changing the Subject: Psychology, Social Regulation and Subjectivity*, edited by W. Henriques, W. Hollway, C. Urwin, C. Venn and V. Walkerdine, 228–52. London: Methuen Publishing.

Hossain, N., and M. Moore. 1999. 'Elites, Poverty and Development'. Background Paper for the *World Development Report 2000/2001* on Poverty, Institute of Development Studies, University of Sussex, Brighton.

International Fund for Agricultural Development (IFAD). 2001. *Rural Poverty Report 2001: The Challenge of Ending Rural Poverty*. Oxford: Oxford University Press.

Jackson, C. 2000. 'Men at Work'. *European Journal of Development Research* 12(2): 1–22.

———. 2003. 'Gender Analysis of Land: Beyond Land Rights for Women?'. *Journal of Agrarian Change* 3(4): 453–80.

Jonasdottir, A. G. 1988. 'On the Concept of Interest, Women's Interests, and the Limitations of Interest Theory'. In *The Political Interests of Gender*, edited by K. B. Jones and A. G. Jonasdottir, 33–65. London: SAGE Publications.

Kabeer, N. 2002. *'We Don't Do Credit': Nijera Kori, Social Mobilisation and the Collective Capabilities of the Poor in Rural Bangladesh*. Dhaka: Nijera Kori.

Kelkar, G., and D. Nathan. 1991. *Gender and Tribe: Women, Land and Forest in Jharkhand*. New Delhi: Kali for Women.

Leacock, E. 1986. 'Women, Power and Authority'. In *Visibility and Power: Essays on Women in Society and Development*, edited by L. Dube, E. Leacock and S. Ardener, 107–35. Delhi: Oxford University Press.

Manimala. 1984. 'Zameen Kenkar? Jote Onkar!'. In *In Search of Answers*, edited by M. Kishwar and R. Vanita, 149–76. London: Zed Books.

Molyneux, M. 1985. 'Mobilisation without Emancipation? Women's Interests, the State and Revolution in Nicaragua'. *Feminist Studies* 11(2): 227–54.

Moore, H. 1994. *A Passion for Difference*. Cambridge, UK: Polity Press.

Moore, S. F. 1978. *Law as Process: An Anthropological Approach*. London: Routledge and Kegal Paul.

O'Laughlin, B. 1995. 'Myth of the African Family in the World of Development'. In *Women Wielding the Hoe: Lessons from Rural Africa for Feminist Theory and Development Practice*, edited by D. F. Bryceson, 63–91. Oxford: Berg Publishers.

Palmer, I. 1985. *The Impact of Agrarian Reform on Women*. West Hartford, CT: Kumarian Press.

Papanek, H. 1989. 'Family Status-Production Work: Women's Contribution to Social Mobility and Class Differentiation'. In *Gender and the Household Domain: Social and Cultural Dimensions*, edited by M. Krishnaraj and K. Chanana, 97–116. New Delhi: SAGE Publications.

Rao, N. 1996. 'Empowerment through Organisation: Women Workers in the Informal Sector'. *Indian Journal of Gender Studies* 3(2): 171–97.

Razavi, S. 2003. 'Introduction: Agrarian Change, Gender and Land Rights'. *Journal of Agrarian Change* 3(1–2): 2–32.

Scott, J. C. 1985. *Weapons of the Weak: Everyday Forms of Peasant Resistance*. New Haven, CT: Yale University Press.

Sen, A. 1990. 'Gender and Cooperative Conflicts'. In *Persistent Inequalities: Women and World Development*, edited by I. Tinker, 123–49. New York: Oxford University Press.

———. 1999. *Reason Before Identity*. New Delhi: Oxford University Press.

Sen, G., and C. Grown. 1987. *Development, Crises and Alternative Visions: Third World Women's Perspectives*. New York: Monthly Review Press.

Sharma, U. 1980. *Women, Work and Property in North-West India*. London: Tavistock Publications.

Strathern, M. 1988. *The Gender of the Gift*. Berkeley, CA: University of California Press.

Tsing, A. 1993. *In the Realm of the Diamond Queen*. Princeton, NJ: Princeton
    University Press.
Visaria, P. 1996. 'Structure of the Indian Labour Force: 1961–94'. *Indian Journal
    of Labour Economics* 39(4): 725–40.
Whitehead, A. 1984a. 'Women's Solidarity – and Divisions among Women'. *IDS
    Bulletin* 15(1): 6–11.
————. 1984b. 'Women and Men, Kinship and Property: Some General Issues'.
    In *Women and Property – Women as Property*, edited by R. Hirschon, 176–92.
    London: Croom Helm.
Wolf, D. L. 1992. *Factory Daughters: Gender, Household Dynamics, and Rural
    Industrialization in Java*. Berkeley, CA: University of California Press.
Young, K., C. Wolkowitz and R. McCullagh (eds.). 1981. *Of Marriage and the
    Market: Women's Subordination in International Perspective*. London: CSE
    Books.

4

Custom and the Courts

Ensuring Women's Rights to Land*

Introduction

Contests over property reflect and shape relationships between people over a period of time as much as between people and resources. They also reflect competing representations of these relationships and notions of the 'community' in specific political–economic contexts (Li, 1996). In many instances, women occupy a disadvantaged position in terms of property rights within the traditional social structures, and in contexts of scarcity, their rights are likely to be the first to be challenged, necessitating the need to protect them. The claims for women's rights to landed property also represent struggles over institutions, status, identities, roles, rules and practices, not just between men and women, but between different groups of men as well. However, the debate is often presented in a polarised, either–or manner – as a struggle between men and women or between statutory law and custom (International Fund for Agricultural Development [IFAD], 2001). I have discussed the problems of presenting the issue of women's land claims and

*This chapter was originally published as an article in the journal *Development and Change* © Institute of Social Studies 2007. All rights reserved. Reproduced with the permission of the copyright holder and the publisher, Blackwell Publishing, Oxford. The fieldwork for the chapter was conducted as part of my PhD research in Dumka district, Jharkhand, and I am grateful to the many men and women who provided deep insights into the issue of women's land rights. I would like to thank Cecile Jackson and Amit Mitra, as well as two anonymous reviewers at *Development and Change*, for their comments on an earlier draft.

secure access as a male-versus-female struggle in Chapter 3;[1] in this chapter I examine the second strand of this polarisation, namely the nature of the legitimisation system. Is there really a choice to be made between statutory codes and customary practices to ensure women's rights?

Internationally, land rights for women gained visibility in the women's movement with the dramatic statement at the United Nations (UN) Women's Conference in Copenhagen in 1980 that women owned only one per cent of the world's resources while constituting 50 per cent of the world's population (UN, 1980: 8). The ground for this had been prepared in 1979 by the UN Convention on the Elimination of All Forms of Discrimination against Women (CEDAW). This included specific clauses on the equal treatment of women in agrarian reform as well as similar rights for both spouses in the ownership, management and disposition of property. With the strengthening of women's movements globally during the UN Decade for Women (1976–85), the exclusion of women from the ownership of land has been increasingly questioned, and legal reform sought to change this position.

In India, this line of argument was articulated in the policy process for the first time in the Sixth Five-Year Plan in 1980 (Government of India, 1980). The debate around women's land rights, however, dates back to immediately after independence, in response to the demand for providing equal rights to women, who had fought alongside men for the country's freedom from colonial rule'. While a comprehensive Hindu Code Bill, proposed by B. R. Ambedkar, the leader of the Constituent Assembly, was rejected, a series of Acts were passed that included the Hindu Succession Act (HSA), 1956, granting Hindu women a share in inheritance (Sonalkar, 1999). While the HSA had some discriminatory clauses (it ignored agricultural land and the claims of married daughters), these have now been removed through a constitutional amendment passed in August 2005 (*Economic and Political Weekly*, 2005: 4487). The Shariat Act, 1937, offers Muslim women an inheritance that is half the share of that of their male counterparts. Since independence, it has been variously amended in India, Pakistan and Bangladesh to include agricultural land (Agarwal, 1994).

Despite the legal provision, a gap between law and practice has persisted (see Agarwal, 1994). This arises to a large extent from the social embeddedness of land and the relational aspects of gender, largely ignored by the statutory codes that treat all people as equal, almost autonomous individuals (Basu, 1999). Yet the failure to ensure property rights to women, which in recent times is seen to have led to a decline in agricultural productivity in a context of men migrating in search of non-farm employment, has pushed policymakers at both national and international levels towards a consideration of more locally negotiated land management systems (Gopal, 1999; Toulmin and Quan, 2000). This is also driven by the asymmetrically gendered formal court processes, with women not having equal access to courts due to lack of time, resources, mobility and judicial bias. Yet local institutions, too, can be hierarchical and highly iniquitous, and the 'resurgence of policy interest in various local and informal mechanisms and institutions for land management', alongside the emphasis on developing land markets, have been identified as threats to poorer women being able to access land on a secure basis (United Nations Research Institute for Social Development [UNRISD], 2005: 13). A key question that arises in this context is one of interpretation – how is law interpreted and by whom?

Faced with such a choice, feminist lawyers and their networks – such as the Lawyer's Collective in India (see Jaising, 1996; Kapur and Cossman, 1996) or the WLSA (Women and Law in Southern Africa) network in seven countries of southern Africa – continue to uphold legal reform as the way forward for ensuring women's rights (Knowles, 1991). In the case of India, feminist researchers such as Bina Agarwal (1994, 2003) and non-governmental organisation (NGO) collectives such as the Working Group on Women's Land Ownership (WGWLO) in Gujarat and the Gender, Livelihood and Resources Forum in Jharkhand also repose greater faith in legal and policy reform than in changing customary value systems, largely patriarchal. The latter see their task as advocating for legal reform to remove discriminatory provisions and encouraging positive action such as the waiving of land registration fees if property is registered in the name of the woman, in addition to enabling women to make their claims. This has led also to a strategy of awareness-raising within the community and providing support on the ground when required (WGWLO, 2005). While a legal framework and recognition are undeniably important in enabling women to make land claims, the role, scope and limitations of such legitimisation systems in given contexts also need to be recognised, as does the problem of separating the material from the social–symbolic realms with respect to land.

Related to this, the concept of a right to land itself needs unravelling. Does it refer to ownership as seen in a legal title and registration in the record of rights, or equally to access, use and varying levels of control, of overlapping 'bundles' of rights – which could be seen as stages in the process of empowerment (Longwe, 1991)? While one may strive towards control as represented by a legal title, there is a simultaneous need to work on issues of social legitimacy, drawing on custom, if needed, to ensure access and use. Ownership in an individual, legal sense can in fact curtail relations between people: 'owners can exclude those who do not belong' (Strathern, 1996: 529). Understanding the processes of claiming absolute rights in land as processes of exclusion could be a useful way of approaching conflicts over land (Cederlof, 2005: 69). Such understandings raise the issue both of collective rights and of collective interpretations of individual rights as forms of social protection, particularly in indigenous communities.

In essence, then, there is a need to examine theories of social praxis in conjunction with theories of jurisprudence, as 'rules of the game' include elements of state law as well as norms and rules evolved from social life and practice. If law is viewed as a social process, it is then difficult to dichotomise between modern and traditional. Yet this dichotomisation continues to dominate global discourse. Apart from the IFAD (2001) *Rural Poverty Report*, the World Bank's landmark 'Land Reform Policy Paper' of 1975 recommended land titling, the abandonment of communal tenure systems and the promotion of land markets as preconditions of modern development. Even though more recently the bank has argued for legal recognition of customary tenure, in practice it continues to finance large-scale land titling and registration projects (Whitehead and Tsikata, 2003), with the majority of land being titled to men (World Bank, 2005).

This chapter is based on my field research with the Santals, a Scheduled Tribe (ST),[2] in a village – called here Bagdiha – in Dumka district, Jharkhand. I aim to demonstrate the temporal and political situatedness of 'law', and the processes of hybridisation that allow a legal right to be actualised, by providing social recognition and validity. Women use different arenas from the extended household and kin group to outside agencies (the courts) to make their claims, with the choice of arena depending on access, legitimacy and available resources, and the expectations of social support or non-support that accompany their particular social and economic location within the community.

What Does Law Really Mean?

In order to reverse the prevalent social and economic inequalities, the democratic state in independent India has sought to plan the core development sectors of the economy. There is thus considerable legislation to support women's rights and policy statements in favour of women as well as other poor and marginalized groups, in a sense providing the space, both legal and administrative, for making claims.[3] While policies may be centralised, governments are not monolithic entities. State policies are interpreted by individual bureaucrats at different levels according to their own ideologies as social actors. Actual outcomes of projects are thus influenced by the everyday practices of bureaucrats and fieldworkers who lie between national policies and local realities (Goetz, 1997).

It is only in the last decade, perhaps in recognition of the 'limits of the centralised state in terms of its knowledge about the complex, functioning social orders' (Scott, 1998: 7), and the need to include local and customary knowledge for effective administration, that the state has been pulling back from the economy, in line also with processes of liberalisation and the operation of global markets. While customary practices should not be romanticised, there is enough practical evidence to show that customs are continually being adapted to new ecological and social circumstances and reinvented in the process of interaction with state authority (Hobsbawm and Ranger, 1983).

Parallel to the development state, the legal system, too, both customary and modern, is embedded in society and social relations. While modern law is seen as a government-enforceable tool that is impartial to individuals in the maintenance of a stable social order, customary law is seen as a set of binding practices of local peoples. Considerable literature on the interlocking of the personal and political dimensions of disputes indicates that such a dichotomisation may not be entirely valid, as every interaction may contain a range of alternatives. An individual may be subject at the same time to rules of the family, kinship and community networks, to rules set by religion and to those of formal state and market organisations including international treaties and project practices in recent times. Each of these can be seen as 'semi-autonomous social fields', with an intermeshing of legal and non-legal norms that may be generated internally but are also vulnerable to rules and decisions emanating from the larger external world (Moore, 1978: 55).

Rudolph and Rudolph note that people behave differently in the private and public realms, and this reflects a way of accommodating traditional and modern forces (1967: 122). For example, while an upper-caste person may not generally eat with a Scheduled Caste (SC) in his or her personal life, they may be forced to do so in a more public, political space. Yet, if there is an expectation that this behaviour should be replicated in the private realm, there is a greater likelihood of conflict and resistance. This appears to be particularly true in relation to property rights, seen as an essential element of kinship systems, yet now sought to be governed by statutory law. In response to overly simplistic models of both state and customary laws, Moore (1986: 4) has pointed out, 'In reality boundaries were not always clear, that mixed systems and intermediate types were commonplace, that transformation and transition were ubiquitous, and that conflict and contradiction were inherent in social life and human thought.'[14]

Rules and laws thus include ambiguities and gaps and are open to a range of interpretations. In the present context, what then tends to happen is that rather than operating as separate fields, the main actors seek to make interconnections between them. What emerges are hybrid systems of jurisprudence, with village leaders often using the state systems to legitimise their viewpoint and vice versa, rather than trying to assert the superiority of one or the other. An account from Papua New Guinea demonstrates how custom is invoked as a legal tool in the courtroom, where it is seen to have a moral weight and be better able to fix responsibility, while what happens at the village level often follows the statutory code (Demian, 2003), which, being more distant, tends to evoke more fear and hence compliance.

Seeing the statutory and the customary as two parallel rather than interconnected systems carries the implication that the basic principles of the two systems differ. While there appears to be an underlying singularity in terms of fairness, justice and equity, what differs is the morality which sets up the framework of interpretation. Modern law, based on universalist generalisations about social reality, tends to deny the collective interpretation of the individual's rights and needs, as shaped by her or his social positionality, which forms the practice of the customary systems. This is because in modern law, the individual is treated as an autonomous entity rather than as part of a larger social domain, embedded simultaneously in community relationships and rules (cf. Rudolph and Rudolph, 1967: 107).

While the dichotomy in legal systems may be more of a myth in practice, it persists in discourse. This discursive distinction plays a major role in shifting the relative bargaining positions of people dealing with one another in these social fields, and, as Meinzen-Dick and Pradhan (2002: 2) note, 'multiple legal frameworks also provide flexibility for people to manoeuvre in their use of natural resources'. Von Benda-Beckmann and van der Velde (1992) have shown in the case of Indonesia that legal pluralism offered opportunities to different groups to pursue different political and economic agendas. The state and customary laws were used respectively by two different ethnic groups in their struggle against each other for economic resources and political equality, rather than in claims for a generalised but non-existent form of 'rights'. While in the Jahaly Pacharr irrigated rice scheme in the Gambia, men used the discourse of tradition to maintain control over land rights and also women's labour (Carney, 1988), in Kenya, women disguised their acts of resistance in the authorised vocabulary and discourse of the state. They used the *harambee* ideology of self-help groups to withdraw labour from household plots controlled by men and use it instead for paid wage work (Mackenzie, 1990). The selective use of the available and recognised legal discourses is also visible in the case of Santal women attempting to claim recognition and rights under the rubric of national policies that provide for equal rights to women, while also trying to manipulate customary law to their advantage.[5] The very diversity of practices gives them room for manoeuvre. Custom then may not always pose a barrier to women's rights to land, as is often argued, especially in the case of patrilineal societies (See, for instance, Agarwal, 1994).

Much of the debate around legal pluralism today is really about the nature of the state in a context of globalisation – how far does the state acknowledge diverse social fields within society or seek collaboration of non-state social fields for the implementation of its laws and policies (Moore, 2001: 107), and what is the distribution of power between these different actors? Strathern (1996) argues that rather than pluralism, this reflects a move towards hybridisation, the picking of different rules and norms from different fields to construct a new code of practice, changing in response to the context. In the remaining part of this chapter, I examine the operation of different rules and norms – legal systems – in practice, extending over a range of arenas from the household and kin group to the courts, to identify both interconnections between different systems of law and processes of hybridisation. I focus particularly on women's inheritance rights through marriage to a *gharjawae* (resident son-in-law) as this is one customary practice that is also recognised in the statutory law governing land relations, namely, the Santal Pargana Tenancy Act (SPTA), 1949, Section 20(2) (Prasad, 1997).

Law in Practice

Bagdiha, a multi-caste village comprising 235 households, lies in the plains, 17 kilometres from Dumka. A daily minibus service to Dumka is run in the morning by one of the *mahajan*s (moneylenders) of Bagdiha. At other times, there is a bus which runs from the road-head, a 5-kilometre walk from the village. Bagdiha has seven *tola*s (hamlets), one exclusively for the Hindu caste groups – the forty-five *teli* and *kumhar* households. The remaining *tola*s are largely composed of the Santals, the dominant tribe of the region, some Kols (another tribe) and several SC households. In this chapter, based on fieldwork carried out over a period of eighteen months during 1999–2000, I largely focus on the Santals, examining the practice of law at different levels, from the kin group to the courtroom (Rao, 2002).

The Household and Kin Group

There is considerable literature on households and intra-household relationships that discuss power and negotiation within the household, based on the relative resources that men and women are able to command (Hart, 1997; Whitehead, 1981). Law is seen as one such resource in struggles over land.

Amongst the Santals, the *gharjawae* is a social mechanism set up to enable a daughter to inherit her father's land. The husband here normally gives up his own land claims in his paternal property and moves to his wife's home. The woman inherits full rights over the landed property, though her children still take the lineage name of her husband. Her father negotiates this arrangement with his male kin and gains acceptance through a ritual village feast. While W. G. Archer (1984 [1946]) has pointed to the flexibilities in customary law in the case of a *gharjawae* – it can be performed by the widowed mother, a second marriage can be performed to a *gharjawae*, more than one daughter can be married to *gharjawae*s – these flexibilities are now being strongly contested. This is especially true since the SPTA of 1949, does not take note of such instances but recognises *gharjawae* only in the absence of a male heir. So we have a situation where a customary practice is absorbed into state legal practice, yet the assumptions in terms of the underlying justifications for this practice are changed.

The struggle here is not within the nuclear household but rather the patrilineage. Several strategies for negotiation have emerged, sometimes in phases over a period of time in order to cumulatively build up the legitimacy for a claim. Chuni Tudu, a widow with two daughters, sought the consent of her husband's brother and his son for the marriage of her elder daughter to a *gharjawae*, but they refused. She therefore got her daughter married in a normal way though seeking support from her daughter's husband for timely ploughing. The conflict, however, has only been postponed, as she would now like her younger daughter to inherit by marrying a *gharjawae*. What she has succeeded in doing, however, is buying time to gain support for her actions from the community, while also attempting to appease the kin by seemingly deferring to their wishes.

Dhaki Marandi was married in a neighbouring village, but her husband brought a second wife, and Dhaki was not treated well, so she returned to Bagdiha. Legally – her husband having sent her back with all her things – Dhaki can get remarried, and in any form. Since Dhaki has no siblings, her mother now wants to get her remarried to a *gharjawae*. By getting a male in the house, they can then improve their own cultivation through timely ploughing. Her male cousins do not help them plough the land; they therefore maintain several heads of cattle to help them negotiate wage labour for ploughing, but the productivity of their land is low due to delays that still occur in securing labour. To get their kin's support, Dhaki has also given them a part of the land, yet they continue to oppose a *gharjawae* marriage for her, because, as things stand, the land would go to them after her mother's death. Her mother knows that a *gharjawae* marriage can be registered in the court, but realises the importance of getting village support, if the right is to be operationalised.

As women's claims to land directly affect the material interests of the male agnates, in a context of scarce resources, it appears difficult for these to be successfully contested within the arena of the household or kin group. At best, temporary solutions can be reached as in the aforementioned examples, but situated within long-term processes of competition, these tend ultimately to work against the interests of the women concerned. The contestation then invariably spills into the more public arenas, at both the village and state levels.

The Village Council

When negotiations fail within the household or kin group, the case is taken to the village council. Miru Murmu, married to a *gharjawae*, had three sons and two daughters. After her death in 1990, her male kin started harassing her sons to drive them away from the village. The main point of dispute was whether the marriage was *gharjawae* or not and whether Miru and her husband were in cultivating possession of the land after the death of her father. The village leaders tried several times to resolve the dispute, their decision in support of the woman's rights. The threats and harassment continued, however, until finally the perpetrators were socially expelled from the community: the family would not be allowed to use the common well or participate in village rituals. But the efficacy of this sanction was undermined by state policy that ensured them access to water and other public services. In January 1999, when her eldest son was returning from the *haat* (weekly market), Miru's male kin finally turned to the use of violence and knifed him to death. A police case was registered, and the male kin were arrested. Interestingly, fear of these 'official' institutions appears to ensure better compliance at the village level than the strength of custom.

Women are not represented in the village council, nor are they present in the courts at the district level as officials, lawyers or judges. Legally they have equal access to the state institutions, but their participation in village meetings is restricted. In the words of the *majhi* (headman) of Bagdiha, in an interview on 31 May 2000:

> When a case involves women, they will narrate everything from the beginning, so it becomes embarrassing for the men. They have to turn their heads away in shame. Women don't participate in the *kulhi durup* [village meeting], as their presence will embarrass their male relatives even further. If a case involves a man, he can be told to cut it short, but with a woman she can't.[6]

Women articulate the nuances of social relationships in great depth, recounting little details that may seem insignificant, but are 'embarrassing' to the male leadership and a threat to their masculinities. They hence exclude them from this space. Women resent their exclusion, yet given its familiarity and accessibility, the village council continues to be the first port of call for negotiation. With a focus on consensus and maintaining dignity for both parties, rather than identifying winners and losers, judgements of the village council are also more likely to be followed (Srinivas, 1962). While tending sometimes to reinforce the 'maleness' of land at the symbolic level, the discourse here nevertheless recognises the material value of land as a key subsistence resource for both men and women.

The Settlement Courts

The settlement court is an intermediate institution, first set up during the second land revenue settlement in the Santal Parganas, supervised by

H. McPherson from 1898 to 1908, to hear and resolve disputes in the process of land titling and settlement of rents. Conducting hearings in local camps, this was seen to be cheaper, quicker and more accessible than the formal courts, yet following a set of universal norms of fairness seen as being in opposition to the traditional structures. During this settlement, many of the cases filed in the settlement courts related to title claims, disputes over who had cleared the land and in whose name it should be registered. These contestations were usually between men.

During the next settlement, supervised by J. F. Gantzer (1925–37), the nature of disputes began to change. While still predominantly between men, they now related to issues of inheritance within kin groups as well as disputes on tenancy agreements. During the current settlement period (1980 onwards), we find an intensification of inheritance and tenancy disputes. The relatively new trend is the preponderance of *gharjawae* registrations, given also its legal recognition, and the contestations around this. Two examples from the settlement records are representative (see Box 4.1).

Women have realised the importance of registration during their lifetime in order to avoid future struggles of the kind faced by Miru. In the event

---

Box 4.1 Contesting settlement claims: *gharjawae*s

Objection 1: Manglu Marandi, son of Safu Marandi, has a *gharjawae*, Boyla Hembrum. Boyla says, 'I was married to Manglu's daughter, Tulsi Marandi, in court. Now her father is dead, and his share should be registered in the name of Tulsi. Bejun Marandi, her male kin, objected that none of Manglu's daughters were married as *gharjawae*. The marriage papers, dated 5 July 1977, were produced. Later, Boyla left Tulsi and married someone else. Bejun said that Tulsi was now no longer *gharjawae*, so she could not inherit. However, as Tulsi stayed on, she was allotted a share.

Objection 54: Bhatu Kisku's daughter, Rasodi Kisku, was married in *gharjawae* form. When her father died, she wanted her name entered in the settlement records. Durga Kisku and Lobin Kisku objected that they did not consider her husband as a *gharjawae*, as he did not stay here or plough the land. She produced a letter from 18 October 1965 validating her marriage in *gharjawae* form and rent receipts from 1983–84 to 1987–88. Dhona Marandi, the former *mukhiya* (government recognised headman), testified that she had a *gharjawae* marriage. The settlement went in her favour.

Source: Adapted from Transfer and Dispute List, 1988–97, Settlement Records, Settlement Office, Dumka.

of a woman's claim being challenged, a notice is sent and a hearing held to decide the case. Women attempt to secure the support of other women in their position and of key men in the village as witnesses. The village leaders were generally supportive of these women, wanting to project their society as fair and just, as opposed to the more patriarchal and restrictive Hindu society.[7] Further, the *majhi* of one of the *tola*s of Bagdiha, himself a *gharjawae*, championed this cause with the other leaders.

In addition to the Settlement Officer, the revenue settlement process involves two other functionaries, who play a key role in influencing the adjudication process: the *amin* who measures the land, and the *karamchari* who is responsible both for rent collections and the evaluation of social security claims such as pensions for widows and the aged. The latter maintains copies of the rent receipts, which form crucial evidence in terms of rival claims to land. While there are differences in the attitudes of these petty bureaucrats, based on their own personal histories and positions,[8] we do find in general a tendency to support *gharjawae* rights – an attempt perhaps to appear 'modern' and above their local caste or ethnic prejudices in line with the national legal framework. As Panti Marandi narrated, 'The *amin* of Guhiajori took me to the settlement camp. He asked me to get my name registered.' Such persons, with access to state information, then replace local mediators, significant in moulding opinion at the village level. Village people too try to establish closeness with those with access to the records[9] and record-keepers, using this as leverage in local power struggles, gaining as a result not just materially, but also in status and prestige.

The settlement courts present a good example of processes of hybridisation, of local and national discourses feeding into each other, to legitimise and strengthen women's land claims. When violence takes over, however, the only recourse is to the courts of law, both civil and criminal. While the former lie in the purview of the Revenue Department – the courts of the Sub-Divisional Officer (SDO), Assistant Collector (AC) and District Collector (DC) – the latter cases are normally filed through the police stations and go directly to the courts of the Sub-Judge and District Judge. Administratively, the former are part of the executive, while the latter are governed by the rules and norms of the judiciary. Yet to uphold their own moral authority, as protectors of all members of the community, women and men, leaders of the village council, usually support women's claims in the courts, both through establishing informal linkages, contacts and arrangements with these 'official' institutions, and also formal presentation of evidence in the court where the case is being tried.

Revenue and Civil Courts

There are perhaps a hundred revenue cases of different types registered in the civil courts of Dumka each month, 75 per cent of them relating to issues of demarcation, tenancy and inheritance. According to the registers of the sub-divisional court, 12–15 per cent of the cases in this category have involved women in the last decade. While oral evidence seems to suggest that contestation has increased since the early 1980s, longer-term court data were not available to confirm this.

The first point of reference for the civil courts is the SPTA which, while seeking to protect *adivasi* (the term used locally for STs) land from alienation by prohibiting all land transfers (Section 20), has provided for women's rights as exceptions to the rule. In the case of a sister, daughter, widowed mother or wife, it provides for a gift or grant with the written permission of the Deputy Commissioner (Section 20[1]). Only in the case of a *gharjawae* is it considered a legitimate right (Section 20[2]). However, following Gantzer, the SPTA represented the *gharjawae* as an adopted son-in-law who inherits the land rather than the daughter.[10] By thus splitting descent group from property inheritance, the ideological from the material, it opened the space for objections from the wife's male natal kin.[11]

Archer had hoped to record as case law the flexibilities in Santal law with respect to women's rights (Singh, 1984: xi). He refers to a note by the DC of Santal Parganas, dated 17 September 1928:

A custom may be developed and modified by custom ... In the Rajmahal, the *Parganait*s Assembly usually find in favour of the widows and daughters when succession disputes are sent to them for arbitration ... By strictly enforcing the existing law, we are practically preventing any possibility of the development of the right of female inheritance. (Archer, 1942–46: Mss Eur F 236/51)

Archer's report was, however, rejected by the government of independent India. In the absence of such a body of case law, the civil courts draw on the advice of the village leaders in deciding cases. Despite the change in form, social and kin relationships thus continue to play a role in determining access to land. Yet the legalisation of their voice, through the SPTA and the court process, gives it a 'public constituency' (Crook, 2001: 43) rather than being an exclusive privilege of elite 'insiders' (Khadiagala, 2001), as has often been the charge against customary institutions. Further, given a largely pro-women national legal framework, village leaders, wanting to present themselves as fair and just, tend to support women's claims to land. If the village leaders for any reason fail to reach a consensus, then the court draws upon the HSA, which provides equal inheritance rights to the widow, sons and daughters in the event of a man's death. In most cases, however, the mere possibility of such recourse to Hindu law paves the way for a negotiated decision.

The key difference with the settlement courts is the intervening role of the lawyers in the civil courts. This is one reason why the Santals often stop attending regularly even the cases they themselves have filed in the court, as they begin to find burdensome the lawyers' fees, payable over a period of several years. Women often file cases as government suits, implying a waiver of legal fees. Yet, if fees are absent, the motivation to argue or resolve the case is minimal, and often such cases drag on for many years. The only woman in Bagdiha who has filed and pursued such a case is the widow Mira Gorain, belonging to the group of Hindu *telis*. While eking out her existence by making and selling *murri* (puffed rice),[12] she is sure of an ultimate resolution in her favour as per the HSA, and hence persists. For a majority of Santal women, the inability to cultivate would in all probability lead to migration from their home. They cannot wait several years for a court decision and hence prefer an immediate decision through social negotiation (Figure 4.1).

Ultimately it falls upon the judge (the SDO, AC or DC), usually a non-Santal, to reach a decision. In cases where witnesses are called, the *karamcharis*, *amins* and village leaders do play an influencing role. But as Moore (1978) has pointed out, while laws are seen as rational and systematic norms by the state, they are open to different interpretations to accommodate the complexities of social life and the different social positionings of the state personnel themselves. While evidence in terms of marriage registration and rent receipts are produced where available, these too are challenged, with land cases argued mainly on the basis of genealogies and migrations, with claims resting on historical, often oral knowledge. Production of this being competitive, some voices carry more weight than others, owing to their social

Figure 4.1 Women negotiating with clerks and lawyers at the district court
Source: Photograph by the author.

position, and as Dhagamwar (2003) points out, courts have often ended up giving judgments in deference to dominant interests. It is no surprise then that the poor, particularly women, see the state as allocating land to and supporting the 'big' people, those able to 'feed' them (Goheen, 1988: 298), and hence prefer the customary courts.

While NGOs have been active both in advocating for women's legal rights to land and in the struggle of *adivasi*s and other oppressed groups against the *mahajan*s, they have not often engaged directly in the legal arena. An exception is the public interest litigation filed in the Supreme Court of India by Madhu Kishwar, then editor of the feminist journal *Manushi*, on behalf of a Ho woman, Maki Bui, in 1982. In its judgment (which came more than a decade later, in 1996), the Supreme Court supported the claims of *adivasi* women to rights in property, based on the general principles of fairness, equity and justice.[13] The male *adivasi* leaders, however, opposed this judgment as an infringement of their customary law and an attempt to undermine the notion of 'community'.

Despite lack of information and access, the utility of legal support in adding authority to women's voice and strengthening their land claims is clear. They may even at some point stop attending the case and yet recognise the value of the courts as a site for the interpretation and reinterpretation of their claims at the local level.

Criminal Courts

Criminal cases range from minor beating (Section 107) and breach of peace (Section 144) to robbery (Section 394) and murder (Section 302). A police complaint is filed, and the case proceeds according to the normal legal process. The court fixes dates for hearings, lawyers are appointed, and the case is argued. While there is an attempt to resolve minor cases within a period of sixty days, most others go on for years.

I referred earlier to the case of Miru, the fundamental premise of which was the questioning of a woman's inheritance. Before the murder of her son, the kin adopted a range of strategies from verbal threats to petty thefts and robberies in order to frighten their cousins and make them give up claims on the property of their inheriting mother. During the last decade, a range of cases, both civil and criminal, were filed, and police protection was sought at different points; yet the murder could not be averted. The core of the dispute was material – competing claims for a scarce resource. It was justified by the use of kinship and descent ideologies – Miru's male cousin had performed the funeral rites for her father. As the next in line in the descent group, his sons now claimed the land as legitimately theirs, justified on grounds of protecting the land for the lineage. Her marriage to a *gharjawae* too was challenged in the process.

Unlike the discourse in the settlement courts or even the revenue courts that lay much greater emphasis on customary law and local practice, and are hence perceived as more accessible by Santal men and women, the discourse in the criminal courts is couched in the language of the Indian Penal Code (IPC). It relies much more on reports from the police than the viewpoints of the local leaders. The police do consult village leaders before making their report, but are easily influenced by bribes, often turning a blind eye to crucial evidence.

The use of legal terminology enhances the dependence on lawyers and makes the role and motivation of lawyers critical. Mostly non-Santal, they tend to look down on their clients. Several interviews with both Muslim and Hindu lawyers in Dumka revealed that they construct Santal men as constantly drunk, good for nothing and getting themselves into unnecessary trouble and Santal women as hard-working but ignorant and promiscuous. They are not really concerned about the longer-term outcomes of the case – for instance, the political implications of securing bail for the killers of Miru's son. If lawyers are progressively motivated, however, they can play a major political role in the judicial process, as during the agrarian struggle in the late 1960s. At this time, the *mahajans* (moneylenders) filed cases of dacoity and loot against the Santals (under Section 395 of the IPC). The period of 1969–72 was one of intense contestation in the courts between the *mahajans* and the Santals. As the Santals could not easily access the official documents needed to fight the cases, a group of lawyers belonging to the Communist Party of India, practising in the Dumka court, used their class and caste contacts to access these records and support their claims. In most cases, they were not paid fees, as the people had nothing even to eat (Rao, 2002).

Unlike the issue of title registrations in the settlement courts, the number of cases brought to the civil and criminal courts by Santal women remains limited, for reasons of time, resources and legitimacy. Village leaders, while supporting women in the settlement and lower revenue courts, discourage them as far as possible from going to the higher courts. Their voice hardly heard here, this is also seen as an affront to their prestige. Instead, they try their best to resolve such disputes locally. Further, while distance from the village does evoke a sense of fear, exclusion of local discourse, especially from the criminal courts, makes it difficult for them to enforce their decisions and influence the final social and material outcomes at the village level.

Legal pluralism, according to von Benda-Beckmann (2001: 48), is an acknowledgement of 'the theoretical possibility of more than one legal order, based on different sources of ultimate validity and maintained by forms of organisation other than the State'. It does not imply a normative preference for one or the other, as the choice of the arena for contestation is ultimately a political choice, determining as it does the access to resources. In practice, however, there is an interpenetration of state and customary laws, as well as a complex relationship between ethnicity, a struggle for identity and these plural systems of law, with the boundaries often blurred.

The Importance of Context

A range of actors – Santal men and women, village leaders, lawyers, petty and higher bureaucracy, judges – participate in the key formal arenas where women's claims to land are contested. While missionaries, NGOs or political party leaders may not directly intervene, representatives of these groups, in their roles as village men or women, carry these views into their other subject positions. The key point to note is not only the presence of multiple actors and multiple discursive arenas, but also the overlapping of different identities and subject positions in these arenas. On account of their particular political affiliations at different moments in history, lawyers, for instance, have been critical in influencing outcomes. *Adivasi* lawyers have often opposed Santal women's rights, seeing themselves as political activists or professional elite, rather than lawyers alone.

Engaged in development interventions, NGOs, on the other hand, firmly support women's land claims. While claiming to represent the voices of Santal women, however, they often diverge both in content and strategy from the client group. While women at the village level seem to prefer staking claims in marital property, NGOs, like the state, have focused on the inheritance of parental property; and while women seem to prefer social negotiation at the local level in the first instance, NGOs emphasise legal reform (Badlao Foundation, 1998). Though progressive from a rights-based perspective to women's equality, there is an assumption here that women do not have rights in customary law. Further, power relations in the 'modern' institutions of state are not questioned, nor are the institutional and cultural biases that prevent women from making their claims.

The Jharkhand Mahila Mukti Morcha (JMMM), a network of indigenous women's groups in Jharkhand, seems to come closer to the view of village women. Some of the groups in the network felt that law and legal reform would not necessarily solve the problem, given the social character of land. Customary law accords unmarried daughters rights in their fathers' land; while maintaining the demand for this, the JMMM is more concerned with marital property. Their position is that, along with a man, his wife's name should also be registered in the land records (Abhiyaan, 1999). If the man wants to separate, then he has to give his wife a share. While largely feminist in their outlook, these groups recognise the embeddedness of property and inheritance in marriage and kinship structures and the need to negotiate therein, if claims are to be realised. This view helps build bridges with male leaders and thus garner support for women's land claims more easily than a position based on the decontextualised principle of equal rights for men and women.

At the same time, the shift in the discourse from property to marriage has been used by *adivasi* leaders to deny women's land claims. The leading political party in the region, the Jharkhand Mukti Morcha (JMM), although constructed on the premise of agrarian change and development, and while supporting gender equality in a broad sense, opposes formal land rights to women, including that of *gharjawae*, fearing 'alienation' of land through mixed marriages. In a patrilineal society, although the mother is a Santal, the effective control of the land is seen to pass out of the lineage and to 'other castes', as the children take the name of the father. While mixed marriage has perhaps been one method of alienation, particularly near major towns, its magnitude does not as yet seem significant (Thakur, 1977) and is definitely not the only reason for alienation. Santals themselves, the JMM leaders recognise the central role of Santal women in the land economy.[14] Yet the economic poverty and the social and political marginalisation of the *adivasi*s vis-à-vis the dominant Hindu groups has led to an emphasis on indigeneity, on socio-cultural difference, as the strategy for political mobilisation to gain access to state resources, and an opposition to women's rights. They are, however, now willing to negotiate more specific rights in marital property, though linked to restrictions on marital choice.

While there are divisions and differences within each of these categories, in the larger policy discourse they appear as sharply opposing voices – one an advocate, another an opponent of the legitimacy of women's land claims. Given this sharp divergence, the 'experts' then seek to build bridges 'which mediate the relations between social movements and the State' (Fraser, 1989: 11). Yet, in translating politicised needs into generalised and depoliticised administrative projects, the nuances relating to women's land claims in marital and natal property, in different environmental contexts and subject positions, do not find adequate reflection in state policy and hence bely implementation.

Conclusion

This chapter has examined both the discourse and practice around women's claims to land in different arenas ranging from the informal household space to the extremely formal judicial courtrooms. The range of actors directly engaging in these arenas are influenced in their views by their multiple subject positionings, as members of a particular political party or social network, in addition to being men, women, Santals, non-Santals, non-literate or professional. Apart from the sometimes overlapping and contradictory ideologies of and pressures on these actors, it is also difficult to separate the discussion on women's claims to land from a complex bundle of issues vis-à-vis the community, markets and state. It is not just a struggle about women's rights to land, but also the identity of the society as a whole, in a context of exploitation, impoverishment and dispossession from resources.

The first point of negotiation remains the extended household and village council; a majority of women who have effectively claimed land have done so through a process of negotiation at this level. Despite being exclusively male, these community institutions do appear more responsive to competing discourses, having as they do a direct knowledge of the local context and relationships, responding on a case-by-case basis, rather than through universal policies. Further, given their marginalisation vis-à-vis the state and the ensuing pressures of the 'modern' legal framework, based on principles of equality (including gender equality) and justice, to prove themselves progressive, they seek to ensure that decisions made at this level are not completely adverse to women's interests.

When violence takes over, the only solution seems to be to appeal to the state – the legitimate enforcers of 'law and order'. Their distance from the village and 'perceived authority' creates fear in the minds of the opponents to a much greater extent than the diktat of the village leadership. In the civil and revenue courts, the officers seek the opinions of the village leadership and adjudicate accordingly; yet this has the stamp of authority and definitely provides weight to women's land claims. In the criminal courts and higher levels of civil justice, however, the local context is largely ignored in favour of the notion of universal rights. The exclusion of local discourse implies that decisions taken here are hardly implemented on the ground.

Law can thus be both empowering and disempowering, depending on the particular perspective from which it is viewed. Legal titling is not necessarily better than the flexible rights ensured by customary practice, as these are legitimised by a sense of social responsibility, while the rights language does not always capture the social embeddedness of women's land claims (Whitehead and Tsikata, 2003). One needs to accept that social relationships, particularly of gender, embrace elements of conflict and competition, as well as cooperation and mutual support (Sen, 1990). The civil code and courts of law see people as individual entities rather than embedded in a network of social relations (Brand, 1998) and hence often fail to arrive at solutions that can be operationalised. They also sometimes miss the collective interpretations of an individual need that form the basis for justifying the claim.

The meanings of land to different groups of men and women are constructed on the basis of their material reality as well as symbolic moorings. Rather than attempting to fix one social reality, or leaving the field completely indeterminate, the way forward could be the pursuit of hybridity – giving legal recognition to socially validated rights as a step forward in the movement towards gender equality.

Notes

1. Agriculture in much of India being a household enterprise, the main argument of Chapter 3 relates to the mutuality and interdependence between men and women in the productive use of land. This often leads to identities based on caste, ethnicity, kinship status, and so on, motivating land claims rather than gender. Further, women's claims to land become effective only when they are socially recognised, and this implies gaining the support of men, including community leaders. Chapter 3 presents evidence to show that men, too, adopt different subject positions and do not form one homogenous group in opposition to women.

2. Article 342, Part XVI, of the Constitution of India provides for public notification by the President to specify the tribes that shall be deemed as STs and hence eligible for special provisions to promote their educational and economic interests. The historical disadvantage of the entire group was thus politically recognised.

3. Apart from the Five-Year Plans, the latest policy statement for women is the National Policy for the Empowerment of Women (Government of India, 2001). Over the last decade several schemes have been launched for the education (Beti Bachao Beti Padhao) and skills development (Mahila Shakti Kendra) of girls and women.

4. O'Rourke (1995) shows how despite the passing of the Land Act in 1963 in Tanzania, the Chagga in Mt Kilimanjaro continued to determine land rights through the local lineage–neighbourhood complex. Stivens, Ng and Jomo (1994) demonstrate for rural Malaysia that women often preferred to postpone the process of registering land, not only because of the expense

involved, but because in the context of high male out-migration, this ensured them access to more land than their share.

5. A documentation of Santal customary law by W. G. Archer (1984 [1946]) is in fact a record of the flexibility in the law in relation to women's rights to land. When raised by women, the male leadership of the Jharkhand and revivalist movements have been forced to legitimise these practices, in the desire to prove the superiority of their traditions in contrast to Hindu institutions' treatment of women.

6. A woman can become a *majhi* if (*a*) her husband is a *majhi* and dismissed for improper conduct or (*b*) her father was a *majhi* and she is his only child. If a woman is a *majhi*, then she can collect revenue and *bheeja*s (ritual offerings) during festivals but cannot participate in the village justice process or outdoor rituals.

7. With a large Hindu population in Bagdiha, comparisons and inter-community one-upmanship is continuous. In the economic realm the Hindus have the upper hand, so one way for the Santals to establish their superiority is through their social and cultural practices.

8. While there are almost an equal number of Santal and non-Santal *amin*s and *karamchari*s, as one moves up the hierarchy, the majority of officers are non-Santals.

9. These are seen as 'objective evidence' in contrast to the subjective perceptions of different actors presented in the village council.

10. 'Objection 1' in Box 4.1 was raised because the *gharjawae* son-in-law is no longer resident of the village; in fact, has married someone else. It was his rights that were recognised rather than the daughter's.

11. Due to strict clan exogamy in marriage, the husband belongs to a different clan or sub-clan from that of his wife, implying that if the *gharjawae* inherited, then the property moved from one clan to another.

12. The returns on *murri*-making are very low, barely 8–10 rupees per day, assuming free fuelwood.

13. In line with international commitments such as the CEDAW, the judgment given on 17 April 1996, in response to writ petitions 5723 of 1982 and 219 of 1986, draws upon the principles of the Indian Succession Act, 1925, and the HAS, 1956, even though they are not directly applicable to *adivasi* women.

14. During the early stages of the agrarian movement, women were placed at the centre of the agrarian reconstruction programme (Iyer and Maharaj, 1986).

References

Abhiyaan. 1999. *Jharkhandi Mahilaon Ki Davedari, Satta Mein Aadhi Bhagedari* (Hindi). Madhupur: Abhiyaan.

Agarwal, B. 1994. *A Field of One's Own: Gender and Land Rights in South Asia.* Cambridge, UK: Cambridge University Press.

———. 2003. 'Gender and Land Rights Revisited: Exploring New Prospects via the State, Family and Market'. *Journal of Agrarian Change* 3(1–2): 184–224.

Archer, W. G. 1942–46. *Archer Papers.* London: India and Oriental Office Collection.

———. 1984 (1946). *Tribal Law and Justice: A Report on the Santal.* New Delhi: Concept Publishing Company.

Badlao Foundation. 1998. *Adivasi Betion Ke Adhikaar* (Hindi). Patna: Alekhan.

Basu, S. 1999. 'Cutting to Size: Property and Gendered Identity in the Indian Higher Courts'. In *Signposts: Gender Issues in Post-Independence India*, edited by R. Sunder Rajan, 248–91. New Delhi: Kali for Women.

Brand, S. M. A. A. 1998. 'Civil Law vs the Mande Conception of Gendered Personhood: The Case of Bamako, Mali'. In *Negotiation and Social Space: A Gendered Analysis of Changing Kin and Security Networks in South Asia and Sub-Saharan Africa*, edited by C. Risseeuw and K. Ganesh, 137–53. New Delhi: SAGE Publications.

Carney, J. 1988. 'Struggles over Crop Rights within Contract Farming Households in a Gambian Irrigated Rice Project'. *Journal of Peasant Studies* 15(3): 334–49.

Cederlof, G. 2005. 'The Toda Tiger: Debates on Custom, Utility and Rights in Nature, South India, 1820–1843'. In *Ecological Nationalisms: Nature, Livelihoods and Identities in South Asia*, edited by G. Cederlof and K. Sivaramakrishnan, 67–77. Delhi: Permanent Black.

Crook, R.C. 2001. 'Cocoa Booms, the Legalisation of Land Relations and Politics in Cote d'Ivoire and Ghana: Explaining Farmers' Responses'. *IDS Bulletin* 32(1): 35–45.

Demian, M. 2003. 'Custom in the Courtroom, Law in the Village: Legal Transformations in Papua New Guinea'. *Journal of the Royal Anthropological Institute* 9(1): 97–115.

Dhagamwar, V. 2003. 'Invasion of Criminal Law by Religion, Custom and Family Law'. *Economic and Political Weekly* 38(15): 1483–92.

Economic and Political Weekly. 2005. 'Groundbreaking Legislation'. *Economic and Political Weekly* 40(41): 4487.

Fraser, N. 1989. *Unruly Practices: Power, Discourse and Gender in Contemporary Social Theory*. Cambridge, UK: Polity Press.

Goetz, A. M. 1997. 'Local Heroes: Patterns of Fieldworker Discretion in Implementing GAD Policy in Bangladesh'. in *Getting Institutions Right for Women in Development*, edited by A. M. Goez, 176–95. London and New York: Zed Books.

Goheen, M. 1988. 'Land Accumulation and Local Control: The Manipulation of Symbols and Power in Nso, Cameroon'. In *Land and Society in Contemporary Africa*, edited by R. E. Downs and S. P. Reyna, 280–308. Hanover and London: University Press of New England.

Gopal, G. 1999. *Gender-Related Legal Reform and Access to Economic Resources in Eastern Africa*. Washington, DC: World Bank.

Government of India. 1980. *Sixth Five Year Plan*. New Delhi: Planning Commission, Government of India.

———. 2001. 'National Policy for the Empowerment of Women'. New Delhi: Ministry of Human Resource Development, Government of India.

Hart, G. 1997. 'From Rotten Wives to Good Mothers: Household Models and the Limits of Economism'. *IDS Bulletin* 28(3): 14–25.

Hobsbawm, E., and T. Ranger. 1983. *The Invention of Tradition*. Cambridge, UK: Cambridge University Press.

International Fund for Agricultural Development (IFAD). 2001. *Rural Poverty Report 2001: The Challenge of Ending Rural Poverty*. Oxford: Oxford University Press.

Iyer, G. K., and R. N. Maharaj. 1986. 'Agrarian Movement in Tribal Bihar (Dhanbad) 1972–80'. In *Agrarian Struggles in India after Independence*, edited by A. R. Desai, 330–61. Delhi: Oxford University Press.

Jaising, I (ed.). 1996. *Justice for Women: Personal Laws, Women's Rights and Law Reform*. Mapusa, Goa: Other India Press.

Kapur, R., and B. Cossman. 1996. *Subversive Sites: Feminist Engagements with Law in India*. New Delhi: SAGE Publications.

Khadiagala, L. S. 2001. 'The Failure of Popular Justice in Uganda: Local Councils and Women's Property Rights'. *Development and Change* 32(1): 55–76.

Knowles, J. B. 1991. 'Women's Access to Land in Africa'. *Third World Legal Studies* (Special Edition): 1–14.

Li, T. M. 1996. 'Images of Community: Discourse and Strategy in Property Relations'. *Development and Change* 27(3): 501–27.

Longwe, S. 1991. 'Gender Awareness: The Missing Element in the Third World Development Project'. In *Changing Perceptions*, edited by T. Wallace and C. March, 149–57. Oxford: Oxfam.

Mackenzie, F. 1990. 'Gender and Land Rights in Murang'a District, Kenya'. *Journal of Peasant Studies* 17(4): 609–43.

Meinzen-Dick, R., and R. Pradhan. 2002. 'Legal Pluralism and Dynamic Property Rights'. CAPRi Working Paper 22, Washington, DC: International Food Policy Research Institute.

Moore, S. F. 1978. *Law as Process: An Anthropological Approach*. London: Routledge and Kegal Paul.

———. 1986. *Social Facts and Fabrications: 'Customary' Law on Kilimanjaro, 1880–1980*. Cambridge, UK: Cambridge University Press.

———. 2001. 'Certainties Undone: Fifty Turbulent Years of Legal Anthropology, 1949–1999'. *Journal of the Royal Anthropological Institute* 7: 95–116.

O'Rourke, N. 1995. 'Land Rights and Gender Relations in Areas of Rural Africa: A Question of Power and Discourse'. *Social and Legal Studies* 4(1): 75–97.

Prasad, B. M. 1997. *Santal Parganas Tenancy Manual*. Patna: Malhotra Bros.

Rao, N. 2002. 'Standing One's Ground: Gender, Land and Livelihoods in the Santal Parganas, Jharkhand, India'. PhD thesis, School of Development Studies, University of East Anglia, Norwich.

Rudolph, L. I., and S. H. Rudolph. 1967. *The Modernity of Tradition*. Chicago: University of Chicago Press.

Scott, J. C. 1998. *Seeing Like a State: How Certain Schemes to Improve the Human Condition Have Failed*. New Haven and London: Yale University Press.

Sen, A. 1990. 'Gender and Cooperative Conflicts'. In *Persistent Inequalities: Women and World Development*, edited by I. Tinker, 123–49. New York: Oxford University Press.

Singh, K. S. 1984. 'Introduction'. In *Tribal Law and Justice: A Report on the Santal*, by W. G. Archer, v–xxiv. New Delhi: Concept Publishing Company.

Sonalkar, W. 1999. 'An Agenda for Gender Politics'. *Economic and Political Weekly* 34(1): 24–29.

Srinivas, M. N. 1962. 'The Study of Disputes in an Indian Village'. In *Caste in Modern India and Other Essays*. Bombay: Asia Publishing House.

Stivens, M., C. Ng and K. S. Jomo. 1994. *Malay peasant women and the land*. London and New Jersey: Zed Books.

Strathern, M. 1996. 'Cutting the Network'. *Journal of the Royal Anthropological Institute* 2(3): 517–35.

Thakur, I. N. 1977. 'Bihar'. In *Alienation and Restoration in Tribal Communities in India*, edited by S. N. Dubey and R. Murdia, 153–79. Bombay: Himalaya Publishing House.

Toulmin, C., and J. Quan. 2000. *Evolving Land Rights, Policy and Tenure in Africa*. London: International Institute for Environment and Development.

United Nations (UN). 1980. *Report of the Second World Conference on Women*. Copenhagen: United Nations.

United Nations Research Institute for Social Development (UNRISD). 2005. *Gender Equality: Striving for Justice in an Unequal World*. Geneva: United Nations Research Institute for Social Development.

von Benda-Beckmann, F. 2001. 'Legal Pluralism and Social Justice in Economic and Political Development'. *IDS Bulletin* 32(1): 46–56.

von Benda-Beckmann, F., and M. van der Velde. 1992. *Law as a Resource in Agrarian Struggles*. Wageningen: Pudoc.

Whitehead, A. 1981. '"I'm Hungry, Mum": The Politics of Domestic Budgeting'. In *Of Marriage and the Market: Women's Subordination in International Perspective*, edited by K. Young, C. Wolkowitz and R. McCullagh, 93–116. London: Routledge and Kegan Paul.

Whitehead, A., and D. Tsikata. 2003. 'Policy Discourse on Women's Land Rights in Sub-Saharan Africa: The Implications of the Re-Turn to the Customary'. *Journal of Agrarian Change* 3(1–2): 67–112.

Working Group for Women and Land Ownership (WGWLO). 2005. *Initiatives on Women and Land Ownership in Gujarat*. Ahmedabad: Working Group for Women and Land Ownership.

World Bank. 2005. *Gender Issues and Best Practices in Land Administration Projects: A Synthesis Report*. Washington, DC: World Bank.

Part III

Migration and Identity

5

Respect, Status and Domestic Work

Female Migrants at Home and Work*

Introduction

It is a matter of respect, that is all.

—Priti, aged 26, a migrant tribal domestic worker in Delhi

Narratives of paid domestic work across time and space point to the dilemmas and contradictions faced by domestic workers seeking respect in their lives. Contemporary accounts of paid domestic work, striving to understand global economic and demographic changes, rarely consider the domestics' desire for prestige and upward social mobility, important constituents of the notion of respect. Rather, they are driven by the expansion of young female migrant workers from poor, undeveloped regions to service the affluent across

*This chapter was originally published as an article in the journal *Poverty, Gender and Migration* © Gender Perspectives on Asia, Developing Countries Research Centre 2007. All rights reserved. Reproduced with the permission of the copyright holder and the publisher, SAGE Publications India Pvt Ltd, New Delhi. The chapter is based on research funded by the Development Research Centre on Globalisation, Migration and Poverty entitled 'Gender Differences in Migration Opportunities, Educational Choices and Well-Being Outcomes'. Thanks to Shrayana Bhattacharya for research support, and Ann Whitehead, Mina Swaminathan and participants at the University of Warwick conference on waged domestic work, in May 2008, for detailed comments on an earlier draft. My thanks also to Amit Mitra for extensive comments on previous drafts of this article and for sharing insights from his ongoing research on migration and to Laura Camfield and the two anonymous reviewers for helping strengthen this work.

the world. This process of globalisation and feminisation of paid domestic work has been attributed to shifts in the structure of the labour market in the developed world with a rise in dual career households (*cf.* Standing, 1999; Kabeer, 2007) alongside cuts in public services limiting the provision of care services to the elderly and young, in a context of both declining fertility and ageing populations (Yeates, 2005; Razavi, 2007).

Respectability is a signifier of class, but always inscribed in gender identities. It involves a complex set of practices, defined by appropriate behaviour, language and appearance, apart from social rules and moral codes, which enable the framing of people and thereby justify the unequal distribution of resources (Skeggs, 1997). Women domestic workers do have a clear knowledge of their class position and social place; yet in their struggle for social mobility, they invest in symbols of respectability as defined by the dominant. This is, however, not a straightforward process, but highlights the ambivalence about giving up their ethnic identities and symbols of respect for elite, middle-class norms of respectability. The ambivalence persists as they realise that gaining the outward signs of material respectability does not automatically lead to a notion of respect as reflected in the treatment meted out by others (Sennett and Cobb, 1973). Respect involves mutuality, which emerges equally from the development of the self and the interaction with and recognition from others (Sennett, 2003), but for these women, there remains a hidden anxiety about the quality of their experience and its legitimisation in society. This cannot be taken for granted, but is negotiated through the interplay of personal character and attributes like age and education, and the larger institutional contexts and social structures both at home and at the destination (including the nature of the placement agency and personality of the employer). Their agency in terms of the 'ability to define their goals and act upon them' (Kabeer, 1999: 438) can then take several forms, ranging from bargaining and negotiation to manipulation, resistance or the more intangible processes of reflection and analysis. Depending on the structures of constraint to be overcome, it can involve both individual and collective action.

Though the identities and status of the domestic workers and their employers are often constructed in opposition to each other (Dickey and Adams, 2000; Moors, 2003; Qayum and Ray, 2003), my focus in this chapter is on the interaction between the identities of the migrant domestic workers in the workplace and in their village home as shaping the shifts in their social position and search for respect through their life course. The physical and cultural separation between the home and the workplace influences domestics' ways of negotiating power relations at both ends, seeking to balance hard working conditions with the prospects of respect at home. Their struggle for respect involves multiple transitions occurring simultaneously in their lives – spatial, social and emotional – and these are not necessarily unidirectional (cf. Punch, 2002). In fact, a sense of agency itself has been seen as a characteristic of the transition to adulthood, including dimensions such as freedom of movement, access to resources and decision-making capacity (Jejeebhoy et al., 2010).

While the market economy leads to a preference for contractual employer–employee relationships, the domestics strive for respect through displaying a sense of selflessness, responsibility and caring and obligation towards others (Skeggs, 1997). They hope that the nurturing of such caring dispositions will be valued and draw respect from their employers; yet the ties of dependence and obligation within the intimate space of the home contribute to the perpetuation of unequal relations of class, ethnicity and gender, what Qayum and Ray call the 'culture of servitude' (2003: 520). At home, however, while their work per se is devalued, their contributions are recognised and their sense of responsibility seen as worthy of respect.

Formal education is seen to provide a clear set of skills useful for future employment and incomes and endowing the status of a respected person. It contributes partially to fulfilling parental and community aspirations in the construction of a respectable identity, as reflected in speech, mannerisms and the possibilities for gaining professional, white-collar employment as civil servants, teachers or health professionals. For the domestic workers, however, it does not provide the requisite skills for employability. Employers value proficiency in mainstream languages, the use of technology and qualities of loyalty and submissiveness (guised as politeness and sophistication) that are not acquired in school. But further, for the domestic worker herself, there is a crisis of respect, in a context where respectability for women derives not just from education, but from its contribution to a good marriage, expected to provide protection, status and freedom from menial labour, with responsibility for the reproduction and well-being of their own family rather than that of others (Ray, 2000).

This chapter highlights the experience of tribal domestic workers both in their rural home and in the urban workplace and their agency in dealing with the contradictions faced between earning incomes and gaining respect across these sites. I also examine how the idea of schooling impacts women's agency and the value for domestic work.

Methodology and Context

The chapter is based on research in Katona village,[1] Simdega district, Jharkhand, a major sending area, and interviews with key informants in Delhi. Katona is a small village with 112 households, 80 per cent belonging to the Kharia and Oraon Scheduled Tribes (STs), a majority Roman Catholic, and the rest belonging largely to backward-class Hindu groups. Literacy levels are high amongst the STs due to the presence of Roman Catholic missionaries since the 1870s, with only 30 per cent of them being illiterate as compared to 68 per cent of the Hindus in the village. Forty-one per cent of the STs, both boys and girls, had attained various levels of secondary education in the mission-run village secondary school and this pattern is reflected in the profiles of the domestic workers too. Yet with uncertain, rain-fed agriculture, the emigration rate is high.

The key occupations and educational and migration profiles of all households were identified through a census survey of the village in October–November 2006. Of the thirty-one domestic workers aged twelve to thirty-six identified, only one was male. The remaining thirty women were live-in domestic workers. Sixty-five per cent of them were below the age of twenty. I therefore decided to focus on the experiences of these women. Parents and members of the household were unaware of the exact location of employment in Delhi, but most women returned home for Christmas each year. A follow-up visit was therefore scheduled in January 2007, when in-depth interviews were conducted with eight of them, present in the village at that time. They spoke of their experiences at the workplace, visits home, emotions and feelings of both being valued and excluded, and although all these dimensions were central to their conception of respect and respectability, they hardly ever used these terms directly in their narratives. Their notions of dignity were instead constructed in relational terms, be it to their employers, family or peers.

The sole male domestic worker was not available, but one other male migrant, formerly in domestic service, was interviewed. In Delhi, I interviewed four employers (not of these domestics) of both live-in and live-out domestics, willing to be interviewed on account of personal contacts, two placement agencies whose addresses and contact numbers were secured from the village homes of the domestic workers and two activists engaged in the mobilisation of domestic workers for recognition of their legal rights. In Simdega, I spoke to local parish priests and social activists engaged in advising, supporting and reporting on the status of migrant domestic workers.

The next section briefly reviews the gendered ideologies of respect and respectability embedded in the arena of domestic work. I then set out the nature and dimensions of the domestic work sector in Delhi, as well as the rural homes and contexts from which the migrant women workers are drawn, before exploring their aspirations, experiences and the contradictions they face in their quest for respect throughout their lives.

Conceptualising Migration for Domestic Work

Despite continuing feminist scholarship on the value of domestic labour, both unpaid 'economic' work (subsistence production) and the unpaid 'care' aspects of social reproduction (the sustenance of human beings throughout their life cycle more broadly, not just servicing male workers)[2], different forms of reproductive work continue to be marginalised. Perceived to have limited repercussions on the rest of the economy, domestic work is ignored, given a low status and left out of work-led entitlements such as social insurance (Elson, 1995).[3] While activities performed in the public realm get socially recognised and valued, work within the home is both invisible and limits opportunities for social mobility. This division of activities and their spatial separation are an essential element of the social construction of gender, with the quite systematic 'non-valorisation of women's labour' ultimately leading to their subordination (Edholm, Harris and Young, 1977: 123). Associated with femininity, domestic workers are often denied their personhood and equality in terms of respect and recognition for their work.

Apart from its spatial, economic and ideological invisibility, reproductive work also has both material elements (labour) and non-material or affective ones, making it difficult to fit into a straitjacket 'labour' discourse. The material includes everyday tasks of cleaning, cooking, washing, feeding, and so on, and the affective relates to 'emotional labour' (Hochschild, 1983). A high degree of stress, from the fear of failing in one's task, of criticism, of displacement is involved, leading to self-exploitation by the worker. This is more intense for live-in workers who do not have the option of walking out and finding other employment immediately like live-out domestics. The very personal, complex and even ambiguous relations of subordination inherent in domestic work then make it not just undervalued but also servile (Anderson,

2000). For Priti, there is a constant tension between personal growth and fulfilling her responsibility towards her family and employers. She said:

> My employers are nice. *Didi* [elder sister] asked me to take the matriculation exam from the open school in Delhi. I was worried about managing studies alongside the housework, so refused. If I study, who will take care of the house? But studying further would get me a better job.

Priti's narrative, full of contradictions, points to her own dilemmas and anxieties. She realises that completing secondary education would get her a more respectable job, as a teacher or an office worker, and would fulfil the expectations of her parents. Despite all the comforts, income and security, she sees domestic work as low status, yet is caught in an inescapable vicious cycle of loyalty to her employers that dampens her future prospects. The emphasis on the construction of a caring self, of one who is responsible, mature and not selfish, as a way to gain recognition as 'respectable' makes it difficult to prioritise her own self-interests (*cf.* Skeggs, 1997). Her employers, recognising her aspiration, have encouraged her to study; yet they have not changed the material conditions of work by appointing an additional person to help with the housework or by playing a greater role themselves so as to relieve the burden on Priti. Afraid of failing in the performance of her duties and being called irresponsible or lazy, she has refrained from pursuing her education.

Despite the contradictions and trade-offs between earning incomes and gaining respect for their work, domestic workers use multiple strategies, often deliberately, to shift the very criteria for understanding respect. The nature of work performed and employer–employee relations are crucial to their experience; yet they speak too of the shifts in broader social and gender relations resulting from particular urban lifestyles, enhanced incomes or consumption and the experience of a new place and culture. These give them a sense of identity and personhood, enabling repositioning within their own cultures. The definitions of work for them extend to their lives beyond the workplace (Parrenas, 2001), changing over time, place and with individual contexts.

Changing Contexts: Bridging the Rural and the Urban

Between 1980 and 2005, India's rural sector stagnated, while the informal urban services sector, especially domestic and care services, grew rapidly

(Rao et al., 2008).[4] While Indian elite in big cities like Delhi always sought support with domestic work and childcare, the current additional demand is not just to meet the needs of working women with higher levels of education (Kaur, 2004).[5] Rather, middle-class women assert upward mobility through withdrawing from domestic and care work and employing 'maids' for this purpose (Kumar, 2003). The domestic worker affirms the status of the woman of the household as manager rather than labourer, reproducing a particular middle-class lifestyle and sense of respectability. With the work taking place within the employers' home, there is an effort to create a self–other contrast, not seen as sharply in other work settings (Dickey and Adams, 2000: 2). Mita, aged sixteen, narrated:

> I did all the housework, cleaning, washing, cooking, making tea, while madam watched television all day. Sometimes she went for a massage at the beauty parlour or to meet her friends. She didn't work, but never helped, even when she invited others home for weekly parties. Unable to cope with the work, I complained to the master. But he got angry and reprimanded me.

Alongside its rapid expansion as a sector of employment, in India, too, domestic work has become feminised (National Institute of Urban Affairs [NIUA], 1991). The 1971 census reported only 37 per cent of the 0.7 million domestic workers in the country to be women (Ray, 2000: 693). Within two decades, the proportions had reversed, with Shramshakti (Government of India, 1988) estimating 1.6 out of 2.3 million domestic workers to be women (70 per cent). National Sample Survey (NSS) estimates for 2004–05 show that while female share of the total domestic work sector is 72 per cent, women constitute 87 per cent of the sub-category of housemaids (Neetha, 2009).

There are several reasons for this feminisation. Men clean and cook in public spaces like offices, shops and restaurants or work as drivers and guards, but lacking submissive attributes, they are seen as threats in the private space of the home. As McDowell (2007: 278) notes, the preference for women reflects their 'supposed attributes of femininity – docility, deference and empathy' as opposed to the 'street bravado and machismo of young men [which] makes them less attractive as potential employees in the interactive service economy'. Apart from employer concerns over safety within the private space of the modern, urban home, the male workers, too, feel that the earnings from domestic work are insufficient to run a household and perform their breadwinning roles. Additionally, the conditions of work and personalised services are seen as demeaning to their own identities as workers. Nisar, aged twenty-six, presently a labour contractor, noted, 'I worked as a domestic with an army officer. When they got transferred, I left their employment. My parents wanted me to get married, but as a domestic worker, no woman wanted to marry me. This is considered demeaning for a man.' Important in his narrative is the gender ideology of respectability, wherein for a man, this comes from not doing 'dirty' work, having independence of means, developing valued skills and abilities and maintaining a 'cultured' life, including marriage and the protection of his wife, conforming to the standards set by the elite (Sennett, 2003; Qayum and Ray, 2003). The move out of domestic work for men has also been made possible by the expansion of alternate employment opportunities.

Feminisation, premised on the availability of cheap and trustworthy female labour, is accompanied by the increasing recruitment of poor, ethnic minority women as domestics, especially from the tribal areas of eastern India. Delhi alone has over 300,000 domestic and related workers (NSS 2004–05). Kujur and Jha (2006) calculate that nearly a third of them are STs. Neetha (2004) further found in Delhi that almost all the live-in maids were migrants of whom 90 per cent were Christian tribal women. They are preferred as live-ins due to the stereotypes of them being simple, honest, obedient and hard-working, all positively valued attributes in domestic service, and hence easier to control than their non-tribal counterparts. Over 50 per cent of such tribal women workers belong to Jharkhand (Kujur and Jha, 2006).[6] Census 2001 data confirm the presence of 38,364 female in-migrants from Jharkhand to urban Delhi, more than double the number over the previous decade.

In live-in domestic work, trust is very important. The worker lives in the home, and therefore employers in Delhi go through agencies to ensure some security. The past decade has seen a jump in the number of such agencies, with estimates varying from 650 to 2650.[7] In Katona, several agencies are active; parents have their visiting cards but cannot contact their daughters despite repeated phone calls. Geeta, a fishworker's daughter, returned after three years in Delhi in September 2007, but had no news of the four girls who accompanied her. To earn additional commission, the agency moved her to a new home every year. The agent collected her wages from the employer. They would not let her go home, and therefore she left secretly and lost a large part of her earnings. Interviews with placement agencies in Delhi revealed that it was common practice for the agency to collect the monthly salary from the employer. Supposedly kept in deposit for the domestic worker, a majority of them received only a small fraction of their wages, and even less, if, like Geeta, they tried to break free of the tied labour relations with the agency.

The agencies are run by local men in Delhi. They usually hire women from the ethnic minority groups as agents (jobbers) in the villages to ensure a steady supply of workers. These jobbers are referred to in kinship terms, but this does not necessarily make them sensitive to the domestic workers' interests. Nina, aged sixteen, noted:

> Seven of us were taken by an 'aunt' to Delhi by train and left in a placement agency. We were confined to a tiny room, allowed out only when some prospective employer came to interview us. I was given some clothes and toiletries by the placement agency for which they deducted the first two months' salary. I worked from dawn to late in the night, cooking for six people, making umpteen cups of tea, cleaning the house, washing clothes and utensils. I slept on the kitchen floor and was threatened with beatings if I complained of fatigue and overwork. I was to be paid 1,200 rupees[8] per month. I left in three months, as I could not stand it any longer, so got only a month's pay. Even this was taken by the 'aunt's' daughter at the station.

Social activists and church functionaries in Delhi and Jharkhand and the families of the migrant women spoke of these 'aunts' becoming prosperous quite quickly through the supply of domestic workers. The agencies provide information, access to jobs and first residence, but in the absence of any regulation, many have turned into grossly exploitative institutions. Given the predominance of tribal Christian women, several denominations of the Church, especially the Catholics, have also set up agencies in Delhi to help recruit and train workers and ensure them a decent wage and living conditions. A few like Sruti have secured jobs in Delhi this way – they get regular leave, both to visit home once a year and on Sundays to go to church, and the agreed wages (Figure 5.1). Church agencies, too, take a commission to meet their overheads, but the worker directly receives the salary from her employer.

How does the world of Delhi, mediated through the plethora of placement agencies, relate to the domestics' lives in their village, Katona, 15 kilometres away from the district headquarters? Rain-fed agriculture is the main source of livelihood in the region. The major crops are paddy,

Figure 5.1 A young woman preparing to leave for Delhi as a domestic worker
Source: Photograph by the author.

maize, groundnut and black-eyed beans. Only 12 percent of the arable land is irrigated making productivity low. Migration is then a key livelihood strategy in Katona, with 25 percent men and 15 percent women migrant in 2006–07. Older men migrated for agricultural work in north-west India or road construction in the border areas, and younger men looked for jobs in factories, as clerks or security guards in Delhi and other cities. For girls and women, these options hardly exist; their hard work in rural areas is seen as preparing them for domestic service in the cities. Some are recruited as nuns by Christian religious orders. Though trained and often placed in respectable jobs, such as teaching and nursing, both their emotional needs and physical mobility are strictly monitored and controlled, similar to those of domestic workers. The justification in both cases is a paternalistic view regarding their need for protection.

Male migrants are usually older and married and female migrants younger and unmarried,[9] pointing to the gendered differences in work–life trajectories for rural men and women. This implies that the biological age is not necessarily an appropriate marker for understanding the multiple and simultaneous transitions in the life of a tribal woman domestic worker. Further, seeing these transitions in a linear pattern from childhood to adolescence and adulthood does not hold true in these ground realities, but is rather shaped by differential life-cycle patterns (particularly puberty and marriage) and gendered social norms, with women expected to eventually settle down with their own families rather than continuing to migrate for work. Dependence and male protection, rather than independence, are for women the ultimate sign of respectability and status acquisition.

Dorothy, schooled up to class seven, one of Katona's first women to move to Delhi in 1986, narrated:

> My father had six years of service left in the army after serving for fifteen years. My grandfather died, and my father took early retirement and came home. I was then in class three. He cultivated some paddy, but this was not enough. There was no money. Being the eldest of seven siblings, I decided to move to Delhi after grade seven, to earn to support my siblings.

For men, migration is important for performing their breadwinning roles, but for women the reasons are more varied, ranging from escaping the chiding of relatives for failing in exams to earning to support the family. Some wished to experience city life before marriage. Others sought to escape the burdens of reproductive work at home. Mita said:

> I had heard about Delhi from the village women working there. They wear beautiful clothes and bring expensive gifts when they come for Christmas. The financial situation at home was worsening. I realised that work was available in Delhi, and one could earn money. I also wanted to see the big city I had heard so much about. I had never attended school, but my brothers did. I felt bad so left without informing them.

Mita's narrative reiterates poverty as a central factor for migration. But it also stresses the multidimensionality of causality, ranging from the personal to the emotional. Attracted by the gifts, she also aspires to see the city before settling in the village. She felt bad that instead of studying like her brothers she worked unacknowledged on the household farm. Feeling neglected, she ran off to Delhi with an agent.

Working life is not easy for the domestics. But they draw from this experience, materially (incomes, skills and familiarity with consumption goods) and discursively (cultural representation), to strengthen their claims for respect. In the next section, I examine the workplace experience and the strategies they adopt vis-à-vis their rural home, to draw out the spatial and social interconnections between them, and how these contribute to their negotiation of respect through their life-course transitions.

Experiencing Domestic Work in Delhi: Narratives of Domestic Workers

Gaining respect at the workplace is the most contested domain in the domestics' life. Employers expect round-the-clock personal service with unwavering intensity. The challenge for the domestics is to meet these expectations yet maintain a semblance of control over their lives. While the hard working conditions and long hours of work are a given, the experience of domestic work is shaped largely by the personality of the employer and the respect and human consideration they show the domestic worker. Priti is very fond of her employers. The fear of any criticism from them makes her work very hard.

> I wake up at 7 a.m., make tea, prepare the two children for school and make breakfast for madam and sir. They leave by 10 a.m. I eat my breakfast, then start cleaning and cooking. This takes up the rest of the day. I go to bed after midnight. Sometimes, I feel so burdened by the work that I begin hating myself. But everyone is not lucky to get to do what they want. The lifestyle is good. I have my own room with an attached toilet. I get good food. I hardly spend any of my earnings on myself, as *didi* gives me all the clothes and toiletries I need.

Priti's salary in 2007 was 2,500 rupees per month, more than the remuneration of the teachers in the village mission-run school. Her lifestyle is good, and she has privacy when needed; yet she resents being a domestic, because her parents and relatives had higher expectations of her. Domestic work, associated with dirt and personal service, is socially stigmatised. Like Priti, Dorothy's employers also treat her well. She perceives her working experience as largely positive, except for restrictions on her mobility. She says, 'I am not allowed to go out except for 3–4 hours once a month. They say it's for my safety and well-being.' Tribal women are stereotyped as simple and child-like. Their lack of fluency in Hindi, the local language, is used to control their physical movement and autonomy, albeit within a discourse of protection.

The use of kinship terms such as 'daughter' or 'younger sister' is a common stratagem to incorporate domestic workers into the private space of the family, while simultaneously defining areas of exclusion. Maternalism and the discourse of kindness and support to the domestic workers, identified as poor women, can perpetuate non-egalitarian, hierarchical relationships between the employer and the employee that facilitate the extraction of unpaid labour, especially emotional labour (Parrenas, 2000: 170; Anderson, 2002). The discourse of being a part of the family reinforces their personal loyalty, while allowing minimal external interaction contributes to preventing social recognition and the organisation of collective voice.

All the domestic workers are unmarried, as marriage constrains continuing with paid domestic work. Prakash worked in a factory, while his wife Sunita was a domestic who had to quit after childbirth. Though responsible for caring for the employers' children, she was not allowed to bring her child to work. In the construction of their relationship with the employer, domestic workers' personal sexual lives and identities as mothers are denied and a child-like dependence and need for protection emphasised. This dependent relationship enables control, for recognising the sexuality of the servant can potentially disrupt the domestic order as adult aspirations are not easy to accommodate and subordinate (Shah, 2000: 107). Marriage confers respectability on women, but domestic workers are often deprived of this option.

Priti's and Dorothy's employers recognised their physical and social needs somewhat, but the majority experience is more like that of Mita and Nina narrated earlier. Many domestics are beaten and ill-treated by the employer. Others do not get a proper place to sleep and are deprived of food. Even when they have some leisure time, they are not allowed to watch TV, a family activity in middle-class homes, or permitted to go out to socialise. The spatial inequality and segregation manifested through food rationing, use of separate utensils, wearing hand-down clothing, sleeping arrangements and being prevented from watching TV signify forms of personalised control and lesser social status of the domestic worker in relation to the employer. They are expected to work sincerely, non-stop, like a part of the family; yet they are excluded from leisure-time activities of family members, thus reinforcing the asymmetrical relationship between them.

Dorothy speaks of playing badminton with her employers' daughter or learning English from her. The participation in such leisure activities constitutes an important element of their identities as people, not just workers. It creates a sense of self-respect and yet is often the most uncertain element of the work experience. In the ultimate analysis, incomes can be claimed, but it is respect in interpersonal relations and mutual recognition, expressed through the granting of personal space, sharing of the same food or participation in leisure activities that are often the hardest to negotiate and defend.

Contributions, Aspirations and Representations: Gaining Respect at Home

In recounting the history of her migration and how her own work and life had changed over time, Dorothy was constantly trying to point to her struggles to gain respect.

> My uncle and aunt moved to Delhi, and I went with them. I initially worked in their house, but was not paid and could not go out. A friend introduced me to a family in Punjabi Bagh. Here I spent eight years. They were very nice people who never made me feel out of place. I was able to send some money home to my parents.
>
> A few years later, my father contracted tuberculosis. I brought him to Delhi and spent 7,000 rupees for his treatment. The doctor asked him not to exert himself, but he had to work in the fields. He died in 1996. The period after my father's death was very difficult. I don't know how I survived those days. I worked so hard to provide for my siblings. My mother worked in the fields, yet she could not manage, so I returned to the village to help. I stayed till 2002. We applied for my father's pension from the army and after much running around started receiving this at the local bank. This income was insufficient to run the household. My youngest brother migrated to Punjab but never sent any money nor kept in touch. Two of my brothers in the meantime got married – one moved to his wife's village and now only one lives here. We couldn't make both ends meet, so I returned to Delhi.

Dorothy's narrative demonstrates her burden of economic and emotional responsibilities. She migrated to Delhi when her father could not support the family. When he died, her remittances were inadequate to tide them through; her mother needed emotional support, and she had to prioritise this element of her responsibility. It is often assumed that sons will support their widowed mothers, but this is not necessarily the case, and as the eldest, Dorothy did so. Taking over the male role of provision and care of her widowed mother, however, strengthened her influence in her village home vis-à-vis her siblings and enhanced respect in the community.

Yet this respect does not come easily. While women's work in the village is valued, paid domestic work is looked down upon and generally accorded low status. Respect then accrues from constructing the discourse around fulfilling responsibilities. Cultivation is insufficient for subsistence and the domestics' remittances become crucial contributors to daily maintenance and quality of life of the rural household, debt repayments and education of siblings. Their financial contributions entitle them to participate in decision-making at home, such as in the education or marriage of their siblings. Simultaneously, they also provide a more legitimate face to female autonomy and independence.

Working conditions are harsh, and thus the migrant domestic workers formulate other criteria of status. This could include the monetary remuneration they receive for their work, substantially more than what they could earn locally; savings; exposure to urbane lifestyles, including dress and personal effects; fluency in a different language and form of speech and familiarity with technology. As Dorothy said:

> I get my salary, 2,700 rupees, in cash. I send this to my mother, who deposits it into my bank account. Earlier I used my savings to finance my father's healthcare, weddings, school fees and household expenditures. I buy gifts from Delhi for everyone when I come home for Christmas. This time I bought a jacket, sweater, saris and watches for my siblings. I thought I would get some utensils, but my mother is scared of the pressure cooker. I am contemplating on getting a solar panel to electrify our home.

Here, respectability is linked to markers of class difference reflected in clothing, consumer goods, having a bank account, understanding technology (evinced in the reference to the pressure cooker and solar panel), language and mannerisms. As these are privileged signs of class distinction, and cannot fully be claimed as signs of status vis-à-vis the employers (Tolen,

2000), domestic workers shift the site of expression to recreate themselves in their rural homes. In contexts of general poverty, the accumulation of money and goods serves as the first marker of respectable status. Apart from these symbols, they also base their claims to respect on their new knowledge, skills and practices. At the workplace, they receive gifts from their employers, a sign of their patronage and higher status; at home, the domestic workers in turn are able to engage in gift-giving rituals based on their higher earnings. The difference, however, is that the latter comes to symbolise mutual dependence and respect, a reciprocal arrangement, though not necessarily equal, but which can ensure the staking of claims to land and other household resources in the future, and thus bind rather than estrange people (Mauss, 1990). The idea of status then needs to be reworked from the perspective of women's respect and their ability to claim a sense of personhood while negotiating unequal gender relations with their families, employers or community. Unless this is done, women's agency on their own terms cannot be understood.

For many, domestic work becomes a career. It is well paying compared to local options and enables higher net savings in contexts where food and accommodation are provided. Nevertheless, they aspire to ultimately leave domestic work as it is perceived as lacking in dignity. It is not seen as a life-long option, even though employers may be kind and, as in the case of Dorothy, include her in their leisure activities. The domestics then consciously work towards developing a range of strategies to ensure their future security, be it gift-giving or saving money in a bank account. In the past, Dorothy had used her savings for her siblings but now hopes to use them to construct a house in the village and set up a small shop. Her connection to the home and construction of a respected identity there is manifested in her aspirations for the future.

The urban–rural contrast in gender relations is important in Dorothy's narrative. Though she speaks of the bonding in the village, she is uncertain about the way her brothers would treat her and whether they would give her a share of the property. She has given them gifts for two decades, but can only hope for reciprocity, as the material and emotional obligations of adult married brothers to their sisters are not so clear. In the city, however, she has seen and experienced much greater equality of gender relations, even though her own freedom of movement was restricted. She did have access to a privileged space in her employer's home, but not as an equal. The experience of urban culture and lifestyle in an upper-middle-class home developed in her a sense of independence and autonomy, of desiring a place of her own before she is too old, rather than depending on marriage as the only form of social support. Experiences such as hers, in terms of the interaction of different worlds, the urban and the rural, the rich and the poor, the material and the social, in shaping elements of identity and agency, and bringing to the fore the contradictions within are often not given adequate consideration in most discussions of domestic workers.

Having been exposed for years to less oppressive urban cultures, Dorothy's aspirations had changed; she was no longer interested in marriage. Priti would definitely like to get married and have a family once she has discharged her responsibilities towards her siblings. She says:

> There are marriage offers from the village, but now people know that I will refuse till my brothers finish studying. I like the city and would like to live here. I told *didi* that I want to marry a Christian, but so far I have not found anyone I like in Delhi.

Priti strongly aspires to either a marriage or a higher-status job in the city to acquire and sustain respectability. Unfortunately, it has not been possible to follow up on Priti's present life trajectory, but none of the thirty domestic workers from the village were married. The exception was Sunita, but she is no longer engaged in paid domestic work. Their aspirations have changed; they desire an urban lifestyle and greater equality and find it hard to settle back in a rural environment, but they also lack the resources required for marriage. A dowry would be needed to compensate for the lack of 'status', but almost all their earnings are exhausted for the maintenance of their rural home and as gifts, leaving them with little for setting up their own household.

In the transition from adolescence to adulthood, the domestics undergo many changes, sometimes simultaneously and not always expected. The first of these are spatial, from the village to the city and back again and relatively easy to understand. Much more complex are the material, social and emotional transitions accompanying such spatial movements, though in non-linear ways. They have moved from a state of hunger to relative well-being, though this is not guaranteed and depends on the employer's personality and their own physical abilities to work. As long as they are able to work and take gifts home, they are respected, but inherent in this respect is a fear of marginalisation the moment they are unable to do so. While marriage is expected as a normal life-course transition within the local context, this often does not occur due to the changing aspirations of the migrant women workers and their desire for equality alongside the structural constraints to marriage faced by somewhat older women.

Their sense of commitment to the family and community and the need for affirmation therein can lead to subordinating many of their personal aspirations, evident in most of the narratives presented thus far. Gaining respect can become a double-edged sword as it can lead to a negation of one's physical self. Many of the domestic workers could opt for lesser wages, but also less strenuous working conditions, by moving to live-out domestic work, if they chose not to send money or gifts home. While individuals who cannot labour are not appreciated, the respect accorded by the community to the domestics seems to be for the tangible benefits they bring rather than the physical and emotional sacrifices they make. The women internalise these patriarchal norms of respect, deeply discounting their own bodies in the process, thereby serving the dual purposes of perpetuating the extraction of women's labour and keeping them in a subordinate position within the larger social order. Respect can also emerge from women's creative associations both at work and at home, but this, too, is hampered at various points: starting from the individualising experience of schooling to the nature of dispersed work, located within individual homes.

Representation, Voice and Respect: The Role of Education

Going by Fraser's (1994: 598) conceptualisation of the principle of gender equality for domestic workers as including income, leisure time and respect, domestic work provides income (some like Dorothy and Priti earning more than teachers in the local high school), but not leisure time (though often women in the village too work long hours) and respect in the workplace. This matters most to the women's sense of identity and personhood. This section briefly explores the ways in which women workers exercise agency to secure recognition and respect for their work, while at the same time shifting the terms of discourse to include respect in other domains of life, especially vis-à-vis their rural home.

At the individual level, education can potentially contribute to opening new opportunities, as teachers, nurses or nuns for girls, but with the growing competition for jobs, education does not necessarily guarantee one (Chopra, 2005). Given their ethnicity, gender and location within the social hierarchy, it is difficult for tribal women to break through segmented labour markets and the power relations therein into new areas of work that can potentially provide transformative respect along with fair earnings. This implies a situation where the acknowledgement and recognition of each other's needs and views are mutual and where one is no longer worried that the treatment from others may injure one's dignity (Sennett and Cobb, 1973). Despite a few narratives suggesting that domestic workers seek to overturn these ways of defining people in terms of respectability, the larger view continues to see education as status-giving. Priti says:

> I have to stay in Delhi till my brothers are studying, maybe another three years, as I have to pay for their education. They want to study. These days without education there are no jobs. I took one of my brothers to Delhi and paid for his driving lessons. He now works in my employer's office.

In talking of the benefits of education, she draws here on elitist and patriarchal notions of cultural capital that perpetuate respectability in terms of particular kinds of work (*cf.* Bourdieu and Passeron, 1977). While migration for domestic and other forms of labouring tasks provides income (economic capital), it continues to be seen as degrading. The differences in the outcomes and experiences of migration may or may not be attributed to education, but clearly educational processes contribute to producing and reproducing social inequalities alongside social respectability through inherent mechanisms of rejection or co-option. Seemingly providing these women some personal confidence to negotiate both at home and in the workplace, the negotiations are limited by the structures discussed earlier – that is, marriage and the necessity of providing incomes on the one hand and gaining 'respect' through these processes on the other.

Domestic workers of all age groups and educational levels struggle to gain respect at home and in the workplace, but their strategies differ. All of them work hard to earn for their family. The younger ones are unable to speak out and negotiate, and thus their only strategy for resisting intense exploitation in the workplace is to flee home. Older women seek to display greater levels of tolerance, diligence and patience, drawing on kinship ideologies to build an interpersonal relationship, but if things do not improve, they feel confident to change employers rather than return home. The oldest women seek stability of employment as a strategy for ultimately being included in leisure-time activities as well, signifying a recognition of their personhood. They also realise that as they grow older it is difficult for them to find new employers, and hence they begin to develop an independent asset base as also emotional- and social-support relationships at home.

Though schooling contributes to enhancing certain skills such as fluency in Hindi, maintaining simple accounts and recording messages, and to this extent confers respectability, it remains individualistic in its philosophy. It is the more informal life experiences that enable migrant domestics to build networks, sharing information and personal emotions. Domestics often travel together in groups from Katona, for the sake of both safety and support, though they lose contact once they are placed in individual homes. Yet they worry about each other. There are instances of older women spending considerable time looking for younger ones from their village who migrated for domestic work but are soon untraceable, caught in the grip of exploitative placement agencies. In Delhi, most of the work-related associations are facilitated by church-based placement agencies; for the others, the only way to associate is by counselling young women seeking work, preparing them for domestic work based on their own experiences and insights. It is these interactions with other domestic workers, often younger, at the workplace, and their families and peers at home that ultimately give these women a feeling of being both valued and respected.

Conclusion

This chapter sought to unpack and highlight the notions of respect embedded in women's agency and their experience of paid domestic work. The experience of such work by young, migrant women is not straightforward, nor always positive, but demonstrates attempts to exercise agency in a context of constraint, influenced by locally determined hierarchies and power relations, personal interactions of domestic service, as well as the larger socio-economic context within which they are located. In the best scenarios, they earn reasonable incomes and are treated well by their employers, but given its association with reproduction rather than skills, domestic work continues to be socially and ideologically devalued.

Yet the women workers have sought to shift the markers of status, delinking it from the nature of work itself and tying it in more closely to elements of consumption, lifestyles, self-dignity and voice at home. Education contributes somewhat to improving workplace negotiation and terms of employment; yet its relationship to respect and involvement in decision-making vis-à-vis their rural households is ambiguous, as it continues to operate within and reinforce the boundaries set by patriarchy. The search for respect is thus often contradictory. It potentially involves compromising with personal aspirations and personhood unless, as in a few exceptional cases, the very basis of this discourse is shifted to one that is transformative for them as individuals but also vis-à-vis the structures within which they are located. The transitions through the life course, from adolescence to adulthood, then entails understanding transitions in 'respects', attributed and perceived, both by oneself and by others, and the actions derived from such perceptions.

Notes

1. All names of respondents and places in the chapter have been changed.
2. See Molyneux (1979), Folbre (1994) and other contributors to the domestic labour debate.
3. The System of National Accounts (SNA) was revised in 1993 to include subsistence work and unpaid, home-based or self-employed work (Hirway, 2005). The production of services, defined as the preparation of meals, laundry, cleaning, shopping, care of children, the elderly and the sick, and volunteer services continued to be excluded.
4. Women paid domestic workers, both full- and part-time, doubled from around 1.25 million in 1995 to over 3 million in 2004–05 (Neetha, 2009).
5. An analysis of the National Sample Survey (NSS) data by education level shows that while at post-secondary levels of education, women's employment has been stable at about 12–13 per cent in urban areas, there has been a rapid expansion for women with less than primary levels of education in 'low-paid jobs, often in a subsidiary capacity, in the service sector, in schools and hospitals or as domestic help in households' (Unni and Raveendran, 2007: 197). Micro studies confirm this (Sudarshan and Bhattacharya, 2008).
6. Jharkhand state has a relatively large proportion of tribal population, locally referring to themselves as *adivasi*s. The south-western parts, consisting of Simdega, Gumla and Ranchi districts, provide the largest number of domestic workers to Delhi. They also have a strong network of missionary schools and long-standing missionary activity.

7. The Delhi Police have licensed 650 domestic help agencies, but according to recent non-governmental organisation (NGO) reports, there are 1,200 registered and 2,650 illegal domestic help agencies in Delhi (Choudhury, 2011).

8. As on 12 March 2011, one Great Britain pound equals to 72.3 Indian rupees, so 1,200 rupees equal to 16.5 pounds.

9. Seventy-five per cent of male migrants were over 18, but nearly half of the female migrants were not yet eighteen.

References

Anderson, B. 2000. *Doing the Dirty Work? The Global Politics of Domestic Labour.* London: Zed Books.

———. 2002. 'Just Another Job? The Commodification of Domestic Labour'. In *Global Woman: Nannies, Maids and Sex Workers in the New Economy,* edited by B. Ehrenreich and A. R. Hochschild, 104–14. London: Granta Books.

Bourdieu, P., and J. C. Passeron. 1977. 'Reproduction in Education, Society and Culture'. London and Beverly Hills (CA): SAGE Publications.

Chopra, R. 2005. 'Sisters and Brothers: Schooling, Family and Migration'. In *Educational Regimes in Contemporary India,* edited by R. Chopra and P. Jeffery, 299–315. New Delhi: SAGE Publications.

Choudhury, Karan. 2011. 'Beware of "Work Less, Fleece More" Domestic Helps'. *Hindustan Times,* New Delhi, 27 February, 3.

Dickey, S., and K. Adams. 2000. 'Introduction: Negotiating Homes, Hegemonies, Identities, and Politics'. In *Home and hegemony: Domestic Service and Identity Politics in South and Southeast Asia,* edited by K. Adams and S. Dickey, 1–29. Ann Arbor, MI: University of Michigan Press.

Edholm, F., O. Harris and K. Young. 1977. 'Conceptualising Women'. *Critique of Anthropology* 3(9–10): 101–30.

Elson, D. 1995. 'Gender Awareness in Modelling Structural Adjustment'. *World Development* 23(11): 1851–68.

Folbre, N. 1994. *Who Pays for the Kids? Gender and Structures of Constraint.* London: Routledge.

Fraser, N. 1994. 'After the Family Wage: Gender Equity and the Welfare State'. *Political Theory* 22(4): 591–618.

Government of India. 1988. *Shramshakti: Report of the National Commission on Self-Employed Women and Women in the Informal Sector.* New Delhi: Government of India.

Hirway, I. 2005. 'Integrating Unpaid Work into Development Policy: Unpaid Work and the Economy: Gender, Poverty and the Millennium Development Goals'. Working Paper No. 838, United Nations and Levy Economics Institute of Bard College, Annandale-on-Hudson, New York.

Hochschild, A. R. 1983. *The Managed Heart: The Commercialisation of Human Feeling.* Berkeley: University of California Press.

Jejeebhoy, S., R. Acharya, M. Alexander, L. Garda and S. Kanade. 2010. 'Measuring Agency among Unmarried Young Women and Men'. *Economic and Political Weekly* 45(30): 56–64.

Kabeer, N. 1999. 'Resources, Agency, Achievements: Reflections on the Measurement of Women's Empowerment'. *Development and Change* 30(3): 435–64.

———. 2007. 'Marriage, Motherhood and Masculinity in the Global Economy: Reconfigurations of Personal and Economic Life'. Working Paper No. 290, Institute of Development Studies at the University of Sussex, Brighton.

Kaur, R. 2004. 'Empowerment and the City: The Case of Female Migrants in Domestic Work'. *Harvard Asia Quarterly* 8(3): 15–25.

Kujur, J., and V. Jha. 2006. *Women Tribal Domestic Workers in Delhi: A Study of Deprivation and Migration.* New Delhi: Indian Social Institute.

Kumar, N. 2003. *Working Conditions of Female Domestic Workers in Delhi.* Delhi: Deshkal Society.

Mauss, M. 1990. *The Gift*, translated by W. D. Halls. London: Routledge.

McDowell, L. 2007. 'Respect, Deference, Respectability and Place: What Is the Problem with/for Working Class Boys?' *Geoforum* 38(2): 276–86.

Molyneux, M. 1979. 'Beyond the Domestic Labour Debate'. *New Left Review* 1(116): 3–27.

Moors, A. 2003. 'Migrant Domestic Workers: Debating Transnationalism, Identity Politics, and Family Relations: A Review Essay'. *Society for Comparative Study of Society and History* 45(2): 386–94.

National Institute of Urban Affairs (NIUA). 1991. *Women in the Urban Informal Sector.* New Delhi: National Institute of Urban Affairs.

Neetha, N. 2004. 'Making of Female Breadwinners: Migration and Social Networking of Women Domestics in Delhi'. *Economic and Political Weekly* 39(17): 1681–88.

————. 2009. 'Contours of Domestic Service: Characteristics, Work Relations and Regulation'. *Indian Journal of Labour Economics* 52(3): 489–506.

Parrenas, R. S. 2001. *Servants of Globalization: Women, Migration and Domestic Work*. Redwood City, CA: Stanford University Press.

Punch, S. 2002. 'Youth Transitions and Interdependent Adult–Child Relations in Rural Bolivia'. *Journal of Rural Studies* 18(2): 123–33.

Qayum, S., and R. Ray. 2003. 'Grappling with Modernity: India's Respectable Classes and the Culture of Domestic Servitude'. *Ethnography* 4(4): 520–55.

Rao, N., A. Verschoor, A. Deshpande and A. Dubey. 2008. 'Gender, Caste and Growth Assessment, India: Report to the Department for International Development, Norwich, UK, DEV/ODG'. DEV Reports and Policy Papers, No. 8. http://www.uea.ac.uk/dev/publications/RPP8. Accessed on 30 August 2022.

Ray, R. 2000. 'Masculinity, Femininity, and Servitude: Domestic Workers in Calcutta in the Late Twentieth Century'. *Feminist Studies* 26(3): 691–718.

Razavi, S. 2007. 'The Political and Social Economy of Care in a Development Context'. Gender and Development Programme Paper No. 3, United Nations Research Institute for Social Development (UNRISD), Geneva.

Sennett, R. 2003. *Respect: The Formation of Character in an Age of Inequality*. London: Allen Lane.

Sennett, R., and J. Cobb. 1973. *The Hidden Injuries of Class*. New York: Alfred A. Knopf.

Shah, S. 2000. 'Service or Servitude? The Domestication of Household Labour in Nepal'. In *Home and Hegemony: Domestic Service and Identity Politics in South and Southeast Asia*, edited by K. Adams and S. Dickey, 87–117. Ann Arbor, MI: University of Michigan Press.

Skeggs, B. 1997. *Formations of Class and Gender: Becoming Respectable*. London: SAGE Publications.

Standing, G. 1999. 'Global Feminisation through Flexible Labour: A Theme Revisited'. *World Development* 27(3): 583–602.

Sudarshan, R., and S. Bhattacharya. 2009. 'Through the Magnifying Glass: Women's Work and Labour Force Participation in Urban Delhi'. *Economic and Political Weekly* 44(48): 59–66.

Tolen, R. 2000. 'Transfers of Knowledge and Privileged Spheres of Practice: Servants and Employers in a Madras Railway Colony'. In *Home and Hegemony: Domestic Service and Identity Politics in South and Southeast Asia*, edited by K. Adams and S. Dickey, 63–86. Ann Arbor, MI: University of Michigan Press.

Unni, J., and G. Raveendran. 2007. 'Growth of Employment (1993–94 to 2004–05): Illusion of Inclusiveness?' *Economic and Political Weekly* 42(3): 196–99.

Yeates, N. 2005. 'Global Care Chains: A Critical Introduction'. Global Migration Perspectives, Working Paper No. 44, Global Commission for International Migration, Geneva.

6

Migration, Representations and Social Relations

Experiences of Jharkhand Labour in Western Uttar Pradesh*

Introduction

> Who can like this work? We work from dawn to dusk, day in and out. Peeling the sugarcane is not easy: the spines make your hands bleed. My employer does not beat me like many others do, but there is no dearth of prods and insults. I don't think I will come next year.
>
> —Manjhi Tudu,[1] a Santal migrant farm servant working in the fields of Ram Chaudhry, a Jat farmer of Kalsi

Every year hundreds of Manjhis from Jharkhand travel to the irrigated high productivity agricultural areas of north-west India, the so-called Green Revolution belt, working arduously long hours to earn what they can. Circular migration, much of it seasonal, comprises an integral part of the livelihood strategies of a large number of poor people living in agriculturally marginal areas (Deshingkar and Farrington, 2009: 1). Some households

*This chapter was originally co-authored with Amit Mitra, an independent researcher in New Delhi, and published as an article in the *Journal of Development Studies* © Taylor & Francis Group Ltd 2013. All rights reserved. Reproduced with the permission of the copyright holder and the publisher, Taylor & Francis, Milton Park, Oxfordshire. The chapter is based on research carried out as part of a larger project entitled 'Gender Differences in Migration Opportunities, Educational Choices and Well-Being Outcomes', funded by the Development Research Centre on Globalisation, Migration and Poverty, whose support I gratefully acknowledge.

barely manage to survive, while a few with some resources accumulate wealth over time (Mosse et al., 2002). It is contended that most would be worse off if they depended solely on local employment (Kothari, 2003; Rogaly and Rafique, 2003), yet the progression from survival to security of livelihoods cannot be taken for granted. Households and individuals are not unified entities. Earnings and savings from migration vary by ethnic group, gender, occupation, wage rates, living costs, contracting arrangements, and debts. In addition to the access to material resources and social networks, individual aspirations and perceptions of work and leisure, time horizons and rates of time preference, and strategies for ensuring future security are central to the experience and outcomes of migration.

Important in shaping livelihood opportunities, choices and outcomes are the nature and role of the democratic state in India. While claiming to be responsible and accountable to the people, especially the poor and vulnerable, it is far from this in its 'everyday practice' (Fuller and Benei, 2001). Notwithstanding processes of liberalisation and democratic decentralisation, the Indian state continues to be driven by elite interests and patronage ties (Corbridge and Harriss, 2000; Corbridge et al., 2005), with informal structures of caste dominance, patronage and brokerage influencing the nature and terms of inclusion in the migration process (Mosse, 2007), especially in a context where spatial, regional, caste and gender inequalities have intensified over the last two decades, as admitted by the Approach Paper to the Eleventh Five-Year Plan (Rao, 2010a).

Meillasoux (1981), theorising the relationship between persistent low wages and migration patterns of rural labour, notes that the implication of permanent migration for capitalism would be the need to pay for both the immediate labour time of the worker and the costs of biological and social reproduction of the labour force. Circular migrants can be exploited by drawing their labour during the long duration when they have no work at home, in a context of mono-cropping, yet have the back-up of their domestic production to meet the costs of family maintenance and reproduction. Such rotating migration establishes a double-labour market, where the labour is divided between self-production at home and production for the employer, while also supporting a discriminatory ideology based on notions of skills, ethnicity and poverty (Meillasoux, 1981: 115).

The Indian National Sample Survey (NSS) data shows that a very high proportion of agricultural labour households actually own land, close to 76–87 per cent in the tribal concentration pockets of Chhattisgarh, Jharkhand and

Rajasthan (Shah, 2009). Their seasonal migration and low wages are assured by a failure of state policy to support largely rain-fed, low-productivity agriculture, to ensure alternate local employment opportunities and basic services, or to implement existing legislation. Laws such as the Minimum Wages Act, 1948, and the Inter-State Migrant Workmen Act, 1979,[2] can potentially protect migrant labour, but mechanisms for putting them into practice, especially in dispersed, rural areas, hardly exist (Breman, 1985, 1996).

This chapter's focus is not on state policy per se, but in conceptualising migration experiences and returns, it is important to locate the debate within the local political economy contexts, as the interaction between local factors and a range of political, economic and social institutions at different levels (macro, meso and micro) shape migrant agency and ultimately their experiences and outcomes within particular contexts (Collinson, 2009). Recent developments in theorising migration and social change have delineated the complexity, contextuality and multi-level mediations of migratory processes with rapid global changes on the one hand and relations of class, gender, ethnicity and other social cleavages that embody hierarchies of power and social status on the other (Van Hear, 2010; Castles and Miller, 1998). In particular, they have focused on the mutual interactions between human agency and structural factors and called for a re-embedding of studies of migration in wider social theory (Bakewell, 2010; Castles, 2010).

These developments, while important, remain largely materialistic in their scope. The ways in which migration shapes the identities and self-representations of both the migrant workers and the employers, and the implications of these symbolic constructions for contesting and renegotiating hierarchical social relations at home and the destination, remain understudied. Issues of dignity, surveillance and control over work are as important in accounts of oppression as conditions of work and compensation, calling attention not just to the non-economic drivers of migration, but equally to the potential gap between real-life experience and its representation. Using the idea of public and hidden transcripts (Scott, 1990), which point to elements of performance as a strategy to resist structures of domination and subordination, we examine how migrant workers use spatial distanciation[3] to represent their work and life in ways that uphold a sense of dignity and self-respect. The effects of this can be seen in both the material and symbolic–normative domains.

Studies of transnational migration have over the last two decades increasingly emphasised the need to understand migrant agency, social relations and economic patterns across source, destination and transit locations (Massey et al., 1998; Collinson, 2009); yet such studies are more limited in the context of internal migration.[4] This chapter seeks to compare the economic processes and labour relations at home and the destination through the lens of the migrant workers' experiences. Apart from working conditions and labour regimes, examining the strategies of control used by the Jat employers and resistance by the Santal labour highlights the deep interconnections between the economic and social relations of production and reproduction and its gendered subtext, within and across three domains – the dominant group of the Jats, the subordinate Santals and the interaction between the two societies.[5] Work and earning is ultimately linked to people's aspirations and hopes for a better life, not just through materially secure livelihoods but in the social relations shaping their lives, the expansion of choices and opportunities and the public recognition of their personal dignity and identities.

The research primarily involved studying a village in depth, here called Mahari, in Jharkhand's Sahebganj district. A village census was conducted between August 2006 and March 2007 to understand local livelihoods and the context of migration. Based on a preliminary analysis of this data, a second round of fieldwork was conducted in June–July 2008. Through in-depth interviews with migrants and non-migrants, mainly Santals (sixteen), but also a few Muslims and Hindus, insights into micro-level experiences of migration and the variables that influence the decisions to migrate were gained. A major stream of migration, in the words of the migrants, was to 'work in' or 'cut' sugarcane in Uttar Pradesh (UP). This migration stream has grown in the last two decades, though lack of official data on such internal migration makes it difficult to estimate the total number of migrants.

A highly developed large village, Kalsi, in Muzaffarnagar district, UP, was identified as the main destination by a large number of the migrants (Figure 6.1). A briefer visit was made to Kalsi in January–February 2009 to understand better the dynamics of migration and the role it plays in the social and political processes of the region. In-depth interviews with four Jat employers, alongside interactions with their wives and other family members, and one Jat jobber were conducted. This last meeting was arranged by a Mahari jobber, who met us in Kalsi.

The Context

Jharkhand lags behind UP, especially its western districts, which form a prosperous agrarian belt, in its levels of development, communication and provision of basic services and civic amenities, with rural poverty estimates of 52 per cent and 43 per cent respectively in 2004–05 against a national average of 42 per cent (Government of India, 2009). Sahibganj district, with a poverty rate of 55 per cent, literacy rate of 38 per cent and immunisation rate of 7 per cent, is amongst India's fifty worst districts in terms of human development and the ninth most 'backward' district overall (Borooah and Dubey, 2007). Muzaffarnagar district, one of India's most prosperous, does better across all these indicators. However, it is amongst the 100 districts with the highest infant mortality rates and lowest female-to-male sex ratios in India (Borooah and Dubey, 2007). Significant gaps and differences exist between and within groups in both areas, with the Hindus in Jharkhand and the Jats in western UP doing better than the other groups across education and development indicators, though worse in gender equality as seen in lower sex ratios.

Mahari, with 330 households, divided into three hamlets, occupied respectively by the Hindus (94 households),[6] Muslims (60 households) and Santals (176 households), reveals a clear distinctiveness of livelihood profiles and well-being indicators according to ethnicity and religious identity. The Santals, classified as Scheduled Tribes (STs) in the Indian Constitution, constitute 9 per cent of Jharkhand's total population but 42 per cent in Sahibganj district. Over 95 per cent of the Santals in Mahari own land and report agriculture as their main occupation. The land is undulating, rain-fed and with little technical support for water management or enhancing yields; the area is largely mono-cropped with paddy during the monsoons. Productivity is low, about 1.5 tons per hectare, against an all-India average of 3 tons per hectare, ensuring food for just a few months after the harvest (Rao, 2008: 149). Irrigated acreage in the Santal Parganas has stagnated at around 15 per cent after independence (Bhalla and Singh, 2001). Migration is hence a virtual necessity and an integral part of the livelihood strategies for the Santals, with at least one migrant from every three households.[7]

The village survey revealed that the largest migration stream (over 70 per cent of all migrants) to Muzaffarnagar district is dominated by Santal men, who leave the village after ploughing their fields and transplanting paddy (in August), to return only the following year before the start of planting (May) (Rao, 2009). Ploughing is a male preserve, but it also confirms their identities as landowners

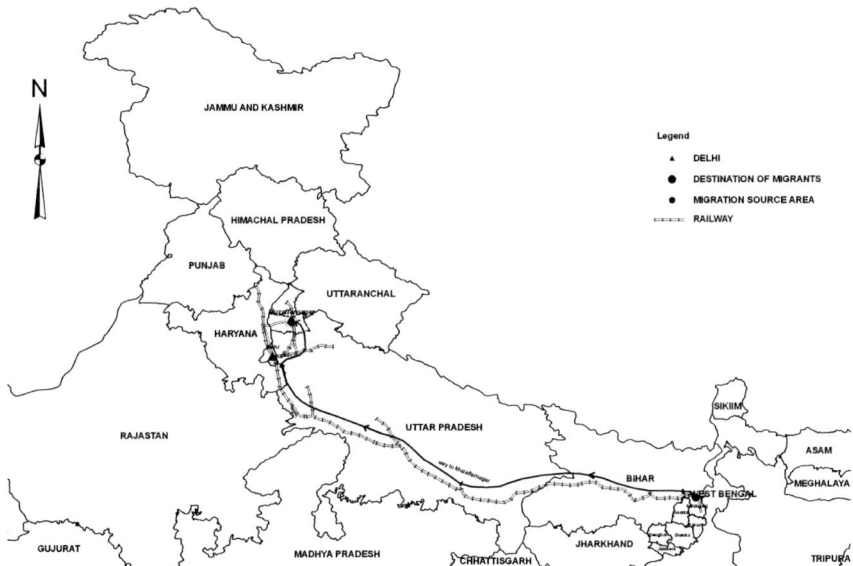

Figure 6.1   Migration map: Sahibganj to Muzaffarnagar

Source: Prepared by the author.

Note: Map not to scale and does not represent authentic international boundaries.

and cultivators (*chasahor*) (Rao, 2008). Wives of the migrants manage all other farm operations – weeding, harvesting, threshing and storage of the grain – and sometimes also work as labour for other farmers in the locality, often Hindu landowners. Where the home cultivation is totally unviable or the plot is too small, the wife may migrate along with the husband. Such instances, however, are still few. Women prefer to migrate to West Bengal, closer to home, for shorter durations of time, for paddy transplanting and harvesting work, given the responsibility they also bear for managing their homes (Rao, 2008).

Schooling in Mahari is poor, and a majority of Santal and Muslim children drop out before completing primary schooling (see Chapter 7). Only seven Santal boys had completed secondary education at the time of fieldwork, and two of them were studying to graduate. In the absence of social contacts in the bureaucracy and money to pay bribes, they found schooling unhelpful in gaining jobs. As Samuel, aged thirty-two, who graduated in 2001, noted:

I was appointed only as a helper in this school on a ten-year contract and a monthly salary of 2,000 rupees.[8] I have to support my family, and this is totally insufficient; yet without money to pay bribes, I am unable to get a job.

Elections to the local government (*panchayats*) were held in Jharkhand only in October 2010. In the absence of a local governance structure which could be held accountable for the functioning of institutions like the school and health centre, or indeed development programmes, their operations have been inadequate.

The Muslims are largely landless, but rather than agricultural labour, they engage in petty trading (in livestock, cloth, household products) and casual labour, both in the locality and in urban centres like Delhi. Several Muslim young men were working in offices (as security guards), hotels, restaurants, and factories in and around Delhi, and a few, like Ahmed, have used this experience to build the social networks needed to turn into labour suppliers themselves. Muslim women do not actively seek work outside the home. While shunned by the Hindus, the Muslims treat the Santals as being lower in status and more 'backward' than them[9].

The Hindus are divided into two groups. The better-off Hindus (including Sah, Thakur and Teli, all classified as Other Backward Classes [OBCs]) have land and education and take up formal and informal white-collar and service-provision jobs as insurance agents, newspaper reporters, teachers, tutors, doctors and moneylenders or work as government contractors. They hire Santals to cultivate their lands, with the women largely playing supervisory roles. There is also a large group of poorer, assetless Hindus who live off the illegal coal trade in the area, alongside some who engage in traditional artisanal work such as pottery (*kumhar*) and iron-smithy (*lohar*). Women help their husbands in the household enterprise, occasionally seeking wage work in the homes of the better-off Hindus. While the Santals work as agricultural labour for the Hindu landlords, there is minimal social interaction between them.

Muzaffarnagar district, in contrast, has benefitted greatly since the adoption of Green Revolution technologies in the late 1960s. Agriculture is highly capitalised, tractors and tubewells are common (Jeffrey, 2003). One of the richest districts in the country, sugarcane and wheat are the major crops and income-earners. The district has eight sugar mills, each governed by a cane growers' society, taking responsibility for the purchase and processing of the cane. Despite some fluctuation in prices and consequently production of sugarcane over the last few years across India, the sugarcane acreage has not declined substantially (Government of Uttar Pradesh, n.d.).

Kalsi's population also consists of three main groups – the Jats, Muslims and *dalit*s. The former two are landowners, seeking to diversify into trade and formal and preferably white-collar employment; the latter are largely wage workers. Amongst the Jats, as Santosh, aged twenty-two, explained, 'It is rare to find an illiterate person, whether a man or a woman, in the present generation.' Schooling has been central to parental ambitions of securing salaried, public sector employment for their sons and hypergamous marriages for their daughters. Yet, given the lack of formal sector jobs, Jat young men over time have either acquired clerical jobs in the informal economy or moved into managerial or supervisory roles in agriculture. Some have gone into businesses, including the 'school provisioning' business. Muslims have focused on strengthening artisanal and trade-based activities rather than investing in education.

Illiteracy is confined to the *dalit*s and Muslims – though with a long history of *dalit* political mobilisation in the region, this too is changing (Pai, 2007). Several *dalit*s have used state affirmative action policies to secure formal sector jobs, and, being close to Delhi, others have migrated for casual work, thus resisting working for the local Jat landlords at low wages. A large number still work locally as casual wage labourers, with their levels of dependence on the Jats, however, having significantly declined (Jeffrey and Lerche, 2000; Leiten, 2003; Lerche, 2003). The Jats and Muslim landowners are interspersed in the main habitation of Kalsi; the *dalit*s live in a separate settlement. Though labour relations are maintained, social interactions between the three groups are minimal.

We will now discuss the evidence on the process of migration itself, the characteristics of the migrant workers, the nature of labour regimes and relations, its implications for wider relations of production and reproduction and their representation at both the destination and the source villages.

The Migration Experience

Most migrants to Kalsi are young Santal men above eighteen, with around 80 per cent of them illiterate. Due to constraints of language and location, lacking both social networks at the destination and financial resources at home, they depend on village-level agents, mostly Muslim youth, to facilitate migration. The work stretches over a period of nine months. The regular cycle is August–September to the last week of May, but in case of need, migrants are brought for a shorter duration from November to March. Incomes are predictable; hence, despite involving hard manual work, such migration offers security in terms of meeting immediate food, health and educational needs.

Ahmed, aged twenty-three, a farm servant for several years, and now a contractor, explained the logic of the migration process:

> There is high demand for agricultural labour in Saharanpur and Muzaffarnagar areas. The boys can easily find work with different farmers. The large farmers don't cheat the labourers as they have to get the work done on time. A labourer can cut about 20 quintals of sugarcane a day. The harvest season lasts from 15 September to 25 March; then the fields have to be cleared and the new crop planted. The weeding is over by May. From June to August, there is not much work so the labourer returns home. At home, there is no electricity for irrigation so we can only produce one crop.

Migrant work, by fitting into the long duration of the lean season at home, enables the workers to earn cash without depriving them of their identity as cultivators. The employers secure round-the-clock labour for relatively low wage payments.

Labour Regimes and Relations

Mahari's Santals all own small plots (84 per cent are marginal or small farmers with less than 2 hectares) and engage in subsistence paddy cultivation based primarily on household labour. While representing themselves as self-employed, owner-cultivators, with insufficient production for survival, the Santals do hire out their labour to the landowning Hindus – men to prepare the land and bunds and women for weeding, transplanting and harvesting. Local wage rates are 50 rupees per day for ploughing, 25 rupees for transplanting and weeding, and 5 kilograms of paddy for harvesting as per village census data. Minoti Soren, aged thirty-five, noted:

> The wages are low, but being in the locality, we get paid. But the women stand nearby and supervise us, ensuring we don't leave early. They grumble, but don't say too much, as they need us to do the work. We get a short lunch break and continue till the evening. Everything is expensive, so we do it.

Wages are low, food limited and services inadequate; yet being in the village, periods of intensive work are interspersed with seasonal breaks and socialisation with fellow Santals, relieving somewhat the harshness of everyday life.

The situation in Kalsi is a complete contrast. Baiju Soren, aged twenty-six, married and with two young children, is the *naukar* (servant) in Sanjay's household. He speaks little and is praised by his employers. Baiju came with seven other migrants brought by Ilyas. He says:

> Ilyas gives money to my parents and wife when he goes home. There is the security that he will definitely find us work here. I studied only till class two, and hence I will not be able to manage on my own. I will take home about 10,000 to 11,000 rupees when I return in May.

This was Baiju's third visit to Kalsi. He highlighted the security and assured earnings instead of the nature or conditions of work and life. Constantly under the gaze of the employer, Baiju could not talk much when we met him at the destination (Figure 6.2). His deference and conformity to the standards was expected and did not necessarily reflect consent; yet it was a way of ensuring that he received his full wages at the end of his stay and that a level of self-respect and dignity was maintained (*cf.* Scott, 1990: 3). Sanjay was upset as the other boy who came with Baiju ran away after three months, though he had to pay the agent his full commission. Sanjay's mother points out:

> That fellow had to be woken in the morning and prodded to work. Look at Baiju. He returns from the fields, chops fodder for the cattle, then goes to sleep. The power comes at 11 pm, he gets up and switches on the water-pumps. He does not have to be woken up. When the water is filled, three hours later, he goes to sleep and gets up on his own.

Estimates of 'Jharkhandi' farm servants in Kalsi vary from 400 to 1,000. Approximately one such servant is needed for every hectare of land. While the labour requirement can be calculated based on area cultivated, estimating the number of migrant labour is harder. This is because each farmer employs one or at most two labourers, and once the labourer is handed over to a farmer by the labour contractor, he stays in his home and has little interaction with his peers. Regulation hardly applies.

Figure 6.2 A Santal labourer working in a sugarcane field
Source: Photograph by Amit Mitra.

The grueling work can stretch up to eighteen hours a day. Cleaning the courtyard, feeding and washing the cattle, cutting fodder, preparing the fields for cultivation, irrigating the crops – in brief doing whatever agricultural or non-agricultural task asked by the employer or any household member. When there is no work in the fields, they are given something else to do, like breaking stones in the field and removing them. Except for Holi,[10] the migrant farm servants do not get weekly holidays. They are not given separate living quarters and sleep in the fields, in the pump house or the verandah of the *gher* (homestead). The fields are used for defecation, and bathing is at the pump house. They do not cook their own food but are given the same from the household: vegetarian food, mainly *roti*s (wheat bread), *dal* (lentils) and a vegetable. But they can eat their fill.

Sugarcane-related work is only a part of the work and, going by the field observations as well as the landlords' versions, makes up only a small part of the tasks performed by the migrant farm servant. Most of the sugarcane is cut and sliced for transportation to the factory by the local *dalit*s working under the *gole* system, wherein they only receive the leafy tops of sugarcane (*gole*) in return for harvesting this crop (Leiten and Srivastava, 1999; Lerche, 1999). Krishan, a Jat farmer in his sixties, explained:

> Earlier, the *kamin*s [workers] would do many things in exchange for payments of wheat at harvest time. This included the barber [*nai*] and the *barbooja*s [a caste that parched grains]. The Jatavs [a sub-group of Chamars][11] would cut and peel the sugarcane and get the leaves and sometimes attend to the bunding work in the fields. But over time all this changed.

Most of the cane-peeling work is family based and still done by the Chamars, preferred in fact to the migrants. The Jat landlords now pay them a wage in addition to the *gole*. The present wage rate in the region is 120 rupees per day plus a meal for seven hours work; yet in practice this varies according to the nature of prevalent patron–client ties. While the Chamars here continue to depend upon the Jats for fodder for their cattle and access to fields in which to defecate, limiting their capacity to bargain for higher wages or obtain speedy and full payment for their labour (*cf.* Jeffery, Jeffrey and Jeffrey, 2008: 4), this to some extent has been set off by the politicisation of the Chamars in western UP since the 1970s (Pai, 2007) alongside the emergence of numerous off-farm employment opportunities. They are employed as daily wage labourers on farms, brick kilns or small industrial units near the village and paid minimum wages. Most farmers stressed that given the low returns from agriculture, engaging locals was unaffordable.

Paralleling trends among rich farmers in Gujarat (Rutten, 1995; Gidwani, 2001), wealthier Jat households now protect their sons from physical work on the land by employing a farm servant, usually a migrant tribal, on a relatively long-term (six to ten months) contract. Explaining this transition, a group of farmers said:

> The tribals work hard, but they are rather weak as they don't get much food at home. But more than that, employing local labour has many problems. First, it is difficult to find someone locally to work for you.

Second, they keep going home [even if they are from some other village] or their relatives keep dropping in. All this interferes with the work. We can't pay them for doing nothing.

The migrants, apart from fulfilling immediate needs, hope to accumulate some savings to help them diversify their livelihoods at home (*cf.* Rodgers and Rodgers, 2011). They strive to purchase assets such as livestock and a bicycle to make local travel easier and to improve the productivity of their own agriculture. Anil Murmu, aged twenty-two, is a case in point. He studied in a mission school but withdrew before completing secondary school. In 2005, he travelled to Kalsi with others from the village to work as a *naukar* on a monthly salary of 1,000 rupees in addition to food and accommodation. He was frustrated as despite his education, the only opportunity for work appeared to be as an agricultural labourer. But this frustration led him to think of other ways in which he could fulfil his aspirations. While working as a labourer, he developed links with other sugarcane farmers and turned into a labour contractor. He took seventeen migrants in 2008, and this gave him a savings of 20,000 rupees. He opened a bank account. He bought a mobile phone as, apart from helping stay in touch with the employers, it is a marker of status. Very few Santals have mobile phones, a privilege of the educated Hindu castes. Yet, in 2009, Anil mentioned giving up labour contracting. Being a tribal, the Jat farmers found him lacking in the communication and negotiation skills necessary for a contractor and preferred others over him. While Deshingkar and Farrington (2009) postulate that, over time, knowledge and experience gained may allow a migrant to move up the ladder from survival to accumulation, clearly this does not hold true in this instance.

In contrast, Ahmed, whom we discuss in the next section, has done better and expanded his networks into Delhi. He explained, 'I come to Delhi every two–three months. I stay with my sister in Govindpuri but go and meet everyone around, even in Gurgaon. It is important to build up relationships.' This points to the complexity of social relationships, including those of authority, at home and at the destination. Anil owns land and is more educated than Ahmed, and while his skills and knowledge are recognised at home, he is unable to command the same authority at the destination. Controlling labour is clearly not enough to gain such authority, not even the accumulation of capital and symbols of wealth such as a bank account and mobile phone. Santals like Anil strive to create relations of reciprocity and redistribution in their desire for social parity and dignity; yet the exchanges at the destination reinforce hierarchies based on ethnicity and language, rather than education or even capital, giving credence to Meillasoux's (1981) contention that identity is crucial to any transaction or Bakewell's (2010) emphasis on structures having a life of their own.

Mediating the Labour Process: The Role of Contractors and Agents

The labour contractors are familiar with both the source and the destination. They operate through a process of subcontracting, with a few large farmers at the destination negotiating labour supply for themselves and others in the locality. Yuvraj of Kalsi is a labour contractor. He visits Mahari and nearby villages annually to recruit labour. Over time, he has developed close links with Ahmed and Ilyas, whom he can rely on for bringing additional labour, if required.

On his role as a contractor, Ahmed says:

> Recently, Yuvraj, the Jat landlord, asked Ilyas and I to be his agents and supply labour from our villages. Each agent has a counterpart at the destination. The farmers who need labour contact Yuvraj, who contacts me. A commission of 3,000 rupees was paid this year for each labourer supplied. Yuvraj takes 500 rupees, and another 800 rupees are spent for travel and food expenses. Of the remaining, I pay 500–1,000 rupees as a cash advance to the labourer. On an average, I save 1,000 rupees per labourer, my responsibility being to ensure that they reach the workplace safely on time and return home at the end of the season. This year I supplied over fifty labourers. Since I belong to Mahari and have been working in Delhi for ten years, people trust me.

There is some variation in the wages paid to the labourers. 'It all depends on the worker's experience and the years he has worked with a farmer,' explains Ahmed. Thus, Sanjay's father pays 1,300 rupees per month for Baiju, who has been working with him for three years now. Apart from the money, everyone in Sanjay's household is emphatic that Baiju gets food thrice a day plus clothes and, once in a while, some alcohol. However, a newcomer would get 1,000 rupees according to Yuvraj, who jokes that there is an 'increment system' here too.

Why do labourers like Baiju then not go directly to employers once they have established links with them as noted in the case of neighbouring Bihar

(Rodgers and Rodgers, 2011)? Landlords like Sanjay say they are willing to pay a part of the commission to the labourers (2,000 rupees instead of 3,000 rupees) but blame the 'lack of education', tribal culture and lack of entrepreneurial skills for not entering into a direct agreement. Without the agent, they are not sure that the worker will actually come and on time. Ahmed and some workers have a different view. According to them, some employers cheat and physically abuse the workers. The system of intermediaries, both at the source and the destination, protects both the workers and the landlords: 'We actually do unrecognised social work (*samaj seva*),' says Ahmed. Rather than being exploiters, they highlight their role in rendering a form of social protection in the absence of any regulation by the state. Being from the same village, Ahmed feels responsible for ensuring that the workers get their dues at the end of their contract. At the same time, if there is a problem with the worker, he also takes the responsibility of providing the employer with a replacement to continue the work uninterrupted.

Interestingly, while contractors like Ahmed perceive themselves as benign social facilitators for their Santal co-villagers, helping them get jobs and earn a living, they also contribute to reproducing the cycle of migration and control for the sake of their own livelihood. They ensure that wages are paid, but contracts are agreed to at a very low level – the cash component being less than a third of the daily agricultural minimum wage. Food and accommodation are seen to make good this gap, but they cannot fully justify the low wage.

Strategies of Domination and Control

Having discussed the working conditions and labour relations of the migrant workers, we now briefly analyse the strategies of the Jats to control the labour, life and social processes of the migrants. Adopting a gendered lens provides new insights into how gender asymmetries both shape and are shaped by the reorganisation of relations of production and reproduction due to migration, though in different ways, in both the source and destination areas.

By assigning tasks to fill up the time of the labourer, the Jat farmers establish control over time use (both work and leisure) and mobility. A discourse is set up of a good servant that stresses hard, uncomplaining work around the clock. The physical arrangements for living and working, which follow from the tasks allocated, ensure segregation of the migrant, allowing few opportunities for socialising with other migrants. The closely watched movement of the labourer to the fields, to home to eat and sleep and to look after the cattle also prevents the snatching of labour by other landlords. As Scott (1990) notes, while servility of the subordinate requires watchfulness and attuning of response to the mood of the power-holder, the dominant too seek to preserve a public reality of unanimity and consent, where contradictions are concealed and discord kept out of sight. One way of achieving this is by keeping the subordinates atomised and under close supervision, abolishing a social realm where 'hidden transcripts' as expressions of frustration, may be generated.

Physical violence is uncommon. Control is established through co-option into the landlord's household. Having visited the source area, many landlords note that the labourers have nothing at home – no work, no food, no clothes – but in Kalsi, they are treated very well, get plenty to eat, what the household does. Free clothes are given, and there is no short-changing on wages. And if the labourer's family back home faces a crisis, like someone falling ill, the farmer sends money immediately. Using the language of kinship, of treating the worker as a member of the household, does not just mask relations of exploitation inherent in class domination but also allows for the over-exploitation of their labour (Meillasoux, 1981: 86; see Chapter 5).

The arduous work at the destination exhausts the migrants. As twenty-five-year-old Manik Murmu said, 'I worked for six months. It is not possible for us to migrate every year as the work is too strenuous. I stayed in the landlord's house and got food but worked every day of each week. There were no holidays.' Instead of demanding better working conditions (and developing class consciousness), the migrants see this as a temporary option for four to five years. Their short time horizons vis-à-vis such migration contribute to a higher rate of time preference, making them accept lower wages and hard working conditions for the immediate security and benefits it provides. This contrasts with the *dalit*s, who are local and, in their longer-term interests, have been able to mobilise and secure wage-rate increases through displaying a lower time preference.

Baiju was more expansive when interviewed in Mahari. Given the social space in terms of unmonitored physical locations, free time and also other people who speak the same language and have had similar experiences, they do discuss the nature of toil, the tough conditions and their counter-strategies including flight, feet-dragging and not returning the next year (Figure 6.3). Flight leads to loss of commission paid by farmer to agent, so it is resented by farmers. And as Ahmed pointed out, 'If a labourer runs away, the farmer not only faces a monetary loss but also stands to lose face in the community. He often becomes the butt of village jokes.' Yet such instances are infrequent; the workers feel assured that they will receive their wage at the end of their contract and can then go home – the need to put up with these conditions is not permanent in their lives.

In Kalsi, migrants' sexuality is controlled by carefully monitoring their movements and also generally not allowing their wives to come unless there are no able women to perform the domestic chores in the farmer's home. Even then, the wages are very low, so it is not a preferred option for Santal women, who stay back to cultivate their fields. Talamai Hembrom, aged twenty-eight, said:

> I got married to Sunil in 2004. We had started living together, which is accepted in Santal society, but his parents disapproved and did not give us any land. His mother feels that I do not work enough at home or in the fields and that I do not clean the house properly. Being

Figure 6.3 Migrants relaxing in Mahari, their home village

Source: Photograph by the author.

landless, we decided to migrate to earn some money. In 2002, I went to Muzaffarnagar with Sunil and worked in the landlord's house. He owned a ration shop which I cleaned. I worked there for nine months and was paid 400 rupees monthly along with clothes and food. Sunil worked in the fields for 900 rupees monthly. We saved 10,000 rupees to build ourselves a home and buy a pair of bullocks. We have leased in some land, so I no longer migrate.

Talamai's narrative raises an interesting issue about the gendered motivations for migration. Women follow this migration stream only when they are landless. Childbirth ends such migration as the costs of reproducing and maintaining a future labour force are not borne by the landlords at the destination. Social reproduction remains the responsibility of the domestic economy. But migration here also challenges the established structures of authority within the village, enabling Talamai and Sunil to make a living despite parental disapproval and denial of a share in the land. Their immediate objective for migrating was saving money to access some land at home, a crucial consideration in reproducing Santal male identity. What then are the implications of these strategies for relations of production and reproduction and their representation at both the home and destination villages?

Representations of Work and Identity

Despite the ground realities of low wages and harsh working conditions, the Santals and the Jats talk about their experiences of the interaction in quite different terms. These are motivated by considerations of status and identity, dignity and self-esteem, much more than the everyday experience of material appropriation and exploitation. Dignity in fact is a public and a private attribute, a source of self-esteem, particularly to be preserved and built in one's closest circle of family and friends (Scott, 1990). In Mahari, the migrants claim they go for sugarcane work, but in Kalsi this is a small portion of what they do. Indeed, the contribution of migrant labour to sugarcane harvesting, unlike in western India, where seasonal migrants have virtually replaced local labour for cutting cane (Breman, 1994), is substantially lower than that of the locals. The rigours of the work and the social indignity of being a farm servant are not mentioned. Amongst the Santals, for an adult male to be a farm servant, who has to perform non-agricultural chores when asked by the landlord, would be considered denigrating, given their self-representations as cultivators (Rao, 2008). It was only by going to the destination that this became apparent.

The Jats, however, claim to be doing a service by employing the Santals and treating them humanely, almost as members of their family. They speak of the intense poverty and lack of infrastructure and services in Mahari and how in comparison the labourers have a comfortable life. Through the public articulation of their generosity and patronage, they justify their claims for legitimacy, as they too cannot take liberties with those symbols in which they have invested and which contribute to their dominant status (Scott, 1990). In striving to sustain a single, unanimous public reality, the extent and nature of the work, including the hard schedules, are not explicitly mentioned.

Renegotiating Gender Relations

These production relations and their representations are intensely connected to the reproduction and reconstitution of gendered social relations at both the source and the destination. For the Jat landlords, hiring a tribal migrant farm servant is both a need and a status symbol. It is a way of accessing cheap labour for essential farm work, keeping the local *dalit* labour in check and adding to their prestige as landlords. Freed from farm labour, their sons can spend their time in education, in urban employment or business activities. Rai Singh, a sixty-two-year-old Jat farmer, with four sons, points to the importance of diversification. His eldest, Jaipal, practises as a veterinarian; the next, Sanjay, works as a temporary foreman in a sugar mill; the younger two sons run a transport business and a fertiliser agency respectively. His wife supervises Baiju, the migrant farm servant, while the daughters-in-law are almost entirely involved in home-making activities.

Many of the tasks traditionally performed by the Jat women, such as animal care, picking dung and collecting and chopping fodder, are handed to the migrant farm servant. The lack of Jat women's mobility is used as a pretext to enhance the labourer's work burden. Kavita, Sanjay's wife, a graduate, is now involved full time in cooking, cleaning, washing and other household chores. Having a farm servant has meant freedom from farm- and livestock-related tasks, but it has contributed to greater restrictions on her mobility. While she has two children, studying in middle school, she is not allowed to go to the market to buy clothes or even to the school to discuss her children's performance. They are allowed to walk between the home and the *gher* – a modern house built on a plot of land on the roadside, used for the cultivation of vegetables for domestic consumption and the keeping of cattle – but only with their saris covering their faces.

Jat women have little voice in their own conjugal relationship. Kavita was keen that her husband give up his part-time blue-collar job in the sugar mill and start an English-medium kindergarten school in the village. 'After all, he is qualified and we have the necessary space,' she said. She was willing to help him in this venture, but to no avail. She could not resist speaking about her second pregnancy, which was aborted following a scan which showed the sex of the foetus to be a girl. This experience had clearly upset her, even though it was several years ago, and she subsequently had a son. Her critique, however, is only possible in private; in public, she performs the deferential role assigned to her.

While status for the household has clearly improved, the employment of a migrant worker has provided an opportunity for further controlling women's mobility and voice, by reducing their visible contributions to the productive process. Most Jat women like Kavita are highly educated and articulate, and yet they are unable to transform their own conjugal relationships in egalitarian ways. In fact, as Rai Singh, her father-in-law, pointed out, 'Girls study more than boys. They are interested in studies. But parents also know that today no one will marry an uneducated girl.' Education here translates into status for the household but does not improve Jat women's control over their own lives (*cf.* Jeffery and Jeffery, 1994). Despite material prosperity, structures of authority and control have intensified in both relations of production and reproduction vis-à-vis the tribal migrant farm servant and their own women. Effective political mobilisation has freed *dalit* workers from such rigid control, though incidents of violent backlash seeking to re-establish this control are also visible.

For the Santal household, the conjugal unit is the locus of production and reproduction of both labour and food. The hard work at the destination for several months, with no breaks, wears the Santal male labourers down. They do come home with lump sum money, which is used for purchasing food, repairing the home, meeting health expenses and, if they are lucky, accumulating assets, all essential for household survival and reproduction; yet the social dimensions of their contributions at home are minimised. During their stay at the destination, communication with their homes and families are limited to occasional messages sent through the agent; their socialisation with fellow villagers is also restricted, limiting opportunities for association or a normal social life.

The possibility of migration and earning a living outside the village, however, provides scope for internal transformation. It enabled Talamai and Sunil to get married, challenging the authority of the kin elders in this process. Sunil's father tried to retain his authority by denying him his share of land, given that he was not consulted in their matrimonial decision. Kinship becomes an ideological frame of reference for justifying social hierarchies through the control of marriage decisions and exchanges, but with the availability of alternatives to land as a productive enterprise and the declining value of local knowledge in the context of interactions with a wider economy and society, these are open to renegotiation.

While norms of seclusion are observed at the destination, these are not carried home as ideals by the migrant workers, as observed in other contexts (Rao, 2012). Tribal polity, marriage systems and culture are here premised on a degree of gender equality and collective solidarity, with both men and women sharing in production and reproduction. However, what has happened is that women's work and responsibilities have intensified during their husbands' absence – managing the farm and the home, earning or borrowing money for everyday expenses, looking after and educating the children. Reproduction and maintenance of the family draws exclusively on women's unpaid work, with enhanced burdens having implications for their health and leisure. Men, too, are drawn into both productive and reproductive work at the destination; this, however, contributes to reproducing Jat identity and status rather than their own.

Conclusions

Migration streams, studied at both the source and the destination, can be a useful tool to understand processes of identity construction and wider social change. Through a study of migrant experiences, this chapter has highlighted the importance of structures, especially of ethnicity and caste identity, and kinship and family relations, in shaping opportunities and livelihood trajectories, with the educated Santals not faring much better than their non-literate counterparts at the destination, a majority never progressing from coping to accumulative migration. Stereotypes of Santals as good agricultural labourers, dating back to the colonial period, get perpetuated, and despite some investment in education, and their landowning status, they are unable to break free from existing social structures and relations of production which almost seem 'to exercise their own causal power, independently of the agency which produced them' (Parker, 2000: 73, quoted in Bakewell, 2010: 1696). While the migrants do exercise agency, the crucial role of ideology, status and identity in shaping migration outcomes challenges the emphasis placed on material resources and economic drivers of migration in earlier studies of circular migration, such as that of Deshingkar and Farrington (2009).

For policy, the analysis presented in this chapter indicates the need to pay attention to not only addressing the material deprivation contributing to regional inequalities, but equally the social drivers and consequences of labour movements across time and space. Women's contributions to agrarian livelihoods in particular need to be acknowledged so that gender asymmetries are not further aggravated.

Also missed are issues of governance and politicisation: why is it that Mahari continues to remain underdeveloped, despite its rich natural resources, and Kalsi so developed? The former has seen widespread mobilisation under the aegis of the Jharkhand movement, though focusing primarily on the control of natural resources – land, water and forests – and breaking relationships often described as being those of 'internal colonialism', that is, vis-à-vis local exploiters (Corbridge, 1988). State corruption, lack of attention to the provision of basic needs, the implementation of developmental programmes and, indeed, decentralisation through *panchayats* have not been questioned to the same extent (*cf.* Corbridge et al., 2005) as in UP (Leiten, 2003). While the role of the state has not been the main thrust of this chapter, by perpetuating subsistence production through the relative neglect of agrarian development in Jharkhand, it plays a central role in maintaining visible disparity between the two regions and giving credence to the Jat discourse of patronage and support to the labour.

With the local *dalit* labour being highly politicised, demanding higher wages and refusing to accept the dominance of the Jats, the landlords of western UP have found a way out by recruiting migrant tribal labour through agents. Employed as farm servants, and set in competition with the local labour, the migrants perform a wide variety of agricultural and non-agricultural jobs under rather harsh conditions. Having a farm servant is also a mark of prestige for the young Jats, who say they are 'farmers' and regard supervision as the main task of farming. The migrant workers contribute to agricultural production at the destination; they also contribute to the production of status for Jat landlords, allowing them to seek opportunities for diversification and upward social mobility.

For the Santals, the fixed contracts and the lump sum that comes at the end of the year provide some security and income. Collecting some symbols of distinction such as clothes (jeans), mobile phones and MP3 players creates the potential for enhancing status. While their immediate needs are met, this stream of migration rarely contributes to substantial accumulation at home or shifts in exploitative labour relations at the destination.

Social relations based on age hierarchies and access to sources of information within the community, as well as gender relations, however, do potentially change. Status reproduction in UP, while facilitating Jat men's engagement in 'modern' economic activities, constrains women to 'traditional' activities outside the labour market, simultaneously enhancing controls over their mobility and voice, confirmed by statistics pointing to declining sex ratios. Amongst the Santals, while daily interaction and joint production are reduced due to male absence for a considerable part of the year and women's workloads increase, they are recognised as producers and their decisions respected. Gender asymmetry is then not just a product of the institutional and socio-political processes underlying migration but also produces them at the same time (cf. Lutz, 2010: 1650).

The interactions between different social groups and economic systems discussed in this chapter point to the centrality of migration in the transformation of gender relations and authority structures, though often in contradictory ways. While embedded in unequal power relations, conceptualising gender as a process, where gender and wider social relations, identities and ideologies are fluid, not fixed (Mahler and Pessar, 2001), enables a deeper understanding of individual agency and social change. Roles change, as do responsibilities, particularly in the case of migration, which involves spatial separation for considerable periods of time (vis-à-vis the home), as well as interaction between different cultures of production and consumption (at the destination).

The gap that is often created between the actual experience and its representation opens the epistemological space for questioning the nature of reality itself. What constitutes 'reality' at a particular place and point in time is not just negated in the safety of the home but also spurs the articulation of alternate realities that seek to reconstitute and renegotiate accepted hierarchies of domination and exploitation. Such a spatial analysis, which focuses on the relations between the household and wider regional processes, between local social formations and rural production systems, between identities as lived experience and their representation, between various forms of agency and resistance, located within particular historical and political contexts, contributes to a more nuanced perspective on migration and its relationship to the social structures of production but equally to social change and transformation.

Notes

1. All names of respondents and places in the chapter have been changed.
2. The Act requires 'establishments' and 'contractors' to be registered with the Government and agreements to be made with the workers. It applies only to those employing more than five migrant workers (Chief Labour Commissioner, 1979).
3. Giddens (1984) uses the term to describe the 'stretching' of social systems across time and space – that is, the interaction with people who are absent in time or space entailed 'the expansion of interaction over space and its contraction over time'.
4. Rogaly et al. (2001)'s work in eastern India is an exception, as is Breman's (1985) work in western India.
5. The Jats are a dominant peasant caste in north India, who took the lead in the spread of the Green Revolution and benefited from the ensuing prosperity. The single largest tribal group in Jharkhand state, constituting 36 per cent of the Scheduled Tribe (ST) population, the Santals have a distinct language, Santali, which was recognised as a national language under Schedule VIII of the Constitution via the ninety-second amendment in 2003, and yet they lag behind in terms of socio-economic status, with a majority still living below the poverty line.
6. The Hindus include several sub-castes, such as potters (*kumhars*), oil pressers (*telis*), ironsmiths (*lohars*), moneylenders (*sahs*), mainly classified as Other Backward Classes (OBCs) in national datasets.
7. Sixty-one Santals, twenty-seven Muslims and thirty-two Hindu men reported their status as migrants during the survey. Amongst women migrants, fourteen were Santal and two Hindu (Rao, 2009).
8. As on 22 January 2013, one Great Britain pound equals to 85 Indian rupees, and one United States dollar equals to fifty-four rupees .
9. The report of the Sachar Committee on the status of Muslims in India (Government of India, 2007) found the STs to be the only group who fared worse than the Muslims.

10. Holi, the festival of colours, marks the start of spring and is celebrated in March every year.
11. While the Scheduled Castes (SCs) (*dalits*) and the STs (*adivasis*, or tribals) are administrative categories, benefiting from constitutionally guaranteed quotas for education and public employment, they are constituted of different sub-castes, tribes and clans, each with their distinct occupations, cultures and lifestyles. The Chamars are the major SC group in the study locality.

References

Bakewell, O. 2010. 'Some Reflections on Structure and Agency in Migration Theory'. *Journal of Ethnic and Migration Studies* 36(10): 1689–1708.

Bhalla, G. S., and G. Singh. 2001. *Indian Agriculture: Four Decades of Development*. New Delhi: SAGE Publications.

Borooah, V. K., and A. Dubey. 2007. 'Measuring Regional Backwardness: Poverty, Gender and Children in the Districts of India'. *Journal of Applied Economic Research* 1: 403–40.

Breman, J. 1985. *Of Peasants, Migrants and Paupers: Rural Labour Circulation and Capitalist Production in West India*. New Delhi: Oxford University Press.

———. 1994. 'Seasonal Migration and Cooperative Capitalism: Crushing of Cane and Labour by the Sugar Factories in Bardoli'. In *Wage Hunters and Gatherers*, 133–211. New Delhi: Oxford University Press.

———. 1996. *Footloose Labour: Working in India's Informal Economy*. Cambridge, UK: Cambridge University Press.

Castles, S. 2010. 'Understanding Global Migration: A Social Transformative Perspective'. *Journal of Ethnic and Migration Studies* 36(10): 1565–86.

Castles, S., and M. J. Miller. 1998. *The Age of Migration*. London: Macmillan Publishers.

Chief Labour Commissioner. 1979. *The Inter-State Migrant Workmen (Regulation of Employment and Conditions of Service) Act, 1979*. New Delhi: Ministry of Labour and Employment, Government of India. https://clc.gov.in/clc/acts-rules/inter-state-migrant-workmen. Accessed on 7 March 2023.

Collinson, S. 2009. 'The Political Economy of Migration Processes: An Agenda for Migration Research and Analysis'. Working Paper No. 12, International Migration Institute, Oxford. https://www.migrationinstitute.org/publications/wp-12-09. Accessed on 10 April 2023.

Corbridge, S. 1988. 'The Ideology of Tribal Economy and Society: Politics in the Jharkhand. 1950–1980'. *Modern Asian Studies* 22(1): 1–42.

Corbridge, S., and J. Harriss. 2000. *Reinventing India*. Cambridge, UK: Polity Press.

Corbridge, S., G. Williams, M. Srivastava and R. Véron. 2005. *Seeing the State: Governance and Governmentality in India*. Cambridge, UK: Cambridge University Press.

Deshingkar, P., and J. Farrington (eds.). 2009. *Circular Migration and Multilocal Livelihood Strategies in Rural India*. New Delhi: Oxford University Press, 2009.

Fuller, C. J., and V. Benei (eds.). 2001. *The Everyday State and Society in Modern India*. London: Hurst.

Giddens, A. 1984. *The Constitution of Society*. Cambridge, UK: Polity Press.

Gidwani, V. 2001. 'The Cultural Logic of Work: Explaining Labour Deployment and Piece-Rate Contracts in Matar Taluka, Gujarat – Parts I and II'. *Journal of Development Studies* 38(2): 5–33.

Government of India. 2007. *Report of the High-Level Committee on Social, Economic and Educational Status of the Muslim Community of India*. New Delhi: Akalank Publications.

———. 2009. *Report of the Expert Group to Review the Methodology for Estimation of Poverty*. New Delhi: Planning Commission, Government of India.

Government of Uttar Pradesh. n.d. 'About District: Muzaffarnagar'. https://muzaffarnagar.nic.in/about-district/. Accessed on 12 April 2023.

Jeffrey, C. 2003. 'Soft States, Hard Bargains: Rich Farmers, Class Reproduction and the Local State in Rural North India'. In *Social and Political Change in Uttar Pradesh: European Perspectives*, edited by R. Jeffery and J. Lerche, 225–45. New Delhi: Manohar.

Jeffrey, C., P. Jeffery and R. Jeffery. 2008. *Degrees without Freedom? Education, Masculinities and Unemployment in North India*. Redwood City, CA: Stanford University Press.

Jeffrey, C., and J. Lerche. 2000. 'Stating the Difference: State, Discourse and Class Reproduction in Uttar Pradesh, India'. *Development and Change* 31(4): 857–78.

Jeffery, P., and R. Jeffery. 1994. 'Killing My Heart's Desire: Education and Female Autonomy in Rural North India'. In *Women as Subjects: South Asian Histories*, edited by N. Kumar, 125–70. Kolkata: Stree Samya.

Kothari, U. 2003. 'Staying Put and Staying Poor'. *Journal of International Development* 15(5): 645–57.

Leiten, G. K. 2003. 'Development Priorities: Views from Below in UP'. In *Social and Political Change in Uttar Pradesh: European Perspectives*, edited by R. Jeffery and J. Lerche, 55–75. New Delhi: Manohar.

Leiten, G. K., and R. Srivastava. 1999. *Unequal Partners: Power Relations, Devolution and Development in Uttar Pradesh*. New Delhi: SAGE Publications.

Lerche, J. 1999. 'Politics of the Poor: Agricultural Labourers and Political Transformations in Uttar Pradesh'. In *Rural Labour Relations in India*, edited by T. J. Byres, K. Kapadia and J. Lerche, 182–241. London: Frank Cass.

———. 2003. 'Hamlet, Village and Region: Caste and Class Differences between Low Caste Mobilisation in East and West UP'. In *Social and Political Change in Uttar Pradesh: European Perspectives*, edited by R. Jeffery and J. Lerche, 181–98. New Delhi: Manohar.

Lutz, H. 2010. 'Gender in Migratory Process'. *Journal of Ethnic and Migration Studies* 36(10): 1647–63.

Mahler, S. J., and P. R. Pessar. 2001. 'Gendered Geographies of Power: Analyzing Gender across Transnational Spaces'. *Identities: Global studies in Culture and Power* 7(4): 441–59.

Massey, D. S., J. Arango, G. Hugo, A. Kouaouci and A. Pellegrino. 1999. *Worlds in Motion: Understanding International Migration at the End of the Millenium*. Oxford: Clarendon Press.

Meillasoux, C. 1981. *Maidens, Meal and Money: Capitalism and the Domestic Community*. Cambridge, UK: Cambridge University Press.

Mosse, D. 2007. 'Power and the Durability of Poverty: A Critical Exploration of the Links between Culture, Marginality and Chronic Poverty', Working Paper No. 107, Chronic Poverty Research Centre, Manchester.

Mosse, D., S. Gupta, M. Mehta, V. Shah, J. Rees and the KRIBP Project Team. 2002. 'Brokered Livelihoods: Debt, Labour Migration and Development in Tribal Western India'. *Journal of Development Studies* 38(5): 59–88.

Pai, S. (ed.). 2007. *Political Process in Uttar Pradesh: Identity, Economic Reforms and Governance*. Delhi: Pearson Education.

Rao, N. 2008. *'Good Women Do Not Inherit Land': Politics of Land and Gender in India*. New Delhi: Social Science Press and Orient Blackswan.

———. 2009. *Gender Differences in Migration Opportunities, Educational Choices and Wellbeing Outcomes* (Research Report, March). Brighton: Development Research Centre on Migration, Globalization and Poverty. www.migrationdrc.org/publications/research_reports.html. Accessed on 15 September 2022.

————. 2012. 'Breadwinners and Homemakers: Migration and Changing Conjugal Expectations in Rural Bangladesh'. *Journal of Development Studies* 48(1): 26–40.

Rodgers, G., and J. Rodgers. 2011. 'Inclusive Development? Migration, Governance and Social Change in Rural Bihar'. *Economic and Political Weekly* 46(23): 43–50.

Rogaly, B., and A. Rafique. 2003. 'Struggling to Save Cash: Seasonal Migration and Vulnerability in West Bengal, India'. *Development and Change* 34(4): 659–81.

Rogaly, B., J. Biswas, D. Coppard, A. Rafique, K. Rana and A. Sengupta. 2001. 'Seasonal Migration, Social Change and Migrants' Rights: Lessons from West Bengal'. *Economic and Political Weekly* 36(49): 4547–59.

Rutten, M. 1995. *Farms and Factories*. New Delhi: SAGE Publications.

Scott, J. C. 1990. *Domination and the Arts of Resistance: Hidden Transcripts*. New Haven, CT: Yale University Press.

Shah, M. 2009. 'Multiplier Accelerator Synergy in NREGA'. *The Hindu*, 30 April, New Delhi. http://www.hindu.com/2009/04/30/stories/2009043055 630800.htm. Accessed on 15 September 2009.

Van Hear, N. 2010. 'Theories of Migration and Social Change'. *Journal of Ethnic and Migration Studies* 36(10): 1531–36.

7

Aspiring for Distinction

Gendered Educational Choices in an Indian Village*

Introduction

There is an ongoing debate globally and in India about the types and nature of educational provisioning and its implications on the dynamics of schooling choice and the reproduction of social inequalities (*Compare*'s Special Issue, vol. 36, no. 4, especially Mehrotra and Panchamukhi [2006] and Tooley and Dixon [2006]). Most studies contrast state and private provisioning in terms of access, costs and quality, rather than explore student and parental aspirations and their perceptions about livelihood opportunities and future well-being. The gender-specific ways in which the social and sexual division of labour mediates the schooling experience are largely disregarded. The much-coveted white-collar employment is not necessarily an outcome of educational investment due to the presence of other constraints for boys, and often not even an aspiration for girls; yet the choice of a particular school and

*This chapter was originally published as an article in *Compare: A Journal of Comparative and International Education* © Taylor & Francis Group Ltd 2010. All rights reserved. Reproduced with the permission of the copyright holder and the publisher, Taylor & Francis, Milton Park, Oxfordshire. The chapter is based on research carried out as part of a larger project entitled 'Gender Differences in Migration Opportunities, Educational Choices and Well-Being Outcomes', funded by the Development Research Centre on Globalisation, Migration and Poverty, whose support I gratefully acknowledge. I would also like to thank the villagers of Mahari, the teachers as well as the district and block officials in Sahebgunj and Borio for their support, and the two anonymous *Compare* reviewers for constructive suggestions and comments on an earlier draft.

the prestige attached to it in itself becomes a marker of social standing and a way of differentiating achievement (Caddell, 2006). Schooling choice can simultaneously be used to either reproduce or transform social and gender inequalities, by excluding the marginalised or providing them an opportunity to gain access to tastes and styles that serve as markers of elite distinction (Bourdieu, 1984).

This chapter explores how people of different social categories (sex, age, occupation, ethnicity) in a village in Jharkhand make educational choices and the way this fits with their distinction aspirations. The village is remotely located, with poor literacy and high poverty rates. It is a mixed-caste village, with populations of Hindus, Muslims and Scheduled Tribes (STs).[1] Social hierarchies and differences are visible in terms of both educational and occupational status across these categories. Despite the presence of affirmative action and welfare policies in favour of the STs, caste Hindus are doing much better than the other two groups. The Muslims and the STs consider attaining education a key strategy to fulfil their aspiration of catching up and competing with the Hindus.

The secondary school certificate in particular is seen as a minimum qualification for most professional jobs; yet in India, few rural boys and girls actually manage to complete their secondary school. At the upper primary level, 50 per cent of enrolled children drop out before completion, with the proportion as high as 65 per cent for ST children (Govinda and Bandyopadhyay, 2007). Additionally, given the differential expectations from and aspirations of men and women across these categories, decisions around schooling remain gendered. While Hindu girls, for instance, may seek schooling in order to make a good marriage (cf. Srivastava, 2006), for ST girls it may involve the ability to negotiate a better deal at the workplace rather than status considerations per se.

Fieldwork for this study was undertaken during July to October 2006, with a follow-up visit in September 2008, as part of a larger project seeking to understand the interlinkages between migration and schooling decisions. All the village households were surveyed to identify occupational and educational patterns across social categories. The population in each social category (Hindu, Muslim and ST) was then stratified by gender (male–female), educational level (below primary–secondary) and migration status (migrant–non-migrant) into eight sub-categories. Two people were selected for in-depth interviews from each of these sub-categories, where available (for instance, there were no female migrants amongst the Hindus and

Muslims in the village and no secondary-level-educated females amongst the STs) to gain a more contextualised picture of aspirations and constraints within particular systems of relationships and practices. Out of a potential sixteen interviews from each social category, based on the stratification, a total of twelve interviews were conducted with STs (eight male and four female), eight with Hindus (four male and four female, all non-migrants) and eight with Muslims (six male and two female). While briefly discussing the schooling experience of the different social categories, the main focus of this chapter is on the numerically dominant yet marginalised STs.

In the next sections I set out my theoretical framework drawing on Bourdieu's notion of distinction and the idea of education as a product that can be creatively consumed. After discussing the village context briefly, I use insights and narratives from the interviews to point out how despite the weight of structural constraints, the marginalised attempt to use the schooling process to challenge and transform existing social and economic hierarchies.

Education as a Strategy for Inter-Generational Mobility

The experience of schooling is often contradictory: it carries the potential for inter-generational mobility, but it can also contribute to reproducing social and gender inequalities and status hierarchies by justifying privilege and attributing poverty to personal failure (Longwe, 1998). Reproduction theorists such as Bourdieu and Passeron (1977) describe how the educational system legitimises the social order and transmission of privilege on grounds of academic certification and merit. Children from poorer and working-class families, from lower castes and tribes, consistently underachieve at every level of the educational system compared to middle- and upper-class children. They are ultimately pushed out of school, and this exclusion and their social destiny is then attributed to the lack of merit. The reasons are seen largely as structural rather than personal: lack of state investment in schools attended by a majority of poor children (and rural schools), issues of language, demeaning attitudes of teachers, low expectations of different groups of children and an irrelevant and biased curriculum, as well as poor health and poverty itself (Kumar, 1993; Bowles, Gintis and Groves, 2005). For girls, schools may sometimes provide more progressive models of gender relations than in the family and an escape from domestic work. Dropouts amongst girls are often linked to cultural practices around puberty and marriage, safety and domestic labour, as evidenced by the fact that girls who stay on in school generally end up performing better.

In a fast-changing rural context, where agriculture is no longer sufficient for survival and meeting the aspirations of the youth, migration is a widespread reality. The debates around gender and migration, as around education, have highlighted how outcomes are linked quite closely to one's social positioning as well as the structure of assets – financial, human and social (Mosse et al., 1999; Breman, 1985), with the socially and economically disadvantaged doing worse than those with some starting resources. However, geographical mobility does also seem to have a connotation in terms of certain key life skills, including the ability to negotiate and survive in unknown contexts, apart from exposure to new cultures, ideas and ways of living. For women, migration often also provides exposure to less oppressive urban cultures and aspirations that include a transformation in hierarchical gender relations (Jackson and Rao, 2009; Unnithan-Kumar, 2003).

While differences in economic standing do contribute to the shaping of aspirations and goals, both educational and occupational, of young people, they do not necessarily accept this as a given, but seek other strategies for mobility, often consumption-oriented. Appadurai attributes this largely to the communication revolution – the rapid spread of information and communication technologies over the last decade – be it the internet or the mobile phones, bringing in their wake a new global culture, linked to the consumption of different types of goods and services as markers of status. People's experience of movement, of accessing new technologies and ideas has resulted in creating a new landscape of aspirations and practice, what he calls the 'capacity to aspire' (Appadurai, 1996: 59).

These larger shifts have led to a decline in the popularity of reproduction as a conceptual tool in the 1990s in favour of a more agentic view of the schooling experience and the ways in which forms of interaction can have both reproductive and transformative potential in particular time-space contexts (Collins, 2009). The same applies to an analysis of gender relations, with domination no longer seen as either static or unidimensional, rather giving weight to women's agency in the development process. Evidence can be found in the case of children from less advantaged backgrounds opting for vocational rather than academic courses, as apart from carrying higher risks of failure, the latter may not be best suited for reaching their goals (Erikson and Goldthorp, 2002; Rao, 2009).

Growing up in environments where there appears to be little hope for mobility, there is a further tendency to rebel against the system rather than conform to it (Willis, 1977; Balagopalan, 2005). The wife of the ST village headman narrated:

> I would send my son to school each morning, but he would stop and play in the fields or forests and return home in the evening. I did not discover that he had never attended school till the end of the academic year. The teachers said he had no brains, but I realised that this was linked to the attitudes of the teachers and his lack of understanding of a largely alienating curriculum.

Even individual acts of exclusion or dropout are then linked to the subjective assessment of the chances of success in an educational system that favours the local Hindu elite; in this case the child's actions varied from parental aspirations. The boy now migrates for wage work; his rebellion has only served to reproduce his class position. Such resistances, however, do have the potential to shift existing norms and practices, not just in the school, but in the wider context of lived experience as demonstrated through several cases in this chapter. This is because resistance can take many forms; it is not just rebellion, but students could also appropriate, select, accommodate or generate their own meanings in specific social spheres (Giroux, 1983: 83).

Bourdieu's (1984) notion of distinction provides a useful way of understanding how people organize their perceptions of social space and social status in terms of a lifestyle that includes a range of cultural practices such as dress, speech, bodily dispositions, tastes, and so on, that are socially valued. While he links this to one's own class position (what he calls 'class habitus'), built into the idea of distinction is a notion of mobility. Hence, while 'culture' could denote an intrinsic disposition, it is equally something that can be cultivated. Objects similarly are not 'objective' in the sense of meaning exactly what their technical characteristics specify; rather they are given value in the world of social uses and the perceptions people have of its value. Education, in particular schooling, can be considered as a 'product' that helps cultivate particular lifestyles, tastes and dispositions that contribute to distinction, while not denying that the experience of schooling and its outcomes do vary with the type of school one attends, one's class position and more broadly one's ethnic, gender and social identity that places a person within existing social hierarchies (Lynch, 1989; Bourdieu and Passeron, 1977;

Bowles, Gintis and Groves, 2005). There is a constant tension between the structural constraints imposed by economic structures, wealth, language and the experience of schooling itself, and the strategies (both conforming and resisting) involved in making it successfully through the system, with pupils also adapting and conforming to school cultures as a way of getting ahead.

While understanding social organisation and positioning owes a lot to Weberian ideas of class, status and power, the idea of distinction helps one break out of these categories, as the strategies for gaining distinction could lie in the realm of ownership and control of property and relations of production, but equally in consumption, social interaction, marriage or indeed education. Migrant youth often return home with mobile phones and MP3 players, or trousers and shoes, and rather than viewing this as conspicuous consumption, they see it as demonstrating 'tastes' and contributing to distinction, in a context where they remain marginalised within traditional forms of ranking. Similarly, the choice of schooling, in particular fee-paying private schools, carries within it varying perceptions of quality, of potential networks and opportunities, apart from differential costs (Rose, 2009). Consumption here needs to be viewed as a social, cultural and moral project (Miller, 1995). The imperatives behind consumption and its experiential aspects emerge as being more than just functionalist, carrying elements of creativity in flaunting one's achievements. While consumption is a marker of social inequality, it can also be a symbol of social success.

New forms of gaining distinction through consumption are now widely visible; yet older forms of cultural capital as reflected in educational attainments have not been given up altogether. When migration is seasonal, less secure and perceived to be a result of desperation or distress, as for the STs in this instance, the earnings contribute to household survival rather than enhancing consumption in any substantial way. The aspiration here is to give up migration or drastically change the quality of migration, and one of the strategies that could make this possible is an investment in education. Most of the better-educated Hindus in the study village are in fact non-migrants, seeking white-collar jobs locally. Higher levels of education are then seen as a core human capability that can potentially lead to both economic security and social status for households that start relatively poor (Nussbaum, 2000).

Gender differences are not explicitly discussed within the ideas of distinction (or indeed reproduction or resistance); yet they are implicitly acknowledged in terms of the differential valuations of roles and their segregation. In India, amongst the Hindu castes in particular, restrictions on women's mobility form an important element of social status, and hence this becomes an aspiration for other social groups too. The only jobs seen as acceptable for women are white-collar jobs, often in the teaching profession, requiring higher levels of education, and these are few and far between. Educational investments in girls, however, are increasing; this is not so much for them to secure jobs as to find well-off marriage partners, bringing distinction both to their natal and marital households through demonstrating the social graces and practices acquired through schooling. Women's migration for work, while enhancing their personal confidence and sense of autonomy, opening up possibilities for changing roles and activities, for developing new skills and experiences, is seen to lead to a loss of status for the family.

Village Context

Mahari village[2] in Sahibganj district is educationally the most backward district in Jharkhand state, with an overall literacy rate of 37 per cent (Government of India, 2001). The village is fairly large with 330 households: 176 ST (primarily belonging to the Santal tribe and some Mahlis or bamboo workers), 94 Hindu (largely Other Backward Classes [OBCs] and a few Scheduled Castes [SCs]) and 60 Muslim households. A railway line set up by the National Thermal Power Corporation (NTPC) to ferry coal from the Lalmatiya coal mines (6 kilometres away in Godda district) to the industrial belt in the neighbouring state of West Bengal divides the village into two. One side is inhabited by the Hindus (who refer to this part as a separate Hindu village) and the other by the Santals, Mahlis and Muslims. The government middle school, health centre, post office, local provision shops and telephone booth are all located in the centre of the Hindu hamlet. The other side of the village has none of these facilities. The village has no electricity or transportation, though private jeeps do operate from the village on market days.

Occupations here are clearly divided by religion and ethnicity, a microcosm of the segregation found at the all-India level (Sachar, 2007: 93). Agriculture and wage labour dominate the occupational profile of the Santals, with the Mahlis engaged in making bamboo baskets for sale. With forest produce now negligible and agriculture at subsistence levels, a large majority of them, both men and women, migrate seasonally to the sugarcane fields of western Uttar Pradesh (see Chapter 6) or the paddy fields or stone crushers in West Bengal for an additional income. The Muslims are primarily petty traders engaging with trading livestock, coal, cloth and other household products as well as umbrella repair, though some also migrate to factories in Delhi and Uttar Pradesh. Muslim women are largely confined to their homes. The Hindus are divided into two groups: the more educated (including the caste groups of Sah, Thakur and Teli) are engaged in teaching, medicine, government jobs or petty contracts; and a large number of the others (Kumhars and other lower-ranked backward castes) are engaged in wage labour, pottery or trading coal. In terms of making a living then, apart from some of the upper-ranked Hindu castes, a majority have insecure livelihoods, moving in and out of the village when the need arises.

A little over 30 per cent of the village population is literate, with 6.5 per cent having completed secondary schooling (grade ten) and less than 1 per cent graduation (Table 7.1). There are large differences by ethnicity and gender, with literacy rates ranging from about 50 per cent for Hindus to 20 per cent for STs and a dismal 1.5 per cent for ST women. This reflects not just poverty, lack of pupil motivation or parental disinterest to persist with education, as is often suggested, but also the forms of exclusion practised in schools, a major one being the language of schooling (*cf.* Subrahmanian, 2005). While Hindi remains the medium of instruction, a majority of the STs are monolingual in

Table 7.1 Literacy levels by ethnicity (population aged six years and above)

	STs	SCs	Muslims	OBCs	Total
Illiterate	486 (80)	26 (41)	132 (62.75)	142 (50.75)	786 (67.6)
Primary (1–5)	81 (13)	18 (28)	62 (29.5)	49 (17.5)	210 (18)
Middle (6–8)	19 (3)	10 (16)	10 (4.75)	46 (16.5)	85 (7.5)
Secondary (9–10)	19 (3)	4 (6)	4 (2)	22 (8)	49 (4.25)
Intermediate (11–12)	1 (0.25)	3 (4.5)	1 (0.5)	14 (5)	19 (1.75)
Graduation (13–15)	2 (0.5)	1 (1.5)	1 (0.5)	6 (2)	10 (0.5)
Post-graduation (16–17)	0	0	0	1 (0.25)	1 (0.1)
Not answered	1 (0.25)	2 (3)	–	–	3 (0.2)
Total	609 (100)	64 (100)	210 (100)	280 (100)	1163 (100)

Source: Village survey (2006).

Note: (*a*) ST: Scheduled Tribe; SC: Scheduled Caste; OBC: Other Backward Class. (*b*) Figures in brackets are percentages.

Santali (Government of India, 2001), making it difficult for these children to learn.

Attendance remains low amongst the STs and Muslims, a further deterrent being the railway track separating their hamlets from the school, making access difficult. While there is no overt discrimination against ST girls, Muslim girls are largely excluded from schooling. There is a trend amongst these groups to access private or religious educational institutions – mission schools in the case of STs and *madrasa*s (Quranic schools) in the case of Muslims. While involving costs, both financial and emotional, they are perceived as sensitive to the needs of the concerned social group, hence providing a more conducive environment for learning.

While the 'consumption' of private education for these groups is almost seen as a necessity, apart from being a mark of distinction, separating as it does those who can afford it and those who cannot, interestingly enough, a majority of the literate Hindus (OBCs and SCs) had attended the local government middle school (up to class eight). After completion, the boys were often sent to the Borio high school to complete matriculation, following which Sahibganj College was a preferred destination for those who continued. It is only in the last few years that a handful of Hindu girls have matriculated from this village. The parents generally expressed a preference for a functioning and accountable government school system rather than relying on increased marketisation (*cf.* Harma, 2009).

In November 2002, the government set up schools 'on demand' in the ST and Muslim neighbourhoods, under the Sarva Shiksha Abhiyan (SSA), or Education for All programme. As the number of children increased, both these schools were upgraded to primary schools in June 2006 and are now listed as new primary schools (NPS) (Figure 7.1). While starting with single teachers, two additional teachers, local Muslim educated youth, were appointed in the Muslim hamlet and one more in the ST hamlet, this time an educated Santal man (the earlier appointee being an OBC from the Hindu hamlet). School buildings and infrastructure have been sanctioned – the school building is already in use in the Muslim hamlet and in the final stages of construction in the ST hamlet. There has clearly been an emphasis on improving access and creating the requisite infrastructure to facilitate learning. Midday meals are also provided to the NPS. A cluster resource centre (CRC) has been constructed in the middle school complex (upgraded in 2007 to a high school) and an academic in-charge appointed in November 2005 to provide academic support to teachers, especially in maths and

Figure 7.1 Eager to learn – children in a government school
Source: Photograph by Amit Mitra.

science. Progress seems to have been made: primary schools set up in each of the hamlets, better infrastructure provided alongside attention to quality through the provision of academic support.

Educational Access and Distinction: Issues and Contradictions

Apart from universalising access, the SSA seeks to bridge social, regional and gender gaps, with active community participation in school management. The SSA framework, in thus recognising education as a social institution, which can perpetuate and reproduce inequalities, focuses on critical dimensions of institutional reforms, community ownership, capacity-building and the role of teachers in the educational process;[3] yet its experience of dealing with social structures or delivering quality education has been uneven. New forms of inequality have emerged even within the structures of the state-run educational system. This has implications for educational choices, as both students and parents are searching for educational opportunities that can help overcome existing structural constraints, failing which they seek alternate strategies for gaining distinction.

Government Schools and the New Segregation

A marked difference is visible between the three state-run schools in the village. The primary school, located in the Hindu hamlet, was upgraded to a middle school as early as 1971–72 and recently to a high school. The school has eight regular teachers, four buildings, drinking water and toilets and a computer room, though the lack of electricity has made this non-functional. All ST and SC children receive free textbooks albeit late and a scholarship to cover their costs. SC and ST girls in grade eight are given bicycles by the Jharkhand Education Department to encourage them to continue their studies. Most of the educated in the village have had their basic education in this school. Table 7.2 provides enrolment figures for 2006 and 2008, pointing to a total withdrawal of Muslim children, explained largely by the existence of a functional and accountable primary school in their hamlet (but also pointing to their absence at post-primary levels) and a fairly stable population from the other groups. Table 7.3 reveals large increases in the numbers of both ST and Muslim children enrolled in the NPS, most of them previously out-of-school. The strategy of having schools within hamlets has definitely helped to boost enrolments and thus meet the objectives of universalising access.

Visits to the two new schools brought out contrasting pictures. While the school in the Muslim hamlet has a proper building, three teachers, a functioning balwadi (day-care centre) for three–six-year olds and a regular

Table 7.2 Enrolments in the Mahari middle school (grades one to eight)

Caste/Ethnicity	Male		Female		Total	
	2006	2008	2006	2008	2006	2008
Harijans (SCs)	11	5	9	6	20	11
Adivasis (STs)	56	84	68	38	124	122
OBCs (Hindus)	117	114	100	91	217	205
Muslims	28	0	0	0	28	0
Total	212	203	177	135	389	338

Source: Information from school (2006, 2008).

Note: ST: Scheduled Tribe; SC: Scheduled Caste; OBC: Other Backward Class.

Table 7.3 Enrolments in the two New Primary Schools (2008)

Caste/Ethnicity	Muslim school			ST school		
	Male	Female	Total	Male	Female	Total
Harijans (SCs)	–	–	–	–	–	–
Adivasis (STs)	38	16	54	41	27	68
OBCs (Hindus)	–	–	–	2	5	7
Muslims	62	57	119	–	–	–
Total	100	73	173	43	32	75

Source: School information (2008).

Note: ST: Scheduled Tribe; SC: Scheduled Caste; OBC: Other Backward Class.

provision of midday meals, the school in the ST hamlet was a complete contrast. The building is yet unfinished, the school officially running in the veranda of the chairperson of the Village Education Committee (VEC). The school has only one teacher, Narain Sah, a Hindu. The chairman said:

I have called him many times, but he doesn't come. The school hasn't opened for the last three months. He says he has to go to the bank or to a meeting or file a report. While officially there are seventy-five children enrolled, there are no studies here. About twenty to twenty-five children go to private and mission schools. I send my three children to the mission school. It is expensive, costing almost 4,000 rupees per year for each child, but what is the alternative?

Two major issues emerge from the chairman's narrative. While community participation, accountability to the user, choice and consumerism are an important part of the discourse of decentralisation, the existing social hierarchies and power relations limit such accountability and choice (Pryor, 2005). Parents, including the VEC, are not easily able to question the teacher or demand accountability from him. Several studies have found teacher absenteeism in government schools to be a major reason pushing the poor towards private education (PROBE Team, 1999). There is a second element at play here which relates to dual enrolments. Children are enrolled in the state school with the hope that they can access benefits such as the midday meals, but in the absence of any teaching or learning, parents, a majority of them illiterate, yet recognising the importance of education both in terms of its quality and social functions, decide to enrol them simultaneously in private schools.

Many parents confirmed that the major cash expenditures incurred by them were on health and education. Bitimai and her husband, Chotu Soren, have some land which they cultivate with paddy during the rains and engage in labouring tasks at other times, earning approximately 3,000 rupees per month. Their son and daughter are both enrolled in the local government school, but their son attends the St James School at Pathra. The cost of schooling, including fees, books and a uniform, works out to approximately 500 rupees per month, almost a sixth of their earnings, so they could not afford to send their daughter there as well. Bitimai said, 'I know the local school is not enough for my daughter. Unless this is supplemented with private tuitions, she will not learn anything.'

This indicates the widespread adoption of private tutoring as a supplement to state school provision, with children receiving tutoring likely to perform better and stay longer in school (Bray, 2006: 521). It is also cheaper than investing in private education. Chunu Hembrom, a Santal contractor and chairperson of the VEC of the Mahari high school, is currently educating his son at Sahibganj College at considerable expense (over 1,500 rupees per month for board and fees). His two daughters go to the village school and for an hour's additional tutoring thereafter to a Hindu teacher, costing him 50 rupees per child per month.

Interestingly, and somewhat inexplicably, while the NPS now have permanent infrastructure, the children in the NPS are not eligible for scholarships. When enrolled in the middle school, these children received scholarships; they are now neither entitled to be enrolled in the middle school nor to scholarships. The headmistress of the middle school, a Santal woman herself, clarified that since the new schools have now been upgraded to primary schools, they each have a clearly demarcated catchment area, and she cannot give admission to children living in the catchment of the ST school, even though she realised that her school was both functional and better resourced than the other. She admitted that the better-off amongst the STs sent their children to mission or private schools, but the rest remained out of school. Lack of choice between the state schools had led to a new segregation based on ethnicity.

Narain Sah, the Hindu teacher of this NPS, explained the difficulties he faced in terms of not only lack of infrastructure and lack of scholarships but also the attitude of the parents, who preferred to send their children to work or graze cattle than to school, not surprising in a context of extreme poverty. He, however, admitted that during the period of July 2006 to October

2007, when there was a second teacher, a local Santal youth, attendance had improved considerably. I had met Samuel during my visit in 2006, an extremely committed and bright young man, who had educated himself with great difficulty, especially following his father's death in 1989, when he was only ten years old. As the eldest son, his mother expected him to take over the family farm. He resisted this pressure as he wanted to study, but two of his siblings paid the price. His elder sister was married, and her husband came to stay to help with the farm, and his younger brother was pulled out of school to help his brother-in-law. Samuel matriculated in 1995 from a mission school, and his graduation in 2001; yet he had been struggling to find a job. According to him, 'I was appointed only as a helper in this school on a ten-year contract, and a salary of 2,000 rupees per month. I have to support my family, and this is totally insufficient; yet without money to pay bribes, I am unable to get a job.'[4] Yet he worked hard in the school, encouraging the children to study, explaining things to them in Santali, till he took up a job as a *gram sevak* (village-level worker) responsible for the implementation of the National Rural Employment Guarantee Programme in an adjacent block. Though still on contract, this brings him a better salary.

This then is the second problem with the NPS. As per official notification, the NPS are only ever entitled to hiring para-teachers.[5] Though young, local and better educated, they remain contract workers, with low salaries, and while sincere about teaching, they are pushed to finding supplementary occupations in order to make a living. One is a journalist, another an insurance agent, a few give private tuitions to children after school. Shekar Sah and several others (all of them Hindu) admitted that they are only able to teach for half a day; the salary of 3,000 rupees per month is insufficient. There has been considerable mobilisation of para-teachers in Jharkhand and negotiations with the government; yet the new guidelines, while allowing for an increase in wages to 5,100 rupees per month, rule against any future regularisation of tenure. The glaring inequality with the regular teachers, often only matriculation pass, but earning three times this amount, has reduced teacher motivation, central to improving educational quality.

Indeed, there is considerable variation amongst the state schools themselves. Under the rubric of universalisation, the poorest have gained access; yet the quality of these new schools remains questionable. Choice is non-existent, as they are excluded from the better resourced and functioning state school, located in the Hindu hamlet. Even though numerically strong, the voice of the STs goes unheard; they are denied benefits, both monetary (scholarships) and in terms of teacher quality. It appears to be in the interest of the elite mediators, both teachers and state bureaucrats, to perpetuate the existing social hierarchies by not adequately redirecting resources to support pupils from the marginalised groups, as this could potentially threaten the interests of the elite (*cf.* Lynch, 1989). To this extent, the state schools do contribute to reproducing social inequality in Mahari.

Yet there is potential for transformation in relations of ethnicity, religion and gender. A clear sign is the large-scale enrolment of Muslim children in the school in their hamlet, in particular girls, and their regular attendance on account of the sensitive teaching and school environment created by the three Muslim teachers, all local youth. During the survey I did not find even a single Muslim woman educated beyond grade four; now there are several girls entering grade five. Even if many of them do not pursue further education, completing primary schooling in itself provides them with some knowledge and skills which their mothers lack. Even in the ST hamlet, the potential for change was evident in the brief period when a Santal youth worked as assistant teacher.

While there is no overt gender discrimination amongst the STs, when Samuel left, the children too, both boys and girls, stopped attending. From the perspective of ST parents, the main purpose of education is to improve their children's futures and provide them the linguistic skills, tastes and social graces that form a sign of distinction and can potentially contribute to both social and economic mobility (including white-collar jobs). While expressing a preference for state schools, when these fail to meet their aspirations, then ST parents find it worth investing in private (mission) education from early on, even at considerable personal sacrifice. They are often not able to afford private school fees or even supplementary tutoring fees for all their children, and in the process of selection, girls generally tend to lose out. There were, at the time of fieldwork, six to seven Santal boys studying in high school, but no girls at this level.

Moving for Education: Private Education in Mission Schools

While some Muslim boys do move to *madrasas* in different cities to pursue their studies and Hindus to cities with private schools, this section focuses on understanding how far the strategy of investing in private education, especially that offered by the missionaries, pays off in terms of status gains for the STs.

The example of Samuel who was first appointed as an assistant para-teacher and later secured a position as a *gram sevak* has been discussed earlier. Most other Santal youth have not been so lucky. Anil Murmu, too, studied at the same mission school but withdrew before his secondary school exams due to ill-health. Once he recovered, he enrolled at the Borio government high school, as his parents no longer had money to send him back to the mission school; a lot had been spent on his treatment. But there was hardly any teaching going on, so he dropped out. In 2005, he travelled to the northern state of Uttar Pradesh (UP) with other boys from the village and started working in the sugarcane fields. He stayed there for close to eight months, working on the fields from morning till night, and received a monthly salary of 1,000 rupees in addition to food and accommodation. He was frustrated, as despite his education, the only opportunity for work appeared to be as an agricultural labourer, and while manual work on his own land was acceptable, working as a wage labourer seemed humiliating. Anil said, 'It would have been better had I not been educated; at least I would not have felt so bad at the treatment I received. With my education, I had hoped to do better.' This frustration led him to think of other ways in which he could gain distinction, distinguishing himself from others of his social group who had been eliminated from the education system much earlier (Bourdieu and Passeron, 1977: 82).

While labouring himself, he used his basic educational skills and the confidence this provided to develop links with other sugarcane farmers and turned into a jobber (contractor), receiving a commission of 3,000 rupees per worker. About half this amount is spent on their transport, railway tickets and other expenses, but the rest is his savings. He took seventeen young men last year, and this gave him a savings of around 20,000 rupees. He has opened a bank account and also bought a mobile phone – a marker of status, as very few Santals have them; rather it appears to be a privilege of the educated Hindu castes. But it is also useful for staying in touch with the employers and getting a sense of the demand for labour. As a school dropout, Anil knows that he can never get a white-collar job, and with poor social contacts, gaining clients, too, is increasingly proving difficult; yet he is using his schooling experience to acquire other signs of privilege in terms of dress, speech and a lifestyle. He dreams of saving enough in a few years to buy a motorcycle – once again a symbol of success – knowing fully that this dream can never be fulfilled through cultivation of rain-fed paddy alone.

Twenty-eight children of school-going age from a total of around 250, or a little over 11 per cent of ST children, are presently going to mission schools, fourteen each to the St James Mission School and the Holy Cross Mission School. Except for two who board at the school, most of these children commute daily, walking for more than an hour each way. Fees are high, ranging from 400 to 500 rupees per month, which the parents can barely afford, as these schools receive no state aid. While ST children are entitled to scholarships in government schools, and this is perhaps one reason they stay enrolled, they do not receive them in the mission schools. The headmaster of St James said:

> Four years ago, the Block Development Officer had been approached for minority recognition and monetary help to the school; he promised to help since the government had formulated a policy on recognising mission schools in Scheduled Areas as part of the Education for All initiative. The local RSS [Rashtriya Swayamsevak Sangh][6] activists heard about this and mobilised people in the area against the school and the work of the diocese. Therefore, the funds did not come through. The only way for us to function is to charge the children some fees to cover basic costs.

The issue does not seem to be one of conversion alone, as a large number of upper-caste Hindus themselves are educated in mission schools. The aim seems to be to maintain their social dominance in the area emerging from their educational achievements, by making such schools, known for their quality, out of reach for the poor.

The *Annual Status of Education Report* (2007) across Indian states has shown that the quality of education or its relevance is not necessarily better in private schools (Mehrotra and Panchamukhi, 2006). It is the discipline enforced on the children and the regularity of teaching, which at least makes them both literate and numerate and able to access opportunities creatively as Anil has done. It moulds them into particular characteristics of distinction, such as forms of dress – shorts, shirt and a tie for boys, with shoes and socks – even though inappropriate to local climatic conditions; in particular forms of speech and linguistic styles such as pronunciation, intonation and phraseology that reflect the social conditions of acquisition and differ substantially from their everyday expression; and in certain sets of values, often alien from their own, though associated with the upper classes in society. So while Anil continues to cultivate at home and work as a labourer outside, he speaks Hindi fluently, sports a trouser and a T-shirt rather than the locally used *lungi* (loincloth), carries a mobile phone and aspires to a motorbike. Adopting particular symbols and characteristics of the upper classes, he hopes, could eventually contribute to a shift in his identity and social standing.

Interestingly, the few secondary school graduates in the older generation such as Chunu, Lakhiram or Babulal, too, were unable to access government jobs, and even though their daily lives were not too different from those of their neighbours, they have insisted on educating their children, based on claims that education has helped their careers and given them a sense of distinction and social standing. One is a successful contractor, one a guard, another teacher. As Bourdieu and Passeron argue, it is the length of education that allows for the 'internalisation of the principles of a cultural arbitrary capable of perpetuating itself once the training has ceased' (1977: 31), and it is further secondary school credentials that give recognition to the authority of learning provided by the school, what they call the 'certification effect' (1977: 165). While not necessarily linked to individual capacities, it helps conserve power and privileges amongst the selected few. While primary schooling does have some gains, especially for girls as discussed in the next section, these are hardly sufficient for boys for gaining distinction in society either through educational careers (including the provision of tuitions) or by accumulating wealth through becoming a successful middleman or contractor. Male primary school graduates are then confined to activities and sectors that belong to the working classes.

There is another route to access private education, and that is to send their children to stay with kin and relatives in towns or locations outside the village that may have better schooling opportunities. The Hindus appear to have been more successful in adopting this strategy. Sheila's son studied till class two in the local government school but was then sent to the district town of Pakur to live with her sister for further education in the Torai mission school. She said, 'The studies are much better than in these government schools. The village school does not even teach English. Everything is in Hindi. There is no discipline and teachers show no interest in the students or teaching.' Clearly, for Sheila, learning English, too, was a mark of distinction and a strategy for keeping ahead of the other social groups in the village.

Amongst the Muslims, the few who are educated, like the three teachers, received free education in *madrasas* outside the state, in Patna and Delhi. Shahid Ansari is a twenty-five-year-old teacher at the NPS located in the Muslim hamlet. He left the local government school after class four and completed his matriculation from a *madrasa* in Patna, which was seen as more convenient and of better quality for his studies. 'My parents worried about my future if I only worked in the fields. Initially they sent me to the local school, but people used to tease me as I was older, and we realized that it was better for me in an Urdu school.' He highlighted the role education plays in migration patterns from the village, especially for men:

> Many Santal and Muslim boys are leaving for schooling outside the village. They have the mission schools, and we have the *madrasas*. Ours are government-run and safe as well. There are a few close by, but it is better for the boys to go and live there, as they can study properly without distraction. My brother is now studying in a *madrasa* in Delhi. Nobody likes to send their children away, but the state of schools is so poor here. What will he do by staying here?

While success stories do exist, the numbers are small. Hardly one or two educated ST youth from the village have succeeded in securing regular, white-collar employment. Given the generally low quality of education, any educational success requires substantial additional investment, mainly in the form of private tutoring. Even if this is managed, the next hurdle comes in securing suitable jobs, those with long-term security, benefits and prospects. Almost all the educated STs in the village, though few in number, mentioned that merit was no longer an adequate criterion for securing a job – large amounts of money were required to pay bribes – and this they lacked.

What is clear is that there are many social dimensions of education which are seen as important both in terms of the experience of education and its contribution to distinction. The discipline, the teaching of English, the focus on studies, the exclusion of manual work – all these contribute to shaping values, lifestyles and people's sense of status and mobility. These markers, however, continue to be framed in relation to masculine identities and the task of provision. For both Hindu and Muslim girls, mobility can be acquired by marrying an educated man, preferably with regular employment. For the STs, where women equally participate with men in the workforce, girls, too, aspire for independent and socially valued careers. Here, however, the weight of mainstream social norms and cultural practices, reflected in school cultures and the high costs of private schooling, appear to be disadvantaging girls and leading to growing gender inequality.

Schooling as a Gendered Process

As visible from Table 7.3, the reorganisation of the schooling system in the village has most adversely affected ST girls. While there was a decline of thirty in the middle school, only twenty-seven joined the NPS. As mentioned earlier, there is no ST girl who has yet completed her matriculation from this village; at most they study up to the primary level. There are several ways of explaining this. First, ST boys themselves have not done too well, so despite the fact that there is no overt gender discrimination amongst the STs, in a general context of male dominance, girls are likely to face even stronger obstacles to success. Boys like Anil have gone in for contracting, but its very engagement with an essentially upper-caste, Hindu, male, public domain makes it an area virtually impossible for ST girls – the exception perhaps could lie in the realm of contracting domestic workers.

The value of private or mission schooling for girls is, however, seen in the sphere of confidence-building, and for this five–six years of schooling are seen as sufficient. Kahan completed her primary education from St James Mission School and was then married. Her in-laws were not good to her; she wanted to assert her independence, so she ran away with a group of ten girls to Delhi in April 2006.

> We were ill-treated by the placement agency, moved from one job to another, not paid a salary or given proper food. In three months, I realised I was pregnant, hence decided to come home – my schooling gave me the confidence to travel back alone. But when I returned, I discovered that my husband had taken another wife. I stayed with my parents till a satisfactory agreement was reached.

While schooling did not help her get a better job or improve her working conditions, it did help her gain confidence to negotiate with her husband and in-laws.

The other girls remained in Delhi, a few returned only in 2008, many of them with only a third of what was their due. None of the others had been to school; they did not know Hindi and could not travel on their own without a woman from the agency accompanying them back. The agency retained some of their wage, the local woman agent took her share, and they came home with very little (see Chapter 5). As Shanti said:

I went due to poverty, so I thought will earn and buy things for myself and my family. My mother was ill, and I sent 2,000 rupees home through the woman who took us, but she never gave them this money. I came home now after two years but didn't get all my dues. I could not really argue for it.

While the access to and treatment in schools is one factor, part of the gender difference in educational attainment also arises from the gendered segmentation of the labour market. The ten girls who migrated for domestic work from this village were all between the ages of fourteen and eighteen, unlike a majority of migrant boys, often married and much older. The purpose for many of them was not to make a career in domestic work but rather to earn some money to relieve the poverty of their households, to accumulate a few personal assets or to escape temporarily from excessive reproductive work burdens at home. As Sita said, 'I was doing so much work at home and was not appreciated at all. Everyone had their demands, so I decided to go to Delhi.' Their future lies in marriage and making a successful home, though this too may include temporary work migration on their own or along with their husbands. Sita has now migrated to the brick kilns along with her husband.

For Hindu girls, a few now completing secondary schooling, the purpose is not to seek jobs but rather to find a groom with a white-collar job. Educated men are perceived to have a preference for educated women to ensure performance of appropriate social roles as befits their status. With an increasing number of educated men, the demand for educated wives is also rising. As Sheila, the *balwadi* worker lamented, 'The day I got admission for pilot training was also the day that my marriage was arranged. What to do, I really wanted to work, but had to sacrifice my career, as marriage is seen as the most important event in a girl's life.'

Conclusion

In this chapter, I have explored the processes through which different forms of schooling are given value and meaning in their everyday use and practice. While higher education is positively associated with prospects for white-collar employment, which continues to be socially valued, there are no guarantees that this will in fact be the outcome of investment in education.

This since the experience of education and its social practice continues to be mediated by personal characteristics of sex, age and ethnicity, as well as one's positioning within the existing class hierarchies. These are not inflexible and yet remain hard to penetrate for the socially disadvantaged such as the STs in a mixed-caste village.

Distinction is measured not just by the consumption of goods and services – in this case, education – but by the social trajectories of its acquisition and its social uses. It is this element that seems to provide the space for the exercise of agency and transforming existing hierarchies in social and gender relations. In this context, mission education appears to have an advantage over acquiring education in government schools or even *madrasas*. Apart from possibly better quality, the mission schools inculcate a set of norms and values, codes of conduct and discipline that conform to middle- and upper-class standards of distinction. Graduates of such schools may end up abhorring manual labour and, even while performing it, constantly seek other alternatives that help them maintain a particular lifestyle and image. This is not easy for the STs, evident from this village study, where barely a handful have escaped into other professions, as they are typically stereotyped as manual workers, with or without schooling.

For women, the picture has been mixed. While few have managed to complete secondary education or even aspire to white-collar jobs, even some basic schooling that provides elementary literacy and numeracy skills gives them a sense of personal confidence, enhancing their bargaining position, at least within their own households, if not with their employers. This is an important gain, as from a perspective of social mobility within the Indian context, this can be acquired not through women's employment but by restricting women to the role of good wives and mothers. And here, too, mission education scores over state schooling, transmitting as it does notions of 'goodness', as seen in terms of discipline, obedience and quiet service, that can help women gain status within their marriages.

While the gains from education cannot be doubted, this chapter has brought out the differences in educational choices, the social meanings and uses of education and also the type of education acquired for people positioned differently within existing social and gender hierarchies. Choice in fact operates at multiple levels: societal, parental and ultimately experienced by the child. The meaning and value attributed to schooling is not fixed; rather, it is contingent on how individuals mediate and respond to lived experiences within existing structures of constraint. In fact, the very act of 'consuming' a particular type of schooling can lead to the acquisition of markers of distinction that can potentially contribute to social and economic mobility.

Notes

1. Article 342, Part XVI of the Constitution of India provides for public notification by the President to specify the tribes that shall be deemed as STs and hence eligible for special provisions to promote their educational and economic interests (Bakshi, 1992). The historical disadvantage of the entire group was thus politically recognised.
2. The name of the village as well as those of the respondents in this chapter have been changed.
3. See 'Sarva Shiksha Abhiyan', http://education.nic.in/ssa/ssa_1.asp (accessed on 24 October 2008).
4. Jeffrey, Jeffrey and Jeffrey (2008: 583–34) note the importance of money, social contacts, then knowledge, in that order for securing government jobs.
5. These teachers are locally recruited, on fixed-wage contracts and not provided much training.
6. The RSS is a Hindu right-wing organisation, particularly hostile to missionaries and church groups in the state, seeing them as responsible for converting a large number of STs to Christianity and thus working against the organisation's cause of creating a Hindu nation.

References

Appadurai, A. 1996. *Modernity at Large: Cultural Dimensions of Globalisation.* Minneapolis, MN: University of Minnesota Press.

Assessment Survey Evaluation Research (ASER). 2007. *Annual Status of Education Review.* New Delhi. Pratham.

Bakshi, P. M. 1992. *The Constitution of India.* Delhi: Universal Book Traders.

Balagopalan, S. 2005. An Ideal School and the Schooled Ideal: Education at the Margins'. In *Educational Regimes in Contemporary India*, edited by R. Chopra and P. Jeffery, 83–98. New Delhi: SAGE Publications.

Bourdieu, P. 1984. *Distinction.* Cambridge, MA: Harvard University Press.

Bourdieu, P., and J. C. Passeron. 1977. *Reproduction in Education, Society and Culture*. London and Beverly Hills: SAGE Publications.

Bowles, S., H. Gintis and M. O. Groves (eds.). 2005. *Unequal Chances: Family Background and Economic Success*. New York and Princeton (NJ): Russell Sage Foundation and Princeton University Press.

Bray, M. 2006. 'Private Supplementary Tutoring: Comparative Perspectives on Patterns and Implications'. *Compare* 36(4): 515–30.

Breman, J. 1985. *Of Peasants, Migrants and Paupers: Rural Labour Circulation and Capitalist Production in West India*. New Delhi: Oxford University Press.

Caddell, M. 2006. 'Private Schools as Battlefields: Contesting Visions of Learning and Livelihood in Nepal'. *Compare* 36(4): 463–80.

Collins, J. 2009. 'Literacy as Social Reproduction and Social Transformation: The Challenge of Diasporic Communities in the Contemporary Period'. Plenary presentation, International Conference on Literacy Inequalities, University of East Anglia, Norwich, September 1–3.

Erikson, R., and J. H. Goldthorp. 2002. 'Intergenerational Inequality: A Sociological Perspective'. *Journal of Economic Perspectives* 16(3): 31–44.

Giroux, H. A. 1983. *Theory and Resistance in Education: A Pedagogy for the Opposition*. London: Heinemann Educational.

Government of India. 2001. *Census of India*. New Delhi: Registrar General of Census, Government of India.

Govinda, R., and M. Bandyopadhyay. 2007. *Access to Elementary Education in India: Country Analytic Review*. New Delhi: National University for Educational Planning and Administration.

Harma, J. 2009. 'Can Choice Promote Education for All? Evidence from Growth in Private Primary Schooling in India'. *Compare* 39(2): 151–66.

Jackson, C., and N. Rao. 2009. 'Gender Inequality and Agrarian Change in Liberalizing India'. In *The Gendered Impacts of Liberalization*, edited by S. Razavi, 63–98. New York and London: Routledge.

Jeffrey, C., P. Jeffery and R. Jeffery. 2008. *Degrees without freedom? Education, Masculinities and Unemployment in North India*. Redwood City, CA: Stanford University Press.

Kumar, K. 1993. *What Is Worth teaching?* New Delhi: Orient Longman.

Longwe, S. 1998. 'Education for Women's Empowerment or Schooling for Women's Subordination?'. *Gender and Development* 6(2): 19–26.

Lynch, K. 1989. *The Hidden Curriculum: Reproduction in Education, an Appraisal*. London: Falmer Press.

Mehrotra, S., and P. R. Panchamukhi. 2006. 'Private Provision of Elementary Education in India: Findings of a Survey in Eight States'. *Compare* 36(4): 421–42.

Miller, D. (ed). 1995. *Acknowledging Consumption: A Review of New Studies.* London and New York: Routledge.

Mosse, D., S. Gupta, M. Mehta, V. Shah and J. Rees. 1999. 'Brokered Livelihoods: Debt, Labour Migration and Development in Tribal Western India'. *Journal of Development Studies* 38(5): 59–88.

Nussbaum, M. 2000. *Women and Human Development: The Capabilities Approach.* New Delhi: Kali for Women.

PROBE Team. 1999. *Public Report on Basic Education in India.* New Delhi: Oxford University Press.

Pryor, J. 2005. 'Can Community Participation Mobilise Social Capital for Improvement of Rural Schooling? A Case Study from Ghana'. *Compare* 35(2): 193–204.

Rao, N. 2009. 'Migration, Mobility and the Assertion of Masculinities in Rural Bangladesh'. Paper presented at the workshop on Learning, Livelihoods and Social Mobility, Brunel University, 13–14 May.

Rose, P. 2009. 'Editorial Introduction: Non-State Provision of Education: Evidence from Africa and Asia'. *Compare* 39(2): 127–34.

Sachar, R. 2007. *Report of the Commission on Social, Economic and Educational Status of the Muslim Community of India.* New Delhi: Akalank Publications.

Srivastava, P. 2006. 'Private Schooling and Mental Models about Girls' Schooling in India'. *Compare* 36(4): 497–514.

Subrahmanian, R. 2005. 'Education, Exclusion and the Development State'. In *Educational Regimes in Contemporary India*, edited by R. Chopra and P. Jeffery, 62–82. New Delhi: SAGE Publications.

Tooley, J., and P. Dixon. 2006. '"De Facto" Privatisation of Education and the Poor: Implications of a Study from Sub-Saharan Africa and India'. *Compare* 36(4): 443–62.

Unnithan-Kumar, M. 2003. 'Spirits of the Womb: Migration, Reproductive Choice and Healing in Rajasthan'. *Contributions to Indian Sociology* 37(1–2): 163–88.

Willis, P. 1977. *Learning to Labour: How Working Class Kids Get Working Class Jobs.* Farnborough, Saxon House: Teakfield Ltd.

Part IV

Livelihoods and Well-Being

8

Displacing Gender from Displacement

A View from the Santal Parganas*

Introduction

Out of the millions uprooted from their habitats involuntarily or otherwise deprived of their livelihood due to development initiatives in post-independent India, the worst affected have been the Scheduled Tribes (STs), or *adivasi*s. They make up about 40 per cent of the displaced even though they account for only 8 per cent of India's total population (Fernandes and Thukral, 1989). The displacement of *adivasi*s from their land is neither a new phenomenon nor is it solely due to infrastructure projects. As we demonstrate in this chapter, with changes in land systems and agrarian relations, *adivasi*s have historically been the losers and have had to migrate to other locations. As outlined by Rebbapragada and Kalluri (2009), the alienation of *adivasi* land to non-*adivasi* traders and moneylenders has been a slow and ongoing process. Thus, forced displacement due to infrastructure projects needs analysing along with slower processes of displacement, often considered to be 'voluntary' processes of out-migration.

This chapter, based on extensive fieldwork in Dumka district in 1996–97, 1999–2000 and 2003,[1] explores the gendered implications of different types of displacement on the Santals comprising 40 per cent of the population of

*This chapter was originally co-authored with Amit Mitra, an independent researcher in New Delhi, and published in *Displaced by Development: Confronting Marginalisation and Gender Injustice* © Lyla Mehta 2009. All rights reserved. Reproduced with the permission of the copyright holder and the publishers, SAGE Publications India Pvt Ltd, New Delhi.

Dumka district, Santal Parganas. Displacement is examined historically, specifically pointing to the implications of displacement on gendered roles and spaces. The analysis takes into account the spatial patterning of resources and their management, the temporal and historical dynamics of land use and livelihood systems, and the gendered relationships between micro and macro processes (McDowell, 2002).

This longitudinal view of gender and displacement, which links macro and micro perspectives, can contribute to development planning and displacement debates. This is because infrastructure development is often 'project' focused and geared towards macro-economic growth. Local micro-factors such as household-level assets and livelihood strategies, levels of education and human capacity or the village-level power distribution are rarely considered, leave alone integrating the project into comprehensive area development plans. An important consequence of this 'project' fixation is that once a project is announced and certain areas demarcated, all developmental activities (such as income generation activities and the provision of basic services) come to a halt, sometimes even before land acquisition. The processes of land acquisition and relocation take years to complete, but the populations are deprived of livelihood activities and basic infrastructure in the interim.

In addition to this temporal disjuncture between land acquisition and resettlement (including the rebuilding of livelihoods), large-scale and sudden displacement due to large projects such as a dam must also be viewed in conjunction with other more gradual processes of dislocation due to both partial submergence and the growing pressures on lands and livelihoods. In sudden displacement, the numbers are finite, and theoretically the affected groups are entitled to compensation and rehabilitation packages. But due to the lack of comprehensive area development policies, *adivasis* and other population groups not necessarily considered as 'project-affected people' are also displaced, albeit in a more protracted manner. This often occurs through a slow but continuous process of alienation, induced either by exploitative market forces or through a process of project dilapidation and decline. This makes it important to distinguish between sudden and gradual displacement from habitats, occupations, livelihoods and cultures. The processes are very much interlinked, and often the gradual displacement is a consequence of the sudden one, even from the sites of physical relocation. While locational displacement can lead to a loss of livelihoods, livelihood insecurity, too, can induce the more gradual processes of dislocation. So one 'big' displacement is followed by a series of small but continuous displacements. This makes it difficult to classify displacement strictly as 'voluntary' or 'involuntary', as what appears to be voluntary, when seen in a historical context, may be involuntary – the only choice in a situation of limited opportunities.

While one-time, sudden displacement involving the permanent loss of land on account of large infrastructure and development projects has been discussed in the literature, there is less attention to the temporary loss of land and the difficulties in identifying the difference between a decision that is voluntary or involuntary. This chapter thus calls for a re-conceptualisation of the nature of displacement and the underlying causalities and comprehensive theorising based on empirical research. Categorising displacement into 'voluntary versus involuntary' might be too simplistic in understanding the processes at work. More often than not, the 'voluntariness' of the displaced people is questionable as people are forced to shift due to factors over which they have no control (see also Baviskar [2009]).

Locating Gender

Women are often the worst affected by displacement, especially those in poorer households and amongst the *dalit*s and *adivasi*s. Their loss goes beyond land and property to encompass their entire livelihood resource base, with the takeover of common lands by industry (Minority Rights Group, 1999: 14). As demonstrated in this chapter, women's use rights over certain lands, which gave them autonomous spheres of control, are wiped out without compensation. Moreover, the loss of forests leads to the scarcity of minor forest produce and fuelwood and destabilises women's incomes. Mechanisation, an inseparable part of industrial development projects, also has an impact on women. The employment generated by the projects comes with hazardous working conditions and low wages and without job security, pushing more and more women into the informal sector. All of this has a direct impact on the food security and health of displaced women.

Men may not necessarily fare better in the contemporary development scenario. Indeed, it is ironic to discuss the rehabilitation of women and men when what has taken place in India can, at best, be described as the mere relocation of populations. Rehabilitation remains a dream for most men and women affected by development-induced displacement. Rehabilitation packages tend to treat both individuals and households as autonomous units, with a clearly identifiable set of interests, and thus fail to take account of their embeddedness in a network of social relations. They club together the entire population on the basis of generalised assumptions about their lives and livelihoods. In reality, there are differences within the 'to be displaced' population regarding not only gender, but also class, caste, ethnicity and age, which affect the collective interpretations of the needs of individuals and households in the community. This process marks the difference between one-time 'involuntary' displacement and other kinds of displacement. The sudden movement reduces the possibility for women to negotiate their traditional rights within the 'rehabilitation package'. For in staking their claims, they stand to be portrayed as opposing the interests of their men and communities. In other kinds of displacement, not only is there no 'rehabilitation package' that can be used to measure the distribution of resources, but the articulation and negotiation of claims, too, remains under-researched.

Against this background, we critically examine the notions of 'displacement' and 'gender' prevalent in contemporary discourses on rehabilitation and resettlement. It is our contention that:

1. Adhering to Micheal Cernea's model of 'impoverishment risks' (Cernea, 1990, 1996, 1997) alone limits the understanding of the displacement processes underway in the country. This is particularly true amongst the *adivasi*s, whose situation must be examined in a historical context. The model ignores the differences within communities as well as the implications of indirect changes arising from shifts in livelihood patterns. Further, it does not consider the changes occurring in an area independent of the project, be they the results of other state policies or issues concerning the wider political economy. Nor does it take into consideration changes in relations between men and women within the community: the displaced are treated as a homogenous category (see also Mehta [2009]).

2. The binary classification of displacement as either 'voluntary' or 'involuntary' needs re-examination. The current assumption is that while development projects displace people 'involuntarily', all other

displacements, often termed as migration, are 'voluntary' or by choice. We question the paradigm of choice(s) available to the poor and the *adivasis*, including women.

3. Much of the resettlement and rehabilitation literature misleadingly treats women and gender synonymously. By essentialising both women and men, these discourses fail to employ gender analysis to examine how displacement processes impact the relationships between men and women, as well as between women and women and men and men. It is important therefore to analyse changes in the construction of both femininities and masculinities to ensure that gender is not displaced from discussions of displacement.

Our conceptual framework, summarised in Table 8.1, points to the contrasts and similarities between different forms of displacement from a gender perspective. It identifies changes in productive and reproductive roles and the implications of this for not just work burdens but also control over resources and consequently gender relations. In terms of locational displacement, a gradual movement can sometimes lead to greater vulnerability for entire households as compared to sudden displacement; the latter often entails a much higher level of gender inequality. In the case of occupational migration, however, while women are generally disadvantaged in the labour markets and cannot avoid reproductive functions, be it at home or at the worksite, where long-term migration is involved, they gain control over some income.

In the next section, we elaborate the distinctions made in Table 8.1, with the caveat that the categorisations are of processes that are not water-tight compartments.

The Mayurakshi Project and Displacement

The Masanjore dam, built in 1955–56 with Canadian assistance on the river Mayurakshi (locally called More), displaced 144 villages in Dumka district. The exact number of people displaced is not known. The dam is 34.4 metres high and 609.6 metres long, and the water is regulated with twenty-one lock gates. The dam generates hydroelectric power and irrigates nearly 50,000 acres of agrarian land in Birbhum and Murshidabad districts of West Bengal.

Table 8.1 Impact of sudden and gradual displacement on productive and reproductive roles and relations

Displacement/ Gender	Locational		Occupational	
	Sudden	Gradual	Long-term	Temporary
Productive roles and relations	Compensation in land, cash, jobs provided to men, but no productive resource to women	No compensation, so lack of assets for both men and women; increase in vulnerability to poverty	Lack of physical assets, so dependence on level of skill and education; usually enter the lowest and least paid levels of the labour market, and subject to poor living and working conditions	Insufficient resource base, indebtedness; women disadvantaged by the gendered nature of labour markets
Reproductive roles and relations	Lack of common property resources (CPRs) increases time taken for reproductive tasks, which become exclusive responsibility of women; breaking of social networks and community ties; lack of social support	Often follow kin and other social networks, leads to some support, but can also enhance work burdens through additional tasks for hosts	Social alienation, possible separation from children; if woman migrates alone; long working hours at low wages plus lack of functioning services in the urban slums, if they migrate as family; new social networks formed at migration site, but based on different, more individualistic values	Increased physical and psychological burden on women for management of home and fields, if men migrate; reproductive tasks at worksite, after work, if women migrate; increased vulnerability to sickness and ill-health due to overwork, with poor amenities; lack of effective social support

The catchment area of the project lies in Dumka district, where over 19,000 acres of land were acquired, 5,000 of which was *baihar*, or lowlands, used for paddy cultivation. Some people lost all their land and had to move to a new location, while others stayed on in their villages, with only a part of their land submerged. Between 1961 and 1981, the numbers of farmers in the region declined from 3.95 million to 2.76 million (Besra, 2002). While there was a rehabilitation package – land for land for the *adivasi*s, a choice of cash or land for non-*adivasi*s, some crop compensation and a promise of improved services including irrigation – there have been loopholes, inefficiencies, fraud and other problems all along.

The Santal Parganas were a part of the Diwani of Bengal, acquired by the English East India Company in late eighteenth century. In order to enhance revenues from the region, following the Permanent Settlement in 1793, the Santals were encouraged by the British to clear the jungle and make the land cultivable. The intense exploitation by the revenue collectors, other colonial officials and moneylenders resulted in the uprising (Santal Hul) of 1855, following which the Santal Parganas district was constituted and exempted from the general regulations of the Bengal province (Roy Chaudhary, 1965). The Santals were allowed privileges like self-governance, control over land distribution and management and dispute resolution. The period that followed saw a series of land settlements (see Chapter 2), both to serve the purpose of revenue collection and to prevent discontent from again leading to violent protests. This is because individual land tenures were transferable and thus valuable, and granting of titles therefore also led to a spate of land alienation from the Santals to the traders. When the colonial government tried to curb this trend, other forms of tenure emerged to bypass the legislation. Individual titling and the establishment of the settlement courts to deal with land disputes also led to the overlooking of women's rights to land.

The empirical material in this chapter is organised as follows: We first examine the gendered implications of permanent displacement through the study of a few villages that were displaced by the Mayurakshi Hydel Project in the mid-1950s. What has been the implication for the livelihoods of households – men and women – who moved from their homes over sixty years ago? Have the conditions of life for them improved or deteriorated? What are the new problems that have arisen in recent years as the project reaches the end of its life? Have more people been forced to move over the years? We then briefly examine the history of land alienation and the ensuing loss of identity of the Santals.

Sudden Locational Displacement

> Our land was submerged in the waters of the dam, and our life in tears

> —Gobindo Soren, Taqipur village, Raniswar block, Dumka district

This statement sums up the feelings of the majority of people affected by the Masanjore dam – both those who were displaced from their villages and those who stayed on.

Gobindo Soren, an eighty-three-year-old Santal (Figure 8.1), organising the resettled people in Raniswar block, Dumka district, around their rights, at the time of writing, raised several issues: the flawed calculation of land for land, poor provision of services, inadequate employment opportunities, and so on. When the notification for displacement was first issued, all *adivasis* were promised 'land for land.' They were brought in trucks to the new locations and allowed to choose their new home site. The total value of the landholding in their original village was calculated on the basis of the quality of land: *dhani* 1 was valued at 2,200 rupees per acre, *dhani* 2 at 1,600 rupees per acre, *dhani* 3 at 1,300 rupees per acre, *bari* 1 at 800 rupees per acre and *bari* 2 at

Figure 8.1   Gobindo Soren and his wife outside their new home
Source: Photograph by the author.

500 rupees per acre.[2] The entire land in the new site, however, was assessed as being *dhani* 2 and valued at 1,600 rupees per acre. As a result, the total land that the displaced people received in the resettlement village was much less than their previous holdings. People in Bisumdih laughed when they showed us their holdings: it was all undulating uplands, where rain-fed cultivation was not possible, yet had been classified as *dhani* 2 by the authorities.

Apart from the loss in total holdings, such classification has also had specific gendered implications. Previously, titles were in men's names at the household and community levels, and *dhani*, or the paddy growing land, was seen to be under men's control. In contrast, women's rights of use over *bari* lands were clearly recognised. They would grow maize, mustard, hemp and vegetables on these plots, close to their homes. Now *bari* no longer exists as a category, so women's rights to land have been wiped out without any compensation.

A further issue relates to the access to common property, particularly forests. Chumki Tudu moved from Bagjuri to Bisumdih when she was twelve years old. In Bagjuri, forests and fruit trees were aplenty, and she collected fruits and other forest produce both for consumption and sale. The family was relatively well-off. The forests are far away in Bisumdih. Chumki goes for wage work to the neighbouring villages and sometimes even to Bengal, which has made life both more insecure and tougher. Her husband added that while the land was good in their earlier home, here it was full of stones and pebbles, and harder work was required to make it productive. Another woman, Sheuli Murmu, moved here with her husband and four young children. Only one survived – food was a problem here – the forests were far away, and the land allocated to them was uncultivable during the initial years until the canal brought water.

Gobindo Soren, who was thirty-five years old at the time of displacement in 1955, and a schoolteacher, noted that once his father died, he gave up his job, as it was difficult for the women to manage in the new location. The lands were not good, forests were far, and the women found it hard to raise additional income despite hard work. But this also meant the loss of a regular income to the household and vulnerability to food insecurity – all impoverishment risks identified by Cernea (1997). So while women seem to have lost both land and common property assets, and to this extent are more dependent on men, men, too, having been cheated of their rightful share, cannot support the household without the full cooperation of the women. For instance, men are now forced to migrate to the brick kilns of West Bengal for labour. It then becomes imperative for the women to single-handedly manage the meagre holdings and care for the children, often under great physical and emotional stress. While the common crisis can enhance mutuality in gender relationships, a lot depends on the site of resettlement. Relationships are not predictable but depend both on personal histories and the environment.

Yet the people here did not remain silent victims. They complained early on (1958–59) to the Irrigation Minister that this land was barren and uncultivable. Without water, they were unable to reclaim much land. In response, they were promised year-round, free irrigation from the Left Bank Canal of the Mayurakshi dam. Until 1965, they received some money for land development, but once the water reached the land, this support was stopped. Further, the fine print of the allotment papers ensured water tax remission only for twelve years, after which they had to start paying for irrigation water. This was not too bad as long as water was available, as they could grow two crops. For the last ten years or so, however, the canal has started silting and is unable to carry its full capacity of water. In the last three years, it has completely broken down, and without water, cultivation is not possible. People have no option but to migrate for work, both agricultural and in the stone crushers in West Bengal. The work is hard, seasonal and insecure, the children fall ill, and often the migrants just manage to save some grains to bring home. Thus, after the initial displacement, consistent struggle did help to secure livelihoods, but there has been a slide back into insecurity as the project runs through its lifecycle, with both men and women having to migrate for employment seasonally, as discussed in the next section.

Class and ethnicity, too, influence rehabilitation outcomes. The Hindus of Kumrabad, who moved to Raghunathpur in Raniswar block, received sufficient land for their homestead and crop compensation for twenty years in cash. The payments were made in parts over five years, and there were several instances wherein the full amount was not paid. Villagers reported that only the few who filed lawsuits got the full compensation. Besra (2002) gives the example of two villages in Masalia block to illustrate this. In Rangamatia village, while 104,459 rupees had been sanctioned, only 18,579 rupees (18 per cent) were distributed, and in Rajmahal, out of the 118,954 rupees, only 20,663 rupees (17 per cent) were disbursed. A lot of this balance money ultimately reverted to the government treasury as unspent amounts.

Uday Ghosh of Raghunathpur admitted that despite lack of payments and tardy payments, they were better off than the Santals, who were cheated outright by the state. In exchange for their cultivable lands, the Santals were allotted wastelands here that were valued as good-quality land. They were not given a choice but had to accept this land. Ghosh himself had considerable land in Kumrabad, but having seen the wastelands being offered here, he opted for cash compensation. At least they were able to set up petty businesses with the cash to keep them going. Several services had been promised – electricity, water for irrigation, jobs. The hydel power station was supposed to produce 4 megawatts of power, a quarter of this for Dumka district. Not only did this not happen, but in 1995, the Bihar government removed its staff from the project and stopped producing hydel power completely. For irrigation, the proposed Right Bank Canal did not materialise, so people on the right bank never got irrigation. The Left Bank Canal was silted up and dysfunctional at the time of the study. Jobs were not forthcoming, and many men now engage in petty trade and business, while others migrate for wage work. There seems to have been a growing invisibility of women, and accessing them, even for a woman researcher, was difficult. They are now almost entirely confined to reproductive roles.

Gradual Locational Displacement Due to Partial Submergence

If this is the condition in the resettled villages, with livelihoods having become extremely precarious in the last three–five years with the collapse of irrigation, the conditions in the partially submerged villages are no better. In Mahadevraidih village of Jama block, the dam submerged a third of the paddy-growing *dhani* land, but the people refused to move. It was a difficult decade, but at least they were not alienated from their homes and community. They used whatever compensation they received to make new fields in the upper reaches of the catchment area of the reservoir and to reconstruct their livelihoods.

Chunda Hansdak's (sixty years old) parents lost all their land. They were offered land in Birbhum district of West Bengal, but refused to move. Instead, they used some of the little compensation received to make new fields in the forest and some for food. They looked for wage work here and there. Hansdak's mother took wood to the market for sale. At times, when there was no food, they borrowed money from the *mahajan* (moneylender). Hansdak was ten years old then. He dropped out after class seven to help his parents with the work. It took almost seven to eight years for their household to stabilise once again, but they were saved the trauma of separation from their village and friends. The forests remained, some new fields were cut, and livelihoods were maintained.

Now they are experiencing a different problem. The dam is silted and nearing the end of its life. Water flows backwards, carrying with it silt and sand. The riverbed is rising, and lands that were not in the submergence zone are now getting inundated during the monsoons. The sand deposits make them uncultivable. Hansdak and his family now fear a new period of displacement and insecure livelihoods, this time without compensation.

In partially submerged villages like Mahadevraidih, women continue to have access to forests, common lands and local markets. This helps them earn small amounts when needed. The reduction in landholdings due to submergence has led to the disappearing of several customary practices including that of gifting land to a daughter or sister by the father or brother – known locally as *taben jom* (see Chapter 3). Not more than 10 *bigha*s,[3] this gift was generally made out of affection or obligation to a daughter or sister, a kind of insurance against a bad marriage. On her death, though her sons were allowed to use the land, the control of this property remained with her patrilyny, rather than passing on to her husband (Archer 1984 [1946]).

Chunda's son-in-law took a second wife. Affronted, his daughter returned to her natal home. She sells leaf plates in the market and engages in wage labour. Chunda feels that as she has a son, when he grows up, they should claim a share of her husband's property, as he himself has only a little land, which his son may not agree to share with his sister. While recognising that *taben jom* is a claim that women can make on their parental property, not only is this considered temporary, but given the shortage of good-quality land, this does not even seem practicable. She can live with them as long as she likes, but Chunda also feels that a good option for her is to get remarried, as she is still young. While these parents care for their daughter, the relative scarcity of land is working to her disadvantage.

Returning to the story of access to common property, this was presented in stark terms in Kumrabad, a predominantly Hindu village. Kumrabad was a big market town before the construction of the dam. Two-thirds of the area were submerged: people left the village and so did all business. The government's promises of jobs, electricity and a new market did not materialise. The government high school was submerged, but no new school was constructed. In 1981, the villagers set up their own school; in 1992, they got funds from the member-of-legislative-assembly (MLA) quota to construct a building, and yet, at the time of writing, this school had still not received government recognition. Common property such as ponds, grazing land, *jaherthan* (sacred groves) and, most importantly, forests, all of which contributed to the livelihoods of the villagers, were lost without compensation.

B. K Pal, a resident of Kumrabad, narrated:

> When Masanjore was being constructed, land was acquired up to a level of 397 feet. The chief engineer had, however, advised the government to acquire land up to 403 feet. This would have meant more land acquisition, more displacement and greater compensation paid out, so it was not accepted. However, during the heavy rains in 1999–2000, there was a flood, and many of the houses were submerged.

In Dumka district, 38,000 houses are said to have been dilapidated by these floods. The villagers here had to leave their homes and move to the primary school building for almost a month. Some lost everything and left the village. Others constructed new houses with help from the government housing scheme for the poor – Indira Awas Yojana (IAY). But clearly life is more insecure. There was one big displacement in 1955 and a complete lack of certainty about the future. No shops, no school, a broken road, no bus service – these are just some signs of the future.

While the problems with compensation and rehabilitation cannot be reversed now, as the trauma and suffering has already taken place, the issue of the new displacement due to enhanced silting and reduced capacity of the dam needs to be addressed. Frequent flooding and submergence of currently cultivable fields, on the one hand, and stoppage of irrigation to the resettled villages, on the other, are issues that need to be attended in more than immediate relief terms. They are clearly not one-off events but will now recur with greater frequency and regularity, until the root of the problem is addressed.

As more land is lost due to siltation and the ensuing flooding of the villages by the backflow of water from the reservoir, the people are left to fend for themselves. There is no initiative for compensating them or even ameliorating their miseries. Even in the resettled villages, without irrigation, the livelihoods are fragile and unsustainable. Women have lost their sense of being and security along with secondary rights to land such as the *bari* plots, forest resources and other customary rights.

Occupational Displacement

We have seen thus far that when people are displaced from their homes en masse, they are often also displaced occupationally because they tend to lose access and control over not only land but also other productive assets. However, this can also be a much slower and individualised process, and historically the alienation of individual land has led to the occupational displacement of many *adivasis*. While some analysts have looked at migration in terms of choice (Todaro, 1969), this appears to be more compelled by circumstances than a result of free will (Breman, 1985; Mosse et al., 2002; Rogaly et al., 2001). In this section, we analyse processes of individual loss of land leading to both long-term and short-term displacement for work and its gendered implications.

Individualised land alienation has a long history, revealed through a study of the various land settlement reports and records.[4] In the annual report for 1882, the Divisional Commissioner for the Santal Parganas, Oldham, observed that 'the bazaar traders of Dumka had gradually absorbed all the Santal settlements in the vicinity ... and that a considerable portion of the lands of cultivators ... had passed into the hands of creditors' (McPherson, 1909: 45). Several people who had migrated to the tea gardens of Assam at this time, ostensibly for a short period, found they had lost their land to the headman or his kin in their own village or to the moneylenders. They had no option but to migrate permanently. Regulation II of 1886 was then passed to stop all land transfers. No further sales took place, but transfers continued in other forms, with *mahajans* getting a foothold in many villages, supported by the police and civil administration. The land survey and settlement operations that followed tried to restrict transfers; yet these have continued until the present day in one form or another.

The Santal Pargana Tenancy Act (SPTA) was passed in 1949, and despite a reiteration of the non-transferability clause, the *mahajans*' exploitation in collusion with the official machinery increased during the next decade. In 1966, a movement evocatively titled the *hul* Jharkhand (Jharkhand rebellion) was launched in Dumka district. It aimed at releasing land and securing debt relief. Apart from *dhan katai* (forcible harvesting), other direct-action strategies included the non-repayment of loans, thefts of grain from *mahajans*' fields and court cases. Mass meetings were held, the word spread through the district and so did the resistance.[5] Women were actively involved in the *hul* Jharkhand, both in the process of planting and harvesting of the fields and in providing food and shelter to their men, who were often on the run. In 1967, a coalition ministry was formed in Bihar with the support of the Communist Party of India (CPI). Though it lasted only eleven months, circulars were issued in favour of the *adivasis* and the oppressed. Many *mahajans* fled the villages, returning only when the movement subsided.

By 1972, the movement was formalised as a political party (Hul Jharkhand Party). Soon after, differences emerged on strategy, financial transactions and leadership, marking the beginning of its collapse. In 1976, Shibu Soren, who had been involved in a movement against *mahajans* in the Dhanbad area (Iyer and Maharaj, 1986), came to the Santal Parganas and relaunched the *dhan katai* movement there. Those who had not yet got back their lands reclaimed them during this period. Shibu Soren was transformed into a folk hero.

The hold of the *mahajans*, however, continued in the arena of forest and water rights. After the *hul* Jharkhand, when the *adivasis* borrowed money, the *mahajans*, afraid now to take land on mortgage, encouraged them to cut down trees for repaying their debts. Most of the forests in the Santal Parganas were destroyed in the 1970s, as reported by several people in the district. The 1980s also saw struggles over forest and water rights. Father Antony Murmu in Borio block of Sahebganj district led a major one. He, along with fourteen other *adivasis*, was shot in police custody on 19 April 1985, in what is known as the Banjhi massacre.

The widespread agrarian and anti-*mahajani* movements in the Santal Parganas and other parts of Jharkhand during the late 1960s and the early 1970s led to a spate of state actions and legislation. In 1969, the Bihar Scheduled Areas Regulation sought to control more strictly the illegal transfers of land,[6] amending the provisions of Section 20 (v) of the SPTA. Soon after, the Bihar Moneylenders Act, 1974,[7] and the Bihar Debt Relief Act, 1976, were passed. However, alienation and transfers still continue and are visible in almost all villages, particularly in the non-Damin areas. See Table 8.2 and Box 8.1 for details of a few villages in Dumka district.

Alongside the process of alienation that accompanied an individualisation of rights to land, women's rights, too, have become increasingly restricted over the years. Reproducing C. H. Bompas' note on the Santal law of inheritance, McPherson (1909: 123), a land revenue settlement officer, noted that daughters got no share of land, and the beneficiaries of land titling were male kin. While the practice of women cultivating was widespread, as noted by McPherson, titling began leading to the creation of exclusionary land systems.[8] Formalisation of rights meant the shrinkage in a range of

Table 8.2 Total village land and extent of alienation (in hectares)

Village	With non-adivasis (in *bigha*)	Pop/hh	Total land	Forest land	Unirrigated	*Gauchar* (grazing land, pastures)	Area not available for cultivation
Titridangal	69						
Bhikampur	14	160/29	125.13	18.25	52.66	2	50.53
Mankapahari	4	124/25	63.69	16.39	30.62	10.09	4.57
J.Paharpur	64	446/81	290.77	89.76	112.96	62.97	19.01
Kodalchalla	33	348/68	185.87	—	137.20	47.02	0.69
Majdiha	12	—/75	183.66	4.11	165.83	9.07	2.45
Kadma	72	649/111	197.44	12	145.09	34.49	15.90 (*khas*)

Source: Agrarian Assistance Association, Dumka.

Box 8.1 The challenges of reclaiming land legally

In eight villages of Jama and Kathikund blocks, with the support of a non-governmental organisation (NGO) (Agrarian Assistance Association [AAA]), land alienation cases involving a total of 231.5 *bigha*s have been taken up. Ramlal Kol of Titridangal village in Jama block filed RM case no. 372/2000-01 in the court of the SDO against Upen Mandal. The order was issued on 20 September 2002. With the support of the village *gram sabha* and the AAA, he could take possession of his land in early 2003. The alienation was long-standing, with the first case being filed as RE case no. 209/78-79, and despite an eviction order passed by the then sub-divisional officer (SDO) on 16 July 1984, he could not reclaim his land due to threats of violence as well as his continued indebtedness and need for cash.

The truth of this became even more apparent when I spoke to the *pradhan* (headman) of Kadhadbil, a village on the outskirts of Dumka, part of which now falls within the municipal area. He is educated and has a petty government job. Yet he was unable to reclaim his own land, alienated many years before, from the courts. Until 1994, he would go regularly for the hearings – it was a great expense. Finally, the court or the lawyers, he is not sure, misled him. Different dates were given to the two parties, and in his absence, the case was settled in favour of the other party. His own lawyer, a non-*adivasi*, was working in collusion with the opponents. This is, in fact, a huge problem reported by many of the *adivasi*s – that the lawyers (a majority of them are non-*adivasi*s) take fees from them, yet work against their interests, as they have in all likelihood taken money from the other side too. Similar is the story of an educated Paharia leader in Gopikandar block. If *adivasi*s who are educated and not really the poorest are unable to use legal processes and institutions in their favour, it is next to impossible for the poorest and resourceless, particularly women, to do so.

flexible and informal rights in land, contributing, in turn, to a re-negotiation of land use and inheritance practices as well as power relations within the 'community' – among individuals, households and kin groups as well as the state.

By 1916, women's land inheritance had become a contentious issue. As distinct from the government position, the local leaders felt that if a man had only daughters, they would be his heirs even after they got married. When a man had sons and daughters, and the sons died without having children, the girls would become the heirs. For a widow, they argued for a life interest in her husband's property, as long as she did not remarry (Bodding, Skresfrud and Konow, 1994 [1942]: 198).

By the next land revenue settlement in 1936, the official understanding of women's rights got further obfuscated. While stating that 'according to Santal *adivasi* law of inheritance, only males can inherit land', J. F. Gantzer, the Settlement Officer, also indicates daughters being recorded as cultivators, where not doing so would have involved real hardship to them (Gantzer, 1936: 22–23).[9] Archer (1984 [1946]) in his survey of 1945–46[10] found in practice a much more flexible system of inheritance and one that was more supportive of women than recorded by Gantzer. The SPTA of 1949, however, repeated the provisions of inheritance recorded by Gantzer, rather than the more liberal systems documented by Archer.

In a context where titling land individually reinforced patriarchal principles to exclude women, at least from the official colonial discourse, the public reassertion of principles of community support was an important counterpoint. At the same time, in light of the erosion of their formal authority (through the establishment of settlement courts), the move by local male leadership to support women's land claims can also be seen as an assertion of their moral authority as protectors of all members of the community – both men and women. A similar situation prevails today, wherein the political movement for a separate Jharkhand state emphasised the value of community institutions and led to a reassertion of their legitimacy and moral authority as a challenge to state structures.

Two related issues arise from the discussion thus far: first, the continuing alienation of *adivasi* land to non-*adivasi* traders and moneylenders and, second, the growing challenge to women's rights to land in instances where the husband is a *gharjawae*,[11] as legitimised by the SPTA (see Chapter 3). While both these trends are not only linked to sudden locational displacement but are historical trends, they get intensified in a context of land scarcity and enhanced competition for a limited amount of land, as is often the case in displacement contexts. Unable to survive on their land, both men and women are then forced to migrate, either for seasonal work or longer-term employment, for a livelihood (Figures 8.2 and 8.3).

The processes of migration are gendered. While it is primarily men who migrate to the stone crushers for relatively longer periods of six to eight months, women migrate for shorter periods of three to four weeks four times a year to transplant and harvest both the *aman* (monsoon) and *boro* (winter) paddy crops in Bengal. Having planted paddy at home, they move to Bengal to earn some rice and cash to tide over the difficult time until their own crop is harvested, while the men stay behind to tend the land. As the output does not see them through the year, they continue to migrate even after the harvest. In the absence of water, there is no second crop. With the household clearly facing survival difficulties, men go too.

Given a choice, men would prefer to stay back in the village and tend whatever little land they have to preserve their identity as *chasahor*, or cultivators. They see migrant work as a loss of status and therefore attempt to project their migration decisions as an adventure to see new places or a strategy

Figure 8.2 Travelling to work as labourers at construction sites

Source: Photograph by Amit Mitra.

Figure 8.3 Waiting for labouring work in town
Source: Photograph by Arundhita Bhanjdeo.

to build capital for investing in their own land. They hence prefer long-term migration to distant locations,[12] usually leaving after ploughing the land for the monsoon paddy and returning before the next planting season. Even though the women undertake all other operations, through the act of ploughing men assert their control over the land and their identity as cultivators. And when unable to make their land productive, they face a crisis of masculinities, often leading to permanent migration or an escalation of violence.

Women's identity as *orahor*, or homemaker, permits them to undertake a diverse range of activities to fulfil their roles as homemakers and contribute to household subsistence – to its food supply, clothes and perhaps for an unmarried girl to build up her dowry. Apart from working on their fields, they thus also undertake wage work when needed, collection of forest produce, raising animals and engaging in the local markets (*haat*s). While Suphal Tudu of Beherakudi village, for instance, tends his land, his wife goes for labour to West Bengal.

In Bardhaman district of West Bengal, the working days are long and the living conditions poor. Ten to fifteen adults are often piled together in a tiny, dark cattle shed. Yet, for these workers, the main advantage over local wage work appears to be that they receive a lump sum payment at the end, which can be used for the purchase of clothes, house repairs and repaying debts or other large expenses. They would never be able to earn enough locally for these purposes. While for harvest work, men and women seem to be employed almost equally, for transplantation work, women are preferred. Unlike the Hindu castes, which tend to withdraw female labour as a sign of status, among Santals, men prefer to stay away from wage work and let women engage in it.

While migration can enhance women's earnings, the trade-offs in terms of social costs are high;[13] hence, the compulsions for migration are also likely to be high.[14] Migration patterns thus reveal the interactions between the micro-context relating to the individual's ability to choose between alternate courses of action and the macro-context, including the political, economic, socio-cultural and resource relationships that constrain such decisions. For men, it often signifies a breakdown in community networks – 'social disarticulation' to use Cernea's term (1997). For women, such migration often tends to strengthen the notion of community – women from different households travel together to the workplace and support not only each other there but also those who are left behind in the village.

Migration, however, works differently for different women, as with men, depending not just on their physical asset base but also on the household composition and other social relations. Women with family support for childcare, for instance, may be able to work longer and earn more. For those without access to childcare, especially female-headed households, it may be more risky and have fewer gains and yet may be the only option for survival. Mariam Murmu, aged forty-five, migrated to Bengal with her daughter for the *aman* harvest. She fell sick there and could not work for six days. For these days, she was neither paid nor given her rations. She brought back only 400 rupees. At home, her elder daughter too had been sick, and her co-wife had pawned a silver ornament for 200 rupees for her treatment. They released the ornament, bought some rice, and the money was finished. She decided not to go for the *boro* planting even though she had no other survival option. She said, 'My daughter and co-wife are both sick. If I go and something happens to them, what is the use?' Clearly the survival risks and the threat of permanent displacement have enhanced support and solidarity amongst women within the extended household and kinship group, where competitive property relations are not involved.

Male migration for long durations also poses difficulties for women. They are left behind to look after the home and children, often with few resources. Remittances are not regular and not necessarily sufficient. They look for wage labour locally or borrow from neighbours and moneylenders, resulting both in tremendous emotional and psychological stress and in enhanced physical burdens of work.

Women have been asserting their land claims, both for its material value and for social security. Land is important for women to fulfil their household maintenance functions within marriage. It is even more crucial in the event of widowhood or marital breakdown, wherein they have to take on the full role of 'provider'. Despite recognition of women's central role in agriculture, women tend to lose because of the symbolic construction of land as a mark of male status, of kinship and masculine identity. This is reflected in symbolic discourses, celebrating male identity, rather than negatively restricting women. Further, in a context of resettlement, where land scarcity is rampant, advancing women's claims becomes even more difficult.

Conclusion

A new draft national rehabilitation policy was formulated in 2006; yet women have once again not been given any place in this policy. This is not surprising: a long line of policies at the state levels as well as of various agencies like the National Thermal Power Corporation (NTPC), formulated through the previous decades, had not given women their deserved attention (Mitra, 2001). Further, caveats have been introduced in the current policies and practices that can deny the displaced land for land in the compensation package.[15]

In this chapter, we have explored the gendered implications of locational displacement due to large development projects – in this case a large dam – which results in a sudden en masse movement alongside longer-term insecurities and sporadic movements set in motion by the initial displacement. We have also analysed the implications of occupational displacement due to land alienation or land scarcity, both short- and long-term. In the case of the large dam, there seems to be not only a deterioration in the living conditions of both men and women in the resettled villages as well as in the villages in the partial submergence area, as the project reaches the end of its life, but also an exacerbation of work burdens imposed on women due to a shrinkage of resources or poorer-quality resources. There has been a loss of access to common property, particularly forests and grazing lands, as well as markets. Alongside a decline in the total land held by the household, women's specific plots of land, namely the *bari*, no longer exist. Finally, in a generalised context of limited land availability, there is an increased questioning of women's customary rights to land. But while in the former case, there is a breakdown in community support and growing individualisation of resources and assets, in the latter, women's networks at least are sustained.

The issue of land alienation is much more embedded in history and the local social context. Given the great deal of social mobilisation that has occurred on this issue, it is a much more contested field, and successes are few and far between for the poorest. (An exception is the Samatha judgment, as discussed by Rebbapragada and Kalluri [2009].) Even though land alienation may not constitute a permanent loss of land, the short-term gendered implications are similar to the case of more permanent displacement. Women specifically have had to work harder to make ends meet, as the gendered nature of labour markets ensures that they are integrated at the lowest levels in the lowest paid jobs. At the same time, they face challenges in making even such land claims that are considered legally and socially legitimate, as in the case of *gharjawae*.

In the contemporary context, it sometimes seems hard to draw the line between voluntary and involuntary displacement. The real issue in terms of gender analysis then becomes examination of the historical processes behind the gradual and sudden displacements and their associated occupational changes. In a specific context, at a point in time, sudden mass displacement is indeed traumatic, while in the long run the impact of the gradual displacement may be as severe. Further, gradual displacement processes already seem to have been in motion when the sudden displacement occurs and continues even after this event. In terms of life chances, then, what seems to matter are also the initial conditions – the skills, educational levels, landholding and tenure patterns and ownership of other assets – apart from the extent of state support provided.

In essence, the development histories of the regions (that is, both the displacement and resettlement sites) and the people become an important factor in understanding the gender implications of displacement, and in fact comprise the settings in which the conventional understandings of 'impoverishment risks' of displacement variously operate.

Notes

1. The 1996–97 study was conducted by me with members of Ayudare, a project of women's empowerment in the Santal Parganas, supported by the

non-governmental organisation (NGO) Adithi; the 1999–2000 fieldwork was part of my PhD research, and the 2003 fieldwork was conducted by me as part of the United Nations Development Programme (UNDP)–Ministry of Rural Development (MoRD)–PRADAN study on laws and policies in Jharkhand. My co-author, Mitra, visited the area several times between 1999 and 2003 in connection with various projects and development interventions by local NGOs. All names of people in the chapter have been changed.

2. Land of five qualities is recorded in the land settlement records: *dhani* 1 refers to lowlands suitable for paddy cultivation, often irrigated; *dhani* 2 refers to medium-quality paddy lands; *dhani* 3 refers to uplands that can be used for rainfed paddy; *bari* 1 refers to homestead plots; and *bari* 2 refers to more distant homestead plots, often wastelands, used for tree crop cultivation.

3. Three *bigha*s are equal to 1 acre.

4. This section is largely based on data and analysis drawn from Rao (2002).

5. In the Damin region, people met, but decided against *dhan katai*. In the absence of other options, they decided not to fight the *mahajans*. Interestingly, while the *hul* of 1855 had started in the Damin region, this time the movement was more intensive in the plains near Dumka.

6. For STs, the period of lease was increased to thirty years from twelve years for immovable property before a transfer was permitted in the records. The District Commissioner was given the powers to evict a transferee without payment of compensation and restore land to the ST *raiyat*. The only exception was for buildings on that land.

7. The government ordered all moneylenders to be registered and to provide a report of their transactions, including money due to them, within thirty days. No reports were received. In fact, most *mahajans* in the village destroyed their records.

8. He says, when the Santal courts became acquainted with the Santal law, they ceased to record women as successors to *jote*s. Before that time, the Settlement Officers following the ordinary settlement rules had recorded whatever cultivators were found in possession and, in so doing, had noted Santal women for a number of holdings (Archer, 1984 [1946]: 683).

9. Gantzer noted in his final report that 'if a female is cultivator of a field, her name should be (recorded) accompanied by that of her father if she inherited the property from him, or by her husband' (Khanapuri Rule 46: 22 in Gantzer [1936]).

10. W. G Archer, a civil servant, was appointed by the British state to enquire into and record Santal law as a reference point for the civil courts. He submitted his report in 1946. It was, however, filed and never published until 1984, when the Anthropological Survey of India and the Indian Council of Social Science Research published it jointly as rich anthropological material on the Santals rather than as a legal text.

11. *Gharjawae* literally means 'resident son-in-law' and refers to particular marriages wherein the husband gives up claims on his father's property and moves to his wife's land. This is recognised by the SPTA, 1949, as a legitimate right for women.

12. The main employer is the Border Security Force. Some men do send money home, but many bring back a lump sum when they return home at the end of the contract, usually for six to eight months. While male income contributes towards meeting large expenses (such as house construction or debt repayments), the entire physical and financial burden for daily maintenance falls on women, leading to overwork, poor health, indebtedness and harassment (Karlekar, 1995; Rao, 2002).

13. Karlekar (1995) includes economic and sexual exploitation, lack of childcare and education, and increased workloads as social costs. At subsistence levels, issues of autonomy can become irrelevant.

14. Breman writes, '[T]o suggest that the *khandeshi* cane-cutters put to work for the season in the fields of South Gujarat, … Halpatis who trek each year to brickworks far distant from their village … leave home because of their own free choice … [is] a grotesque distortion of social reality' (1996: 201). Rao and Rana (1997) reach a similar conclusion regarding women seasonal migrants from the Santal Parganas. These studies focus on the poor. While they are not forced to leave their homes in legal terms, they are faced with a lack of alternatives hence lack choice.

15. Recent Supreme Court judgments on the Sardar Sarovar dam have referred to the Oversights Group report (Shunglu Panel report), which argues in favour of cash compensation in lieu of land. (Iyer, 2006).

References

Archer, W. G. 1984 (1946). *Tribal Law and Justice: A Report on the Santal.* New Delhi: Concept Publishing Company.

Baviskar, A. 2009. 'Breaking Homes, Making Cities: Class and Gender in the Politics of Urban Displacement'. In *Displaced by Development: Confronting Marginalisation and Gender Injustice*, edited by L. Mehta, 59–81. New Delhi: SAGE Publications.

Besra, V. 2002. 'Masanjore and After'. *Hor Sambad* (in Santali), Department of Information and Public Relations, Jharkhand Government, 15 November.

Bodding, P. O., L. O. Skresfrud and S. Konow. 1994 (1942). *Traditions and Institutions of the Santals*. New Delhi: Bahumukhi Prakashan.

Breman, J. 1985. *Of Peasants, Migrants and Paupers: Rural Labour Circulation and Capitalist Production in West India*. Oxford: Oxford University Press.

———. 1996. *Footloose Labour*. Cambridge, UK: Cambridge University Press.

Cernea, M. M. 1990. 'Poverty Risks from Population Displacement in Water Resources Development'. HIID Development Discussion Paper No. 355, Harvard University, Cambridge, MA.

———. 1996. 'The Risks and Reconstruction Model for Resettling Displaced Populations'. Keynote address, International Conference on Reconstructing Livelihoods, Refugee Studies Programme, University of Oxford.

———. 1997. 'The Risks and Reconstruction Model for Resettling Displaced Populations'. World Development 25(10): 1569–88.

Fernandes, W., and E. G. Thukral (eds.). 1989. *Development, Displacement and Rehabilitation*. New Delhi: Indian Social Institute.

Gantzer, J. F. 1936. *Final Report on the Revision Survey and Settlement Operations in the District of Santal Parganas, 1922–35*. Patna: Superintendent, Government Printing.

Iyer, G. K., and R. N. Maharaj. 1986. 'Agrarian Movement in Tribal Bihar (Dhanbad) 1972–80'. In *Agrarian Struggles in India after Independence*, edited by A. R. Desai, 330–61. Delhi: Oxford University Press.

Iyer, R. R. 2006. 'Narmada Rehabilitation: OSG Report and After'. *The Hindu*, 1 August 2006. http://www.thehindu.com/2006/08/01/stories/2006080102780800.htm. Accessed on 1 November 2007.

Karlekar, M. 1995. 'Gender Dimensions in Labour Migration: An Overview'. In Women and Seasonal Labour Migration, edited by L. Schenk-Sandbergen, 23–78. New Delhi: SAGE Publications.

McDowell, C. 2002. 'Involuntary Resettlement, Impoverishment Risks, and Sustainable Livelihoods'. *Australian Journal of Disaster and Trauma Studies* 2. http://trauma.massey.ac.nz/issues/2002-2/mcdowell.htm. Accessed on 16 June 2008.

McPherson, H. 1909. *Final Report on the Survey and Settlement Operations in the District of Santhal Parganas, 1898–1907.* Calcutta: Bengal Secretariat Book Depot.

Mehta, L. 2009. 'The Double Bind: A Gender Analysis of Forced Displacement and Resettlement'. In *Displaced by Development: Confronting Marginalisation and Gender Injustice,* edited by L. Mehta, 3–33. New Delhi: SAGE Publications.

Minority Rights Group. 1999. *Development, Equity & Justice: Report on a Roundtable.* Ahmedabad: SETU Centre for Social Knowledge and Action.

Mitra, A. 2001. 'Land Acquisition and Compensation Policies: How They Treat Women'. In 'Women's Empowerment Policy and Natural Resources: What Progress?' Paper presented at workshop organised by the Planning Commission, Government of India, and the Overseas Development Group, University of East Anglia, Norwich, New Delhi, 18–19 May 2001.

Mosse, D., S. Gupta, M. Mehta, V. Shah and J. Rees. 2002. 'Brokered Livelihoods: Debt, Labour Migration and Development in Tribal Western India'. In *Labour Mobility and Rural Society,* edited by A. de Haan and B. Rogaly, 59–88. London: Frank Cass.

Rao, N. 2002. 'Standing One's Ground: Gender, Land and Livelihoods in the Santal Parganas, Jharkhand, India'. PhD thesis, School of Development Studies, University of East Anglia, Norwich.

Rao, N., and K. Rana. 1997. 'Women's Labour and Migration: Case of Santhals'. *Economic and Political Weekly* 32(50): 3187–79.

Rebbapragada, R., and B. Kalluri. 2009. 'The Samatha Judgement: Upholding the Rights of Adivasi Women'. In *Displaced by Development: Confronting Marginalisation and Gender Injustice,* edited by L. Mehta, 249–69. New Delhi: SAGE Publications.

Rogaly, B., J. Biswas, D. Coppard, A. Rafique, K. Rana and A. Sengupta. 2001. *Seasonal Migration for Rural Manual Work in Eastern India.* Norwich: School of Development Studies, University of East Anglia.

Roy Chaudhary, P. C. 1965. *Bihar District Gazetteers: Santal Parganas.* Patna: Secretariat Press, Bihar.

Todaro, M. P. 1969. 'A Model of Labor Migration and Urban Unemployment in Less Developed Countries'. *American Economic Review* 59(1): 138–48.

9

Enhancing Women's Mobility in a Forest Economy

Transport and Gender Relations in the Santal Parganas*

Introduction

The Santal Parganas in Jharkhand (erstwhile south-eastern Bihar)[1] was reorganised in 1981 into five districts, Dumka (which is the divisional headquarters), Deoghar, Godda, Sahebganj and Pakur. The Santal tribals constitute a large proportion of the population and are also spread across several adjacent districts of Bihar, Odisha, Madhya Pradesh and West Bengal. The Santal Parganas have three distinct tracts. About a third of the area consists of partially forested hills, running from north to south, and valleys with small villages and clearings for cultivation. Half is rolling country in the west and south-west, with long ridges, intervening depressions, rocks or scrub jungle. The third tract is the rice-cultivating plain between the Ganga and the hills. The area was once rich in forests of different types, which are now restricted to small pockets.

*This chapter was originally published in the *Indian Journal of Gender Studies*, vol. 9, issue no. 2 © Centre for Women's Development Studies, New Delhi, 2001. All rights reserved. Reproduced with the permission of the copyright holder and the publishers, SAGE Publications India Pvt Ltd, New Delhi. The study on which this chapter is based was part of an International Forum for Rural Transport and Development (IFRTD) project on 'Gender and Rural Transport'. I acknowledge the IFRTD's support, both financial and conceptual, in developing the methodological framework. I thank executive secretary Priyanthi Fernando for comments on an earlier draft. My sincere thanks to Munni Hembrom and Santoshini Hembrom, senior cadres of Ayo Aidari, a local tribal women's organisation, and Kumar Rana for support in data collection.

Dumka was connected to the rail network only in 2011, but the division has a fairly good system of roadways. Major towns are linked by buses; yet the bullock cart remains the main form of local transport, particularly for goods. As ordinary carts cannot negotiate the steep hills and boulders, people generally walk. Bicycles are gradually increasing but are exclusively used by men. Women have no option but to walk from their village, at least up to the roadside.

The population is mostly rural; three towns were recorded in 1901, rising to twelve in 1981. Many missionary societies run educational and medical institutions in the district. Mainstream society considers the Santals as labourers in agriculture and construction. For generations they have been employed to clear the land and work in the tea plantations of the north-east, as well as in agriculture and construction in eastern India. Literacy was low at 37.26 per cent for men and 14 per cent for women in the region in 1991. This is likely to be even lower for the Santals and Paharias despite the designated tribal schools. In 1993–94, there was great enthusiasm for the National Literacy Mission's adult literacy campaign. Women were also organised to form savings groups named Jaago Behena (Awaken Women) and Didi Bank (Elder Sister's Bank). However, the lack of adequate post-literacy and continuing education programmes have led to a rapid decline into illiteracy.

The district population has increased since 1901, as reflected in every decennial census except in 1921 when there was a decline due to epidemics of cholera, smallpox and malaria. Despite an improvement in health services after independence, the establishment of primary health centres (PHCs) and sub-centres and the setting up of a malaria control unit, malaria and diarrhoeal diseases continue to be major reasons of mortality due to lack of proper drainage systems (leading to waterlogging) and unsafe drinking water. In Jadopani, one of the villages studied, five–ten adults die due to these diseases every year. The PHC at the block headquarters is ill-equipped for both diagnosis and treatment. Further, without any transport from the village, it is difficult for sick persons to reach the PHC. Villagers usually bring the sick when it is too late to save their lives. Till twenty years ago, the local people used medicinal plants from the forests to cure many of these diseases, but with deforestation many of these plants have disappeared. People's faith in medicinal herbs has also declined due to the exploitative rituals that are often associated with the practice of traditional medicine.

The Santals were originally a communitarian people, with all lands and forests considered as common property. The basis of this system was the village that was collectively settled. The leader, or *majhi*, administers the rights, rules and ceremonies of the community. The more or less hereditary institution of *majhi* is recognised officially for collecting rents and reporting crimes. Most village issues are discussed and decided locally by the *panchayat*, or the council of village elders headed by the *majhi*. Punishment by Santal law is usually not very severe. One of the exceptions is the case of intimacy between a Santal girl and a *diku* (non-Santal) boy, where the offenders could be excommunicated from the society. This tradition really developed as an attempt by the Santals to maintain their social purity and solidarity and prevent the transfer of Santal lands to non-Santals. After independence, and the formation of community development blocks, the people were asked to go to the block office for all their basic needs and provisioning. As a result, the community spirit that is essential for meeting their own small needs has gradually declined.

The Situation of Santal Women

According to Santal customary law, women are 'objects' or 'property' to be transferred from the father to the husband. If a woman commits any offence, the father or husband is held responsible. Hence, women do not have any claim over the movable or immovable property of the father or husband. The law did, however, provide maintenance for widowed women, unmarried girls, divorced daughters and wives. This was codified during British rule, in 1922–23, and after independence by the Santal Pargana Tenancy Act (SPTA) in 1949. The SPTA has interpreted Santal customary law somewhat mechanically, virtually ruling out possibilities for women to inherit land (Rana and Rao, 1996).

Traditionally, in the absence of a male heir, a man could get a daughter married to a *gharjawae* (a son-in-law formally adopted at the time of marriage as a son) who would stay in the girl's village and sever all links with his own family. The land can then be legally transferred to the daughter. In actual practice, even if a *gharjawae* is taken, the male agnates (who would inherit property in the absence of a *gharjawae*) rarely allow the couple to live peacefully, and muscle power is often used to harass and drive them out of the village. A widow gets no share and is virtually homeless upon her husband's death unless she has a son. Many cases in the Dumka courts today relate to property disputes involving *gharjawae*s.

Making the plight of women worse is the Santal practice of marrying more than one woman. If the first wife agrees to the marriage, she is given some gifts as an insurance against friction; if she does not, she receives nothing. Deprived of the right to inherit land, quite frequently victims of polygamy, and thrown out of the house without any maintenance, a large number of Santal women are forced to lead unimaginably hard lives without resource support.

As in other patriarchal societies, within the gender division of labour, ploughing, hunting, sacrificing animals and other ritual ceremonies are exclusive male preserves. Within the household, however, apart from all the maintenance functions, it is the woman who collects paddy, borrows seed grain, negotiates loans, goes to the market and in general manages the household. There are no restrictions on her mobility as the household manager.

Survival and Livelihood Strategies

Agriculture and the collection and sale of forest produce used to be the mainstay of the Santal economy. Over the years, with the decline of forest cover and lack of substantial improvement in agriculture, the Santals have been forced into local and migrant wage employment. Indeed, livelihoods today are finely balanced between the availability of forest produce, land ownership, the ability to cultivate land and wage employment. Table 9.1 shows the high degree of wage labour in the district as a whole, ranging from less dependance in Gopikandar block, which still has considerable forests and forest produce, and high dependance in Jarmundi, which lacks forests and forest-based artisanal or trade activity. Since the major focus of this study was on women's transportation needs in a forest economy, villages in Gopikandar

Table 9.1 Primary occupation of households in twenty-one villages of Dumka district in 1997

Block	Agriculture	Labour	Service	Artisan/ Trader	Others (MFP)	Total
Gopikandar	210	101	8	43	30	392
Jarmundi	75	257	4	1	—	337
Dumka	291	273	21	4	11	600
Grand total	576	631	33	48	41	1329

Source: Rao (1999).

and the adjacent Ramgarh block of the district were selected. In these areas almost 38 per cent of women and 25 per cent of men are dependent on the forests for their survival (Rao, 1999: 144).

Transport, Livelihoods and Gender Relations

Despite severe deforestation in this area, the Santals still depend on the remaining forests as a supplementary source of livelihood for survival, especially in lean summer months: the collection of fuelwood; food such as roots, berries, greens and mangoes; medicinal herbs; and forest produce such as *mahua*, *sal* seeds and leaves, tamarind, *kendu* leaves, construction poles for further processing and sale. They also cultivate a rain-fed crop, usually paddy and maize.

The forest economy is primarily a female one, with women responsible for collection, processing and sale of forest produce. As forests dwindle, they have to walk longer distances to the field and forest for collection, carrying back the produce as headloads. Firewood, leaf plates, puffed rice, vegetables and liquor are also carried as headloads to market. Roads have now been constructed, but there is no regular transport. A few villages have a single bus service during the day, which can perhaps take them one way to the market. The buses are crowded with passengers, particularly on market days, and refuse to carry women carrying large, heavy loads. The majority of villages in the interior and hilly areas are inaccessible, and even bullock carts find it difficult to traverse the slopes. Motorbikes are rare. A few bicycles are now found in these villages, but they are entirely controlled and used by men.

Significantly, the marketing of firewood and fruits (mangoes and jackfruit) is now gradually being taken over by men, who carry the produce on bicycles. This has reduced women's transport burden and time pressure, but the negative consequence is that they have lost control over the income from selling the firewood and fruits that they collect. This study analyses this development and its impact on women's income, status and gender relations.

The state's intervention in transport provisioning seems to be restricted to road construction. Metalled roads facilitate the development of public transport, buses, trucks and other heavy vehicles, but if not maintained properly, the roads become unusable except by heavy vehicles. In several parts of Dumka district, the metalled roads are in a pathetic condition – perhaps nobody has looked at them since their construction in the 1940s and the 1950s. The metalled road to Kurumtand village is used by only one bus plying to the interior villages, and that too once a day! Those who walk and ride bicycles or bullock carts prefer to use the field by the roadside. A gravel or pebble road might be softer on the feet, but muddy roads could become slippery and unsafe during the rains. It seems that transport provisioning has been limited to connecting villages to towns in order to meet the needs of the market rather than those of village women.

Research Questions

To understand the linkages between transport provisioning, livelihoods and gender relations, a small study was conducted in Dumka district in the first quarter of 1998. The major questions addressed relate to the consequences of changes in the socio-economic and environmental context on the transport roles and responsibilities of women and men. Specifically, the issues addressed were

1. the extent of women's transport burden (distance, time, load and frequency) for both work purposes (for example, marketing forest produce and wage labour) and for household maintenance (like fuelwood, food and water collection);
2. the existing transport provision, how it is used and whose needs it meets;
3. recent changes in transport provision, both formal and informal, and how they have affected gender relations and transport tasks; and
4. the scope of non-transport interventions (drinking water supply, fuelwood plantations) to reduce women's transport burden.

Exploring some of these questions could help fill gaps in information on gender issues in women's mobility and rural transport and point towards context-specific strategies and interventions that address rural women's needs and priorities.

Methodology

Three villages were selected for detailed study: (*a*) an interior forest village with no proper road or means of transportation (Jadopani), (*b*) a village connected once a day by a jeep to Dumka (Pandhini Duma) and (c) a roadside village (Mohalo). Jadopani and Mohalo are in Gopikandar block, and Pandini Duma is in adjoining Ramgarh. In all three, the people's major source of livelihood was collection and sale of forest produce. The context and situation of each of the three villages was studied, including a population listing covering characteristics, major occupations and transport needs of all the households available at the time of the study. A few sample households were selected for detailed interviews to understand the workloads, time-loads and consequent transport needs of both men and women.

An important methodology adopted for this case study was participant observation. Many of the trips were made by the researcher along with the respondents in order to correctly estimate the time spent by them for particular tasks, nature of the journey, distance, type of path, and so on. Not only was this a very interesting exercise, but it provided an insight into the tough daily routines of the women, who are dependent on forest produce for their survival.

The following section presents the issues raised in the context of each village and includes some brief case studies to give an insight into the daily routines and living conditions of tribal women and men. The last section highlights some of the key lessons and elements for policy emerging from the village studies.

Village Studies

Jadopani Village

Jadopani is an interior, tribal village with two tribal groups and two major hamlets at different topographic levels, with nineteen and twenty-four households, respectively. The lower hamlet is inhabited entirely by Santals; the upper has a mix of a few Santal and Paharia households. Other Paharias live in smaller groups of two to three households, scattered on the hilltops near the jungle. There are clear contradictions and conflicts between the two groups and the rich and the poor in the village. Almost all the households own some land. Only a few in the lower hamlet, however, have land beside the stream and can hence irrigate it for summer paddy, in addition to their major rain-fed crop. This has made them more prosperous than those in the upper hamlet. Members of a fourth of the households engage in seasonal wage labour, but migration for survival is negligible. Not many own bicycles, bullock carts or other forms of transport, as the path to the village is rocky, steep and difficult to negotiate with a vehicle.

The village *majhi* (headman) is among the more prosperous Santals. The Paharias particularly felt that the Santal headman did nothing for them but was interested only in the lower Santal settlement. The Paharias have only one well located at a distance of almost 1 kilometre. The ten-minute walk to collect water has to be made at least three times in the morning and two to three times in the evening. During the summer months, April and May, when this well dries up, they have to fetch water from the stream. Carrying water uphill is a difficult task. There is a handpump near the headman's house but not in their hamlet. The headman, however, said that attempts at boring a well in the upper settlement had struck the rock crust but no water. He had got government loans sanctioned for house construction for twenty-three Paharia households. Service provisioning was difficult, according to him, as they lived in scattered groups in the jungle.

The Santals in the upper hamlet, too, are poor and mainly depend on the collection and sale of forest produce, apart from a little cultivation. Each family has about 30–40 *mahua* (*Madhuca latifolia*) trees allotted to them in the *jamabandi* (land settlement), which is a major support for the food and income it provides. A household can earn 500–1,000 rupees from the sale of *mahua* seeds, fruits and liquor in the lean summer months. The Paharias are poorer than the poor Santals. They do not have land and depend upon shifting cultivation in the forests and selling firewood. (The better-off households also have better access to education and health, the services of the health worker and the PHC doctor. Poorer households with less access often end up paying high fees to private doctors.)

Being high up in the hills and surrounded by forests, some forest produce is available all the year round seasonally (Table 9.2). This gives the people (especially women) some supplementary income for meeting daily needs throughout the year and prevents them from migrating in search of employment. Despite this, most of the Paharias and poorer Santals have taken food loans from the local moneylender at Gopikandar. They have to return it with 50 per cent interest within a year.

Lukhi Murmu is a widow with three daughters and a son. Her husband had cleared 2 *bigha*s of land in the jungle, but after his death, she was unable to cultivate it as she had to take care of her young children. She would go to the forest twice a week and collect *sal* leaves, make these into leaf plates and

Table 9.2   Seasonal calendar of forest produce

Month	Produce
January	Firewood, sal leaves
February	Firewood, sal leaves
March	kendu, mahua flowers, firewood, sal leaves
April	Mahua flowers, raw mango, tamarind, bel, kendu fruit, firewood, sal leaves
May	Kendu leaves, mango fruit, firewood, sal leaves, mahua fruit
June	Mahua flowers, mushroom, firewood, sal leaves, wild vegetables
July	Mushroom, sal leaves
August	Vegetables, sal leaves
September	Vegetables, sal leaves
October	Roots, firewood, sal leaves
November	Roots, firewood, sal leaves
December	Roots, firewood, sal leaves

sell them in the local markets, also twice a week. Now, with her daughter making leaf plates along with her, they save one person's earnings to purchase clothes, footwear, and so on, and spend the rest on daily food needs. The markets are 10–15 kilometres away, and virtually the entire day is spent on the trip on market days.

At the wedding of her eldest daughter, she arranged for the son-in-law to be *ghardijawae*[2] and was able to resume cultivation. The condition of their household improved till he suddenly died of disease in April 1997. Once again the family is in a precarious condition, back to selling leaf plates. Even though women here are well acquainted with agricultural practices, due to the difficult terrain and the taboo on women ploughing, they find it hard to manage the cultivation without the support of men.

One of the women interviewed, Durghi Maharani, a Paharia, took the researcher along their daily routes to the well, the fields and the forests. The well was just over ten minutes on foot along a narrow path. Durghi does two trips in the morning and two in the evening, carrying two pots of water on each trip. From the well, we walked across the fields, belonging to the Santals, and into the forest. It was dense, green and very beautiful, but the climb up the hill was steep. Going down the other side, in the middle of the forest, was a little stream, and beside that Durghi and her husband had cleared a small plot of land for cultivation. Some 2 kilometres from their house, it took almost half an hour to reach. They mainly grow pulses. A crop had just been harvested in February and was being carried home on their heads by women and on their shoulders by men.

The Paharias still practise shifting cultivation. For the next year another plot of land was being cleared. While we waited, Durghi collected some wood for fuel, *dantvan* (tooth twigs) for cleaning teeth and *sal* leaves for making plates for home use, which she bundled up to carry. The plot would be cultivated for a year and then left to rejuvenate. The shifting cultivation practised by the Paharias is quite systematic, well planned and not destructive. Durghi apparently makes four to five trips to the forest every day to collect fuelwood, *sal* leaves and other produce. From December to June, the work in the forests peaks, as she must stock fuelwood and *sal* plates for home use and sale during the rainy season when it is difficult to go to the forest. During the monsoons, they are also busy with their own cultivation and agricultural wage labour.

When Durghi takes fuelwood to the Gopikandar market, her husband goes to the weekly Amrapara *haat* (local market) about 20 kilometres away with poles of wood needed for construction work. He can carry four poles, each sold for ten rupees. He leaves the previous evening and stops overnight on the way. The next day, after selling the poles, he returns home by night-time. Though the poles are sold only once a week, he goes to the forest three or four times a week for collecting them, as these too are stored for sale in the monsoon months.

The women market fuelwood as headloads; the men market poles transported on their shoulders. Roles, income and modes of transportation differ for women and men. Women make many more trips to the forest collecting produce for sale and home consumption; men are mainly concerned with collection for sale. Walking is the only form of transportation for both men and women in Jadopani. Very few use bicycles. As the tracks from the village to the roadhead are rocky and steep, it is difficult to balance a loaded bicycle (Figure 9.1).

The intensity of workloads varies with the size and structure of the family. While there is a fairly clear gender division of tasks, these are shared by members of the same sex. In case there is only one woman in the household, the entire burden of household tasks including the collection of water and fuel falls on her. Even house repairs and maintenance, such as coating with a layer of mud, to be done in the summer every year, is entirely the woman's responsibility. She is hence unable to engage in any other forest-related activity.

Figure 9.1 Head-loading firewood along village paths

Source: Photograph by Arundhita Bhanjdeo.

The study of Jadopani village brings to light the intensity of women's daily transport burden, almost six to ten hours spent in collecting water, fuelwood and other forest produce as well as on work in the fields. All household maintenance tasks fall into women's domain. This includes not only housework but also earning income to buy oil and spices. Ostensibly, the men are responsible for providing grains for the family (they are assisted by women in household agriculture), besides wage-labour tasks and the sale of certain kinds of higher-value forest produce. Men's transport burden for marketing may be higher as they walk longer distances, carrying heavier loads, but this is not done daily. The remote location, the poor track and scarcely any means of transportation mean that most tasks have to be carried out on foot by both men and women. There is scope for non-transport interventions like providing a well closer to the upper hamlet to reduce women's transport burden.

Mohalo Village

Mohalo is a roadside village, in Daldali *panchayat*, well connected by bus to both Dumka and Pakur. Four or five overcrowded buses operate each way every day but do not take people with loads. Nearly 50 per cent of the households own a bicycle. The PHC at Gopikandar is reachable by bicycle or bus. Bicycles are also used for going to government offices in the block headquarters, to the market, and for carrying loads of wood for sale. The bicycle is exclusively a male asset.

We were able to meet thirty-four of about sixty households in the village and collect some preliminary information. Of these, twenty-nine were Santal, four Paharia and one from a higher caste. Most of the households had some land but were unable to cultivate it properly; twelve households had leased out a part of their lands, often forced to do so as collateral for loans taken from moneylenders. In all, twenty-one households were indebted, mostly for purposes of seed or consumption. Wage labour and migration, however, are not high in this village.

In Mohalo, both men and women go to the forest for collecting fuelwood, which is sold in the local *haat*. This is a major aspect of their household economy. Women are primarily responsible for collection of water, food preparation and household maintenance. The four handpumps on the road are often in disrepair, so the women have to go to the stream 2 kilometres away. There are also two wells located near the stream. Men graze the cattle in the fields near the village and chop and bundle the wood for sale in the markets. Depending on the size and composition of the household, several men also assist their wives in a few household tasks such as cooking and childcare. If they have a bicycle, they play a more active role in marketing, otherwise they go along with the women to the weekly market. Both men and women carry two loads of fuelwood 10 kilometres to the local weekly market at Kharoni. Some men take daily bicycle-loads 19 kilometres to Pakuria. They get ten to twelve rupees for a load at Pakuria and eight rupees at Kharoni. The men often get harassed by the Forest Department officials and, if caught, end up paying a fine of 150 rupees.

We accompanied one couple, Barsa Kisku and Lukhi Marandi, on their daily trip to collect firewood. The forest is 6 kilometres from the village, and it took almost an hour to get to the hilltop. A forest adjacent to the village is being protected by the villagers themselves for the future, and fuelwood collection is not allowed here. All the households collect fuelwood from the hilltop plot, which had been marked by the Paharias for cultivation. In shifting cultivation, vegetation is cut but generally not uprooted, so the forest regenerates fast. The couple spent several hours cutting the wood, arranging and bundling the long pieces. The woman then took the *heavier* bundle on her head, and the man the lighter one on his shoulder. The logic of this is that on a steep slope it is difficult to maintain one's balance with a shoulder load, and men are unable to carry the wood on their heads.

It was quite an experience watching the couple slowly finding their way down, holding onto roots and stems for balance. When there was difficulty maneuvering due to the thick vegetation, the husband following behind helped by moving the bushes and branches so the woman could pass. At one point there were steep rocks. The couple had to put their loads down. The woman went first, and then her husband slowly passed the bundle. She pulled it down, balanced it against a tree, then put it on her head again. It was a treacherous journey down the hill, and the couple moved slowly and carefully. They rested only after we reached the plain land outside the forest. At this stage the man untied his sandals from the bundle of wood and put them on. The woman did not have any footwear.

We had started for the forest at 11 a.m. By the time we returned, it was 4 p.m. The couple's children were at home, and though young, they were habituated to the absence of their parents as going to the forest was a daily routine. After returning home, the woman started on her household chores, while her husband settled down to the task of cutting the logs and preparing bundles that could be carried to the market the following day. The sale is done by both the man and woman. Lukhi goes only to one weekly *haat* at Kharoni. Her husband uses his bicycle to sell wood thrice a week at Pakuria, taking two bundles on each trip. At the rate of ten rupees per bundle, he earns 60 rupees per week from the sale of fuel wood.

Some men who own bicycles, even go daily to sell wood, leaving the task of collection to other family members. Most of the Santal men use their bicycles only for carrying firewood to the local markets. Several non-tribal traders purchase the loads and then transport these to the district headquarters, Dumka, where they are sold at almost double the price. The Santals are afraid of harassment by police and forest guards, as the sale of fuelwood is illegal (despite this being the mainstay of their livelihood). The non-tribals are more confident of handling such situations. Market access for produce is therefore not only determined by access to transport, but also by complex social relations based on gender, caste and class, as also other factors such as the number of working women and men in the household.

This village study of Mohalo, like Jadopani, shows the importance of the household structure and gender relations in determining the relative transport burdens of men and women. In the case of a nuclear family, it is not enough for the man to undertake only the marketing function; he has also to help and support the woman in collecting forest produce for sale. This is, however, not the case in larger households with more than one adult woman, where the women take care of the forest-related activities, while the men are more likely to be engaged in agriculture or wage work, only providing assistance in marketing if required.

An attempt was made in this village to understand whether the phenomenon of bicycle-loading of fuelwood by men had affected intra-household relationships in any way, and if so how. This exploration is quite important as traditionally the collection and sale of forest produce has been in the women's domain. As a consequence, the income from forest produce, too, has been women's income. With men doing the selling, have expenditure priorities changed? Have decision-making roles changed? Is the society becoming more patriarchal?

In the case of Barsa Kisku, after selling the wood at Pakuria, he usually buys rice, vegetables, pulses, oil and spices for the house. Having two young children, he realises the importance of proper care and food for them and also helps Lukhi with childcare and cooking. This seemed to be the rule rather than the exception amongst the head-loaders of this village. In one household, Budhan Hembrum actually makes two trips to the Kharoni *haat* on market day so that he can reduce the trips to Pakuria and go on more days to the forest to collect firewood. By and large, the men do spend the money earned through the sale of firewood on household necessities, but the women no longer have access to cash for any of their personal expenses. If there is a surplus, the men spend it on their own needs or sometimes on alcohol.

Being as yet a recent phenomenon, it is difficult to comment on the long-term implications of the shift of marketing functions to men, in terms both of women's mobility and status within Santal society. While losing direct control over income, at the moment at least, it is a relief in terms of workloads and transport burdens for already overworked women. How best they are able to negotiate intra-household gender relations in the future to maintain their position of relative equality would be worth watching.

Pandhini Duma village

Pandhini Duma is a small village of twenty-three Santal households. The road to the village is poorly maintained. A daily jeep service connects the village to Dumka. There is plenty of land in the village, and the primary occupation is agriculture. The bulk of the land, however, is upland, and not very productive. The paddy-growing lowlands are limited. The village headman has a large family and only about 3 *bigha*s of paddy land. He provided deep insights into the process of land alienation in the village, with most of the lowlands being transferred to non-resident non-tribals about a hundred years ago. He blamed the Paharia tribe for destroying the forests. Now the women had to walk more than 5 kilometres for fuelwood.

In a listing of thirteen households available in the village at the time of the study, we found a third of them very poor and perpetually indebted to the moneylender. Four households had taken loans for seed, household and medical expenses at an interest rate of 50 per cent for six months. In the absence of a primary school in the village, only two out of thirty-three children go to school. Women from six of the households migrate seasonally to labour on West Bengal's irrigated paddy lands. Three men accompany the women, ostensibly to protect them! The major reason for migrating in mixed groups is the increased incidence of physical harassment and violence on women when they travel alone.

When we reached the village in the morning, it was deserted. Several couples were working on the threshing floor on the village outskirts, and many of the women had gone to the forest. Around noon, groups of women and girls started returning from the forests. Firewood collection takes five to six hours, so they must leave home around 6 a.m. The women go to the forests almost every day in order to store fuelwood for their consumption during the rains. Any surplus is sold in the weekly market. This is not very common any more, as collection itself is a difficult task. One man who had gone with his wife was bringing the fuelwood back on a bicycle, but this was not easy on an uneven path. The women also collect some *sal* leaves to use as plates at home.

There are some open-cast coal fields about 10 kilometres away. Several men go there regularly, cut the coal and bring it for use at home, as well as for sale. A bag of coal sells for 50 rupees in the local market. It sells for 150 rupees in Dumka, but they rarely go to Dumka as the effort is too great and the road bad. Most men who go to the coal fields own bicycles and use them for transporting bags of coal. Of the thirteen households studied, nine had bicycles; one household had two and another three. This is directly related to the number of adult males in the household. Women have no access to the bicycles.

Several people from the village now migrate to Bengal seasonally in groups of about ten. They take the jeep to Dumka and the bus from there to Bengal. On other occasions, they take a bus from the next village, 3 kilometres away, but when migrating they carry luggage including a few pots and pans, so the jeep is preferred. The regular jeep users, however, are the non-tribal traders and professionals such as schoolteachers or nurses working in the area.

A detailed study of the gender division of tasks revealed that contrary to one's perception of rural life, both men and women here arose at 4 a.m. The men took the cattle to graze around the village; the women cleaned the house, brought water and cooked the morning meal. The well is close by; yet they have to collect six to eight pots of water, and this takes more than half an hour. The grain had just been harvested in January. By the time the men returned, the women had finished their household chores. After having a light meal, both the men and women went to the threshing floor, about 1 kilometre outside the village. For almost the entire day they thresh, collect the grain, bundle the chaff and transport it home. This is seasonal work and completed in a few days. In this village, the exclusive task for women is going to the jungle and for men to the coal fields. The distances are nearly the same, and the loads as heavy, but men use bicycles and the women walk.

Maino Hembrum is a widow who lives with her two children, a daughter aged twenty and a son aged seventeen. During the study, Maino's daughter was in Bengal, where she had gone for the harvest work. When asked to describe a day in her life, the first response was that it varies with the season. In rural India, particularly the Santal Parganas, life changes drastically in each season with the change in availability of forest produce, employment, and so on. At this time, Maino gets up in the morning and quickly finishes with cooking and cleaning the house. She then goes thrice to the well, fetching two pots of water each time. During the summer months, this well dries up, and then she has to go 3 kilometres away to fetch water. When her daughter is at home, she helps with this work. By 7 a.m., Maino is ready to go to the threshing floor. The straw has to be bundled up and brought home. If she does four to five trips every day, this task is completed within a week.

Maino does not migrate to Bengal, but she regularly looks for wage labour, both agricultural and non-agricultural, in a large village, Dando,

2 kilometres away. Though they have some fields, she does not spend too much time on their own cultivation. The output is always low as the lands are not of very good quality. In labour work she can earn up to twenty rupees per day and one snack of puffed rice. It is almost 8 kilometres into the interior of the forest, so she goes only once or twice a week to collect fuelwood (mostly for home consumption) and *sal* leaves for making leaf plates. Going to the forest virtually takes the whole day. If she does not go out to work as a labourer, she makes leaf plates at home. When a sufficient number are made, she sells them to any trader passing by rather than going to the market for this purpose. Maino's son has a bicycle and uses it for getting coal. At the time of the study, he was helping his mother with agricultural work, so he was not going to the coal field. He usually goes once or twice a week, and then the earnings from coal are sufficient for their weekly provisions of oil, spices, pulses and vegetables.

As in the other villages, the composition and size of the family makes a lot of difference to the women's workload, which is shared more equally by same-sex members of a household. It is also possible to reduce transport burdens, and hence the women's transport needs, indirectly by providing infrastructure and services, such as a reliable source of drinking water within the village. Though most households in the village have bicycles, as in Mohalo, this is exclusively a male asset. Some women travel long distances but never ride a bicycle, which could substantially reduce their commuting time to work sites in neighbouring villages. This has never been discussed till now.

Issues and Lessons

Employment and Transport

Women's livelihood strategies, employment opportunities and related transport needs are seasonal (Table 9.3). From November to May, people depend on the collection and sale of forest produce (which is more diverse in Jadopani and restricted to fuelwood in Mohalo). The rest of the year they depend on their own cultivation and some wage work. Their transport needs are more local in nature, from the village to the forests, fields and markets. In Pandhini Duma, however, there seems to be a greater dependence on wage work and seasonal migration as part of livelihood strategies. As

Table 9.3 Seasonality in employment

Month	Jadopani	Mohalo	Pandhini Duma
January	Sohrai festival, firewood collection	Festivals (Sohrai) and celebrations	Sohrai festival, migration to Bengal
February	Sal seeds and sal leaf plates	Firewood collection, wage work	Digging soil, wage labour
March	Mahua, sal leaf plates	Mahua collection	Wage work
April	Mahua, leaf plates	Mahua, leaf plates, mango, tendu	Digging soil, collecting coal
May	Mahua kernel, kendu leaves, sal leaf plates, fruits, non-agricultural work	Mahua kernel, leaf plate, mango, firewood	Own cultivation
June	Own cultivation, agricultural labour, vegetables	Own cultivation, mahua kernel	Own cultivation, agricultural wage labour
July	Own cultivation, maize harvest, wild vegetable, mushroom	Own cultivation, wage work,	Own cultivation, migration to Bengal
August	Firewood, leaf plates and mushrooms	Own cultivation, vegetables	Harvest of maize
September	Harvest work	Own cultivation, firewood	Paddy harvest
October	Own harvest, agricultural labour	Own harvest, wage work, firewood	Agricultural labour, own cultivation
November	Agricultural labour, harvest, firewood	Own cultivation, wage work, firewood, leaf plates	Migration to Bengal
December	Post-harvest work, firewood, leaf plates	Own cultivation, wage work, firewood, leaf plates	Migration to Bengal

seen in the village profile, trips to the forest are necessary, but due to the distance, forest produce is no longer a source of earnings, though it does provide support for household subsistence. The search for wage work and outside sources for earning incomes leads to a need for long-distance transport to surrounding villages, the coal fields or still further, as in the winter for migration.

The daily and more regular journeys of women are to the forests, fields and markets, as well as to the source of water, whether well, stream or handpump. Women in this region mainly carry loads on their heads, whether from the forests and fields or to the markets. Fodder collection is not one of their tasks, as the cattle are largely left to graze in the fields and forests. In some cases, for wage work particularly, the journeys may be to neighbouring villages and towns or, in the case of migration, to more distant destinations.

Household Structure and Transport

An issue that emerges strongly from this study is the relationship of household size and composition with the transport needs and burdens of different members of the household, both women and men. The transport needs are actually a corollary of the gender division of tasks and responsibilities. The tasks of women and men are quite distinct in most instances, with men responsible for providing the basic grains and women for all other household maintenance functions, including finding food supplements. There is, however, a practice of sharing tasks among members of the same sex and also among men and women in nuclear families. The exception is ploughing, an exclusive preserve of men, which makes it difficult for women-headed households to engage in agriculture in the absence of an adult male. It is possible to hire male labour, but this is not reliable in terms of availability, and it also depends on the household's ability to make cash payments for labour. In this rural forest-centred economy, more hands or a joint family, especially with a larger number of women, actually appears to be more beneficial than a nuclear family in terms of sharing tasks and transport burdens.

Transport Provision

Transport interventions have been few. The state provisioning has primarily related to road construction and setting up bus routes. These address the needs of the market rather than the transport needs of village women in performing their daily tasks. Even where transport services do exist, as in Mohalo, the women, or for that matter even men, with loads, are not allowed in the buses. In Pandhini Duma, the major users of the daily jeep service to Dumka were non-tribal traders and professionals such as schoolteachers who needed to commute to the villages. It was rarely used by the local tribals, the one exception being in the case of transport needs for migration.

The Regional Transport Authority (RTA), located in Dumka and headed by the Divisional Commissioner as its ex-officio chairperson, enjoys full powers with regard to the issue of route permits and other control measures. Some of the stated criteria for decision-making by the RTA are: (*a*) routes are decided mainly according to public need and demand; (*b*) the bus owner's views on the profitability of the route are taken into account; and (*c*) the RTA invites applications from bus owners for different routes; however, they are also free to suggest new routes. As the Bihar State Road Transport Corporation does not respond to applications, in practice the RTA deals primarily with private owners and accommodates many of their demands. The profitability of routes for private owners thus tends to get more weightage than public need. This implies that the routes are developed in response to the needs of the market rather than of the local people. The RTA, however, fixes and monitors the fares for the region, which according to them are lower than elsewhere in Bihar.

It is clear from the list of routes that very few buses are intended to connect the interiors with the towns. Moreover, even where these routes exist, they are not operational. For the sake of the permit, many bus owners have taken the interior routes, but ply only on the main road. This was also unofficially confirmed by the District Transport Officer. According to a bus owner, it was difficult to ply on the permitted routes, due to poor road conditions in the interior areas of the district. He further felt that the women head-loaders preferred to walk to the markets even if there was a bus on the route in order to save money. At Mohalo, however, we learned the contrary.

In case of the informal transport interventions such as the introduction and use of bicycles to reduce the burden of head-loading, this too has not directly benefitted women. First, the area being very poor, and the society basically patriarchal, the acquisition of any asset goes first to the men. While this has meant that the task of taking the loads to the market is gradually shifting to the men wherever they own bicycles, the impact of this is as yet not very clear. While most of the men interviewed do spend the money earned from the sale of the forest produce in the markets on household necessities, women lose direct control over the income. As the cash does not come into their hands, they are unable to save for emergencies or utilise it for their personal expenses. The women, however, continue with the task of collection from the forest on foot as the steep and narrow paths make bicycles difficult to use.

Areas for Policy Intervention

Transport for Collection Needs

Given the region's difficult terrain, it may not be possible to address many of women's transport needs through transport interventions alone. Attempts to protect and regenerate village forests, as is being done in Mohalo, could help in reducing transport burdens relating to the collection of forest produce in the future. Improving the field paths and providing small carts or wheelbarrows could ease the burden of carrying loads, mainly seeds and the harvested crop. As agriculture is mostly rain-fed and manured by free-grazing cattle, other inputs are low. If, however, one projects the transport needs in a context of possible changes in agricultural practices (with agriculture becoming the mainstay of rural livelihoods), then these needs too would arise.

Transport for Market Needs

The issue of linkages to distant markets needs to be seriously addressed. Bicycles are, of course, one option, but as discussed in the village case studies, access to bicycles does not necessarily mean access to the best markets or access to all irrespective of gender, caste and class relations. The non-tribal traders carry wood and coal to market in Dumka town, but the Santals are unable to do so, constrained by poverty, lack of capital and resources, and unequal social relations. Even among the Santals, the men with bicycles have greater freedom to stay away from the house for longer periods of time, fewer household maintenance responsibilities and access to better markets than the women. Having to return home as soon as possible, with no staying power and no access to transport, Santal women also get the lowest prices for their produce. From this broader perspective, sensitive to poverty, development and social relations, there are several options:

1. Special bus trips on market days for women carrying loads: In Kerala, where women fish vendors (with wet and smelly loads) were not allowed to board regular buses, such a special service is being provided to help them bring fish from the harbour into town.
2. Collectivisation of marketing: Collective sale of the produce of several people is extensively practised by traders who go from house to house in a village, collecting leaf plates, fruits, mushrooms, and

so on, from the women and taking these by bicycles or vans to the market. Women receive a lower price when they sell the produce to such traders. The Santal women are experienced marketers, and it may be possible for them to transport their produce (other than fuelwood because of its bulk) to market through a collective arrangement. Indeed, this might increase their bargaining power in the market vis-à-vis other market forces.

3. Improvement of paths: The road construction policy has mainly linked towns and market villages with each other. Roadside villages, such as Mohalo, have benefitted, but more by accident than intention. Even a market-driven policy has to pay greater attention to improving the paths connecting interior villages, such as Jadopani, with the main roadhead. In such a case, even if state-run buses cannot be provided to all villages, people have the option of hiring their own transport.

4. Transport for social needs: The state of health care is dismal in this area, with several deaths due to malaria or diarrhoea each year. The staff of the network of health sub-centres find it difficult to regularly visit the villages under their jurisdiction due to the distances from the roadhead and lack of transport. Not many 'professionals' are prepared to spend hours walking to the villages concerned. If at least the paths were improved, more people might be able to use bicycles or motorcycles. It would also be easier to bring sick people from the village to the PHC.

Conclusion

This study has highlighted several significant features regarding women's mobility, transport needs provisioning and gender relations in the forest-dependent villages of Dumka district. First, despite a clear gender division of roles and activities, particularly in household maintenance functions (collecting drinking water, fuel for home consumption, cleaning and cooking are primarily women's tasks), both men and women are equally engaged in the collection of forest produce for sale. Second, the rigid gender division of household tasks is largely mediated by the size and structure of the family. In a nuclear family, men do take on several roles, particularly cooking and childcare. It is notable, however, that men usually do not undertake tasks such as collecting water, which involves a transport burden over a distance. Third, existing transport provisions mainly cater to the needs of the market and particularly to the needs of professionals commuting to work or trade between markets. Apart from the long-distance transport needs of Santal women and men, for local or migrant wage employment, other transportation needs for marketing forest produce are not addressed. Bicycles are slowly emerging as a mode of transport, but without well-maintained paths and infrastructure, their use is limited. At present, they are also essentially male assets.

Given this situation, a combination of non-transport interventions (for providing basic services such as water, education and healthcare facilities in the villages) along with innovative transport and organisational interventions are urgently required to ease the transport burdens of the local Santal population, particularly for the women, without adversely affecting gender relations. The present role shift in the marketing of certain forest produce, from women to men with bicycles, has reduced women's transport and time burdens but has meant that women have lost control over the income from the sale of such produce, which they continue to collect. Clearly, transport interventions have a complex impact on gender relations, people's livelihoods and natural resource management practice.

Notes

1. The Santal Parganas were part of Bihar till the formation of Jharkhand.
2. In this system (different from *gharjawae*), the son-in-law stays in the wife's village for a certain number of years.

References

Rana, K., and N. Rao. 1996. 'Gross Injustice'. *Hindustan Times*, 17 October.
Rao, N. (ed.). 1999. *Owning Their Land: Rights of Santhali Women*. New Delhi: Friedrich Ebert Stiftung.

10

Mothers, Daughters and Well-Being

Contentment and Conflict amongst the Santals*

Research on 'well-being'[1] has progressed from an exclusive focus on individual, 'objective' outcomes (such as literacy and schooling, health and nutrition, and the ability to work and earn an income, as conceptualised in the *Human Development Report*) to being 'a process that comprises material, relational and subjective dimensions' (White, 2010: 170). Varying with history, geography, across time, space and life cycle, the concept of well-being captures the dynamics of the relationships between these different elements in people's lives (White, 2010: 170).

However, a focus on binaries of poverty–wealth, well-being–ill-being, happiness–unhappiness persists in development discourses. Efforts to move people out of poverty (Narayan, 2009) often stress the material dimensions of people's lives, ignoring the relational, emotional and non-material, which are equally important for a person's well-being.

Families are major sites of gendered socialisation during childhood. Children observe the actions of their parents and as they grow older are socialised into gender roles, learning and reproducing, but sometimes challenging, particular roles and responsibilities. Relationships are crucial in this process – with parents, siblings, peers and others. One of the key concerns expressed by parents relates to the life chances and future well-being

---

*This chapter was originally published in *Disciplinary Dialogue on Social Change: Gender, Early Childhood and Theatre* © Nitya Rao 2016. All rights reserved. Reproduced with the permission of the copyright holder and the publishers, Centre for Women's Development Studies (CWDS), an autonomous research institute supported by the Indian Council of Social Science Research (ICSSR), New Delhi.

of their children. The normative expectation of 'maternal altruism', where mothers are primarily responsible for the care of children and maintenance of the household, however, poses a dilemma for women. While the well-being of her children is indeed a very important priority for a mother, she has to make choices: how far can she really be herself, how important is it to socialise the child, especially the daughter, to lead a life without bearing some of her own trials and tribulations, or is it preferable to sacrifice her own identity and possibly emotional well-being for the sake of the material well-being of her children and gaining a life of peace (*cf.* Ahmed, 2014)? Women have to negotiate functional boundaries and work out the extent to which deviations are permissible, within the larger context of patriarchy. When my own daughter was born, a dear friend of the family, now no more, sent me a congratulatory card, in which she wrote, 'Never stop being yourself for the sake of your daughter. She will appreciate you for who you are, not what you gave up for her sake'.[2]

While there has been a lot of attention to the mother–son relationship, especially in the context of debates around son preference in India, less is known about the mother–daughter relationship, perhaps because of its plurality, ambivalence and continuities (Hirsch, 1981), and the fear of exposing our pain, longing, nostalgia and struggles to retain our own identity. What little exists relates to urban, middle- or upper-class, educated women, able to reflect on and write about their lives and relationships.

In this chapter, I seek to add to this literature, exploring the relationships between mothers and daughters, and how it contributes to the shaping of well-being for both. While conscious of my own positionality as an urban, educated woman, and informed by my own experiences and relationships with both my mother and daughter, this chapter is based on long-term, ethnographic work amongst the Santals in Dumka district, Jharkhand. It focuses specifically on unpacking the gender norms in relation to notions of 'reciprocity' amongst the Santals. As I explore in this chapter, patrilineal inheritance practices relating to property and identity intensify the dilemmas and contradictions mothers and daughters face (Rao, 2008). A social context of male dominance reflected in institutions, both formal and informal, and relationships, force women to choose between the material and emotional aspects of relationships, especially vis-à-vis their daughters, at particular moments in time.

Yet the relationship is an important one because while material resources are exchanged between fathers and sons, a lot of the business of social reproduction takes place between mothers (or indeed fathers) and daughters. At times of ill-health or crises, daughters are called upon to support their parents, not just as an obligation, but as the result of a relationship built on notions of reciprocity and care, on emotional rather than material foundations. At the collective level, we have examples from the anti-dowry movement in urban, middle-class India which encouraged parents to take their daughters' voices seriously (Sen, 1994), treat them as one of their own, rather than *paraya dhan* (someone else's property). At a more individual level, my own research amongst *dalit*s in Tamil Nadu revealed daughters' willingness to support their mothers, often abused, both financially and emotionally (Rao, 2014).

After briefly explaining the methodology and setting the context in the next section, I explore a few key dimensions relating to mother–daughter relationships conceptually and their links to well-being, before offering some tentative conclusions.

Methodology and Context

This chapter is informed by long-term associations built over fifteen years, in two villages, in different agro-ecological settings of Dumka district – one in the plains and one in hilly, forested terrain (Rao, 2008). Dumka district, the headquarters of the Santal Parganas division, has a majority Santal population. Despite small improvements, Santal literacy rates remain far below those of other social groups (Census, 2011; see Table 1.1). Poverty and food insecurity are high. Santal women participate equally with their men in agriculture and other productive activities involving engagement with both labour and product markets. Mainly small-scale farmers, poor-quality land, inadequate water (except during the monsoons) and lack of inputs have led to agriculture remaining low in productivity. Malnutrition and indebtedness are near-universal, and growing Maoism (an ultra-left, violent resistance movement) in the district has further restricted employment opportunities locally. Seasonal migration is rampant for both men and women – men often for longer periods to more distant locations in north India (see Chapter 6).

Inheritance is patrilineal and residence generally patrilocal. There are instances where the husband stays in his wife's village for a certain period of time or even a lifetime (see Chapter 3). The Santal customs in fact describe seven forms of marriage, ranging from arranged marriage and simple remarriage (following widowhood or separation) to elopement. Separation is common, with almost a third of the women and men I encountered in their second or third marital relationship. Separation could be initiated by either men or women, and the causes often seemed insignificant. Women even mentioned their sense of not being valued or loved by the husband as a cause for separation (see Chapter 2).

The high levels of marital mobility reflect a situation where women stand up for their rights, their dignity and their spaces, demanding mutuality in marriage. But in a patriarchal society, this often leads to parting with the children, with a potential negative effect on their own sense of well-being. While sons are left with the father, daughters are moved to the maternal grandparents or maternal uncle. In one stroke, in such situations the daughter loses both parents. There is a loss of trust, a letting down, in a psycho-emotional sense, but this also has material implications – in terms of her education, the food she gets and the work she has to do in her new home. Motherhood then is perhaps the one element that could lead to compromise in an unhappy conjugal relationship.

In this chapter, I also draw on a specific piece of research on well-being, conducted with households with three living generations of men and women, in 2006–07. Thirty-one households were identified in the two clusters of villages. While all Santal, the sample is skewed in favour of the educated, often Christian, and those with regular employment, usually as teachers in state schools. Life expectancy is lower amongst the poor, those dependent on agriculture or wage labour, making three generations hard to find in these households.

A hundred and thirty-eight people (sixty-one men and seventy-seven women) were interviewed. The numbers reveal excess male mortality, especially in the oldest generation. In fact, there were not more than a handful of men above the age of forty-five in the more remote, hilly cluster of villages, pointing to the importance of location in mediating the relationship between the personal and the material. The interviews began with questions on the individual's view on happiness and life satisfaction, and were followed up with questions on various dimensions of well-being such as work, assets, education, health, marital relations, social standing, politics, identity and others that they raised. Each interview took close to two hours.

The responses were ambiguous, especially in relation to feelings of happiness or unhappiness. For instance, for men, their sense of happiness and satisfaction with life was linked to appreciation of the efforts they were making in fulfilling their 'provider' roles – namely ensuring the food security of their family. In a context of rain-fed agriculture, high rates of indebtedness and lack of inputs, this was not guaranteed, but conditional on nature, their efforts and relationships. The uncertain realities of people's lives points to the problems of averaging across indicators to arrive at indices such as the gross national happiness index. Mooted first by the Kingdom of Bhutan to emphasise the importance of the environment and people's psychological well-being and community relationships, and not just economic or material development, it nevertheless masks differences within communities and over time. Further, people's priorities shift in accordance with their positionality (economic and social) and stage in the course of life.

Women placed importance on reciprocity and status, which included both material and emotional support vis-à-vis their larger family. Reciprocity for them includes support to parents, grandparents, siblings, children and grandchildren both in financial or material terms, as well as love, care and affection. It also includes the absence of quarrels and conflicts within the family. Status includes the ability to work, to earn, to have a stable job, to accumulate assets, have children and successfully overcome adversity and difficulties. While men too laid emphasis on their children's well-being, for them it was linked to educational attainments, performance in school and the ability to get a job. Women articulated a more general notion of their children doing well, including their education, their ability to get good marriage partners, their ability to get a job and have a happy family life.

In this chapter, I focus particularly on the nature, meanings and construction of reciprocity and status in the mother–daughter relationship. I give voice to women, both mothers and daughters, telling their stories without imposing any value judgement on their actions or emotions.

Understanding the Mother–Daughter Relationship

A key role for a woman is that of a mother. The biology of childbearing is in many ways seen to be responsible for the gendering of roles and division of work in society. Women are typically seen to be more concerned with private lives and reproducing the family, and men with public spaces of decision-making, politics and engaging with the markets. The central role of motherhood in women's lives has been held responsible for the subordination of women (Edholm, Harris and Young, 1977). While not devaluing motherhood per se, examples of women resisting social domination in myriad ways and in 'everyday' forms, often very subtle, point to the need to question some of these stereotypes. Through the case studies presented in this chapter, I demonstrate how women manipulate patriarchy, accepting certain elements to resist others.

At a more collective level, too, the women's movement has been struggling to gain recognition for women as 'persons', refuting the idea of a family as existing by 'nature' (cf. Ortner, 1974). There is nothing innate about biology, traditions, necessity or norms that make women better placed to provide love and care compared to other members of the household (Nussbaum, 2000). While the family does have virtues, emotions, attachments and affiliations are central human capabilities (Nussbaum, 2000), and it is hard to imagine ourselves as separate, individuated selves. The family, however, can be a major site of oppression – of violence and abuse, of potential discrimination and gender inequality in nutrition, health and educational opportunities. Recognising this duality in the role of the family as a source of solidarity as well as neglect, the women's movement in India has raised their voices for reproductive choices and rights on the one hand, while demanding social support especially in terms of childcare services on the other.

Rich (1976), by pointing to the silence around the mother–daughter relationship in her controversial work, set off considerable feminist, interdisciplinary work on this theme. While the mother–child relationship is perhaps the essential human relationship, it is often blamed for the domestication, confinement and subordination of women across contexts. As a result, it has contributed to a burden of maternal guilt, a constant reviewing of whether they have failed their children or could have done better.

What then is meant by the nurture of daughters? At one level, it is trust and tenderness, a love not of the old 'sacrificial' kind, but rather one that shows courage. While there is no end to the limits that society imposes on women, the most important thing one woman can do for another is to expand her sense of possibilities, her understanding of choices that she can make and the implications of these. It is important for the mother 'to refuse to be a victim' (Rich, 1976: 246). This in fact corresponds to the concept of well-being, which is seen to ultimately be about people's goals and aspirations, and about the choices they make in trying to achieve these goals (cf. Gough, McGregor and Camfield, 2007). The quality of the mother's life and her struggle to expand the surrounding spaces demonstrates to her daughter that these possibilities exist. Yet the struggle for physical survival, a reality for many poor women in India, and the Santals, demonstrating the fighting spirit to their daughters almost always means absence, even long-term separation from the child. It may involve migration for work; it may also mean leaving the child with a maternal uncle or grandparents during their critical growing-up years.

There is likely to be the deepest love but also the most painful estrangement between mothers and their daughters, a shared knowledge, but also a desire to be free of each other (Hirsch, 1981). The collection of oral testimonies from working-class or lower-middle-class (British) women reveals how many women hated their mothers for constantly being tired, overworked and oppressed, yet doing exactly the same vis-à-vis their daughters (McCrindle and Rowbotham, 1977: 4). If mothers were strong and independent, resisted their domestication and subordination, this too appeared selfish and was construed as neglect by the daughter, especially in her early years – more so, if the daughters ended up in mothering roles vis-à-vis their younger siblings. In retrospect, many of them saw these same actions as worthy of respect.

The birth of a daughter is not celebrated in most communities across India. For the mother, it can have several consequences – from the extreme and painful act of infanticide, to, more commonly, a period of neglect, and in some circumstances of being devalued as a wife, having to accept another wife or even separation. Sona's mother[3] recounts how the most difficult time in her life was when she gave birth to her third daughter – the failure to produce a son almost put her future in jeopardy. Fortunately for her, the next child was a son. The relationship with daughters then is often conflictual, but also changes over a lifetime. While some see closeness developing in later years (Fischer, 1986), others see this period as more demanding and difficult (Barnett, 1988). In their study of a group of adult, employed daughters, between the ages of twenty-five and fifty-five, Barnett et al. (1991) found that quality of the daughter–mother relationship significantly impacted the daughter's subjective well-being and levels of distress. The same probably holds true for the mother.

Gulati and Bagchi (2005), exploring the lives of educated Indian women, including many academics, isolate several key elements in mother–daughter relationships. First of all, given the engagement of women with a large number of kin, it often became difficult to disentangle the relationship of oneself with one's own parent. Secondly, while several of these women made hard choices in terms of their careers as well as family life, the sense of satisfaction or happiness they express emerges not just from 'externally recognised success', but rather from having 'established a sphere of autonomy where they could make decisions that nurture themselves as well as others'

(Gulati and Bagchi, 2005: 10). What many of these women remember is the strength of their own mothers and grandmothers in dealing with both family crisis such as the death of a husband and related internal dynamics, as well as external social change. This included risky ventures such as negotiating with the bureaucracy and police in refugee camps after partition or providing shelter to Muslim strangers from across the border.

An important defining moment for women, especially in a patrilineal, patrilocal context, is marriage – preparing the daughter for marriage (which implies also a break in daily contact with people with whom she is closest), arranging the marriage and post-marriage support. Despite the rhetoric around the sanctity of marriage, numerous examples of failed marriages exist, influencing in turn the relationship between mother and daughter. It becomes a test of their support and understanding for each other. Children are their proudest accomplishment; yet relations with children are often distorted due to their own lack of personal space as well as voice in influencing marriage decisions (Gulati and Bagchi, 2005: 19).

When speaking to women in the field, what commonly emerged was the coexistence of love and resentment. In isolating the causes of resentment, one is confronted by the contradictions inherent in patriarchy – the gendered access to resources it entails – and the choices it then poses in fulfilling material expectations. As some of the stories reflect, when mothers resist patriarchy and are punished through material deprivations, the daughters instead of challenging the structures of patriarchy, challenge or resent their mother. The notions of 'maternal deprivation' are constituted not just of material deprivation but also the feeling of helplessness to support one's child, particularly one's daughter. It is this contradictory element in women's relationships within patriarchy, the ways in which female experiences (both of mothers and daughters) are shaped by male structures (Hirsch, 1981), which are explored in the rest of this chapter. The purpose is to highlight how 'well-being happens in relationships' (White, 2010: 171), the implications of relational shifts for women's emotional well-being and in turn ensuring their basic human capabilities (to use Nussbaum's phrase).

Perceptions of Reciprocity: Insights from the Field

The tensions between marital fulfilment and motherhood in a Santal woman's life play out most significantly in the relationships they build with their daughters, in material terms at least, as sons are expected to be taken care of by their fathers. I start this section with a focus on the feelings and emotions of the daughter, which range from hatred to resentment, from understanding to intimacy, often changing over time, depending on how their own futures work out. In presenting these cases, I explore the interlinkages between material, personal and relational aspects of well-being that they highlight. I then turn to the perspective of the mother.

Hating Her Mother

Sheela, aged sixty-five, is a retired primary school teacher. She is educated, soft-spoken, helpful and reflective, well-liked by most people in the village. In 2010, she was elected *sarpanch* (head or leader) of her village local government (*panchayat*). I lived with her family in the village, and she became one of my closest friends. Her narration of her relationship with her mother, whom she hated, was poignant. Sheela's father, a schoolteacher, earned a meagre salary of 60 rupees per month. Yet he had four wives. The eldest had a daughter; Sheela was born to the second. The third wife had three children, and the fourth did not stay long with her father, finding the situation oppressive. While the social system allows polygyny, clearly this is not straightforward for the women concerned. Some may accept and adjust, while others resent the apparent absence of love and reciprocity from their spouse.

They were poor, her father did not have much land, and this too was disputed by his brothers. Yet he insisted on educating all his children. Sheela and her elder sister (by his first wife) studied for a year or two in the local village school and were then admitted to the Moharo Mission School. Her father paid the fees, even though they had often to cut down on the food they ate at home. She recalled how other children would bring snacks from home to the hostel, but she never brought any. Both sisters studied hard, and ultimately both got jobs as teachers.

When her father married a third time, her own mother got upset and started demanding a share of the property for her upkeep. Sheela begged her mother not to insist, as this would affect their household condition and potentially her education. Yet her mother persisted in her claims creating a permanent rift between them. While deep down she resented the social system which allowed polygyny, her anger was directed at her mother, whose actions (challenging her husband) potentially affected her personal interests. When she came home from school, she had to listen to the bantering of her stepmother who resented the fees being paid for Sheela's education. She grew up hating her mother, yet admiring her father for his commitment to education and to treating all the children equally.

Sheela felt that even though she was the only child, her mother preferred to take advice from others, harming their family's well-being in the process. After Sheela got married, her mother came and stayed with them, cultivating her share of the marital land. Sheela was annoyed, but being the only child of her mother, she could not throw her out of the house. She apologised to her father for the behaviour of her mother, as the relationship with her father was central to her well-being. After his retirement in 1980, with failing health, her father and his third wife came and lived with them for six years, and this gave her an opportunity to reciprocate her feelings for him. Just the fact that her stepmother looked after her father until his death has enabled a shared intimacy between them. She still visits her stepmother, who lives on the outskirts of Dumka town (with her son). She also takes pride in maintaining a range of relationships and affiliations, especially with her siblings: her sister, with whom she studied, was also her closest confidante. Her brothers, all employed, maintain cordial relationships and visit her occasionally.

This narrative of a fragile, emotional relationship is not due to marital mobility but reflects the tension of being in a polygynous household. When her father married a third time, if her mother had left him and moved away, perhaps Sheela's future would have taken a different turn. She may not have been able to continue her education; she may have had to work in the home of her maternal grandparents (as Maki's daughter Surajmani, discussed in the next section, did). Her mother claiming a share of the property, of course, made life difficult for the rest of the family, but things could have been worse for Sheela herself had her mother left the village. At least now her father, committed to the cause of education, continued to support all his children, without discriminating against her because of her mother's claims. Perhaps it was also a man's guilt – and recognition of his responsibility as a provider.

While polygyny is an affront to the woman's identity, and one can understand why Sheela's mother was determined to fight for her rights, for the children, it provided a strong support base. Sheela's stepsister, as long as she was alive, and stepbrothers have been a source of great emotional support. When one looks at the case from a gender perspective, rather than from the woman's perspective alone (see Chapter 3), the father's position becomes somewhat more complex and ambiguous. To compensate for his shifting sexual and emotional needs, he was willing to provide equally for all his wives and children, helping develop a sense of sharing and camaraderie amongst them. This semblance of equity and justice creates a dilemma for the mother – resisting the system only served in this case to evoke the resentment of her daughter, as their material and personal interests were opposed to each other, at that moment in time.

Daughter's Sense of Desertion

Surajmani, aged eleven in 2006, was an unhappy child. She never knew her father, as her mother, Maki, left her marital home just before Surajmani was born. Maki was eighteen then, ill, and her husband had no money for medical treatment. She returned to her parents' home. Her daughter was born, but her husband never visited; instead he remarried. Maki was deserted. When Surajmani was seven, she decided to marry a man from a neighbouring village. She hoped to keep her daughter with her, but her failure to conceive again led to quarrels with her husband and mother-in-law, who refused to allow Surajmani to stay with them. She too did not want her daughter to see her being abused. Maki wanted to educate her daughter and give her all her love, but they barely managed to meet once a month. Outwardly, Maki seemed reconciled to this separation, keen to build a new family and a new life. Her main concern when we spoke was not her daughter but rather the difficulty in conception, as reproductive failure could probably result in another failed marriage.

Marriage for her appears to be the only way to build a home of her own. Maki is a strong woman, and while living in her parent's house, over the past several years, she engaged in hard work. She would migrate several times a year to Bengal in search of seasonal agricultural work. Even now she works on the fields of her second husband and also makes and sells liquor in the bi-weekly local market. Despite her economic independence, she cannot imagine life as a single woman, as this she feels will deny her a 'home' of her own. Her parents barely have any land, and she has three brothers with whom it would have to be shared. The choices of women such as Maki get shaped by patrilineal inheritance practices that deny the daughter a share of her parent's property – the contours of emotional and personal well-being thus set by material constraints.

But more importantly, Maki cannot face the psychological state of rejection, the feeling of not being wanted. She does not want to be like her mother. Her father brought a second wife twenty years ago, from one of his migrations to Bengal, yet her mother stayed on with her four children. Her father gave her mother a larger share of his less than an acre of land, so she could feed the children. He also helped her plough the land. He built himself and his new wife a separate house next to hers. Her mother chose to accept this option – it gave her some security, and she had the children, which gave her social respect. While motherhood helped her realise her identity, it also closed down the exit option. Instead, she internalised her well-being as the happiness of her children.

But for Maki, still young, having a man is important, and a reaffirmation of her femininity. A reciprocal relationship, with a man who cares for her, is crucial for her personal well-being. She would not be happy as a mere 'working body', fulfilling the role of a mother. Her marriage gives her material security yet is also a source of dejection. She is worried that if the marriage does not work, she would not only be rejected as a woman and a wife yet again, but would also in the meanwhile have earned the resentment of her daughter and hence failed as a mother too.

Surajmani lives with her grandparents. Her mother's remarriage was a moment of intense distress, sadness and loss. The only person in whom she could confide was her friend, another girl from the village. While her grandparents are kind, after her mother moved to her second husband's village, there was one set of hands less to work, so she was roped into helping with a range of household tasks. Her main job, however, was to take the cattle out to graze each day, so even though she wanted to go to school, she could not. While she loves her mother very much and meets her once a month, she feels lonely in her absence and resents the fact that her mother got remarried and left her behind.

The emotional abandonment of the daughter by the mother has material consequences as well, in a context of poverty. Her mother completed her primary education, but Surajmani was unable to pursue her own aspirations. She sees her friends in school, and she knows that her lack of education will affect her life chances. While she has enough food to eat, she is not optimistic about her future – it can only be a hard life filled with manual work. Interestingly, during a recent visit in February 2015, though I could meet neither Maki nor Surajmani, I learnt that Maki had left her second marriage and was now remarried a third time, while Surajmani too was married in a neighbouring village. According to her grandfather, she was happy.

And such cases are not isolated ones. Baha is twenty-eight years old. She was married when barely twelve, and a few years later she had a son. When her son was three, her husband died. She stayed with her in-laws to look after her son, but her father-in-law tried to rape her. This upset her father, it became a matter of pride, and he brought her home. The child was left behind; being a male he would inherit his father's property. Baha was miserable, but in the clash of male egos, that of her father and father-in-law, she could do nothing. Two years later, her son died of illness; she knew it was from neglect.

Her parents then started pressurising her to remarry; she was only twenty. She was not keen, but a man from the same village had lost his wife, and so she got married to him. While her parents are kind to her, she feels that they cannot understand her pain and feelings. She never got an opportunity to study, and she was married early. She lost the child she had. Her husband is a nice man and helpful, but they have had no children. She worries about this, as once he went to Bengal for seasonal agricultural work and there had an affair with another woman. He was fined and apologised for his behaviour, but like Maki, reproductive failure is clearly a concern in terms of her future security.

Baha understands the attitude of her mother, who was herself abandoned as a child. Baha's grandmother was not happy with her first marriage, so she moved out. She was then deserted by her second husband, after she gave birth to a daughter. Her grandmother got remarried a third time when her mother was about ten years old but left her mother behind in her natal home. A few years later, however, she took her daughter to stay with her in her new marital home. She did not have any more children; her husband, much older, accepted Baha's mother as his daughter. Through hard work, her grandparents gradually built up assets in the form of food stocks, goat and cattle. As her grandparents grew old, they came to stay with Baha's parents, bringing their cattle with them. Her grandfather died four years ago, but her grandmother continues to live with her mother's family, they feed her and take care of her, and in return use her cattle for their cultivation. Baha feels that perhaps it is the childhood experiences of her mother, both of being abandoned for a while but then finding a new father and moving to a new home, that made her insist that Baha get remarried and make a new life for herself.

These two examples bring to light a range of extremely complex themes. Both Maki's and Baha's mothers supported them in their separation and widowhood, giving them a place to stay, and encouraging them to find new partners. They were concerned about their daughters' futures, wanting them to get remarried and find love and happiness in their lives. For the younger women, this meant abandoning their children, failing in their role as mothers, in an attempt to find themselves as women and secure their futures as wives. While Maki's daughter is alive, and now married herself, Baha's departure from her marital home led ultimately to the death of her child. As mothers, they cannot forgive themselves. At times, this gets expressed as anger against their own mothers, for what they see as improper advice and a failure to protect their own children.

The stories are not straightforward. The older generation of women were seeking to help their daughters, projecting their 'own ambivalence about being female in a patriarchal culture' (Hirsch, 1981: 206). They did not just bargain with patriarchy but also tried to reformulate and redefine its rules. Baha's mother and grandmother were perhaps more successful in this than Maki's mother, although she too managed to secure access to land for herself and her children, albeit a small plot. The daughters, however, end up blaming their mothers for not giving better counsel, for forcing a separation between mother and daughter (son in the case of Baha), rather than finding alternate pathways that could continue to nurture these bonds and relationships.

There appears to be a generational shift too on what constitutes well-being and the contours of reciprocity entailed. It is important to point out here that this is bounded by class position and geographical location. While both were poor, Maki's mother lived in the plains village, with a small plot of land to cultivate, and Baha's mother in the forested cluster of villages, dependent on both land and forests for survival. With diversified livelihood opportunities including seasonal migration prevalent in the former, social bonds had already started to weaken, in contrast to the latter village. The general levels of social reciprocity and its correlation to the ability to access material resources also contributes to the shifting terrain of relationships between mothers and daughters.

Mothering Options: Material versus Emotional Needs

Given the link to material resources and personal security discussed in the last section, it seems clear that mothering and the 'maternal' is a social and not a biological category. It is constituted of what mothers do rather than what they are. 'Maternal thinking' can then be separated from the 'ideology of womanhood [which] has been invented by men' (Ruddick, 1980: 345), and in fact the term 'mother' can be extended to include shared parental care. This thought is rather more radical than the current emphasis on motherhood and fatherhood as complementary (Sriram, 2016), which itself is an improvement on near exclusive parenting by the mother. In this section, I explore different elements of 'maternal thinking', to use Ruddick's phrase, vis-à-vis their daughters.

Providing Material Support

Hopni, sixty-five in 2007 (died in 2012), had a daughter, Nachni, and a son. When the son was about eight, he died of illness, and soon after, so did her husband. She was close to her daughter, wanted to stay with her and get her married to a *gharjawae* (resident son-in-law) when she came of age. However, her husband's male kin got wind of these plans and made it clear that they would not allow her daughter to inherit her father's land. Hopni was at a loss on how to proceed and ended up marrying a man from a nearby village. He did not let her daughter stay with them, as he already had a son, so the girl was moved to her maternal uncle's home. The uncle got Hopni's daughter married when she was still very young, but this marriage did not last. A few years later she married again. Hopni's second husband died in the late 1990s, and since then, she has been helping her daughter in myriad ways. When Hopni's stepson started resenting her support to Nachni, she demanded a partition of the property. Her grandson stayed with her to help with the cultivation. She gives any surplus to Nachni's family, as the latter's alcoholic husband is unwell and unable to do much work.

Although there were a few years when she and her daughter were separated from each other, the villages being close, they continued to meet. Hopni felt that by entering the second marriage, she was able to access property, which she could now use to help her daughter. This could have been much more difficult in her first marital home, where there were many more people interested in the property. While perhaps at that moment of remarriage she failed in her role as a mother emotionally, she feels that this has been compensated for. Over the past two decades, both materially and emotionally, while not having much herself, she has been the main source of support for her daughter. Hopni negotiated a host of power relations, with the marital kin of her first husband (somewhat unsuccessfully in terms of securing her share of property) and with her stepson (in securing a partition of her husband's property), to support her own daughter better negotiate her marriage and maintain her household.

Resisting Remarriage

Despite the acceptance of secondary unions, and its common occurrence, several women have resisted remarriage. The main reason is the priority they give to mothering. Jhumri is a case in point. She was widowed at the age of thirty, ten years previously, a mother of two young daughters – the elder aged ten and the younger barely four. There was a lot of pressure on her to get remarried – she was young; she had only daughters, who would ultimately get married, so she needed to build a new life for herself. She refused, precisely because of the fear that a new husband might refuse to support her daughters, and she could not bear the thought of leaving them behind. She therefore fought for her share of her husband's property to maintain herself and her children. This was not easy, as she had no sons.

The support of her parents was crucial in enabling her to fight for her share of her late husband's property, permissible in Santal customary law, as long as the widow does not get remarried (see Chapter 2). She cultivates her land and engages in wage labour, but occasionally if she is in need, her parents give her food or cash. She is educated up to grade nine and was determined to educate both her daughters. The elder one was in college, living with her maternal grandparents, from whose home travelling to college was easier. Jhumri's father retired from the army, and from his pension, he contributes partially for her elder daughter's education. She is very grateful to them for this support, as she knows that singlehandedly it may have been difficult for her to meet their educational needs in addition to all the daily necessities. Jhumri has chosen a life of struggle, and of independence, mainly to give her daughters all she has and the best chances in their own lives. They recognise this and study hard.

A second instance is Sona, aged forty, who too was widowed about ten years ago; although a mother of six children at that time, the eldest daughter married, but the youngest less than a year old. On her husband's death, Sona faced harassment from her relatives – she was called a witch, abused and isolated. Yet she never thought about remarrying, having five children to bring up. She is very close to her eldest daughter, Lalita, aged twenty, who, along with her husband, helps her cultivate the land, especially ploughing it for her on time (Figure 10.1). This was not easy for Lalita, as she too had to manage all the household tasks in her marital home. Yet she realised that at this moment, her mother needed her support. Lalita clearly recognises her mother's role in educating her (up to grade eight) and in supporting her

Figure 10.1 A mother and daughter helping each other prepare the land for sowing

Source: Photograph by Arundhita Bhanjdeo.

marriage to a man of her choice. Apart from cultivation, Sona engaged in wage labour and brewed and sold liquor, in order to feed her children. In return for the support from Lalita and her husband, Sona gave them a field to cultivate for their own use. Mother and daughter meet every week in the local market and exchange news and confidences. They remain as close as they have ever been, both with their independent families to nurture.

What Do These Life Stories Tell Us about Well-Being?

The life stories discussed in this chapter point to the difficulties of generalisation, of assumptions of 'good' and 'bad', as they each have a story to tell in terms of choices made in particular contexts and at particular moments in time. Yet patterns can be detected – the search for economic security (in the context of extreme poverty), age and positionality of the women concerned, the number of children, their age and sex, and the responsibility demonstrated by the husband or father as 'provider', to name a few. Facing resistance from her marital kin, an older woman like Hopni, for instance, remarried, hoping through this move, to help her daughter in the longer term. Each decision – should they separate or claim their share of property in case their husband brings a second wife, should they remarry or not if widowed – however, involves certain trade-offs, when analysed from the perspective of well-being – between material, personal and relational concerns.

The choices women have, how far they can push the boundaries and deviate from the norm need to be located within an understanding of the social systems and structures, and how these are changing in the context of larger political and economic changes. In the forest cluster, the erstwhile Damin-i-koh, the voice of the *majhi* (headman) and community leaders was much more respected than in the plains, where even minor complaints are now lodged with the police and courts (Rao, 2008). Women then potentially have greater voice in the hilly tracts, with some of their customary entitlements likely to be respected, to maintain local peace and a sense of fairness within the community. This, however, cannot be generalised, as over the last decade, with the construction of a road through the forest, and enhanced interaction with the 'outside' world, perspectives are changing. While seen as a society with relative gender equality, the examples presented in this chapter reveal that this claim may be far from the truth. Women need to fight for their rights; these are not automatically given to them. Their ability to fight is shaped by their economic (in)security, social standing and kin support, within the diverse ecological contexts in which they live. Without understanding the microcosm of women's lives and contexts, it is difficult to understand their everyday struggles and resistances, to create a better life for themselves and eventually their daughters.

Why have I focused only on the mother–daughter relationship and not on the primordial mother–son one? First of all, the quality of the mother–son relationship is of an entirely different order. The son is expected to look after the parents in their old age and, in many ways, to ensure her position and security in future years; the mother does not fail to shower favours on her son. There is clearly a material dimension to this relationship, an expectation of future returns. Further, in a patrilineal and patrilocal society, the son normally lives close to the parents, in the same house or in a different house in the same compound, so maintaining a cordial relationship becomes a necessity from a practical standpoint as well.

Daughters, on the other hand, not merely leave home upon marriage, but are also not expected to contribute in any significant way to the lives of their parents in their old age. In the absence of material obligations, the relationship between a mother and a daughter tends to be honest, reflecting feelings of love and hate, of conflict and support, and provides an insight into the emotions of women, as they feel and experience them. There could be errors of judgement in this process that lead to tensions between the mother and daughter, but neither has much to gain from sustained conflict; in a sense, both occupy subordinate positions within a patriarchal social system. When things go wrong in the daughter's life, she may blame her mother for not giving her proper advice or, indeed, for misguiding her. This is particularly the case when it comes to conjugal relations and their different understandings and expectations of it, from their particular subject positions – as a mother and as a wife (possibly also a mother herself).

Starting from this insight, the chapter has further pointed to the contradictions and conflicts between women's interests as women, and women's interests as mothers. Mothering is a significant life experience for women and often they tend to choose this identity over others. Living up to the identity of a mother is, however, not easy, as the cases here demonstrate, and often involve lives of struggle and hardship, of compromise and acceptance of abuse, even rejection.

This takes us to the multiple understandings of the notions of emotional pain and well-being. Women in different positions have different perceptions of well-being at particular moments in time. The choices and decisions are hard, for the mother but also the daughter. Some of their own dilemmas in 'bargaining with patriarchy' (Kandiyoti, 1988) are then projected on to their daughters. While the mother is concerned about the welfare of her daughter, the daughter is perhaps looking for a different type of support. It could be affirmation of her marriage, inspiration to carry on fighting to improve the relationship, rather than backing out of it. Of course, when the daughter is young, if the mother prioritises her own emotional well-being, this could potentially lead to physical separation. While justified in terms of future material support, this can be emotionally painful nevertheless (Rao, 2012).

An unexpected finding is the difference in the way these women define their rights and identities in contrast to the urban, middle-class feminist movement in India. The women discussed in this chapter have struggled to expand both their sex-related and employment-related capabilities to use Nussbaum's phraseology. They have struggled to push the boundaries of patriarchal control, for themselves, and for their children, often having to choose one struggle over the other. Compromising on their personal interests does not make them less conscious or aware of their selves; clearly it is an informed, though constrained, choice. It is an attempt to forge new opportunities for care through developing new forms of affiliation. An exploration such as this one into mother–daughter relationships then provides us with deeper insights into the nature of women's choices, the factors influencing their exercise of agency, and the outcomes of these choices. Often it is harder lives.

Notes

1. McGregor (2008) has defined it as a state of being, which arises when human needs are met, one can act meaningfully to pursue one's goals and can enjoy a satisfactory quality of life.
2. Personal communication with Rosalind Wilson, March 1988.
3. All names of people and places in this chapter have been changed to maintain anonymity.

References

Ahmed, F. E. 2014. 'Peace in the Household: Gender, Agency, and Villagers' Measures of Marital Quality in Bangladesh'. *Feminist Economics* 20(4): 187–211.

Barnett, R. C. 1988. 'On the Relationship of Adult Daughters to Their Mothers'. *Journal of Geriatric Psychiatry* 21: 37–50.

Barnett, R. C., N. Kibria, G. K. Baruch and J. H. Pleck. 1991. 'Adult Daughter–Parent Relationships and Their Associations with Daughters' Subjective Well-Being and Psychological Distress'. *Journal of Marriage and the Family* 53: 29–42.

Edholm, F., O. Harris and K. Young. 1977. 'Conceptualising Women'. *Critique of Anthropology* 3(9–10): 101–30.

Fischer, L. R. 1986. *Linked Lives: Adult Daughters and Their Mothers*. New York: Harper and Row.

Gough, I., J. A. McGregor and L. Camfield. 2007. 'Theorising Well-Being in International Development'. In Well-Being in Developing Countries:

From Theory to Research, edited by I. Gough and J. A. McGregor, 3–43. Cambridge, UK: Cambridge University Press.

Gulati, L., and J. Bagchi (eds.). 2005. *A Space of Her Own: Personal Narratives of Twelve Women*. New Delhi: SAGE Publications.

Hirsch, M. 1981. 'Mothers and Daughters'. *Signs* 7(1): 200–22.

Kandiyoti, D. 1988. 'Bargaining with Patriarchy'. *Gender and Society* 2(3): 274–90.

McCrindle, J., and S. Rowbotham (eds.). 1977. *Dutiful daughters: Women Talk about Their Lives*. London: Allen Lane.

McGregor, J. A. 2008. 'Well-Being, Development and Social Change in Thailand'. *Thammasat Economic Journal* 26(2): 1–27.

Narayan, D. 2009. *Moving Out of Poverty: The Promise of Empowerment and Democracy in India*. London and Washington, DC: Palgrave Macmillan and World Bank.

Nussbaum, M. 2000. *Women and Human Development: The Capabilities Approach*. New Delhi: Kali for Women.

Ortner, S. B. 1974. 'Is Female to Male as Nature Is to Culture?' In Woman, Culture, and Society, edited by M. Z. Rosaldo and L. Lamphere, 68–87. Redwood City, CA: Stanford University Press.

Rao, N. 2008. *Good Women Do Not Inherit Land: Politics of Land and Gender in India*. New Delhi: Social Science Press and Orient Blackswan.

———. 2012. 'Breadwinners and Homemakers: Migration and Changing Conjugal Expectations in Rural Bangladesh'. *Journal of Development Studies* 48(1): 26–40.

———. 2014. 'Caste, Kinship and Life-Course: Rethinking Women's Work and Agency in Rural South India'. *Feminist Economics* 20(4): 78–102.

Rich, A. 1976. *Of Woman Born: Motherhood as Experience and Institution*. New York and London: W. W. Norton and Company.

Ruddick, S. 1980. 'Maternal Thinking'. *Feminist Studies* 6(2): 342–67.

Sen, I. (ed.). 1994. *A Space within the Struggle: Women's Participation in People's Struggles*. New Delhi: Kali for Women.

Sriram, R. 2016. 'Harnessing Fathering Potential to Ensure Child Wellbeing'. In *Disciplinary Dialogues on Social Change: Gender, Early Childhood and Theatre*, edited by N. Rao, 151–78. New Delhi: Academic Foundation.

White, S. C. 2010. 'Analysing Well-Being: A Framework for Development Practice'. *Development in Practice* 20(2): 158–72.

Part V

Policy and Politics

11

Vision 2010

Chasing Mirages*

Introduction

Jharkhand, created as an independent state in November 2000, produced *Vision 2010* – a statement of policy directions for the new state. The state's first chief minister, Babulal Marandi, had identified increasing socio-economic disparities – more than 56.8 per cent of the population living below the poverty line (as against 36 per cent for India in 1996–97), lack of road connectivity in more than 60 per cent of villages, 54 per cent literacy rate (42 per cent in the tribal sub-plan area that includes 112 out of 221 blocks in Jharkhand, spread in eleven districts out of twenty-two) and 85 per cent of villages having no electricity – as key problems confronting the state, along with the challenge of extremism.

Marandi, during his tenure, had seemed increasingly attracted by the 'Asian strategy' for development, particularly that adopted by Singapore. Along with an eleven-member team, he undertook a tour of Singapore, Malaysia and Thailand in December 2002 (Prasad, 2002b). Thereafter he proposed a trip for Jharkhand legislators to China and South-East Asia: 'Legislators will be sent to foreign countries to observe the developments there to change their mindset' (Indo-Asian News Service [IANS], 2003). These trips have been funded from the state's exigency fund, meant for emergency purposes (Prasad, 2002b).

*This chapter was originally published as an article in the *Economic and Political Weekly*, 3 May 2003 © Nitya Rao 2003. All rights reserved. Reproduced with the permission of the publisher, Sameeksha Trust, Mumbai.

Turning Jharkhand into another Singapore is indeed a commendable objective, but perhaps it is time to reflect on the key ingredients of Singapore's success and ask whether these are reflected in the actions or even in Jharkhand's vision document. What have been the measures taken to counter the human costs in terms of displacement and shrinking access to natural resources that would accompany a process of rapid growth? With many thousands starving to death or dying of diarrhoea and malaria, the answer sadly is predictable.

I discuss briefly in this chapter the key elements of the East Asian 'miracle', and then point towards the lack of both clarity and commitment in the *Vision 2010* document as well as in the actions of the state government to date, in terms of these key elements.

Development Strategies in Asia

Remarking on Singapore's achievements in the introduction to his lecture at the Institute of Southeast Asian Studies in Singapore, Amartya Sen said, 'This country's success in economic development as well as in building a vibrant and harmonious multicultural society has been exceptional' (1999a: 3). The success of the region lies not just in enhancing the productivity of international trade, but rather in its emphasis on basic education as a prime mover of change as well as conscious measures for cultural integration of the Malays, Chinese and Tamils (Seen-Kong, 1983). The new features of the 'Asian strategy' included the wide dissemination of basic economic entitlements through land reform, education and training, essential medical facilities, and credit that allowed for a wider sharing of social opportunities, thus leading to the participation of a majority of the people in the process of economic expansion and social change.

While poverty still prevailed, this strategy led to an expansion of human capabilities, facilitated economic and industrial expansion by improving people's productive capacities, while at the same time leading to an improvement in the quality of life. Even the World Bank, with its focus on the 'market' to boost growth, has acknowledged the role of state-led public action, particularly education, in leading to 'the Asian economic miracle' (World Bank, 1993)[1]. It has admitted that these are the only economies that have 'high growth and declining inequality' (World Bank, 1993: 3).

In the case of Singapore, in the decade from 1972–82, poverty declined from 31 to 10 per cent, in India from 54 to 43 per cent. During this period, the Singapore government had to demonstrate to its people that the benefits of growth would be shared. Attempts to reduce inequalities in basic wealth were an important component of this development strategy. Thus, workers cooperatives were formed to give workers a stake in the economy, such as the 'fairprice supermarket cooperative' with over 240,000 members, 'comfort taxis' and many others. Similarly, a massive public housing programme was undertaken. The National Wages Council was set up in 1972 with representation of both the government and trade unions to keep the inter-industry wage structure stable. By the early 1980s, provision of child-care services was expanded to enable women to participate equally in the economy (Phongpaichit, 1988). The building of a merit-based and competent civil service as well as improving relations between business and the state (including encouragement to small and medium enterprises) assisted the rapid economic growth and demographic transition.

By the mid-1980s, 5 per cent of gross national product (GNP) was allocated to education, a bulk of it for basic education. Universal, high-quality, basic education helped close gender gaps in education. In the late 1990s, an increase in income inequalities became visible. Higher incomes are clearly linked to higher education; therefore, in order to stabilise income inequalities, there may now be a need for the state to intervene in maintaining equal educational opportunities at the higher level as well (Peebles and Wilson, 2002). In 2001, the state announced its intention to retrain workers and upgrade their skills, along with redistributive policies such as tax rebates and subsidised credit for the poor. With the exception of Kerala and West Bengal, most Indian states have neglected basic education and healthcare, as well as redistribution and reduction in income inequalities, and this has become a barrier for using opportunities of global trade and exchange as well.

While Singapore, a small country, has no agricultural sector, perhaps a lesson to be drawn from other East Asian countries is the simultaneous focus on basic education, land reform and improving agricultural productivity and public action to foster development. I turn now to briefly discuss the *Vision 2010* document of Jharkhand and analyse how far it fits this strategy.

Development Challenges Facing Jharkhand

Jharkhand is rich in natural resources – forests, minerals and abundant land. It has a diverse population consisting of *adivasi*s (27.7 per cent),

Scheduled Castes (8.4 per cent) and other groups, as well as several religious denominations – Christians, Muslims, Hindus and animists. Yet more than half its population lives below the poverty line; gaps between the rural and urban areas are wide, as also between different groups of the population. Along with Bihar, it has been identified as the most food-insecure state in the country (M. S. Swaminathan Research Foundation [MSSRF] and World Food Programme [WFP], 2001). The *Vision 2010* document admits to a 52 per cent deficit in food grain production as well as 230 gram per capita daily availability as against 523 grams for India as a whole (*Vision 2010*: table 8).

The challenge of development includes both the elimination of persistent and endemic deprivation, as well as the prevention of sudden and severe destitution, a result of economic inequality rather than a lack of food supply (Sen, 1999b). In May 2002, a series of starvation deaths were reported in Palamau district of Jharkhand. The Minister for Land Reform and Revenue dismissed these reports as baseless; yet an independent team of researchers who attended a public hearing in July of the same year in a few affected villages found the situation disturbing (Bhatia and Drèze, 2002). Total lack of health facilities, clean drinking water or employment opportunities during a drought year, accompanied by an extended period of low food intake, malnutrition and hunger-related diseases, seemed to have led to the deaths.

This is clearly not an isolated example. My own fieldwork in the Santal Parganas during 1999–2000, with repeat visits in May 2001, December 2002 and March 2003, reveal a similar picture. Lack of water for irrigation leading to a shortfall in self-cultivated food, lack of employment opportunities, lack of health services, clean drinking water, a total collapse of the public distribution system (PDS) and lack of welfare services, all contribute to chronic malnutrition and death due to disease. In 1999–2000, several thousands of people died of *Plasmodium falciparum* (cerebral malaria), and several more of diarrhoea.

Swaminathan (2000) has shown that undivided Bihar had the highest rate of malnutrition in the country in 1992–93. Thirty-one per cent of children were severely undernourished and 62.6 per cent moderately undernourished in the age group 0–4 years, as against an all-India average of 20.6 per cent and 53.4 respectively. This can partly be explained by the very poor, virtually non-existent PDS in the state, with only 1.2 per cent of households even partly dependent on the PDS for their food requirements (Swaminathan, 2000: 43). Annual per capita food grain offtake at 2.29 kilograms was the lowest in the country. One might argue that the situation has changed now with the formation of Jharkhand.

Unfortunately, this is not what field experience shows. While the PDS has improved marginally in 2001–03, with tighter targeting guidelines, identification of the beneficiaries itself is a nightmare for local governments in districts and blocks where large numbers of the population do not have enough to eat. For instance, according to calculations based on national guidelines, ninety households would be eligible for the Annapurna Scheme, or receiving grains free of cost, in Gopikandar block of Dumka district. This translates as one household per village. Yet in many of my fieldwork villages alone, there were at least five households that had not more than a single meal a day even at the best of times. Yet none of them possesses a ration card (Rao, 2002: 271). The same applies to most villages in this largely tribal-dominated block. Meenakshi et al. (2000) show the headcount ratio of poverty for Scheduled Tribes to be much higher than for the general population in Bihar. In such a context, targeting can only become counter-productive, with the better-off accessing benefits rather than the poorest (Kumar and Corbridge, 2002). In more than ten villages I visited in Dumka and Deogarh districts of the Santal Parganas in March 2003, I found that the poorest still did not have ration cards!

Yet the *Vision 2010* statement does not prioritise food security. The vision is to make the state self-sufficient in food production through a focus on irrigation development, scientific farming and sustainable agriculture. Alongside this, there is a focus on commercialisation, export orientation and market development through the promotion of horticulture and floriculture, as well as developing support infrastructure for the storage, preservation and marketing of agricultural produce. The slant is very clearly in favour of developing cash crops and agricultural markets rather than ensuring equitable distribution of food, which requires a combination of land reform, improving agricultural productivity and ensuring food distribution. It is now well recognised that self-sufficiency in food production, while being an essential condition, does not ensure food security and prevent destitution. The strategy is hence likely to exclude the poorest and most marginal – *adivasi*s in remote areas, women-headed households, and so on. This is more so because these groups lack land titles and hence access to agricultural credit from banks to improve agricultural production.

The only reference to food security comes way down as the twenty-fourth point in the list of twenty-seven strategies, and refers to sufficient and efficient food storage capacity up to the village level and a responsive distribution infrastructure owned and operated by the community. Community-based distribution systems are, however, yet to be developed with adequate safety nets for the most vulnerable.

There is also no reference to land reform. In the Santal Parganas, land reform has two major components: (*a*) distribution of government lands to the landless and marginal farmers and (*b*) restoration of alienated lands to the *adivasi*s.[2] One sees tardy progress on both fronts in Dumka district. Despite the government decision to provide 2,500 rupees as legal aid to an *adivasi* trying to reclaim alienated land, only eleven cases were resolved in 2002–03. While alienation of *adivasi* land is visible in almost every village of Dumka district, delays and costs of the legal process, as well as threats at the local level from the powerful, prevent many *adivasi*s from coming to the courts. If the government was really serious about restoring alienated lands, then grassroots-level revenue officials – the *karmachari*s as well as village-level workers – could easily be used for this purpose.

While not addressing the issue of land, one strategy that has been used is employment generation for the educated unemployed through the allocation of local buses to cooperatives of ten tribal youth on the line of 'comfort taxis' in Singapore. In the absence of any training in accounts or maintenance, however, including the setting aside of depreciation costs, as soon as there is a maintenance problem, these buses are being transferred to the non-*adivasi* bus owners and operators in the district. Yet if one considers this a positive intervention, one wonders why the same concept of tribal cooperatives is not applied to other resources, particularly in the case of mining operations. In 2001–03, since Jharkhand was formed, over 120 stone mines and crushers were given licenses in Dumka district, mostly to non-*adivasi* investors and contractors. Not only is this in contravention of the Samatha judgment of the Supreme Court in 1996 that stated that mining leases in tribal areas should only be given to cooperatives of tribals, but it also keeps the tribals here as daily wage labourers, working in hazardous conditions, rather than giving them a share of the benefits from the 'development' process!

Social Development

A second key priority in line with the 'Asian strategy' should be investment in basic health and education, to develop the capacities of the population to make use of social and economic opportunities and contribute to the growth of Jharkhand. Here, *Vision 2010* turns into a depressing document for those who welcomed the formation of Jharkhand state as a step towards progress. There is no clear prioritisation of education and health. In fact, the strategies for education come after commitment to industrialisation, power supply, highways, transport and urban development. The trip to Malaysia mentioned earlier was meant to negotiate a financing arrangement for the state capital project! And the health strategies follow education.

The vision for education was to ensure that all children were in school by 2005 and completed five years of schooling by 2010, to reduce gender gaps in literacy by at least 75 per cent and to increase the literacy rate from 54 to 85 per cent by 2010. The targets are commendable, and so are the strategies in terms of recognising the need to improve school infrastructure, quality of education as well as involvement of parents and villagers in the management of schools through the *panchayati raj* (elected local self-government) institutions. The remaining strategies deal with higher and vocational education. Let us look at what has happened during the period between August 2000 and the time of writing in 2003 towards achieving the vision at the level of the school.

With the announcement of the Sarva Siksha Abhiyan (SSA, or universal education campaign), there has been an effort to extend education provision to remote areas. Rather than filling teacher vacancies and strengthening the government school system, however, there is a trend towards privatising education – in this case, handing over the responsibility for education provision to a local teacher or a local non-governmental organisation (NGO). The issue of quality then remains a question mark. What is especially worrying in Jharkhand is the rapid expansion of schools that provide an education shaped by the Hindutva ideology. Rashtriya Swayamsevak Sangh (RSS)-linked networks have been active in utilising the SSA resources to expand their network of schools in remote rural and tribal areas. Systematic, district-wise workshops have been conducted in the last six months to strengthen the 'NGO network' affiliated to the RSS.

These networks are cadre-based and hierarchical, and there is no scope for dissenting voices. Involvement of parents and villagers in school management then remains a distant dream. Principles of democracy are not a part of the political culture. Even Bihar had conducted *panchayat* elections by the time of writing, but Jharkhand had been postponing the elections, which were finally conducted in 2010. Strengthening democracy and freedom of speech is not one of the priorities of the vision statement either. In fact, there are several examples wherein freedom of speech has been actively restricted by the government, even leading to police firing on dissenters (Prasad, 2002a). Sen (1999b), in fact, has emphasised the role of democratic governance and political freedom as being responsible for preventing large-scale famines in India after independence, unlike some of the Asian countries like South Korea and Indonesia.

I would like to deal briefly with the health strategies before concluding with a comment on multi-culturalism and social diversity. There is in the vision statement an emphasis on free access to primary healthcare, affordable secondary and tertiary healthcare, eradication of tuberculosis (TB) and malaria, reduction in infant and maternal mortality rates, universal immunisation coverage for infants and pregnant women, and access to potable drinking water in all villages. The record in 2001–03 somehow does not convince one of the commitment to these goals. The budgetary allocation for public health for 2002–03 was only 879 crore rupees, or less than half the education budget.

Bhatia and Drèze (2002) found a lack of primary healthcare facilities, lack of TB treatment and lack of potable drinking water in the villages they visited. In Dumka district of Santal Parganas, the primary health system has a 44 per cent vacancy rate in sanctioned posts for doctors. There are hardly any doctors in the remote rural postings, auxiliary nurse midwives (ANMs) are unable to regularly visit the villages under their charge, and primary health centres have no drugs and poor facilities and hence largely remain unused (Rao, 2002). Several people, especially children, died of malaria in the villages where I stayed for my fieldwork in 2001 and 2002. Lack of potable drinking water and lack of adequate food make them prone to endemic diseases, and lack of cheap and good quality healthcare leads to death.

Once again, the absence of an accountable local government makes the primary health system largely ineffective. And institutional changes making for a transparent, accountable and effective government do not seem to be forthcoming. On the contrary, there is a move towards an authoritarian police state in the name of curbing extremism. As Heyzer (1983) has pointed out, in the case of Singapore the major negative aspect was the highly authoritarian state that subordinated the interests of its workers, especially women and migrants, in the first phase of export-led industrialisation due to its dependence on international capital. To an extent, it made up for this through widespread social provisioning. This not being the case in Jharkhand, an authoritarian state and lack of political voice are likely to be major obstacles in the path of equitable development.

Conclusion

I would like to conclude at the point where I started, namely Sen commending the building of a multi-cultural and vibrant society in Singapore. Jharkhand has this potential; however, the events of the latter half of 2002 have shown the political climate to be divisive rather than celebrating multi-culturalism. I refer here to the domicile policy for government jobs introduced by the Chief Minister in June 2002, giving preference to *adivasi*s (28 per cent) and other *moolvasi*s (original settlers, around 36 per cent) in government jobs. Even though the actual benefits are limited, this measure has succeeded in splitting the society vertically, pitting non-*adivasi*s against *adivasi*s (*Economic and Political Weekly*, 2002). In addition, by denying Christian *adivasi*s the right to benefit from reservations, a Christian–non-Christian split has been created amongst the *adivasi*s. There were incidents reported of Christian *adivasi*s being forced to leave villages where they had resided for many generations. Similarly, in Ranchi, tensions were created between *adivasi*s and Muslims, and in the ensuing violence, six people were killed (Prasad, 2002a).

In conclusion, if at all there is a lesson from the Asian economies including Singapore, surely it is to recognise the interconnections between economic facilities, political freedoms and social opportunities. Yet these are lessons the political leadership of Jharkhand appears not to have learned. The vision of growth and poverty eradication, too, is then unlikely to be met.

Notes

1. See also Evers, Dicken and Kirkpatrick (1990) on the successful combination of market-based development and state planning in Singapore.
2. Interview with Deputy Commissioner of Land Reform (DCLR), 5 April 2003.

References

Bhatia, B., and J. Drèze. 2002. 'Starving Still in Jharkhand'. *Frontline* 19(16): 3–16.

Economic and Political Weekly. 2002. 'Jharkhand: Creating Schisms'. 27 July.

Evers, B., P. Dicken and C. Kirkpatrick. 1990. 'The Role of Producer Services in Development: The Case of Singapore'. DP 17, University of Bradford.

Heyzer, N. 1983. 'International Production and Social Change: An analysis of the State, Employment, and Trade Unions in Singapore'. In *Singapore Development Policies and Trends*, edited by P. Chen, 105–28. Singapore: Oxford University Press.

Indo-Asian News Service (IANS). 2003. 'Jharkhand MLAs to Go Abroad to Change Mindset'. *Times of India*, 11 January.

Kumar, S., and S. Corbridge. 2002. 'Programmed to Fail? Development Projects and the Politics of Participation'. *Journal of Development Studies* 39(2): 73–103.

Meenakshi, J. V., R. Ray and S. Gupta. 2000. 'Estimates of Poverty for SC, ST and Female-Headed Households'. *Economic and Political Weekly* 35(31): 2748–54.

M. S. Swaminathan Research Foundation (MSSRF) and World Food Programme (WFP). 2001. *Food Insecurity Atlas of Rural India*. Chennai and Rome.

Peebles, G., and P. Wilson. 2002. *Economic Growth and Development in Singapore: Past and Future*. Cheltenham, UK: Edward Elgar Publishing.

Phongpaichit, P. 1988. 'Two Roads to the Factory: Industrialisation Strategies and Women's Employment in South-East Asia'. In *Structures of Patriarchy: State, Community and Household in Modernising Asia*, edited by B. Agarwal, 151–63. New Delhi: Kali for Women.

Prasad, M. 2002a. 'Marandi Digs in Heels on Domicile, Toll Touches 6'. *Indian Express*, 26 July.

———. 2002b. 'Marandi Borrows to Beg for Investment'. *Indian Express*, 9 December.

Rao, N. 2002. 'Standing One's Ground: Gender, Land and Livelihoods in the Santal Parganas, Jharkhand, India'. PhD dissertation, University of East Anglia.

Seen-Kong, C. 1983. 'Ethnicity and National Integration: The Evolution of a Multi-Ethnic Society'. In *Singapore Development Policies and Trends*, edited by P. Chen, 29–64. Singapore: Oxford University Press.

Sen, A. 1999a. *Beyond the Crisis: Development Strategies in Asia*. Singapore: Institute of Southeast Asian Studies.

———. 1999b. *Development as Freedom*. Oxford: Oxford University Press.

Swaminathan, M. 2000. *Weakening Welfare: The Public Distribution of Food in India*. New Delhi: Leftword Books.

World Bank. 1993. *The East Asian Miracle: Economic Growth and Public Policy*. Oxford: Oxford University Press.

12

Agricultural Research and Extension in India

Changing Ideologies and Practice*

Introduction

The Indian Agricultural Research Institute celebrated its centenary in 2005. Having spent my early childhood at the institute's campus in New Delhi, I was tempted on this occasion to explore the original intention of the institute, set up in 1905 in Pusa in Darbhanga district of Bihar, and the state of agricultural research and extension now, 100 years later, in parts of Bihar that now constitute Jharkhand. This chapter is divided into two sections. The first, based on archival research, provides a historical account of the setting up of the institute – the motivations and purpose as well as the choice of site in Bihar. The second part is based on primary research in Dumka district of the Santal Parganas. The research, however, was conducted in 1999–2000, prior to the formation of Jharkhand, and presents both village-level data on agricultural production and constraints to productivity gains as well as the current status of agricultural extension, reorganised as part of the National Agricultural Technology Project (NATP), supported by a loan from the World Bank.

---

*This chapter was originally published as an article in *Economic and Political Weekly*, 26 March 2005 © Nitya Rao 2005. All rights reserved. Reproduced with the permission of the publisher, Sameeksha Trust, Mumbai.

The Historical Context

Different parts of India had faced serious famine conditions in the last quarter of the nineteenth century. In response to the reports of Famine Commissioners in 1878 and 1898, and John Augustus Voelcker's mission in 1889–90, the imperial government of the time, which had already reconstituted the Department of Revenue and Agriculture and initiated some measures for agricultural improvement, decided to focus more specifically on agricultural research and extension.[1] In October 1901, J. Mollison, Deputy Director of Agriculture, Bombay, was appointed as Inspector General of Agriculture for India, and for his assistance, a botanist and an entomologist were also appointed. But still a need was felt for a full-fledged research laboratory, in order to find ways to combat the famine situation. The idea of a research centre was thus already under consideration when Henry Phipps of the United States visited India, and on seeing the conditions, he came forward with a donation of 20,000 pounds to be devoted to 'whatever object of public utility (preferably scientific research)'. In accepting this generous offer, it appeared to then British Viceroy, George Nathanie Curzon, that 'no more practical or useful object could be found to which to devote a portion of this gift, nor one more entirely consonant with the wishes of the donor, than the erection of a laboratory for agricultural research'. Phipps expressed his warm approval of the decision and generously added a further sum of 10,000 pounds to his original contribution.[2]

While the natural choice for this research station appeared to be Dehradun, where the available agricultural experts were already at work and which appeared more suitable for chemical and bacteriological work due to its cooler climate, there was a proposal from the government of Bengal, offering 1,280 acres of land on the government estate of Pusa in Darbhanga district for this purpose. The advantages appeared to be the diversity of the land, including a low-lying tract in the south, uplands for grasses and grazing in the centre and a tract beside the river Gandak. The heat was not too severe in this region either. A special committee was therefore set up under the presidency of J. O. Millner, secretary to the government of India, Department of Revenue and Agriculture, to evaluate the two proposals and make a decision on the location of the proposed agricultural research station. The committee unanimously decided on Pusa in a meeting held at Calcutta (present-day Kolkata) on 5 March 1903.

There were a range of reasons behind this decision. First, Pusa's varied soils were suited for experimenting on a wide variety of crops, while the climate and soils of Dehradun were not typical of any important agricultural tract in the country. Secondly, Pusa was also the site of an agricultural college, focusing on provision of quality higher education in agriculture and creating a pool of specialist teachers and researchers (at that time all imported from England), and the usefulness of combining research and teaching in a single premises seemed clear. Thirdly, agricultural research needed an experimental farm, not available in Dehradun. With modern conveniences like cold incubators, exceptional work needing a cool climate could be conducted, though a small laboratory could also be maintained at Dehradun for this purpose. And finally, located as it was in a densely populated agricultural tract, it was hoped that dissemination would be faster and more effective.[3]

In a note dated Simla, 4 June 1903, Curzon explained to George F. Hamilton, Secretary of State for India, the reasons for the choice of Pusa for the agricultural research station. Proposals were also made for a range of staff, including a principal for the institute. Coventry, a Bihar planter, who had come to India in 1880, was identified as an appropriate candidate due to his agricultural experience, administrative skill and familiarity with Indian conditions. The proposal was sanctioned by the Secretary of State on 14 August 1903, and construction of buildings was initiated soon after.

Before laying the foundation stone for the institute in March 1905, Curzon noted in his discussion of the annual budget, wherein he had allocated 20 lakh rupees for agricultural research, experimentation, education and demonstration:

> The stone which I am to lay at Pusa in two days' time will, I hope, be the foundation stone not only of a fabric worthy of its object, but also of a policy of agricultural development henceforward to be systematically pursued in good years and bad ones, by the Government of India: so that a time may one day arrive when people will say that India is looking after her greatest living industry as well, let us say, as she is now looking after her greatest inherited treasure, viz, her ancient monuments.[4]

In his opening speech, Curzon emphasised that it was not enough to study the agricultural problem, but to bring the results of research to the knowledge of the cultivators of the country. In addition, rural schools, before imparting agricultural training, should give 'children preliminary training which will make them intelligent cultivators, will train them to be observers, thinkers and experimenters, and will protect them in their business transactions with the landlords to whom they pay rent and the grain dealers to whom they dispose of their crops'.[5] So there was a two-fold aspect – agricultural research and education of the farmer was to rest on a basis of good primary education.

There is further correspondence in relation to the establishment of a Board of Agriculture for India as per government of India's resolution number 8, dated 29 February 1904, which states that the Secretary of the Board would be an officer selected from the staff of Pusa. It clarified that the board would not control the institute, but the annual meeting of agricultural experts from provinces would enable exchange of ideas and learning for improvement of agriculture in the country.

There are several points to note in the aforementioned records. First, the need to systematically pursue the objective of agricultural research and development, as with over 75 per cent of the rural population still dependent on agriculture and allied activities for their livelihood (Dev, 2003), this is perhaps still the greatest 'living industry' in India. The second key objective relates to the issue of extension services and the need to bring this research knowledge to the cultivators, based on a foundation of good basic education. While in India today there are rapid advances in universalising primary education through the Sarva Siksha Abhiyaan, what continues to be ignored is the need for primary education to be relevant to the needs of the mass of Indian people, both men and women, still farmers by profession.

Post-independence state policies in relation to agricultural research and extension have varied. While not given much importance during the first two Five-Year Plans, following the poor harvests of 1965–66 and 1966–67, a fresh impetus was given to agricultural investment, particularly in support of the Green Revolution. Alongside investment in irrigation infrastructure, investments were also made in research and extension, with the setting up of a range of innovative programmes such as the Lab to Land, the Krishi Vigyan Kendras (KVKs), and so on, in the 1970s (Planning Commission, 2003).

Various analyses of the Green Revolution have pointed to the heightening inequalities as a result of the new technologies. While north-west India was seen to do well, agriculture in eastern India appeared to stagnate. West Bengal appears to have come out of this agrarian impasse in the past three decades, primarily due to its land reform programme and massive investments by the state government in irrigation provision.

What about Bihar – the state where the research centre was established in 1905 in preference to Dehradun? What is the state of agricultural development as well as extension services?

The next section is based on my fieldwork in Dumka district over a period of eighteen months in 1999–2000. I had an opportunity to collect data on agricultural production for the district as a whole as well as for two villages in two different blocks of the district where I was conducting ethnographic research. I interviewed block-level agricultural officers as well as the Dumka project director of the then newly set up NATP.

The State of Agriculture in Dumka District

Forty per cent of the total land area of Dumka district is agricultural land, of which 25 per cent is lowland, 33 per cent midland and the remaining 42 per cent upland (District Agriculture Office [DAO], 2000). Despite a range of national agriculture development policies, Dumka continued to be marked by low productivity (less than 5,000 rupees per hectare) and very low growth rates (less than 1.5 per cent) from 1961 to 1991 (Bhalla and Singh, 2000).

There are several reasons for this. The irrigated area as a percentage of gross cropped area dropped from 17.3 to 3.6 per cent in the Santal Parganas between 1931 and 1971 (Sengupta, 1982: 23) and was 7.5 per cent in 1991, according to estimates provided by Bhalla and Singh (2001). This is despite the fact that the Santal Parganas have fairly good rainfall, about 1,367 millimetres per year, based on the average from 1901–50, recorded at 24 rain-gauge stations set up across the area (Roy Chaudhary, 1965: 36), and further rainfall data corroborate this information, with 1,298 millimetres for 1960, 1,225 millimetres for 1970 and 1,398 millimetres between 1994 and 1999. Despite problems with averaging rainfall data, the availability of water is conducive to the taking of one or more crops in a year. Lack of attention to rainwater conservation has, however, led to surface run-offs and the possibility of taking only a single crop.

For Bihar as a whole, on the other hand, the proportion of gross irrigated area to gross cropped area increased from 17.9 to 19.5 per cent between 1931 and 1971 (Sengupta, 1982) and further to 40 per cent in 1991 (Bhalla and Singh, 2001). In addition to differences in agro-ecological conditions between the Santal Parganas and north Bihar, explanations for this drastic reduction in the former vary from institutional changes leading to the decline in traditional irrigation systems in the Santal Parganas (Sengupta, 1980, 2000) to arguments of sheer neglect of the region by the Bihar government (Munda, 1988). As a consequence, agricultural productivity (of monsoon paddy) at 1.5

tonnes per hectare in Dumka is much lower than for Bihar at 2.3, and India at 3 tonne per hectare in 1998–99 (DAO, 2000). Interestingly, despite high irrigation potential and fertile soils, Bihar itself lags behind other states of India in productivity of rice and wheat (Ballabh and Pandey, 1999).

Coming back to Dumka, while 27.7 per cent of the land was double-cropped in 1961, predictably this declined to 11.5 per cent by 1991, improving marginally to 15 per cent in 2000 (DAO, 2000). One of the implications of this continued dependence on rain-fed paddy alone has been an enhanced commoditisation of labour. Until 1961, agricultural labour constituted only 10–11 per cent of the agricultural labour force in the Santal Parganas as compared to around 30 per cent for Bihar (Government of India, 1961). In 1991, this increased to 17 per cent, and in 2000 to 20 per cent in Dumka district (DAO, 2000).[6] It needs to be mentioned here that as the sale and purchase of land are not legally permitted by the Santal Pargana Tenancy Act (SPTA), 1949, most Santals own some land, though with division over generations, the landholding size is declining. The Santals see their identities as cultivators rather than labourers; therefore Santal men particularly prefer to stay at home and tend to their fields, if this is possible, while women increasingly migrate to West Bengal for seasonal agricultural work. The attachment to land as a symbol of status hence provides a clue to the increasing contestation over land in the region and the desire to retain their identity as cultivators. Why then has agriculture not improved?

Evidence from the Study Villages

Based on data collected from two villages, Chuapara, a remote upland village, and Bagdiha, a plains village, I discuss the patterns of production, outputs and crop cycles as well as trends relating to agricultural intensification. While the output estimates based on crop-cutting during 1999–2000 reveal that the productivity of paddy in the district varied from 2,300 kilograms per hectare (920 kilograms per acre) for high yielding varieties (HYVs) to 1,500 kilograms per hectare (600 kilograms per acre) for improved varieties (DAO, 2000), in my sample the output varied between 175 kilograms per acre and 1,125 kilograms per acre (Rao, 2002).[7]

The lower output relates not just to output in the uplands but also lowlands that are indifferently cultivated for a host of social reasons. As Chutki, a widowed woman with two daughters in Bagdiha, said, 'My output is low as the transplanting was delayed. We had to interrupt our own work for two weeks to engage in wage labour as there was nothing to eat at home or any cash to hire in male labour.' The higher outputs refer generally to lowlands, but also reflect the household's investment in the land, in terms of better-quality seeds, fertilisers and labour time (Figure 12.1). Sital Marandi, a village leader, and his wife, Kanali, who did engage in wage labour occasionally, invested most of their time in improving and nurturing their own land. Their output per acre is a little more than the district average for HYV production. The difference between the two villages was considerable as well as amongst households.

Clearly, peasants do seek to readjust farming practices in order to improve their food supply and security;[8] yet this seems to be governed by social and structural rather than technical factors (Byres, 1977). Such an understanding can go towards explaining why even with similar qualities of land there are variations in output between different households. Productivity is not just a function of the inputs and resources invested, but a reflection of differences in household structure, capacities and social arrangements, of risks and

Figure 12.1   A Koeri farmer with his vegetable crop

Source: Photograph by Arundhita Bhanjdeo.

vulnerabilities, of the balance between returns, security and status.[9] A possible reason for the low growth in agriculture is perhaps the lack of attention by policy interventions to such factors. The block-level agricultural officer, for example, provides seeds or fertilisers to those who can come to his office at the block,[10] thus ruling out the poorest, often women-headed households, with neither the time nor resources to visit the block office. Even when he visits villages, it is very unlikely that he will be able to speak to such people. I once found that the village-level worker (*gram sevak*) had been to Chuapara and prepared a list of the poorest households for granting of Integrated Rural Development Program (IRDP) loans. The list did not include the names of any of the households whom I had found to be the poorest in the village. On making some enquiries, I found that given the lack of resources to either pay a bribe or, indeed, to visit the block office several times in order to complete the paperwork, these households had not even tried to get their names on the list!

At this point, it may be appropriate to describe the pattern of agriculture in the two villages. Agriculture to the Santals means paddy cultivation, *khet* (field) implies paddy land, and rice is considered food. However, the land use and cropping patterns are much more complex than this. Five qualities of land are listed in the land records.[11]

In terms of the crop cycle, the paddy seeds are planted in June, transplanted to the fields in the month of July and harvested in November, thereafter being threshed, dried and stored for consumption. Where resources are available, a second crop of wheat or potato is grown on the *dhani* (paddy) lands in Chuapara. In Bagdiha, these lands are left fallow after the paddy harvest. While the land is ploughed by men, the transplanting is generally done by the women. Harvest, threshing and other post-harvest operations are performed jointly. While the women thus contribute as much as, if not more than men to the production of paddy, it is seen as men's contribution to the household and fulfils their identity as cultivators and food providers.

Bari technically means the homestead plot. Usually a smaller plot and close to the house, it is considered a part of women's domain, a resource contributing to the performance of women's household maintenance functions. Men's role in the *bari* is restricted to ploughing the land. Before planting the paddy seeds, women plant maize in their *bari*. After paddy transplantation, by August, the maize crop is ready to harvest. This provides them with food till the early varieties of paddy are harvested towards the end of September. Soon after, the women plant mustard seeds in the same *bari* plots, which mature by December, are harvested after the main paddy crop and are used for the production of oil. Many households, such as Lakhiram Marandi's in Chuapara, produce enough oil for their own consumption. A few households grow some vegetables as well. While the *bari* in many ways seems better utilised than the *khet*, it is not considered as 'land' and has no value in exchange relationships.

The second crop, where it is taken, is often a cash crop and, like all cash crops, is risky. In 1999, due to heavy rains, the *ghangra* (black-eyed bean) in Chuapara succumbed to a pest attack,[12] and output was low. Most of the households had taken small seed loans for the crop. Few households got enough to repay the *mahajan*, and for the majority the debts mounted up. Rasi Tudu could not even return the seed he had borrowed; hence, his daughter went to work for the household of the lender. Dudhwa Kol was planning a wheat crop but had to give up his plans as he had no cash to purchase the seeds. Crop decisions are then based on a complex combination of factors, such as available labour surplus, quality of land, capital requirements, revenue regime, terms of cash advance, subsistence needs and not the individual choice or motivation of the farmer.

I turn now to briefly examine trends in intensification–extensification in my study villages. Boserup (1965) was one of the earliest to propose that more intensive farming technologies tend to occur with rising population density. Rural population growth shortens fallow periods, increases investments in land, induces manuring to maintain soil fertility and promotes specialisation in production. Others have observed that intensification is not driven by population growth alone, but also policy changes relating to technology, institutions and markets (see review by Carswell [1997]).

The evidence from Bagdiha and Chuapara, however, contradicts this proposition. Rather than intensification of agriculture and technological improvement, rising population and consequent decline in per capita landholding has led to an increase in disputes around land, especially in Bagdiha.[13] The desire to extend holdings has meant displacing other claimants, leading to greater contestation, even violence. Further, while there is no apparent shortage of water, and the infrastructure in terms of wells does exist, agricultural intensification and the production of a second crop do not seem to be the norm. Historical evidence from the district gazetteer (O'Malley, 1910) points to the prevalence of double cropping as a rule rather than an exception. Right until the early 1980s, it was practised in Bagdiha. Grain *golas* (granaries) functioned to provide seeds for the *rabi* crop, forests provided supplementary incomes, and seasonal migration to Bengal was limited. This system seems to have collapsed, pointing to the collapse of public provision of agricultural services (inputs, credit, extension and irrigation), on the one hand, and the playing out of power relations in a context of growing individualisation of interests, on the other.

Further, double cropping would mean intensified work roles for both men and women, depending on the particular crop cycle (Duvvury, 1989). While men now see greater security in investing in off-farm income sources such as contract work or government employment,[14] with no control over either the output or decision-making, women prefer to migrate to Bengal during the *rabi* season to earn a wage under their control. Clearly then, land here is prized for the status it gives, the sense of identity and rootedness, rather than its economic value. Resistance to intensification and the willingness to contest extension reflect struggles over status, over the social–symbolic meanings of land between castes, kin and genders.

In Chuapara, in contrast, some people do take a *rabi* crop of wheat and potato, especially those with lands near the stream, which can hence be easily irrigated, or black-eyed beans on the hill slopes. Here, the constraint is a different one – a constraint of capital and labour. In 1999, on account of the failure of both paddy and beans, most households were already indebted and did not have the financial resources to invest in the *rabi* crop. Statements from the lead bank revealed that during 1999–2000, actual crop loan disbursals were only 33 per cent of the target for *kharif* paddy and 17 per cent for winter wheat or potato. Capital was thus not forthcoming from banks either. In terms of labour, during the winter months, women are engaged in the collection and sale of forest produce. The rate of returns from this appears higher than from the labour-intensive *rabi* crop.[15]

Current Agricultural Extension Scenario

Dumka district was selected for the World Bank-supported NATP in 1999. A district-level agency, Agricultural Technology Management Agency (ATMA), was set up in order to decentralise technology dissemination. Key line departments of agriculture, animal husbandry, horticulture and fisheries, research organisations, non-governmental organisations (NGOs) and agencies associated with agricultural development in the district are members of the ATMA. With a leaner structure, the idea is that public extension will operate till the block level, after which private service providers including NGOs, farmers' associations and other para-professionals would take over. The underlying concept is one of 'social learning' which reflects shared learning of interdependent stakeholders in preference to a top-down approach, in order to arrive at a more desirable outcome (Leeuwis and Pyburn, 2002: 11).

The two major goals of the ATMA are the replication of proven technologies (success stories) and the assessment and refinement of new research findings for generating new success stories. In terms of the first goal, success stories are first to be identified, followed by exposure visits for selected farmers. As per the document, 'It is important that such exposure visits are made … only for those farmers for whom it is likely to be relevant. It may be worthwhile if concerned farmers are asked to contribute a part of cost towards such visit so that their genuine interest is ensured'.[16]

One of the major strategies for agricultural development is intensification through double cropping (MANAGE, 2000). The project document repeatedly emphasises the motivation of the farmers (organisation into groups of only interested farmers) on the one hand and the skills required as being either managerial or technological on the other. To quote, 'It is proposed that one person at block level (agricultural officer) would be identified and trained on the first skill (about management aspect) so that farmers would be advised on changes to be considered in relation to the choice of enterprises in the overall farming system. Afterwards, the farmers could go to the concerned technical person within the line department for advise/training regarding technical aspects of the proposed enterprise' (Figure 12.2).

Four types of agro-ecological situations (AES) have been identified in Dumka district. After discussions with groups of farmers in one village of each AES, the following strategies were identified.[17] For the rain-fed uplands, the main strategy identified is awareness generation to grow a second crop. For the rain-fed midlands, the strategy is to enable farmers to diversify to linseed and sunflower. The rain-fed lowlands appear to have the maximum potential, and it is hoped to introduce improved varieties of paddy, maize, pea, gram, wheat and potato and transfer the latest technology available. While the introduction of HYV paddy followed by linseed and *masoor* has been advised for the irrigated midlands, there is a peculiar problem in the command area of the Mayurakshi project, namely the conversion of lowlands into marshy land, due to the flowback from the dam, which makes it difficult to plough the fields. As I found during research in January 2003, much of this land is now uncultivable, and has been so since 1999–2000, often forcing

Figure 12.2 Training in row-planting techniques
Source: Photograph by Arundhita Bhanjdeo.

people to move (see Chapter 8). Despite policy commitment to a holistic farming systems approach rather than the earlier commodity-oriented approach (Sharma, 2002), there seems to have been little attention paid to this problem in terms of strategies for securing the livelihoods of people who were once cultivators.

Clearly, the project has not engaged with the social or material resource issues in the field, discussed earlier, and is still looking for technical–managerial fixes to the problem of low productivity. As Scott (1976) pointed out, the rich (including the policymakers) see the poor as not cultivating because they are not interested and become lazy once they have enough food; they do not see the material difficulties of lack of capital and resources or the social contestation for power and status.

Conclusion

Perhaps it is time to think back to the notion of agriculture as a 'living industry'. Land and agriculture are an integral part of people's lives and identities, a reflection of their status, wealth and labour, and not just a matter involving some technical or managerial tinkering. People do know their interests; yet they are constrained by a range of factors, both individual and structural. In this context, the neo-liberal analysis of the causes for low productivity that underlies the agricultural extension system – lack of individual motivation rather than constraints of capital and labour – appears to be quite off the mark.

The role of public agricultural research to enhancing productivity as well as contributing to poverty reduction has been substantial after independence (Joshi, Pal and Birthal, 2002; Fan, Hazell and Thorat, 1999), though the performance of extension has been controversial and reformed on several occasions. Farmer-to-farmer contact is useful, as is the role of NGOs for outreach. The recognition of the need for agricultural extension to be close to people is thus commendable. However, a strategy of shifting public funds to NGOs and other private service providers can disadvantage marginal regions and groups, especially women. While there have perhaps been some winners from the new extension system as envisaged in the NATP, there have been at least two losers: research seems to have been undermined (especially as farmer-driven questions as in the Mayurakshi case discussed earlier do not really seem to be finding a place on the research agenda), and groups and genders, lacking access to resources, are unable to 'participate'.

Notes

1. The department was tasked to combat famine by promoting conditions to prevent its recurrence. This included steps to increase gross produce by technical improvement of agriculture and extension of irrigation; to regulate demands on produce by the state and moneylenders through a revenue policy and controls on alienation of land; and to encourage diversification through supportive emigration policies to Assam and South Africa. MSS EUR F111/494, p. 2.
2. No. 26 of 1903, Section B, MSS EUR F111/495, pp. 1–2.
3. No. 26 of 1903, Section B, MSS EUR F111/495, p. 4.
4. MSS EUR F111/494, p. 11. In the case of the Santal Parganas, the Deputy Commissioner (DC) from 1886–1900, Richard Carstairs, noted that water storage reservoirs and distributaries had been neglected in preference for expenditure on maintaining land records and fixing rents. Maintaining

water and forest resources could, however, provide the best safeguards against famine (Carstairs, 1912).

5. MSS EUR F111/494, pp. 9, 11.

6. For India, Mukherjee (1999) notes an increase in the proportion of agricultural labourers from 24 to 44 per cent during 1961–91 for women. For men, the proportion rose from 15 to 21 per cent of male work force. Forty per cent of male workers continued to be listed as cultivators as against 34 per cent of women in 1991. While noting the same trend, Visaria (1996: 334) based on the National Sample Survey (NSS) shows an increase of the proportion of male agricultural workers from 21 to 26 per cent from 1961 to 1987–88, and women from 24 to 33 per cent.

7. Though the data were collected quite carefully, a note of caution is needed. While very low output levels can be explained by factors such as delayed ploughing and planting, another explanatory factor is definitely under-reporting. In both the villages, the most vulnerable families engaged in a process of staggered harvest, cutting the crop little by little from the fields as it ripened, threshing, drying and consuming it immediately.

8. A lot of HYV cultivation has come into Bagdiha through the regular migrants to Bengal. They have also learnt the techniques of fertiliser and pesticide application from this exposure.

9. On the basis of six African poverty assessments by the World Bank, Whitehead and Lockwood (2000) conclude that inadequate access to land is rarely in itself a cause for poverty. See also Doss (2001).

10. He does not have access to a vehicle to transport these inputs to the villages.

11. The *dhani* 1 are the most prized lowlands, well irrigated and best suited for paddy. *Dhani* 2 are the midlands, but often the distinction with *dhani* 1 is merely for purposes of rent calculation. It is these two that are really considered as 'land' (*khet*) by men and can be mortgaged out for purposes of taking loans and advances. *Dhani* 3 are the uplands, unirrigated, but where it is still possible to cultivate paddy. *Bari* 1 and *bari* 2 are superior and inferior varieties of homestead land, respectively.

12. During my fieldwork year, there was excessive rain in September–October, when the paddy crop was ripening, leading to a heavy loss in output. There was also considerable hardship in terms of the collapse of houses, leaking roofs, loss of source of drinking water, and non-availability of dry firewood and hence cooked food. While overall the rainfall was not excessive, its concentration over a few days led to losses rather than a surplus.

13. It remains a puzzle, however, as to why despite growing demands for land, the net sown area in the district shows a decline. Perhaps there is a shift in land management strategies in favour of creating new paddy lands, leading to the consequent abandonment of less productive uplands.

14. Most of the Hindus in the village are not cultivators; yet they are generally better off.

15. At least two members from the households that had planted a *rabi* crop had to move to live in the fields as the wheat was ripening, to both guard and nurture the crop.

16. The source document is no longer available on the official website of the ATMA. The ATMA is now described as 'responsible for all technology dissemination activities at the district level' (ATMA, n.d.).

17. For a district like Dumka, given very few NGOs with professional expertise and an absence of *panchayati raj* institutions, the extent of both participation and dissemination is constrained by following an NGO group model.

References

Agriculture Technology Management Agency (ATMA). n.d. 'About ATMA'. http://www.atmadumka.co.in/index.html. Accessed on 28 April 2023.

Ballabh, V., and S. Pandey. 1999. 'Transitions in Rice Production Systems in Eastern India: Evidence from Two Villages in Uttar Pradesh'. *Economic and Political Weekly* 34(13) (27 March): A11–A16.

Bhalla, G. S., and G. Singh. 2001. *Indian Agriculture: Four Decades of Development*. New Delhi: SAGE Publications.

Boserup, E. 1965. *The Conditions of Agricultural Growth: The Economics of Agrarian Change under Population Pressure*. Chicago: Aldine Publishing Company.

Byres, T. J. 1977. 'Agrarian Transition and the Agrarian Question'. *Journal of Peasant Studies* 4(3): 258–74.

Carstairs, R. 1912. *The Little World of an Indian District Officer*. London: Macmillan Publishers.

Carswell, G. 1997. 'Agricultural Intensification and Rural Sustainable Livelihoods: A "Think Piece"'. Working Paper No. 64, Institute of Development Studies, Brighton.

Dev, S. M. 2003. 'Agriculture, Employment and Social Sector Neglected'. *Economic and Political Weekly* 38(14): 1353–56.

District Agriculture Office (DAO). 2000. *Land Use and Production Data.* Dumka: District Agriculture Office.

Doss, C. 2001. 'Designing Agricultural Technology for African Women Farmers: Lessons from 25 Years of Experience'. *World Development* 29(12): 2075–92.

Duvvury, N. 1989. 'Work Participation of Women in India: A Study with Special Reference to Female Agricultural Labourers, 1961 to 1981'. In *Limited Options: Women Workers in Rural India*, edited by A. V. Jose, 63–107. New Delhi: International Labour Organisation.

Fan, S., P. Hazell and S. Thorat. 1999. 'Linkages between Government Spending, Growth and Poverty in Rural India'. Research Report 110, International Food Policy Research Institute, Washington, DC.

Government of India. 1961. *Santal Pargana District Census Handbook*, parts I–II. Patna: Directorate of Census Operations.

Joshi, P. K, S. Pal and P. S. Birthal. 2002. 'Contributions of Agricultural Research'. *Economic and Political Weekly* 37(13) (30 March): 1193–95.

Leeuwis, C., and R. Pyburn (eds.). 2002. *Wheelbarrows Full of Frogs: Social Learning in Rural Resource Management.* The Netherlands: Koninklijke Van Dorcum.

MANAGE. 2000. *Strategic Research and Extension Plan of Dumka District.* Prepared by the Agricultural Technology Management Agency (ATMA), Dumka district, under guidance of the National Institute of Agricultural Extension Management (MANAGE), Hyderabad.

Mukherjee, M. 1999. 'Women and Work in India: A Collage from Five Decades of Independence'. In *From Independence Towards Freedom*, edited by B. Ray and A. Basu, 56–79. New Delhi: Oxford University Press.

Munda, R. D. 1988. 'The Jharkhand Movement: Retrospect and Prospect'. *Social Change* 48(2): 28–58.

O'Malley, L. S. S. 1910. *Bengal District Gazetteers: Santhal Parganas.* Calcutta: Bengal Secretariat Book Depot.

Planning Commission. 2003. *India's Five Year Plans: Complete Documents.* New Delhi: Academic Foundation.

Rao, N. 2002. *Standing One's Ground: Gender, Land and Livelihoods in the Santal Parganas, Jharkhand, India.* Norwich: University of East Anglia.

Roy Chaudhary, P. C. 1965. *Bihar District Gazetteers: Santal Parganas.* Patna: Secretariat Press.

Scott, J. C. 1976. *The Moral Economy of the Peasant.* New Haven, CT: Yale University Press.

Sengupta, N. 1980. 'The Indigenous Irrigation Organization in South Bihar'. *Indian Economic and Social History Review* 17(2): 157–89.

———. 1982. 'Background of the Jharkhand Question'. In *Fourth World Dynamics: Jharkhand*, edited by N. Sengupta, 3–39. Delhi: Authors Guild Publications.

———. 2000. 'Negotiation with an Under-Informed Bureaucracy: Water Rights on System Tanks in Bihar'. In *Negotiating Water Rights*, edited by B. R. Bruns and R. S. Meinzen-Dick, 137–61. London: ITDG Publishing.

Sharma, R. 2002. 'Reforms in Agricultural Extension: New Policy Framework'. *Economic and Political Weekly* 37(30) (27 July): 3124–31.

Visaria, P. 1996. 'Structure of the Indian Labour Force: 1961–94'. *Indian Journal of Labour Economics* 39(4): 725–40.

Whitehead, A., and M. Lockwood. 2000. 'Gendering Poverty: A Review of Six World Bank Poverty Assessments'. In *Gendered Poverty and Well-Being*, edited by S. Razavi, 115–44. Oxford: Blackwell Publishing.

13

Conflicts and Contradictions

Land Laws in the Santal Parganas*

Introduction

During fieldwork in the Santal Parganas in February 2006, I was one day accosted by a policeman – the head of the local *thana* (police station). He was visiting the village where I was staying to talk to the *parganait* (leader of a group of villages) about the tense situation in the area. There were press reports on the growing activities of Naxalite groups in the region, he said, led by 'civil elements from outside'. Training in the use of firearms was being organised and an atmosphere of violence being created in this otherwise peaceful region.

I soon realised that he was talking about the neighbouring *panchayat* (village council) of Pachwara in Pakur district, which has witnessed strong resistance to a large coal mining project in the last three years. I was told that compensation has now been paid out in cash and the resistance broken. Work was on full swing on the project, and it was now only a few people who were creating problems – these were the Naxalites, who needed to be arrested at the earliest!

This brief encounter raised a number of issues: How had the state actually managed to acquire land and get an agreement on cash compensation from the local *adivasi* people? Was any dialogue ever held or was this agreement a one-sided one? Was this solution not in contradiction to the existing

*This chapter was originally published in *Legal Grounds: Natural Resources, Identity, and the Law in Jharkhand* © Nandini Sundar 2009. All rights reserved. Reproduced with the permission of the copyright holder and the publisher, Oxford University Press, New Delhi.

protective land policies, as legalised through the Santal Pargana Tenancy Act (SPTA) of 1949? And was it not a gross violation of the Supreme Court's Samata judgment of 1997?

The fundamental issue behind these questions seems to be one of differing conceptualisations of land in cultural and political terms by the local people and the state, including the meaning of and principles underlying the notion of non-alienability of land in today's context. Economic growth and 'national development' require additional resources, whether minerals or land, for power generation, construction, industry or infrastructure development. Both industry and government make a strong case for the extraction and use of resources which are ostensibly being 'wasted' in 'undeveloped' and 'remote' *adivasi* regions such as Jharkhand. This view of land use and development, however, differs from local *adivasi* understandings. For the *adivasis*, apart from food production, land is valued for its ability to provide security and reinforce a sense of personhood (Rao, 2008). It offers them access to credit, to labour and other exchange entitlements, apart from public visibility, bargaining power and enhanced status. It is not only a material resource, but much more – it is a cultural and symbolic resource, essential to social identity and the achievement of a political voice (Peters, 2002: 160).

While there is considerable debate around legal pluralism and the flexibility it offers people to manoeuvre in relation to claims over natural resources (Meinzen-Dick and Pradhan, 2002; Benda-Beckmann, 2001), there is also recognition that much of the dichotomy persists as a discursive resource rather than as practice on the ground. Rules and laws, whether created by the state or local customary institutions, include ambiguities and gaps and are open to a range of interpretations, often used in struggles over economic resources and political equality. While in the Jahaly–Pacharr irrigated rice scheme in the Gambia, men used the discourse of tradition to maintain control over land rights and also women's labour (Carney, 1988), in Kenya, women disguised their acts of resistance in the authorised vocabulary and discourse of the state. They used the *harambee* ideology of self-help groups to withdraw labour from household plots controlled by men and use it instead for paid wage work (Mackenzie, 1990).

In the present context, however, what tends to happen is that rather than operating as separate fields, the main actors seek to make interconnections between them, picking particular rules and norms to create a new code of practice. What emerge are hybrid systems of jurisprudence (Strathern, 1996). With village leaders often using the state systems to legitimise their own viewpoint, the purpose is not to assert the superiority of one or the other. An account from Papua New Guinea demonstrates how custom is invoked as a legal tool in the courtroom; it is seen to have a moral weight and thus better able to fix responsibility, while what happens at the village level often follows the statutory code, which being more distant, tends to evoke more fear and hence compliance (Demian, 2003).

What becomes clear is that engagement with state rules and their contestation is critical for securing both one's material needs and social identities. It is a struggle over the power to construct 'authoritative definitions of social situations and legitimate interpretations of social needs' (Fraser, 1989: 107). Only by engaging in the process of interpretation and legitimisation of what constitutes a need claim is there a chance of it being heard and eventually satisfied.

It is the tensions around and varying conceptualisations of land and its alienation that I interrogate in this chapter. I begin by examining the case of the Pachwara coal mining project mentioned earlier, alongside other instances of both alienation and resistance, exploring the contradictions in SPTA and the extent to which its non-transferability clause, as embodied in Section 20, has been able to protect *adivasi* land and property. Despite the difficulties of contesting their claims against those in positions of power, both political and economic, the local *adivasi*s and other marginalised groups have persisted in their efforts to establish their conceptualisation of land as legitimate. I briefly examine the possibilities offered by the land governance institutions in the region to support rather than negate the rights of the local people to their land and property.

The fieldwork for this study was conducted in the Santal Parganas in March and April 2003, followed by repeat visits in January 2004 and January–February 2006. Two districts were selected for the study: one scheduled (Dumka) and the other non-scheduled (Deogarh). While villages spread over six blocks of Dumka district were covered, two blocks were covered in Deogarh. Village visits involved both individual interviews and group discussions on customary norms and practices, how laws and government policies function in practice, mechanisms for dispute resolution, extent of tenancy and alienation of land, and struggles around land restoration. Apart from the village visits, I held discussions with a range of government officials at the district level, lawyers, non-governmental organisations (NGOs) and activists, in order to understand the intricacies of legal provision and its functioning in practice. In addition to examining the current land records of the villages visited, records of revenue cases in the court of the Sub Divisional Officer (SDO) and relevant case law were referred to, where possible. I also collected various administrative orders. This was, however, a particularly difficult process as all these orders were not available on file, but secured through a range of personal contacts.

Pachwara: A Recent Case of Land Acquisition

The Pachwara coal-mining project in Amrapara block of Pakur district undertaken by Panem Coal Mines Ltd, as a captive electricity provider to the Punjab State Electricity Board, exemplifies the state's attitude towards *adivasi* rights to their resources. The central block of the Pachwara project envisages forty-four years of open-cast mining to extract 289 million tons of coal, bringing the Jharkhand government an annual royalty of 100 crore rupees. The mines would take over 640 hectares of *raiyati* (cultivable, under private title) land, 360 hectares of forest land and another 100 hectares of wasteland, apart from grazing lands and river. Compensation would be paid on a pro rata basis as per calculations made under the Land Acquisition Act (LAA), 1894, amounting to 50,000 rupees for the first acre of land, 30,000 rupees for the next two acres and 20,000 rupees for land beyond 3 acres. It is stressed, however, that a person receiving compensation forgoes all claims to employment and vice versa. In any case, eligibility for employment in a mechanised mine requires certain technical qualifications, which not many of the local *adivasis* possess. The rehabilitation package includes 'land for land' only for the homestead and not for agricultural land. Given that land in the Santal Parganas is largely non-transferable and non-saleable (Section 20, SPTA), the displaced villagers would be unable to acquire land elsewhere even if they received the compensation money.

Here, the land acquisition notification has been issued as per the LAA. The *gram sabha* (the village general body under the *panchayati raj*) was, however, not given any information prior to this notification (as per Section 5a), even though survey operations have been going on in the area since 1985. People in the affected villages (nine revenue villages covering 13 square kilometres) hence organised themselves to protest such takeover of their land without proper discussion and appropriate rehabilitation. A writ petition was also filed in the Jharkhand high court, Ranchi (6348 of 2003) by the Rajmahal Pahad Bachao Andolan, but was unfortunately dismissed on 19 August 2005. The court judged that due process had been followed: the compensation package had been finalised and even accepted by the concerned people.

While the villagers were not against the extraction of coal per se, they were demanding both consultation and involvement in this process. This is not only legitimate by all standards of natural justice, but actually stipulated by the Panchayat (Extension to Scheduled Areas) (PESA) Act, 1996, which requires consultation with the Gram Sabha before granting of prospecting licenses, mining lease and other concessions in respect of minor minerals. Section 41 of the SPTA in relation to the transfer of vacant or 'waste' lands has a similar provision. While India is not a signatory to the Indigenous and Tribal Peoples Convention, 1989, of the International Labour Organization (also known as ILO Convention 169), concerning the rights and privileges of indigenous and tribal people, by international custom, these rights include consultation, compensation for damage and benefit-sharing.

To counter the charge of non-consultation, the government organised a meeting in Pakur in March 2003. Villagers from adjacent areas such as Gopikandar block of Dumka district were taken to Pakur for this meeting, rather than those from the project villages. But even in these non-affected villages, most people were opposed to the project. Only one family, a man and his two children, from Chuapara, a village where I have undertaken long-term field work, went to this meeting. They were each given a watch, 50 rupees and food, and asked to sign a paper. This is now being shown as consent given by the local *adivasi*s to the project, though few of those affected by the project were actually present.

I could not personally meet the project manager, as the situation in the area was tense. Given the harassment from the police and the *dalal*s (contractors or middlemen), the people too resorted to self-defence tactics and allowed only known visitors with prior information to enter the area. I was, however, told by one of the members of the People's Union for Civil Liberties (PUCL) team (which conducted an enquiry from 25 February to 11 March 2003) that the officer representing Panem, which has been granted the lease, had been promised Central Reserve Police Force (CRPF) support, if necessary, to get the work started (PUCL, 2003: 23). The polarity in views is undeniable: the only way left for the state to negotiate the use of their land with the *adivasi*s was by resorting to the armed forces and the barrel of the gun. In the following year, small amounts of money were regularly distributed to the local *adivasi*s, especially on market days, to break their resistance. Following the high court order on the writ petition, displacement seemed inevitable, so most of the villagers accepted their compensation cheques. Now only a few protesters remain, and they have been labelled 'Naxalites'.

In response to the PUCL team pointing out that such transfer of land was illegal under Sections 20 and 41 of the SPTA, the District Collector (DC) of Pakur seemed to think that it was 'perfectly legal and necessary for development' (PUCL, 2003: 6). It is worth mentioning that following the Samata judgment,[1] the National Commission for Scheduled Castes (SCs) and Scheduled Tribes (STs) also issued a directive on this matter. In keeping with the spirit of the law, the then Divisional Commissioner of the Santal Parganas, wrote to the Advocate General, Jharkhand, for reconsideration of the project. She was, however, soon transferred from her post.

> From the documents enclosed it is apparent that a perpetual and grave contempt of the Honourable Supreme Court Order dated 11.07.1997 … is being committed by not following the clear and unambiguous order of the Honourable Supreme Court and therefore it is stated that all mining operations in the Scheduled Areas of Santal Parganas Division especially those in the… districts of Pakur and Sahebganj must be stopped forthwith. (Memo no. 71, Res. dated 27 April 2001)

The villagers were emphatic that they were not against development. A village headman summed up, 'We too believe in development. If at all the minerals have to be extracted from our fields, we will do it ourselves when we are capable' (PUCL, 2003: 9). People whose livelihoods are affected by such mining projects clearly need to be a partner in the project itself and share in its long-term gains, rather than being displaced with small amounts of short-term compensation. Worse perhaps is the breakdown of discourse resulting from the labelling of oppositional voices as 'Naxalites'. For the state, they are to be immediately arrested to prevent them from aggravating social tensions, rather than providing an opportunity to discuss alternate viewpoints. Before going deeper into the issue of land, in particular agricultural land, I briefly examine Section 20 of the SPTA that assures non-alienability of *adivasi* land.

The Legal and Policy Framework: Issues of Praxis

Despite the contemporary official imagery of *adivasi*s as 'manual labour', visible on construction sites and the border roads, and as agricultural wage labour, economic, political and social relationships in the Santal Parganas have historically been mediated through land. The *adivasi*s – in particular, the Santals – were brought into the region in the early part of the nineteenth century to clear the land and initiate cultivation (Orans, 1965).[2] To enable control over land and facilitate revenue collection, the colonial state gradually formalised and privatised land titles by the early twentieth century, through a process of land survey and revenue settlements. Yet the local populations, during this entire period, resisted the taking over of the land administration by the state. The most important resistance movement was perhaps the Santal Hul of 1855, which, though brutally repressed, was effective in highlighting several elements of exploitation and harassment of the local people. A separate district, the Santal Parganas, was created as a result[3] and granted some autonomy in systems of resource control and decision-making. This and later struggles repeatedly emphasised the integration of resources, especially land, with *adivasi* social, cultural and political institutions, representing a different way of life and different principles of social organisation, based on the notion of 'community responsibility' rather than 'individual rights' (Singh, 1966; MacDougall, 1985).

Resistance led to state attempts at appeasement of the *adivasi*s, both through protective legislation and special development programmes. One finds then a series of land laws and policy notifications that sought to protect the *adivasi*s from alienation of their land, especially to the *mahajan*s (moneylenders) and revenue collectors (Appendix 13A). The SPTA was passed soon after independence in 1949, largely following the provisions for tenancy, land management and inheritance as recognised and recorded by these earlier laws and regulations. Despite this, the decade after independence saw an increase in exploitation by the *mahajan*s, in collusion with the official machinery, and led in the 1960s to a further period of agrarian unrest. In the Santal Parganas, this resistance, in the mid-1960s, was called the Hul Jharkhand. Supported by a group of lawyers affiliated to the Communist Party of India (CPI), the Hul Jharkhand was able to secure and confirm legal rights to land to the *adivasi* owners, who had come to believe that it no longer belonged to them but to the moneylender (Rao, 2008). This ultimately fed into the political movement for a separate Jharkhand state led by the Jharkhand Mukti Morcha, the slogan of which was control over *jal, jungle aur jameen* (water, forest and land).

On 2 August 2000, the central parliament approved the Bill for the reorganisation of Jharkhand as a separate state. The Bharatiya Janata Party (BJP) and its allies formed the first government in November 2000, rather than the Jharkhand specific parties which had fought for statehood. The *Vision 2010* document outlines some of the policy directions and emphases of the new state. A preliminary reading reveals a focus on commercialisation, export orientation and market development, both in the agricultural and industrial sectors. Dealing with food security, inequities in resource distribution and control, and destitution do not appear as priorities (see Chapter 11). One of the first steps taken by the new government was to set up an all-party committee to review the existing land legislation and suggest amendments as needed, as the non-transferability of land was seen as the biggest obstacle to economic growth and development.

> A Santal headman in one of the villages visited said, 'Babulal Marandi [Chief Minister of Jharkhand from 2000–03] has the body of an *adivasi*, but the head and mind of a Marwari [a trading group]. He does not care about our land but is trying to give it to big industries. His policies are targeted to suppress the *adivasi*s. First, buses have been given to cooperatives of ten tribal youth. But their certificates have been retained, so they cannot apply for any other job, probably till such time as the loan component [70,000 rupees] is repaid, if ever. Second, schools have been built, but new teachers have not been appointed and the existing teachers are overloaded with other work; hence, hardly any teaching takes place. Educational achievements of *adivasi* children continue to be low. On top of that, liquor sales have now been legalised, so drinking has greatly increased. The policy seems to be to keep the *adivasi*s drunk and uneducated.

The priorities of the state and the *adivasi*s are clearly diverging: to the latter land remains more than a productive resource, a key element of their social and cultural identity, the foundation of their struggle for a separate state. The Jharkhand government, led by an *adivasi*, does realise this, yet is seeking to divert attention in other directions to avoid the spotlight falling on the crucial issue of alienation and mechanisms for dispute resolution.

The Santal Pargana Tenancy Act, 1949

Section 20 of the SPTA, which ensures non-transferability of land, has been the main source of dispute in recent times. According to Section 20,

'No transfer by a *raiyat* of his right in his holding or any portion thereof, by sale, gift, mortgage, will, lease or any other contract or agreement, express or implied, shall be valid unless the right to transfer has been recorded in the record-of-rights' (Prasad, 1997: 30). Section 20, however, does provide for a few exceptions:

1. gift to daughter or sister, with previous written permission of the DC;
2. grant of not more than half of the area of his holding to his widowed mother or wife for her maintenance after his death with the previous written permission of the DC;
3. transfer in favour of *gharjamai* or *ghardijamai*;[4]
4. lease for the purpose of an excise shop for not more than one year, with the previous written permission of the DC; and
5. restoration of land transferred through fraudulent means.

While land is thus not generally transferable, exceptional cases are allowed, with the permission of the DC, taking account of the prevailing 'customs'. Most of these exceptions interestingly relate to women's rights and reflect the existence of customary practices in relation to women in different subject positions. The DCs, however, have rarely used their position to ensure women's rights, primarily due to the difficulty of proving uncodified 'custom', especially in the face of contestation by male kin. This is a shortcoming of the SPTA, but then one needs to recognise that the SPTA is a tenancy act and not a personal law.[5] At present, women's rights have social recognition, but there is no legal obligation, the wording used being that of a 'gift' or a 'grant'. In most of these cases, women are deprived of their legitimate claims. The exception is *gharjamai*, wherein the husband gives up claims on his father's property and moves to his wife's home. The land then is recorded in the name of the daughter (see Chapters 2, 3 and 4 for a fuller discussion of women's rights to land).

Fraudulent Transfers and the Restoration of Land

In the rest of this chapter, I focus on Sub-Section V of Section 20 that allows the DC, in the event of discovering fraudulent transfer of land belonging to an ST, to give reasonable opportunity to the transferees and then evicts them, with or without payment of compensation, and restores the land to the transferor. There is, however, a provision that if the transferee has occupied the land for more than thirty years (as per the amendment brought by Section 6 of the Bihar Scheduled Areas Regulation Act, 1969) and constructed substantial structures on it, he may be allotted that land on payment of adequate compensation. Earlier the limitation period was twelve years.[6]

One direction for analysis is of course to look for legal loopholes, and these exist in plenty. The specification of time period is one example. A lot of people in fact 'manufactured' documents known as *kurfa* showing occupancy dated between 1935 (when the last land settlement by J. F. Gantzer was finalised and was hence a reference point) and 1937 (twelve years before the passing of the SPTA in 1949). The 1969 amendment, by specifying the time period as thirty years, did not solve this problem and instead allowed for *kurfa*s dated between 1935 and 1939 (thirty years preceding 1969). What should instead have happened was that the time period should not have been specified at all (as in Section 42 of the SPTA)[7] and the revenue authorities should have been given powers to annul any transfer of land belonging to an ST *raiyat* by fraudulent means. This not being the case, instances of false *kurfa* continue, and illegal transfers are regularised, especially near urban centres.

The discussion thus far, however, raises more substantive issues of interpretation: what is considered false or fraudulent, for instance, and from whose perspective? This is because local understandings of land tend to be context-specific rather than universal in application. In this section, I consider two contemporary examples. I first deal with the issue of credit and the continued dependence on moneylenders, who charge exorbitant rates of interest, the inability to repay leading to the alienation of land. I then examine issues of urban development and the rapid growth of stone quarrying to meet the demands of construction, which have a similar outcome. Both these examples help examine the divergent meanings and interpretations of land alienation in a largely rural context, where over 90 per cent of the *adivasi*s are dependent on agriculture for their livelihood.

Credit Needs and the Loss of Land

The existence of Section 20 means that land cannot be used as collateral to get loans from banks. With few other assets that can be used as collateral, and faced with a serious problem of default in a context of severe poverty and deprivation, banks have been unwilling to lend to *adivasi*s, except in the case of government rural development schemes that have a subsidy component. This has led to the continued dependence of *adivasis* on moneylenders for their credit needs. By the 1960s, a large number of Santals had been reduced to working as labourers for the *mahajans*, often on their own lands. As one of the leaders of the Hul Jharkhand protest that followed, Kunjiram Tudu, said:

> *Mahajans* controlled almost all the land of the Santals. If a person borrowed 100 rupees, he would record it as 300 rupees. As the Santal had nothing in the house, he got an order from the civil court and confiscated the crop. People started losing their land. Many people ran away to Bengal during this period. The police and the courts supported the *mahajan*. (Bagnol village, 21 December 2000)

The movement aimed at releasing land as well as securing debt relief. Apart from *dhan katai* (forcible harvesting), other direct-action strategies included the non-repayment of loans, thefts of grain from *mahajans*' fields and court cases. Mass meetings were held, the word spread through the district, and so did the resistance. In 1967, a coalition ministry was formed in Bihar with the support of the CPI. Though it lasted only eleven months, circulars were issued to facilitate the restoration of alienated land and debt relief in favour of the *adivasis* and the oppressed. Several of the *mahajans* fled the villages, returning only when the movement subsided. This and other anti-*mahajani* movements in other parts of Jharkhand during the late 1960s and the early 1970s led to a spate of state actions.[8]

Legislation was passed to regulate moneylending and provide debt relief in the form of the Bihar Moneylenders Act, 1974, and the Bihar Debt Relief Act, 1976. The government ordered all moneylenders to be registered and to provide a report of their transactions including money due to them within thirty days. No reports were received. In fact, most *mahajans* in the village destroyed their records. The SPTA was also amended by Section 2 (a and b) of the Santal Parganas Tenancy (Supplementary Provisions) Amendment Act, 1975, known also as the Bihar Act 17 of 1976. According to this amendment, ST *raiyats* with the previous sanction of the DC (and non-ST *raiyats* without previous permission of the DC) could 'enter into a simple mortgage in respect of his holding or a portion thereof with any Scheduled Bank within the meaning of the Reserve Bank of India Act 1934, or a society or bank registered under the Bihar and Orissa Cooperative Societies Act, 1935' (Prasad, 1997: 30). Further, a holding or portion thereof could be sold in accordance with the procedure laid down in the Bihar and Orissa Public Demands Recovery Act, 1914, for the realisation of such loans. However, in the case of an ST *raiyat*, this could only be sold to another ST.

In practice, however, despite the amendment, problems remain. First, since only those with land titles can get loans, this rules out women and other groups without land titles. Secondly, while the banks do now issue threats to defaulters, the process of taking over and selling their land is indeed very difficult. They use the Public Demand (PD) Act to file certificate cases, and they have to pay court fees; yet usually there is no recovery, so they lose both the credit given and the fees paid (Table 13.1 provides the status of certificate cases in Dumka district). Banks by and large then hesitate to lend to the *adivasi*s, as revealed by the low credit-deposit ratios in Dumka district. While this has improved from 24 per cent in 2001–02 to 33 per cent in 2005–06, it is still way below the target of 60 per cent (Annual Credit Plan, 2005–06, Dumka).

Field visits revealed a widespread problem of indebtedness resulting in land alienation. As a poor SC man in a village in Deogarh district, said:

We take loans from the *mahajan*s at an interest of 10 per cent per month. Often we give him our land on *satta* [the local term for *bhugatbandha*⁹]. If there is a dispute and we try to resolve it within the village, he will not listen to the judgment. Court is the only solution, even though it is very expensive for us. And usually, it is those with resources who get the judgment in their favour. Yet what is the option for us?

Several SC and backward caste households have lost their land to the *mahajan*s for over twenty years, and all attempts at repossession through the courts have failed. Even leaders of the Hul Jharkhand admitted that while a lot of land was recovered during the movement, some still remained

Table 13.1 Certificate cases

	Cases pending: 1.4.01		Cases filed after 1.4.01		Total disposed 2001-2	
	No.	Amount	No.	Amount	No.	Amount
Banks	3666	2.60 crore	1357	62.02 lakhs	468	93.19 lakhs
Total	4992	3.95 crore	1654	1.48 crore	546	1.01 crore

Note: Of the cases settled, 272 cases were within five years and 129 cases within five–ten years.

unclaimed. They estimate that 25 per cent of the land reclaimed may have reverted back into a situation of alienation.

The new Jharkhand government, given the slogan of *jal, jangal aur jameen* underlying its very formation, put up a notice about land restoration outside the treasury building in Dumka. This offers 2,500 rupees as legal aid and 5,000 rupees per acre as support for resuming agriculture on restored land. None of this money had, however, been sanctioned or distributed till 2003. Village visits revealed the existence of considerable land that has been alienated and not yet restored – lacking resources, both time and money, the *adivasis* who have lost their land are unable to make their claims successfully.

Ram Kol of a village in Jama block has not cultivated his land for close to twenty-five years. He first filed a case against the moneylender Bipin Mandal (Mandals are classified as Other Backward Classes [OBCs] in the region) in 1978 (as RE case[10] no. 209/78–79). An eviction order was passed by the then SDO on 16 July 1984; yet he could not reclaim his land due to threats of violence as well as his continued indebtedness and need for cash. He must have been to the different courts more than twenty times, spending anything between 30 rupees and 300 rupees on each trip. Once again, he filed RM case[11] no. 372/2000–01 in the court of the SDO, and the order in his favour was issued on 20 September 2002. He has finally been able to take possession of his land in early 2003, largely due to the encouragement and support of the village gram sabha and a local NGO, both of whom have steadily stood by him.

Taking hope and encouragement from this case, the Paharias of a neighbouring village also decided to try and reclaim some of their land, alienated to Vinay Mandal of Gamra village more than twenty–thirty years ago. In 2001, they tried to cultivate their own land and would not allow Vinay Mandal to plough. He, however, filed a case under Section 107 of the Criminal Procedure Code against them. This led to an engagement in the court, which was costly and time-consuming and which they could not have managed without the support of the NGO, the same one which had helped Ram Kol to recover his land. Another Paharia, Badwa Grihi, narrated his story with the courts. He had an earlier case with Vinay Mandal and, when he tried to cultivate his land, was threatened by him. The revenue *karamchari* asked him to file a case in the court of the Circle Officer (CO), which he did. The case ran there for three–four years, and then at the SDO's court for another two years. At that time, there was a settlement camp in this block, and the SDO sent him there. Badwa secured a decree in his favour. He was able to cultivate for a year, and was then again threatened, so he fled to Assam, and Vinay Mandal started cultivating his land again. A lot of money has been spent, and yet there has been no final settlement, the dates for hearings constantly being extended. The court practice is not easy to grasp or deal with in reality. Even though the government is now offering legal aid, this is to be given post-facto – ordinary people cannot bear the expenses for all those long years! Even when decrees are secured, the problem of implementation still remains, as the opposing party is usually the economically stronger one.

The truth of this became even more apparent when I spoke to the *pradhan* (headman) of a village on the outskirts of Dumka, part of which now falls within the municipal area. He is educated and has a petty government job. Yet he was unable to reclaim his own land that had been alienated many years ago. Till 1994, he regularly attended court hearings, despite the expense. Finally, the court or the lawyers, he is not sure who, misled him. Different dates were given to the two parties, and in his absence, the case was settled in favour of the other party. His own lawyer, a non-*adivasi*, was clearly in collusion with them. This is in fact a huge problem reported by many of the *adivasi*s – that the lawyers (a majority of them are non-*adivasi*s) take fees from them, yet work against their interests, as they have in all likelihood taken money from the other side too. An educated Paharia leader in Gopikandar block gave me a similar story. If *adivasi*s who are educated and not really the poorest are unable to use legal processes and institutions in their favour, clearly it is next to impossible for the poorest and resourceless.

Alternate legal systems can only be drawn upon if they are seen to be legitimate. In most of these cases, land has been alienated to non-*adivasi*s by both SCs and STs. The party that has taken the land does not see customary practices as legitimate, so the only option is to engage with state law. As per the SPTA, transfer of land from an *adivasi* to a non-*adivasi* as debt repayment is clearly 'fraudulent practice', and while an order is therefore likely to be ultimately issued in their favour, the process of law is time-consuming, manipulated by the better-off and difficult to enforce on the ground. The poor then often see the law as helping the rich (Goheen, 1988), and yet there is no option but engagement.

According to government records, a total of 3,132 cases were filed up to 2001–02. Among these, 1,952 cases were approved and 1,165 rejected. Only fifteen cases were carried over to 2002–03, and three new cases filed in the current year. Of these, seven have been resolved and eleven remain in balance. The DC (land reform) admitted that information was a problem; however, this appears to be an excuse for inaction. Information on pulse polio reaches every village, so it is not clear why information on the restoration of alienated land does not. Why are the revenue *karamcharis*, who have in-depth information of every village, not made in charge of collecting information on alienation? Putting up a board outside the treasury building in Dumka is hardly a sufficient strategy to spread information. These questions raise serious issues of intention in addition to interpretation.

Urban Development and the Quarrying of Stones

As already mentioned, the non-transferability of land in the Santal Parganas as per the SPTA is being represented as a barrier to industrial and urban development in the region. The opinions on liberalising the SPTA, however, continue to be sharply divided. While government officials, non-*adivasi* professionals (including lawyers) and the parties in power clearly support a move to liberalise the legislation (seeing this as hampering 'development'), local *adivasi*s as well as poorer Hindus and Muslims, NGOs, *adivasi* professionals and the Jharkhandi political parties have been opposed to such a move, fearing the rapid decline of *adivasi*s into landlessness.[12] While the all-party committee set up for reviewing the law faces strong opposition to its proposals for amendment, the problem remains on several fronts. One such relates to urbanisation, with the formation of Jharkhand state having given a fillip to the setting up of a range of administrative and professional institutions in the urban and peri-urban areas, such as training institutes, branch offices of business establishments and NGOs, leading to increased demands for land.

Since 2000, houses have rapidly been built on three times the municipal areas of Dumka and Deogarh, all on non-transferable *raiyati* land. Poor people, in need of money, have been pressurised to write *danpatra*s, or gift deeds, in favour of a third party, claiming them to be close friends or kin. The deed claims to donate some land to a needy and poor relative. This document does not have legal validity as it violates Section 20(v) of the SPTA, and hence potentially the land can be reclaimed by the owner at any time. The illegal nature of the transaction disadvantages the *adivasi*s as the buyers offer a lower price for the land, due to the risk involved in terms of insecurity of lease and the additional investment required for the construction of a house. The courts, as mentioned earlier, are, however, hardly seen as reliable, in ensuring repossession of the land if the need arises. The mafia element has now entered land transactions, taking over land at cheap rates and 'selling' them for a profit.

This is the story emerging from village after village close to Dumka town. A lot of people from other parts of Jharkhand or even from other states (especially Bihar) now reside in these villages, with 95 per cent on *danpatras*. They are all employed in Dumka. It is interesting that only 10–15 per cent of the *adivasi*s have such employment; a majority continue to be engaged in agriculture and wage labour. About a third of the land in these villages has now effectively been sold, but the price received was perhaps one-fourth of the real value of the land, had it been saleable. There have so far not been any disputes, but the headman and some of the other residents of Kadhadbil village were despondent: 'In any case we have given up our land. If this had been legal, we would at least have got a correct price.' At present, only the homestead, or *basodi* land, is legally transferable, and this is very little in quantum. They cannot stop the trend; yet seeing the surrounding villages loose some of their best land to outsiders, the community here has made some rules in relation to *danpatras*. They have agreed not to transfer cultivated fields but try and make transfers only on the roadside.[13]

The Samata judgment does note that the purpose of special laws was to protect the *adivasi*s from moneylenders and contractors. Hence, if an amendment is needed in these special laws for the sake of urban or industrial development, then the respective chief ministers should draft a policy for their state and then seek amendment from the parliament. While there is no further discussion on amending the law, there is a rampant illegal process working against the interests of the *adivasi*s. As some of the lawyers in Dumka said to me:

There is a lot of government land available, only 30 per cent of the land is *raiyati* land, so why take that?[14] Why can't the land that is not used for agriculture be used for other development purposes? Also, if the government does need *raiyati* land for urban development, then this should be acquired under due process of law through the Land Acquisition Act, 1894, with proper compensation rather than allowing illegal private transactions.

Of course, this too is problematic, as revealed in the Pachwara case discussed earlier.[15] As land is not transferable, hence alternative land virtually impossible to acquire, how the future livelihood security of those displaced would be ensured needs to be carefully worked out.

This issue of fair compensation and understanding the multifarious processes of alienation has again arisen in the context of a rapid expansion of stone quarries, with more than 120 of them having been established in Dumka district between 2000, when Jharkhand was formed, and 2003, when this study was undertaken.[16] According to the District Mining Officer, mining leases are granted under the Bihar Mining Concessionary Rules, 1972, with approval of the DC. As underground mineral rights are vested with the government, they receive a royalty per truckload of stones removed. Concerned with a rapid loss of livelihoods and large-scale migration of *adivasis* from the area, the Association for Weaker Adivasis Enhancement and Rural Development, Sahebganj, filed writ petition no. 842/2001 in the Ranchi high court, requesting a stay on the renewal of old and granting of new mining leases till such time as the mining rules were revised. The Advocate General of the state, however, issued a letter of clarification (no. 724 dated 16 June 2001) to the DCs of Sahebganj and Pakur districts in the Santal Parganas, stating, 'Though the case was pending, the high court had not passed any interim order of stay for the mining leases already granted nor passed any order restraining the state of Jharkhand from either refusing or granting any fresh lease.'[17] The granting of leases has therefore continued apace, the revenues from royalty reaching a record of 2.12 crore rupees for Dumka during the year 2002–03.

According to the SPTA, any transfer of *adivasi* land is illegal, with the exceptions outlined in Section 20, confirmed by the Samata judgment in the context of transfer of land for mining. In the stone quarries, too, no formal transfer of land was taking place, though the owner of the land made a 'private agreement' with the contractor to clear his land of stones. The lease agreement is usually for five years or a maximum of ten years; it is informal and not controlled by the state. Discussions with stone quarry and stone crusher contractors in Sikaripara block of Dumka district revealed ambiguity regarding the time period of the lease agreement and the amount of money paid for the land on which the quarries and crushers were located. Estimates varied from 3,000–5,000 rupees per *bigha*,[18] and the time period ranged from five to twenty years. While there are a few Santals amongst the quarry contractors and owners, the majority are not *adivasis*. The people in the region, mostly *adivasis*, are poor, so in return for some cash to meet their consumption and credit needs, they agreed to make affidavits and hand over their land to the contractors. In most cases, the affidavits say that the land is rocky; hence, they are seeking help from the contractor to clear it of stones and make it cultivable!

The stone quarries have raised a range of issues around wages, health hazards, common property and the social character of the population itself. While the government minimum wage rate is 64 rupees for an eight-hour working day, the contractors usually make the workers work longer hours for a lower rate of 45 rupees per day. This has been facilitated by the fact that almost half the workers on the quarries are migrants from outside the district. Some of the villages have now started organising the workers to demand minimum wages, but threats of not being given work in a context where there is a large pool of labour waiting for work make such organisation difficult. The prevalence of silicosis and other health problems due to pollution and the dust from crushers are well known. The Mining Rules therefore have a list of requirements such as the construction of a protective wall, provision of protective gear, and so on, to reduce the adverse health impacts. In all the crushers I visited, neither was there a protective wall (12 feet high as per the rules) on all sides of the crusher nor were the workers, mainly women, given any protective gear. The activity being fairly recent, the long-term health impacts are yet to be felt.

An unexpected problem was raised in one of the villages I visited. A group of local youth reported that the mine owners were throwing the mud dug out of the quarry on the *gauchar*, or common grazing land, of the village, and this was now a big heap and totally unusable for grazing purposes (Figure 13.1). Maintaining their cattle had become a problem for the villagers. They met the DC, who asked the CO to enquire into the matter and file a report. The CO never visited the area but filed his report at the behest of the contractors. The grazing land is now virtually lost without any compensation. Without cattle, agriculture itself is also at risk, affecting all cultivable lands. Cultivation has already declined, particularly of pulses such as *arhar* and *kurthi* that were grown on the lands now being quarried. These pulses are too expensive to purchase in the market, and hence a major source of protein has literally vanished from local diets. While perhaps production from the land has never been sufficient for all their needs; yet apart from

Figure 13.1 Waste dumped on grazing lands near stone quarries in Dumka
Source: Photograph by Amit Mitra.

ensuring a minimum food security, it gave poor villagers access to credit and other resources, as well as bargaining power vis-à-vis other groups. As landowners, they were recognised and visited by government functionaries and revenue officers at least occasionally. Now without the land, they seem to have dropped out of the radars of the state and other public agencies; they feel totally marginalised, their voices unheard, if not ignored.

The villagers who have lost their land to the quarries are reduced to wage labourers. Some get jobs locally in the quarries and the crushers. Despite low wages, there has been a sudden spurt of cash flowing into the local economy, resulting in the growing consumption of liquor as well as a rise in sexual crimes. This was evident to me on my visit in 2003, when at 10 a.m. in the morning, there was already liquor being sold and consumed, a sight that I had rarely seen in the area since 1995 except, of course, during market days.

In terms of land policy, it is clear that a lot of land is being taken over by the quarry contractors through private agreements or land developers through *danpatras* that are not only illegal as per the SPTA, but which also deny the owner a fair compensation for the use of his or her land. This is being supported by the silences of the state, which in many ways condones this illegal alienation of *adivasi* land to fulfil its vision of development. The *adivasi*s, though resourceless, have been organising to protest these fraudulent transfers. There have been a few successes as in the case of Ram Kol, but these are few and far between. Interestingly the reversals due to the nexus of contractors, bureaucrats and political leaders, largely non-*adivasi*s, has not stopped the *adivasi*s from continuing to resort to official mechanisms including judicial intervention. These appear to be a part of everyday lives, and despite the odds, the only way to claim recognition as citizens, with rights that need to be protected and respected by the state apparatus.

Institutions Governing Dispute Resolution

Several comments have already been made in the previous sections on the functioning of the courts and their inability to resolve disputes around land satisfactorily. While exploring the functioning of the judicial system is beyond the scope of this chapter, I want to briefly draw attention to the diversity of laws and institutions that deal with land, and the social relations involved, adding to the complexity of processes of dispute resolution.

*Adivasi*s, a majority of them Santal, constitute almost a third of the population of the Santal Parganas. The rest include Hindus (46 per cent, both SCs and BCs), Muslims (18 per cent) and Christians (2 per cent). Land transfer amongst the Hindus is largely governed by the Hindu Succession Act, 1956, which entitles all children (including daughters) to inherit an equal share of their father's property (following an amendment in August 2005). Its clear articulation of inheritance rights enables people including women to approach the legal courts for justice. A review of cases filed in the court of the SDO, Dumka, over the last ten years revealed that a majority of the women involved with land cases in the court were Hindu women. It is also interesting to note that due to the differences of both caste and class amongst the Hindus, local dispute resolution mechanisms have all but collapsed, and use of the legal courts, with all its costs, delays and complexities, is common practice. In fact, the number of such disputes between the rich and the poor Hindus increased markedly after 1980, when the survey and settlement operations began in the Santal Parganas. Many people for the first time realised that they owned particular plots of land, which they had assumed had long since been alienated to the richer landlords. It is not only the *adivasis*, but even the poorer Hindus, especially the SCs and the BCs, who were glad that land was not transferable in the Santal Parganas. Otherwise, they would today have no land left and be landless wage labourers for the large landlords, as is the case in most other parts of India.

Muslims, like the Hindus, have a clear inheritance law as per the Shariat Act, 1937, that entitles daughters to inherit half that of sons. Even though there is inequity in shares, a legal share is ensured to both sons and daughters. Unlike the Hindus, Muslim women, however, are not making claims to their share of the land. In one village with a significant Muslim population, they clarified, 'Agriculture is not our primary occupation, as we do not have much land for cultivation. Our men are engaged in petty business. There is hence no point in making a claim for land.' Still, if there is a dispute, they try to resolve it locally, with the help of the *pradhan* of the village, and only in the last resort, do they go to the courts. In fact, revenue court records reveal only very few cases filed by Muslims.

The Santals, as already mentioned, have no codified personal law, the SPTA being a tenancy Act. The central government can, by notification, bring the Santals under Hindu law; however, such a measure has been opposed by the Jharkhand movement. The result of lack of a codified personal law is particularly adverse for women – as while customary law does allow for a range of circumstances in which women can inherit land, this is hard to prove in a court of law (Archer, 1984 [1946]). Perhaps it is because of the absence of a codified personal law and the reliance of land inheritance and transfers on customary practices that community institutions for resolving land disputes continue to exist (see Chapter 4). Most claims made by women, in the event of polygyny, divorce or widowhood are in fact resolved at the village level. An in-depth study in two villages of Dumka district revealed that while only 1.5 and 4.5 per cent of women were recorded titleholders, 11 and 12.5 per cent had actual control over land (Rao, 2008). Interestingly, customary institutions have usually supported women's claims to land because in supporting what is seen as fair in 'custom', though challenged on grounds of resource scarcity, they are in fact attempting to re-establish and boost the legitimacy of their own status within society.

This is particularly crucial in light of the present discussion on the meanings of alienation, where *adivasis* are struggling to establish the legitimacy of their claims for 'community control' vis-à-vis state efforts to take over their land in exchange for differing levels of individual compensation. Conflating their struggle for securing their authority in the sphere of land distribution and management with women's struggles for land offers the community leaders advantages in terms of retaining their distinct identity, projecting an image of 'fairness', as well as maintaining a social security mechanism, in a context where state provision is lacking.

It is worth mentioning that this is not a new struggle but one that goes back to the McPherson settlement of 1909, which for the first time set up settlement courts to resolve land disputes, hitherto the exclusive domain of local customary institutions (Bodding, Skresfrud and Konow, 1942). The settlement courts, like other judicial bodies under the colonial government, took a rather rigid, patriarchal view on women's land rights. Hence, right from the start, the issue of women's rights was one that was championed and used by the customary institutions to establish their own legitimacy. It demonstrated their commitment to fairness and upholding the rights of all members of the community, men and women.

Yet a range of courts too are used, from the temporary settlement courts, set up to hear and resolve disputes at the local level during the survey and settlement process, to the civil and criminal courts. While in general very few *adivasi* women have approached the courts for their rights and prefer a quick settlement in the community (as land is a key livelihood resource for them), there are a few who have filed cases, and while there is often no judgment, they use it as a threat against the male kin. Most of these are within *adivasi* groups, so the different legal systems can be manipulated to their advantage.

As mentioned by several people, they often discovered that they were the owners of particular plots of land through the settlement courts, which, being both local and informal in process, not requiring the intervention of lawyers, were more accessible to them. The civil courts lie in the purview of the Revenue Department – the courts of the SDO, the Assistant Collector (AC) and the DC, and are most commonly used in land alienation cases. All these follow the provisions of the SPTA.

If there is violence of any kind, however, police complaints are filed, and the cases go directly to the courts of the Sub-Judge and the District Judge. Criminal cases range from minor beating (Section 107) and breach of peace (Section 144) to robbery (Section 394) and murder (Section 302).

The court fixes dates for hearings, lawyers are appointed, and the cases are argued. While there is an attempt to resolve minor cases within a period of sixty days, most others go on for years. Unlike the settlement courts or even the revenue courts, the proceedings in the criminal courts are couched in the legalistic and official language of the Indian Penal Code. Less accessible to the Santals, local notions of legitimacy or fairness are hardly taken into account.[19]

Conclusion

The SPTA forms the basis for governing land relations and transactions in the Santal Parganas. Given a history of land alienation from the *adivasi*s to the non-*adivasi*s and the exploitation of the former by a range of vested interests, including traders and petty bureaucrats, the Act (through Section 20) has sought to protect *adivasi* rights to land by making all land in the region non-transferable. There are, however, a few exceptions to this clause, primarily in relation to women's land claims. After independence, a few amendments have been made to facilitate conditional mortgage to banks (1976) as well as to stop any fraudulent transfer that was still taking place (1969).

Loopholes, however, remain, both in implementation and the very interpretation of what is considered fraudulent practice. Several land lease, mortgage and gift arrangements, such as the gifting of land through *danpatra*s in the urban and semi-urban areas, have emerged to bypass the Act, resulting in the alienation of land belonging to the poorer *adivasi*, Hindu and Muslim residents of the region. While cases can be filed under Section 20 of the SPTA for restoration, and some legal aid too is being currently offered for such cases, the legal process being time-consuming, slow and expensive, has not helped many people recover their land.

In the last few years, there has also been considerable transfer of land through privately negotiated, temporary lease arrangements for stone quarrying and crushing, from *adivasi*s to outside contractors. This has no doubt helped generate local employment. Yet it has also raised issues in relation to the terms of employment, particularly wages, health hazards, the destruction of common property (such as grazing lands being used to dump the mud from the quarries) and the long-term implications in terms of the sustainability of local livelihoods, in a context where alternative livelihood resources are hardly available.

In line with its new industrial policy, the government is also acquiring land for mining and other developmental activities through private enterprise, without appropriate compensation or attention to the long-term livelihood security of the *adivasi*s. Apart from issues in relation to the rehabilitation package, the process adopted seems to be in gross violation of the Supreme Court's Samata judgment (1997) that required mining operations in scheduled areas to be conducted in consultation with and preferably with the participation of the local *adivasi*s (through cooperatives). Neither of these recommendations has been given any consideration at all. While the SPTA is seen to hamper industrial and urban development, it needs to be recognised that it is the SPTA that is responsible for the fact that there are still proportionately few landless people in the region. While not well off, they are at least able to survive. It is not surprising then to find a mushrooming of protest movements, using a range of techniques from direct action to applications for administrative or legal redressal in response to the new emphasis on industrial and urban development and to the exclusion of rural livelihoods.

As land becomes increasingly scarce and there are multiple demands on it, conflicts and disputes will only increase. The first attempt is always to resolve them locally, but if violence erupts, or the dispute is between members of different communities, then there is no option but to use the legal process. Yet there is much to be desired from the functioning of the courts. As one lawyer noted, in 95 per cent of the cases, the parties stop attending after some time. Apart from the difficulties in court procedures, there is also no way of ensuring that the order given finally is implemented at the village level. The party with power, both economic and social, tends to get the better deal in practice. This includes the locally dominant but also institutions of the state.

A final plea in lieu of a conclusion – more than 80 per cent of the population of the Santal Parganas are dependent on land and agriculture as their primary source of livelihood. State policies and institutions need to recognise that the meanings of land diverge depending on the perspective adopted. With few alternatives in sight, land and natural-resource-based sectors of development that have the potential to benefit large numbers of people should be prioritised, rather than adopting a strategy of economic growth based on private investments and profits. Strengthening agricultural development and social security can contribute to securing the livelihoods of a majority of the *adivasi*s, at present at the bottom of the social and economic hierarchy.

Appendix 13A

Major Landmarks in Land Legislation and Settlement in the Santal Parganas

1855	Act 37, which led to the creation of a separate district of Santal Parganas, removed from the operation of the general laws and regulations
1872	Santal Pargana Settlement Regulation III, which recommended a land survey and settlement, restored powers of the village headman and limited interest rates to 24 per cent
1873–79	First land settlement under the guidance of Browne Wood, which demarcated village boundaries, identified community rights and fixed rents in consultation with the headman
1886	Regulation II to stop all land transfers – if a person had occupancy rights for twelve years, however, land could then be transferred to him or her
1898–1907	Second land settlement under McPherson – individual rents were fixed for the first time and settlement courts set up to resolve disputes
1922–35	Third settlement under J. F. Gantzer – this report was the precursor to the Santal Pargana Tenancy Act (SPTA), 1949
1948	Bihar Privileged Persons Homestead Tenancy Act, 1948, granting titles to artisans on occupancy of twelve years
1949	SPTA passed soon after independence to protect the rights of the local people, especially Scheduled Tribes (STs) over their land and common resources
1969	Bihar Scheduled Areas Regulation Act, which aimed to control continuing land transfers by extending the period under consideration from twelve to thirty years
1976	Santal Pargana Tenancy (Supplementary Provisions) Amendment Act (also known as Bihar Act 17 of 1976) to allow mortgage to banks in line with the procedure of the Bihar and Orissa Public Demands Recovery Act, 1914
1977	14 October: Bihar Gazette Notification on a new survey and settlement

1989	Amendment to the Bihar Privileged Persons Homestead Tenancy Act, 1948, restricting its application in the case of non-transferable land in scheduled areas such as the Santal Parganas

Notes

1. While the SPTA provisions are detailed in the next section, the main contention of the Samata judgment was that mining operations in *adivasi* areas can only be conducted through state mineral development corporations in partnership with cooperatives of *adivasi*s. Further, 20 per cent of the net profit should be spent on education, health and communication services and the general upliftment of the local *adivasi*s.

2. With the advent of colonial rule in 1765, and particularly following the Permanent Settlement of Bengal in 1793, the need was felt by the colonial rulers to enhance revenues from land. As the Paharias were unwilling to give up forest-based activities and take to settled agriculture, in 1818, the Damin-i-koh was constituted as a *khas mahal* (government estate) and the Santals encouraged to reclaim and settle land for cultivation.

3. Act 37 of 1855 made this into a separate district, removed from the operation of the general laws and regulations. It contained both the hilly Damin-i-Koh tracts (that include parts of Dumka, Godda, Pakur and Sahebganj districts and were demarcated in 1832 as a reserve area for the *adivasi*s) and the plain lands that were *zamindari* estates attached earlier to Birbhum.

4. Literally meaning a house son-in-law, this is a situation where after marriage a girl stays in her natal home with her husband and inherits natal property.

5. There is a need to amend the Santal Civil Rules, 1946, to introduce women's inheritance or, indeed, draft a separate personal law for this purpose.

6. Section 27 of the Santal Parganas Settlement Regulation, 1872, adopted in Section 20(v) of the SPTA.

7. According to Section 42, the DC may at any time eject any person who encroached upon or acquired agricultural land in contravention of the provisions of this Act.

8. For further details on Hul Jharkhand and the agrarian movement in the Santal Parganas during the 1960s and 1970s, see Rao (2008).

9. *Bhugatbandha* refers to a lease of land that is legally recorded and the maximum duration of which can extend to six years as per Section 21 of the

SPTA. It is almost totally restricted to Hindu and Muslim groups, who are legally not allowed to acquire land in any other form.

10. Raiyati Eviction, or RE, cases relate to unauthorised encroachment.

11. Revenue Miscellaneous, or RM, cases are related to demarcation, tenancy and inheritance issues and constitute 75 per cent of all cases filed in the revenue courts.

12. More recently, the political parties have taken an ambiguous stand, supporting land acquisition for the purposes of industrial and urban development.

13. This resolve appears to have weakened, and during a visit in January 2023, I found the city expanding and large rural tracts taken over for infrastructure and institutions.

14. Recent agricultural statistics put this at 39 per cent, while 17.5 per cent of the land area consists of non-cultivable wastelands.

15. Under the LAA, compensation is calculated on the basis of the capitalised value of the output for fifteen years. In the case of *basodi* land, the average rate on which such land has been transferred in the previous three years is taken into account for fixing a price.

16. The total number was 190, only 70 quarries having existed prior to the formation of Jharkhand.

17. Translation mine from the original Hindi.

18. Three *bigha*s make an acre of land.

19. Following several years of harassment over a land dispute, Miru's eldest son was killed by her male kin in January 1999. They were arrested, but being stronger in financial terms, they were able to pay for lawyers who secured bail for them. This was resented by the villagers, since this family had consistently gone against the diktats of the village council and was all out to destroy Miru's family. The court, however, paid no heed to the social threat created by granting them bail.

References

Archer, W. G. 1984 (1946). *Tribal Law and Justice: A Report on the Santal.* New Delhi: Concept Publishing Company.

Benda-Beckmann, F. von. 2001. 'Legal Pluralism and Social Justice in Economic and Political Development'. *IDS Bulletin* 32(1): 46–56.

Bodding, P. O., L. O. Skresfrud and S. Konow. 1994 (1942). *Traditions and Institutions of the Santals.* New Delhi: Bahumukhi Prakashan.

Carney, J. 1988. 'Struggles over Crop Rights and Labour within Contract Farming Households in a Gambian Irrigated Rice Project'. *Journal of Peasant Studies* 15(3): 334–49.

Demian, M. 2003. 'Custom in the Courtroom, Law in the Village: Legal Transformations in Papua New Guinea'. *Journal of the Royal Anthropological Institute* 9(1): 97–115.

Fraser, N. 1989. *Unruly Practices: Power, Discourse and Gender in Contemporary Social Theory.* Cambridge, UK: Polity Press.

Gantzer, J. F. 1936. *Final Report on the Revision Survey and Settlement Operations in the District of Santal Parganas, 1922–35.* Patna: Superintendent, Government Printing.

Goheen, M. 1988. 'Land Accumulation and Local Control: The Manipulation of Symbols and Power in Nso, Cameroon'. In *Land and Society in Contemporary Africa,* edited by R. E. Downs and S. P. Reyna, 280–308. Hanover and London: University Press of New England.

MacDougall, J. 1985. 'Land or Religion? The Sardar and Kherwar Movements in Bihar, 1858–95'. New Delhi: Manohar.

Mackenzie, F. 1990. 'Gender and Land Rights in Murang'a District, Kenya'. *Journal of Peasant Studies* 7(4): 609–43.

McPherson, H. 1909. *Final Report on the Survey and Settlement Operations in the District of Santhal Parganas, 1898–1907.* Calcutta: Bengal Secretariat Book Depot.

Meinzen-Dick, R., and R. Pradhan. 2002. 'Legal Pluralism and Dynamic Property Rights'. CAPRI Working Paper 22, International Food Policy Research Institute, Washington, DC.

Orans, M. 1965. *The Santal: A Tribe in Search of a Great Tradition.* Detroit, MI: Wayne State University Press.

Peters, P. 2002. 'Bewitching Land: The Role of Land Disputes in Converting Kin to Strangers and in Class Formation in Malawi'. *Journal of Southern African Studies* 28(1): 155–78.

Prasad, B. M. 1997. *Santal Parganas Tenancy Manual.* Patna: Malhotra Bros.

People's Union for Civil Liberties (PUCL). 2003. *PUCL Enquiry Report, 2003, Pachwara Coalmining Project, Conducted by P.A. Chacko, Anant Hembrom, Md. Rehman and B.N. Upadhyaya.* New Delhi: People's Union for Civil Liberties.

Rao, N. 2008. *Good Women Do Not Inherit Land: Politics of Land and Gender in India*. New Delhi: Social Science Press and Orient Blackswan.

Singh, K. S. 1966. *The Dust-Storm and the Hanging Mist*. Calcutta: Firma and KL Mukhopadhyay.

Strathern, M. 1996. 'Cutting the Network'. *Journal of the Royal Anthropological Institute* 2(3): 517–35.

Part VI

Conclusion

14

Looking Ahead

Policy Implications for Equitable Development

Introduction

The state of Jharkhand was formed in August 2000, a result of the long-standing movement against large imbalances in the distribution of resources – with contestations over ownership of *jal* (water), *jangal* (forest) and *jamin* (land) – and an assertion of tribal identity and self-determination (Jewitt, 2008). Jharkhand was faced with adverse initial conditions – low average income, high incidence of poverty and little social development (World Bank, 2001). More than twenty years after its formation, there have been significant improvements in human development and multidimensional poverty indicators like literacy, health, sanitation and nutrition. But what has this meant for the *adivasi* populations of the state, their identity, culture and knowledge? What has it meant for the aspirations and well-being of women and youth?

The *Vision 2010* document of Jharkhand, while recognising a 52 per cent deficit in food grain production, with half the per capita availability of food in comparison to the national average, aspired to convert Jharkhand into another 'Singapore' (see Chapter 11). At the same time, in line with the government of India's priorities, the government launched a State Agriculture Plan (2008–09 to 2011–12) to improve agriculture infrastructure, ensure adequate credit flow and implement capacity-building measures (Nabard Consultancy Services, n.d.). The Jharkhand Economic Survey, 2016–17, points to the impressive growth rate of the state between 2011–16, higher than the national average (6.8 per cent) and only lower than that of Gujarat, Mizoram and Tripura between the financial years 2011–12 and 2015–16 (8.8

per cent). For the financial year 2015–16, the growth rate at over 12 per cent was much higher than the national average at 7.6 per cent.

Following the NITI Aayog's (National Institution for Transforming India) ambitious blueprint for 2032 (published in 2016), the Chief Minister of Jharkhand committed to working on eliminating poverty, doubling farmer's income by 2022 and ensuring sustainable development in Jharkhand (Swaniti, 2017). A new Vision document prepared by the Confederation of Indian Industry in 2011 emphasised three key areas: minimum quality of life, governance, and sustainable economic development. The vision remains a top-down one, driven by the elites, largely non-*adivasi*, bureaucrats and the private sector. *Adivasi* voices and priorities are largely missing.

The chapters in this book have outlined the gendered opportunities and pitfalls confronting the Santals in relation to access to resources, especially land; livelihood opportunities; the experiences of migration, education and social well-being; and the politics of policymaking over the past two decades. In this chapter, I look back to the development context of Jharkhand and the changes since its formation, pointing to both what has worked and what has not, and for whom. I then provide a few examples of the implications of this development trajectory for *adivasi* women and youth in particular, and highlight the need to recognize their agency and aspirations, treating them as equal citizens, rather than as 'beneficiaries' of state support, reduced to mere numbers in project reports. In the final section, I present a few reflections on potential future directions for research, policy and action.

The Changing Development Context

Jharkhand is home to abundant biodiversity and fertile land, with forests accounting for over 29 per cent of its land area. While agriculture is the mainstay of the rural population, the state contains some 40 per cent of the country's mineral reserves (including coal, iron ore, bauxite, limestone) (Swaniti, 2017). The rich reservoir of natural resources and biodiversity has attracted considerable investment in industries, mines and various thermal and hydel projects by large corporations. Yet Jharkhand is one of eight states in the 'Hindi heartland' known for its socio-economic and demographic backwardness. Economic growth has clearly not been enough to ensure the inclusion of its Scheduled Tribe (ST) population into mainstream institutions, in both the political (state) and economic (market) domains. Their numbers have declined from 32.6 per cent in 1991 to 26.2 per cent of the population in 2011, pointing to an inflow of other (non-*adivasi*) population groups into Jharkhand but also the eviction and displacement of *adivasi*s from their lands (Lahiri-Dutt, Balakrishnan and Nesar, 2012). This decline is observed most acutely in the Santal Parganas districts (Baraik, 2019). Intensification of the historical marginalisation of the *adivasi*s, which the creation of the state of Jharkhand had sought to redress, has led to a range of responses from communities, especially young people – from migration to other states in search of opportunities for securing their livelihoods to a withdrawal from active citizenship by joining the ultra-left Maoist movement.

As if to compensate for state repression, in 2013, the Jharkhand Tribal Empowerment and Livelihoods Project (JTELP) was initiated in fourteen districts, with financial support from the International Fund for Agricultural Development (IFAD). The project highlighted the principles of the Jharkhand movement – *jal, jangal, jameen* (water, forests, land), adding to this *janwar* (animals) and *jan* (people) – and sought to work on community empowerment, integrated natural resource management and livelihood enhancement. Claiming to have reached over 200,000 *adivasi* farmers, substantially improving their agricultural incomes, and contributing towards building community institutions, the project closed at the end of 2021 (IFAD, 2022). While empowerment, or even development, is a process of change, which should reflect an expansion of freedoms and choices for those involved, across space and time, the state's conceptualisation of these processes appears to be both directive and delimited. It raises questions about the goals and vision of the state, and how they compare to the needs and aspirations of communities and individuals on the ground.

Interventions for education and skill development provide insight into the nature of development efforts being undertaken to build human capacities, for instance. The current government has launched the Marang Gomke Jaipal Singh Munda Overseas (MGJSMO) Scholarship Scheme, which provides five youth from ST, Scheduled Caste (SC), minority and Other Backward Class (OBC) backgrounds in the state scholarships to pursue higher education in prestigious universities in the United Kingdom and Ireland. The MGJSMO scheme seeks to identify and promote talent for academic excellence, and while worthwhile, it is a far cry from the realities of children and young people living in the remote and rural parts of the state, seeking collective identity as much as, if not more than, individual success. Undoubtedly, considerable progress has been made in terms of basic education, as noted in Chapter 1; yet inequalities of physical (in)access, linguistic exclusion and gender-related deprivation persist (Baraik, 2019), amplified further by schemes such as the MGJSMO.

Recognising the low level of educational outcomes, especially for *adivasi* youth, those residing in rural areas and in the Santal Parganas region of the state, the Jharkhand Skill Development Mission Society (JSDMS) has launched a range of vocational schemes for skilling youth to enhance their employability. The state government, between 2017 and 2019, also organised Global Investors Summits, signing more than 200 memoranda of understanding (MOUs) with industries across the world to set up units in Jharkhand. The skilled human resource requirement for these industries was supposed to be fulfilled by the youth in the state (Press Trust of India [PTI], 2021a). An ambitious target of establishing 200 government industrial training institutes (ITIs) by 2021 was set (Government of Jharkhand and PHD Chamber of Commerce and Industry, 2019). However, at the time of writing, the ITI portal of the government still lists the number of ITIs at 58 (Directorate of Employment and Training, n.d.).

The Jharkhand skills gap study (2012–17 and 2017–22) uncovered several constraints faced by the *adivasi*s, including gender-specific concerns (National Skill Development Corporation [NSDC], n.d.). Most young women cited the lack of vocational training institutes close to their homes as a barrier, alongside the absence of suitable job opportunities. As discussed in several chapters in this book, dignity and respect are central to the lives and livelihoods of Santals, as is the case for other tribes in the state and, indeed, globally. Labouring jobs, with little control over their bodies or work, may be essential for survival, but they would not be an obvious choice, in terms of investments in shaping their future life pathways. Breaking out of the colonial stereotype of Santals, and *adivasi*s more generally, as 'manual labour' has been a key element in their struggle for identity.

In December 2021, the Jharkhand labour and employment minister informed the state assembly that Jharkhand had reached the highest level of joblessness among the five neighbouring states and stood fourth in the country in terms of unemployment rate since the COVID-19 pandemic hit the country. In a span of two years during the pandemic, the employment exchanges saw a rise in 638 per cent of applications by youth. He also informed the assembly that none of the 645,844 jobless people registered with forty-three employment offices in the twenty-four districts got jobs; nor were they receiving any unemployment allowance (PTI, 2021b). While deeply saddening at a personal level, this admission brings to the fore questions about the development vision being pursued by the state over the last two decades. Are there lessons that can be learnt and more bottom-up pathways adopted?

This question becomes urgent when we turn to the data on food and nutrition security in the state. A rapid assessment conducted by a group of civil society organisations in 2018 revealed that 50 per cent of the population did not have enough food for their needs (Welthungerhilfe, 2019). The public distribution system (PDS) plays a crucial role in reducing food insecurity by distributing food grains at subsidised rates and acting as a safety net, especially for the poor and vulnerable (George and McKay, 2019). In Chapter 11, I had noted a total collapse of the PDS in the Santal Parganas, the siphoning of grains into the open market, a situation that persisted till the implementation of the National Food Security Act, 2013, in mid-2016 (Drèze et al., 2017). The state government's experiments at addressing localised corruption through the introduction of compulsory Aadhaar-based biometric authentication, or direct benefit transfer (DBT), provide a sobering saga of inclusion and exclusion errors. In mid-2017, the state found 11.6 lakh ration cards to be 'fake' as they were not linked with Aadhaar cards. Many households lost their access to subsidised food, and Right to Food activists in Jharkhand reported deaths due to hunger and malnutrition between September 2017 and June 2019. Though the cancellation was retracted following protests from civil society, the human costs were high. Jharkhand recorded the sixth highest proportion of exclusion from welfare benefits due to Aadhaar-related issues in the country (Totapally et al., 2019). In a similar tale, the government transferred food subsidies into the bank accounts of PDS beneficiaries who had to travel (multiple times) to the bank to withdraw cash and then buy rations from the PDS dealer. For widows, the elderly and manual workers, this became a nightmare, initiating a period of hunger. The scheme, fortunately a pilot, was rolled back in October 2018, after nearly a year of protests by the local people and various activist groups.

These experiments with fragile lives, people with little voice in the political or economic mainstream, demonstrate the gaps between the government and its *adivasi* people. While some progress cannot be denied, Jharkhand today has the third highest prevalence of stunting and wasting in children aged below five and the highest levels of anaemia among women aged between fifteen and forty-nine (International Institute for Population Sciences [IIPS] and ICF International, 2017) (see Table 14.1).

Table 14.1 Nutrition indicators in Jharkhand as per the National Family Health Survey (NFHS)-3, NFHS-4 and NFHS-5 (per cent)

Indicators	NFHS-3 (2005–06)				NFHS-4 (2015–16)				NFHS 5 (2019–20)			
	India	Jharkhand	STs	SCs	India	Jharkhand	STs	SCs	India	Jharkhand	STs	SCs
Under-five stunting	44.9	49.8	54.5	53.7	38.4	45.3	48.8	52.2	35.5	39.6	44.9	40.8
Under-five wasting	22.9	32.3	39.5	28.5	21.0	29	34.4	30.8	19.3	22.4	25.2	20.9
Underweight children	40.4	56.5	64.2	56	35.8	47.8	55	54	32.1	39.4	46.4	41.1
Anaemia in children (six to fifty-nine months)	78.9	70.3	79.5	76.8	58.6	69.9	78.4	71.9	67.1	67.4	72.8	70.7
Anaemia in women of reproductive age (fifteen to forty-nine)	56.2	69.5	85.0	72.6	53.1	65.2	75.0	66.4	57.0	65.3	72.0	66.1
Women with below normal BMI (< 18.5 kilograms per square metre)	33	43.0	47.2	39.2	22.9	31.5	34.9	34.8	18.7	26.2	28.0	29.2
Men with below normal BMI (< 18.5 kilograms per square metre)	28.1	38.6	42.1	41.1	20.2	23.8	29.0	24.6	16.2	17.1	17.9	17.2
Infant mortality rate (IMR) (per 1,000 live births)	57	69	N/A	N/A	40.7	43.8	N/A	N/A	35.2	37.9	N/A	N/A

Source: Compiled by the author with data from NFHS-3, NFHS-4 and NFHS-5.

In fact, the National Family Health Survey (NFHS)-5 records anaemia in children and women of reproductive age at an alarming 67 per cent and 65 per cent, respectively. The situation is worse for STs and SCs, where 73 per cent of children and 72 per cent of women of reproductive age are anaemic. According to the World Health Organisation (WHO), if in a population, the prevalence of anaemia is 40 per cent or higher, it constitutes a severe public health problem (*The Telegraph*, 2021).

The Expert Committee on Tribal Health, set up by the Ministry of Health and Family Welfare and the Ministry of Tribal Affairs, conducted a first-of-its-kind examination of inequity in health faced by the *adivasis* of India to recommend ways of addressing it. The report of the committee concluded that *adivasi* communities face the 'triple burden of disease' and that 'tribal health must receive first and the highest attention' (Government of India, 2018). The experts pointed to the near complete absence of community participation and lack of consideration for the needs and aspirations of the *adivasi* communities in the planning, design and implementation of health services.

Despite this expert committee recommendation, the heavy-handed, top-down approach, apparently only seeking to shift numbers, rather than improve the lives of people, has continued. In December 2016, the Jharkhand government launched double fortified salt (DFS) to fight anaemia, where households were given 1 kilogram of the iron and iodine fortified salt at 1 rupee per month through the ration shops run under the PDS. The programme touched twenty-six million people in the state till March 2019, when it was replaced by the distribution of iron folic acid (IFA), calcium and albendazole tablets under the aegis of the centre's Anaemia Mukt Bharat programme. The beneficiary list constituted pregnant and lactating women, children and adolescents (Ray, 2019), leaving out the rest of the population. However, in 2021, ignoring the micronutrient supplementation, the central government adopted a 'cost-efficient way' of addressing malnutrition by distributing iron fortified rice through the PDS (Kumar and Shekhar, 2021). A fact-finding study found adverse effects of this on people (especially *adivasi*s) with sickle cell disorders (SCDs) and thalassemia (Accredited Social Health Activist [ASHA] and Right to Food Campaign, 2022).

Food is an essential part of local cultures and ecosystems. Medicalising it and removing control of their food from local communities rarely leads to sustainable solutions for the problems of undernutrition and malnutrition. On the contrary, it can exacerbate problems, as in the case just discussed.

Traditional foods obtained from the local ecosystem can be powerful sources of nutrients and improve dietary diversity (Ghosh-Jerath, 2016, 2018). The invisibility of such foods and an absence of a holistic conceptualisation of nutrition and health grounded in the local ecological and social environments is apparent in the aforementioned policy measures. Even if well-intentioned, they appear to be knee-jerk reactions rather than located in people's lives and cultures. It is indeed shocking that a state with a significant *adivasi* population, governed by all (except one) *adivasi* chief ministers, has no systematic documentation of the various forest foods available in different seasons or their nutritive values. Along with the experience of civil society groups, drawing on indigenous knowledges of uncultivated forest foods, practices involving the preservation of indigenous seeds or the cultivation of local grains including millets could ensure healthier diets that are both accessible and sustainable.

So What of Gender Roles and Relations in the State?

In terms of human development indicators, as noted in the previous section, women and those from the STs lag behind men, especially from 'other' communities. Only a third of women have ten or more years of schooling as against 50 per cent of men. A third of women are also married before the age of eighteen years (Table 14.2). Despite these constraining factors, women's physical mobility, at 48 per cent, is better than the national average of 42 per cent, with women able to go alone to markets, health facilities and places outside their village or community. Women's physical mobility is considered an important metric of women's autonomy, empowerment and agency (Mehta and Sai, 2021). The state's figures highlight women's willingness and ability to participate in social, political and economic institutions on an equal basis. Why they are excluded then remains a puzzle.

The data presented in Table 14.2 confirm that women in Jharkhand are engaged in both productive and reproductive work, with some access to assets and decision-making control. While these data are not disaggregated by ethnicity and caste, it is likely that the figures will be more favourable for women belonging to STs. Though gender equality may not exist, there is clear evidence of a degree of mutuality and cooperation amongst men and women, albeit 'asymmetric' (Nelson, 2016). While women are not recognised officially as farmers (*chasahor*), they are nonetheless 'farmers', with skills and

Table 14.2 Indicators of women's agency (per cent)

Indicators	NFHS-3 (2005–06)		NFHS-4 (2015–16)		NFHS-5 (2019–20)	
	India	Jharkhand	India	Jharkhand	India	Jharkhand
Female population aged six years and above who ever attended school	58.3	46.3	68.8	61.1	71.8	64.5
Literate women	55.1	37.1	68.4	59	71.5	61.7
Literate men	78.1	68.5	85.7	79.7	84.4	81.3
Women with ten or more years of schooling	22.3	15.1	35.7	28.7	41.0	33.2
Men with ten or more years of schooling	N/A	N/A	47.1	40.2	50.2	46.6
Women aged twenty to twenty-four married before eighteen	47.4	63.2	26.8	37.9	23.3	32.2
Women who have money and can decide how to use it	44.6	60	41.7	40.2	51.2	51.9
Women who have a bank or savings account that they themselves use	15	6.9	53.0	45.1	78.6	79.6
Women who know of a microcredit programme	38.6	25.5	40.8	40.7	51.3	61.0
Women who have taken a loan from a microcredit programme	4	1.9	7.7	5.2	11.1	13.5
Women allowed to go to the market, health facility and outside the village alone	33.4	36.6	40.5	41	42.3	48.3
Women who own a house and/or land alone or jointly	N/A	N/A	38.4	49.7	43.3	64.2
Women who have a mobile phone that they themselves use	N/A	N/A	45.9	35.2	54	49

Source: Compiled by the author with data from NFHS–3, NFHS–4 and NFHS–5.

knowledges that are fast being eroded due to this very non-recognition (Rao, 2008).

In the now familiar top-down style, in 2018, the state launched a micro drip irrigation project with Japanese support in nine districts to improve farmers' incomes by enabling them to grow three to four vegetable crops in a year. Women farmers from this project were at the forefront of supplying vegetables to cities during the COVID-19 pandemic through an app developed by the Jharkhand State Livelihoods Promotion Society (JSLPS) (Japan International Cooperation Agency [JICA], 2020). The focus is on enhancing incomes and productivity through technical and managerial solutions, and while this is important, there is less emphasis on recognizing the skills and contributions of women as farmers, their agency and aspirations (Rao, 2017).

The denial of women's agency, treating them as labouring bodies or 'beneficiaries' at best, has led to everyday resistances to the efforts to 'empower' them from above. Such resistance is, however, met by patriarchal violence, couched in terms of 'social sanctions by the community'. Incidents of branding strong women as witches, or dain, and killing them has taken the lives of 523 women between 2001 and 2016 (Dey, 2017). Despite the existence of the Prevention of Witch (Dain) Practices Act, 2001, eighteen to twenty cases continue to be recorded each year. Punishment under the Act remains an inconsequential fine of 1,000–2,000 rupees and imprisonment of three months to one year, an indicator of state impunity to violence against women. In 2020, the state government launched Project Garima, which adopts a curative approach to provide social, economic and psychological support to enable the women accused of witchcraft to overcome the trauma and move ahead with their lives. This is a classic example of not just blaming the women for the violence they encounter, but equally denying their agency by creating a medical–therapeutic mechanism to address, or silence, their concerns. As argued by Fraser in the context of the United States welfare system, the juridical–administrative–therapeutic state apparatus tends to substitute 'monological, administrative processes of need definition for dialogical, participatory processes of need interpretation' (1989: 156).

While undoubtedly low literacy, poor healthcare services and a lack of exposure contribute to the continued and systematic violence against women, solutions that medicalise the problem, deny women's agency or, indeed, the space for dialogue are unlikely to work. Attempts to generate awareness through collaborative methods in the local language, listening to women, engaging local youth and frontline workers, and ensuring equal representation and voice are potentially powerful tools to move beyond stereotypes on a path towards gender equality.

The strategy of promoting collectives or self-help groups (SHGs) of poor women and building strong grassroots institutional platforms, supported by the Ministry of Rural Development's National Rural Livelihoods Mission (NRLM), appear to offer some 'spaces for engagement' to rural women (Cox, 1998), enabling them to break out of dependency relationships. The SHG movement can be traced back to the 1980s when several non-governmental organisations (NGOs) started experimenting with social mobilisation, organising the rural poor into groups for mutual benefit, solidarity, empowerment and poverty reduction. Drawing on the principles of saturation and inclusion, the NRLM's stated aim is to empower women by enhancing their access to financial, technical and marketing services, and building capacities and skills for gainful and sustainable livelihoods. Around 84 million rural households in India have been mobilised into 7.7 million women's SHGs as of June 2022. In Jharkhand, a separate and autonomous society, the JSLPS, has been established by the state government to work as the nodal agency for effectively implementing the NRLM vision.

Interestingly, the JSLPS is focusing on building women's capacities as entrepreneurs and collectivising them into informal production clusters engaged in agriculture and allied activities. Agriculture in Jharkhand is primarily rain-fed; hence, the women in these groups are encouraged to cultivate horticultural crops and medicinal plants instead of staples like rice for their entrepreneurial ventures. Lac, *tassar* and other forest-based products are also grown or collected from the forests by women based on the agro-climatic context of the region, then processed, packaged and sold. Around sixty indigenous products manufactured by SHGs in Jharkhand are sold under the brand 'Palash', some of which are also available on e-commerce platforms such as Amazon and Flipkart (Ranjan, 2021a). During the COVID-19 pandemic, a mobile app called Palash Mart was launched to enable women to generate income by delivering products to consumers' doorstep. Credit linkages have enabled many women to set up small businesses and shops, with greater control over the income earned alongside autonomy in decision-making over credit. At the same time, participation in these groups has added to women's time burdens, and excluded the poorest, those with young children and those belonging to STs and SCs (Kumar et al., 2021). It raises the question of what empowerment means for these groups of women, whether it can be measured only in relation to material outcomes such as income or more broadly in relation to their agency, intrinsic knowledge and capacity to adapt to rapid changes in their everyday lives.

The COVID-19 pandemic severely impacted the livelihood opportunities of the SHGs, especially the non-farm livelihoods of women entrepreneurs (Raman, 2021). The grim reality of interstate migrants walking home long distances following the sudden national lockdown, however, also brought to light inspiring stories of solidarity and support (Tankha, 2021). In Jharkhand, women in SHGs responded to the uncertainty and chaos by running community kitchens, distributing ration kits, stitching and distributing masks and protective equipment, manufacturing sanitisers, and supporting rural households in setting up kitchen gardens to ease the broken supply chains. More than twelve lakh people – the poor, destitute and migrant workers – were fed every day through 6,900 Mukhya Mantri Didi Kitchens and Daal Bhaat Centres during the lockdown, taking special care of hygiene parameters (Ranjan, 2021b). The masks and sanitisers produced by the women were sold to medical stores for greater outreach (*Times of India*, 2020).

Several anecdotes exist around the role of SHGs in bringing about social change in their communities, especially when it comes to addressing gender-based discrimination. While the state provides support to SHGs under Project Garima to conduct awareness drives against the social practice of witchcraft, for instance, women use this opportunity to challenge violence against women more broadly. In Kolebira block, Simdega district, women went to the police station to ensure the safety of a woman who was being threatened and beaten by some people in her village in the name of witchcraft (Ranjan, 2021c). In Deoghar, SHGs have formed a separate forum called the Ekta Mahila Vikas Manch for raising their voice against violence on women. This forum provides information and moral support to women in distress and also builds linkages with the District Legal Service Authority to seek legal support in cases of violence against women (Devi, 2019). The SHGs here have a supportive institutional ecosystem in the JSLPS and civil society organisations (CSOs) who are willing to back them in their struggle for identity and justice, beyond the access to credit and other material resources. This will be a 'long march' as the formal and informal law enforcement systems are not yet ready to respond to women's claims for equality (Kumbhakar, Kindo and Narain, 2021).

And What of Land and Assets?

Jharkhand as a new state was carved out of the southern part of the state of Bihar on 15 November 2000, the result of a long struggle for justice (Upadhyay, 2009). Yet today the *adivasi*s are confronted by a globalised world, seeking to boost economic growth and enhance rural peoples' livelihoods through rapidly expanding capital-intensive industry, as evident from the various Vision documents. This strategy has only contributed to intensifying conflicts around land ownership, acquisition, alienation and conservation.

Amongst the *adivasi* communities, land is valuable for its ability to produce food, provide access to credit and other extension entitlements, but equally secure their identity (Rao, 2008). Alienation from their land therefore means the loss of cultural identity and political–economic status – the very basis of their survival – and has therefore always evoked protests and resistance (Sharan, 2009). During the colonial period, the response of the state was to recognise *adivasi* rights through the land survey and settlement operations (Singh, 2019), leading ultimately to the passage of legislation – the Chotanagpur Tenancy Act (CNTA) in 1908 in response to the Birsaite movement and the Santal Parganas Tenancy Act (SPTA) in 1876 following the Santal Hul. Both these Acts seek to regulate and largely prohibit the transfer or sale of *adivasi* land to non-*adivasi*s and have succeeded in keeping the percentage of landless people relatively low (see Chapter 13). In addition, other laws that safeguard *adivasi*s from alienation from their lands and forests are the Scheduled Area Regulation (SAR) Act, 1969; the Coal Bearing Areas Act, 1967; the Scheduled Castes and the Scheduled Tribes (Prevention of Atrocities) Act, 1989; and the Jharkhand Right to Fair Compensation and Transparency in Land Acquisition, Rehabilitation and Resettlement Rules, 2015.

Despite this plethora of protective legislation, *adivasi*s have continued to be displaced due to legal loopholes, allowing the state to acquire this land for 'public purpose' (Corbridge, 1991), including both mineral extraction and industrial development. While courts were set up under the Scheduled Area Regulation (SAR) Act to hear disputes and restore illegally alienated *adivasi* lands, accounts of their misuse led to the Chief Minister announcing their closure in 2015. However, following widespread protests, the courts did not close down; instead, two more SAR officers were appointed to strength the institution (*Business Standard*, 2016).

While the state has been forced to respond to the assertion of *adivasi* identity, it is nevertheless clear that this is at odds with its pro-industrialisation development policy, often benefiting the rich at the cost of both the poor and the environment. An important tool to attract investment from industries, encouraged by the central government, is the creation of 'land banks' – large tracts of land kept under the control of governments to be given mainly to private organisations for future development. The government has claimed three categories of land under this scheme: common lands such as playgrounds, village paths and land meant for grazing of animals; sacred groves (Sarna, Deshavali and Jaherthan); and forest land whose entitlements were supposed to be given to the *adivasi*s and other traditional forest dwellers. Nomenclature on village survey maps was changed to reflect these community lands (*gair majarua*), over which villages and communities had customary rights, and which remain central to their livelihoods (for farming, grazing, collecting forest produce), as government land (Anwar, 2019). In the Santal Parganas region, the community forests, flush with fruits, greens and mushrooms during the monsoon months from June to September ensure a degree of food security during this 'hunger period'. The inclusion of such lands into land banks makes local livelihoods precarious, apart from ignoring the collective rights and identities of the *adivasi*s over their ecosystem.

The creation of land banks in Jharkhand preceded the Global Investors Summit organised by the Bharatiya Janata Party (BJP)-led state government in 2017. The government earmarked 21 lakh hectares of land for its land banks; however, neither were people consulted nor physical surveys conducted (Sushmita, 2022). The then government attempted to amend the CNTA and the SPTA to make it easier to acquire land for these land banks and thereafter hand them over to industries. The amendment Bills were passed in the state assembly through a voice vote in November 2016. As in previous instances, once again there was mobilisation against this amendment by the *adivasi*s, with support from civil society, land rights advocates as well as political parties (PTI, 2017). Draupadi Murmu, now president of India, then governor of Jharkhand, in response to 192 petitions against the amendments, returned the Bills, questioning their merit for the *adivasi* community. However, the Raghubar Das-led BJP government sought in 2017 to bypass this setback by amending the Right to Fair Compensation and Transparency in Land

Acquisition, Rehabilitation and Resettlement (Jharkhand Amendment) Act, 2017, diluting the importance of 'social impact assessment' and the 'consent' of the *gram sabha* (the village general body under the *panchayati raj*) prior to acquisition (Kiro, 2018). These attempts at reshaping *adivasi* rights gave rise to huge protests, popularly known as the *pathalgadi* movement, wherein *adivasi*s declared the *gram sabha* the only sovereign authority and banned 'outsiders' from entering their villages.

The *pathalgadi* movement once again brought to the fore the long-standing challenges and struggles of *adivasi*s, particularly around land alienation, through a democratic assertion of their rights (Xaxa, 2019). Messages displayed on plaques included excerpts from the Panchayats Extension to Scheduled Areas (PESA) Act, 1996, which empowers the *gram sabha*s with decision-making control over the use of natural resources in the village, including minerals, waterbodies and minor forest produce (Singh, 2019). It became clear that *adivasi*s would continue to oppose land acquisition, given the rootedness of *adivasi* culture and identity with land, alongside their dependence on land-based resources for sustaining their lives and livelihoods (Lahiri-Dutt, Balakrishnan and Nesar, 2012). The union government launched the Swamitva Scheme in April 2021 to ensure streamlined planning and revenue collection and provide clarity over property rights by creating digital records of immovable properties of rural residents. Under the scheme, villagers with personal property cards would become eligible to avail the benefits of legal aid, relief from encroachment, bank loans, and so on. Pilot villages in Khunti district opposed the scheme. They were filled with suspicion and mistrust when consent of the *gram sabha*s was not taken before starting the mapping work, as the villages are all governed by the PESA Act (*Prabhat Khabar*, 2022). The current government in the state has since put the scheme on hold.

The Indian state has created contradictory narratives of *adivasi* identity and their relationship to their environment, simultaneously portraying them as protectors and the original inhabitants of the forest and labelling them as encroachers and major contributors to deforestation (Davidsdottir, 2021). The life cycle of the *adivasi*s is based on natural resources; their coexistence is therefore central to social reproduction. Acquisition of their lands for ambiguous 'public purposes' without the consent or stake of these communities not only causes physical alienation and displacement but also destroys their identity, history, culture and livelihoods (Sharan, 2005). Uncertain rehabilitation and compensation arrangements, as discussed in

Chapters 8 and 13, accelerate the process of deprivation of the *adivasis*, while also denying associated rights such as that of women over landed property.

Youth Aspirations and the Need for Constructive Engagement

Youth are central to creating pathways to sustainable development across the world. While surveys report youth aspiring to move out of agriculture and agrifood sectors, one needs to ask why this is the case. Agriculture and allied sectors are often presented as 'traditional' and 'backward', where economic returns are low, and by and large focus on manual work rather than skills and knowledge. Most youth, in the absence of alternative employment, however, end up as food system workers. If the status and perception of the sector can be improved, making it both more rewarding economically and stimulating intellectually, youth can be agents of change for transforming food systems, making them sustainable, resilient, equitable and healthy (High Level Panel of Experts on Food Security and Nutrition, 2021). The COVID-19 pandemic highlighted the crisis in the current global and local food systems and the need for an urgent and systemic transformation (Glover and Sumberg, 2020).

While there is no dearth of 'schemes' for youth empowerment and entrepreneurship, they miss the critical element of 'agency' and 'aspirations' that play out across space and time. The very first government of Jharkhand announced support for youth collectives to run local transport services. Young people had to surrender their school certificates for participating in such groups, which often never took off or proved unviable. They were constrained in their entrepreneurial ventures by their *adivasi* identity (see Chapters 7 and 11) – the dominant social construction of Santals as 'labour' rather than 'entrepreneurs'. More recently, in 2019, the government of Jharkhand launched the Tejaswini: Socio-Economic Empowerment of Adolescent Girls and Young Women project, with World Bank support, to provide market-driven skills training and secondary education to adolescent girls and young women in the age group of fourteen to twenty-four years. Young women are organised into community-based platforms ('clubs' and 'cluster centres') to come together for regular activities, counselling and guidance, life-skills education, livelihood support services, and information on and access to broader services and training opportunities. While it is too soon to pass judgement on this time-bound scheme, the fundamental principle of understanding and responding to the needs of these young women appears to be missing. My research assistant and companion from many years ago, an educated young woman, with many skills, aspired to be a teacher, but she was never 'selected'. Many Santal youth, especially women, aspire to secure state jobs rather than work in risky enterprises. They are fully aware of the social and economic constraints they face, most of all their intersecting identities as *adivasi* women.

Before closing, I would like to narrate a recent personal experience, one that raises hope in the agency and capacities of the youth. Supported by the Global Research Translation Award (GRTA) 'Meeting the SDGs' at the University of East Anglia, where I am based, we set up CHIRAG (Creative Hub for Innovation, Reciprocal Research and Action for Gender Equality), an action research project with Santal youth, towards the end of 2019. Aimed primarily at addressing issues of food and nutrition security in their communities, we worked with Lahanti Club, a group of local Santal youth in the Chakai block of Jamui district, Bihar, adjacent to the Santal Parganas region of Jharkhand, facilitated by the NGO PRADAN (Professional Assistance for Development Action). When we first met, this youth group was trying to support the learning outcomes of Santal children through after-school classes and activities, conducted in their local language, Santali. Using participatory workshops, discussions and training, including the use of cameras to document their local culture, biodiversity and food practices (Rao, Narain and Sabir, 2022), moderation of and content development for a mobile-based interactive voice response system, community theatre and food fairs, we jointly developed bespoke content for interactive and digital media platforms, but also methodologies for the equitable sharing and exchange of knowledge. The youth started documenting local practices with a digital camera, talking to village elders, reflecting on their own practices, questioning their beliefs and arriving at a narrative that they wanted to share through their short films. Lahanti Club has created more than fifty short films on seasonally and locally available food and traditional recipes and archived them on their YouTube channel (Figure 14.1).

These interactions helped the rural community, particularly the youth, engage with myths, taboos, assumptions and opportunities within their local knowledge systems and practices, food cultures, biodiversity, seasonality and livelihoods. Participatory theatre, for instance, or the screening of the films they had produced encouraged debate and dialogue around people's historical practices and how and why they have shifted, the strengths and limitations of traditional practices, and how these need to be modified and reshaped in

Figure 14.1   Women members of Lahanti Club and a local self-help group using a digital camera

Source: Photograph by Arundhita Bhanjdeo.

the present context. This dialogical process provided them space to generate local, indigenous and intergenerational knowledge that was recognised as legitimate, but equally to present their knowledge and practices creatively through 'modern' digital and other public platforms. The selection of one of their films for the International Science Film Festival, 2021, and another for the Table-to-Farm video challenge organised by the Youth Alliance for Zero Hunger in the United Nations (UN) Food Systems Summit, 2021, provided much-needed recognition, motivating them to pursue their creative endeavours for achieving their own development vision. While better understanding their local and traditional knowledge systems which were gradually becoming invisible and unacknowledged in the market-driven economy, they are now able to identify local concerns, conduct surveys and collect feedback from their community on a range of issues. Willing to speak out, they now stand as the voice of their community, aspiring to be heard and taken seriously.

Looking Ahead

Much has been achieved since the formation of Jharkhand, and yet several puzzles remain. Despite rich biodiversity, the willingness to work hard and the relative mobility of women, why does Jharkhand lag behind the rest of India in terms of basic food and livelihood security, especially of its *adivasi* population, in whose name the state was created? The chapters in this book, based on research over the past two and a half decades, provide some insights but also lessons for future research and action.

Perhaps the most important insight is the recognition of the everyday agency of women and men in these communities; their constant struggle to survive, in a political–economic context that perpetuates myths about their intellectual backwardness while seeing them as valuable sources of 'labour'. STs and SCs in India constitute a much higher proportion of the labouring poor in the country, whether in their own localities or as 'footloose' migrant workers, relative to their population numbers. There is clearly a systemic discrimination in place, despite the constitutional provisions of equality for all, irrespective of gender, race, class and ethnicity. The *adivasi*s in general, and women in particular, are constantly striving to move from a situation of dependence through expanding their spaces of negotiation, albeit incremental, both individually and collectively.

Second, within modern educational systems, we are often bound by linear definitions of 'development' or even 'knowledge'. Empowerment is understood as a set of characteristics, which can be measured, rather than more relational and subjective processes or models of personhood. Land, as I have argued, is more than a material asset; it has symbolic meanings in terms of identity and status. As a result, people's interests go beyond enhancing productivity of the land in terms of yields and crop mixes. Land also has meanings beyond privately owned plots, particularly for women, who are equally dependent on the biomass from common property resources, whether forests, pastures, ponds or rivers, for meeting their livelihood needs. They understand the synergy between different elements of the ecosystem – nature and people – and the need to nurture each other. This may appear akin to an ecofeminist position, but rather than romanticizing women as the protectors of nature, I argue for the need to legitimise their knowledges and practices and engage with the challenges these pose to top-down directives. They present an alternate worldview, a recognition of identity, and suggest pathways for sustainability and resilience.

So where do we go from here? For researchers, we need to critically examine the methodologies we use and the conclusions these lead to. Going beyond the debate on quantitative-versus-qualitative methods, and the measurement of outcomes, we need to reflect on the processes on the ground, learning from Freirean methods of action and reflection (Freire, 1970). This will enable engagement with emic perspectives, critical for finding workable solutions to the multiple crises of social reproduction we confront today – of leading lives that are no longer sustainable – in both practical and metaphorical terms. The dominance of externally designed and driven policies, which often fail due to divergent visions, problems of conceptualisation rather than implementation, are nonetheless used to blame the 'victims', reinforcing stereotypes of 'lazy' and 'backward' *adivasi*s.

In policy and action, there is need to challenge dominant perspectives that refuse to recognize the identity struggles of those labelled as poor and marginalised. This includes women and, more so, *adivasi* women. While presenting some positive examples from the Jharkhand State Livelihoods Mission, it needs to be mentioned that the guidelines and norms are usually generic, applicable across the country, not contextualised to local cultures, knowledges or resources. Women are discouraged from taking on leadership roles beyond their SHGs, joining the economic or the political mainstream. Rather, they are directed towards 'caring' tasks, of cooking and feeding, of engaging with petty commodity production or petty trade. While seeking to 'empower' women, these approaches often do not meet their 'needs' in terms of securing their identities. The power women seek reflects dignity and reciprocity, not dominance and control. Yet they do break out, even in this instance, forming solidarity networks to combat both the interpersonal and structural violence they confront in their daily lives.

Young women and men provide a ray of hope. Rather than imposing restrictions and boundaries on their creativity, we need to recognize them as agents of change, giving them voice and opportunity to express and live their vision. Too many youths have been lost – some to migrant destinies which destroy their lives; others to frustration expressed in Maoist struggles, arrested and confined to prison cells. They can no longer be taken for granted as 'fronts' for capitalist investments, wherein they only stand to lose. Rather than providing them predetermined 'projects' to manage, they need control and authorship over their lives. The youth are rediscovering the power of collective action, with equality rather than chauvinism as its base. And in this lies the future.

References

Accredited Social Health Activist (ASHA) and Right to Food Campaign. 2022. *Report of the Fact Finding Visit to Jharkhand, on Rice Fortification in Government Food Schemes.* 8–11 May. https://www.greenpeace.org/static/planet4-india-stateless/2022/05/8fbfa50f-final-fact-finding-report-jharkhand-rice-fortification.pdf. Accessed on 15 September 2022.

Anwar, T. 2019. 'Jharkhand's Land Bank: Injustice to Adivasis Continues'. NewsClick, 18 June. https://www.newsclick.in/Jharkhand-Land-Bank-Adivasis-Tribes-Revenue-Land-Reforms. Accessed on 27 October 2022.

Baraik, V. K. 2019. 'Dimensions of Tribal Education and Employment in Jharkhand: Linkage of Educational Level and Industrial Category'. *Jharkhand Journal of Development and Management Studies* 17(3): 8159–74.

Business Standard. 2016. 'Special Courts for Tribal Land Rights to Continue in Jharkhand'. 28 January. https://www.business-standard.com/article/news-ians/special-courts-for-tribal-land-rights-to-continue-in-jharkhand-116012801238_1.html. Accessed on 26 October 2022.

Confederation of Indian Industry. 2011. *CII Vision Document: Jharkhand@2022: A Sustainable Development Vision.* https://indiaat75.in/wp-content/themes/Indiaat75/myassets/pdf/national_and_state_vision_document/Jharkhand.pdf. Accessed on 15 September 2022.

Corbridge, S. E. 1991. 'Ousting Singbonga: The Struggle for India's Jharkhand'. In *Colonialism and Development in the Contemporary World*, edited by C. Dixon and M. J. Heffernan, 153–82. London: Mansell Publishing.

Cox, K. R. 1998. 'Spaces of Dependence, Spaces of Engagement and the Politics of Scale, or: Looking for Local Politics'. *Political Geography* 17(1): 1–23.

Davidsdottir, E. 2021. 'Our Rights Are Carved in Stone: The Case of the Pathalgadi Movement in Simdega, Jharkhand'. *International Journal of Human Rights* 25(7): 1111–25. DOI: 10.1080/13642987.2021.1878351.

Devi, B. 2019. 'Women of Jharkhand: Fighting Violence against Women'. https://www.pradan.net/sampark/women-of-jharkhand-fighting-violence-against-women. Accessed on 26 October 2022.

Directorate of Employment and Training, n.d. 'Govt. ITIs'. https://iti.jharkhand.gov.in/Director_Portal/Institutes/ITIColleges.aspx. Accessed on 7 November 2022.

Drèze, J., N. Khalid, R. Khera and A. Somanchi. 2017. 'Aadhar and Food Security in Jharkhand: Pain without Gain?' *Economic and Political Weekly* 52(50): 50–59.

Fraser, N. 1989. *Unruly Practices*. Cambridge, UK: Polity Press.

Freire, P. 1970. *Pedagogy of the Oppressed*. Middlesex: Penguin Classics.

George, N. A., and F. H. McKay. 2019. 'The Public Distribution System and Food Security in India'. *International Journal of Environmental Research and Public Health* 16(17): 3221. DOI: 10.3390/ijerph16173221.

Ghosh-Jerath, S., A. Singh, M. S. Magsumbol, T. Lyngdoh, P. Kamboj and G. Goldberg. 2016. 'Contribution of Indigenous Foods towards Nutrient Intakes and Nutritional Status of women in the Santhal Tribal Community of Jharkhand, India'. *Public Health Nutrition* 19: 2256–67. DOI: 10.1017/S1368980016000318.

———. 2018. 'Estimates of Indigenous Food Consumption and Their Contribution to Nutrient Intake in Oraon Tribal Women of Jharkhand, India'. *Food and Nutrition Bulletin* 39(4): 581–94. DOI: 10.1177/0379572118805652.

Glover, D., and J. Sumberg. 2020. 'Youth and Food Systems Transformation'. *Frontiers in Sustainable Food Systems* 4. DOI: 10.3389/fsufs.2020.00101.

Government of India. 2018. *Tribal Health in India: Bridging the Gap and a Roadmap for the Future*. Report of the Expert Committee on Tribal Health. New Delhi: Ministry of Health and Family Welfare and Ministry of Tribal Affairs. https://nhm.gov.in/nhm_components/tribal_report/Executive_Summary.pdf. Accessed on 15 September 2022.

Government of Jharkhand and PHD Chamber of Commerce and Industry. 2019. 'Rising Jharkhand: Skill Development to Spur Socio-Economic Growth'. https://www.phdcci.in/wp-content/uploads/2019/01/Rising-Jharkhand-Skill-Development-to-Spur-Socio-Economic-GrowthUpdated.pdf. Accessed on 15 September 2022.

High Level Panel of Experts on Food Security and Nutrition. 2021. *Promoting Youth Engagement and Employment in Agriculture and Food Systems*. Rome: High Level Panel of Experts on Food Security and Nutrition.

International Fund for Agricultural Development (IFAD). 2022. 'Jharkhand Tribal Empowerment and Livelihoods Project'. https://www.ifad.org/documents/38711624/40330956/India+1100001649+JTELP+Project+Completion+Report_1.pdf/908f63ab-dc18-a51e-abdc-22ccc959249f?t=1657295425340. Accessed on 24 October 2022.

International Institute for Population Sciences (IIPS) and ICF International. 2017. *National Family Health Survey (NFHS-4), 2015–16: India*. Mumbai: International Institute for Population Sciences.

———. 2021. *National Family Health Survey (NFHS-5), 2019–20: India*. Mumbai: International Institute for Population Sciences.

International Institute for Population Sciences (IIPS) and Macro International. 2007. *National Family Health Survey (NFHS-3), 2005–06: India*. Mumbai: International Institute for Population Sciences.

Japan International Cooperation Agency (JICA). 2020. 'Connecting Farmers with Consumers' Delivery of Fresh Vegetables to Consumers in Ranchi amidst COVID-19 Pandemic'. https://www.jica.go.jp/india/english/office/topics/press200430.html. Accessed on 24 October 2022.

Jewitt, S. 2008. 'Political Ecology of Jharkhand Conflicts'. *Asia Pacific Viewpoint* 49(1): 68–82.

Kiro, A. K. 2018. 'Opposition Unites to Fight BJP on Land Act Amendment in Jharkhand'. 22 June. https://thewire.in/rights/opposition-unites-to-fight-bjp-on-land-act-amendment-in-jharkhand. Accessed on 26 October 2022.

Kumar, N., K. Raghunathan, A. Arrieta, A. Jilani and S. Pandey. 2021. 'The Power of the Collective Empowers Women: Evidence from Self-Help Groups in India'. *World Development* 146. DOI: 10.1016/j.worlddev.2021.105579.

Kumar, R., and V. Shekhar. 2021. 'Rice Fortification Is an Effective Way to Combat Anemia'. 28 October. https://www.thehindubusinessline.com/opinion/how-to-combat-anemia-effectively/article37196547.ece. Accessed on 16 September 2022.

Kumbhakar, K., M. Kindo and N. Narain. 2021. '"Mujhe Nyay Chahiye, Paise Nahin": A Collective's Fight for Justice'. https://www.pradan.net/sampark/mujhe-nyay-chahiye-paise-nahin-a-collectives-fight-for-justice. Accessed on 24 October 2022.

Lahiri-Dutt, K., R. Balakrishnan and A. Nesar. 2012. 'Land Acquisition and Dispossession: Private Coal Companies in Jharkhand'. *Economic and Political Weekly* 47(6): 39–44.

Mehta, V., and H. Sai. 2021. 'Freedom of Movement: Studying Women's Mobility in North India'. *Urbanisation* 6(1_suppl): S77–S114. DOI: 10.1177/24557471211022566.

Nabard Consultancy Services. n.d. 'Jharkhand State Agriculture Development Plan: 2008–09 to 2011–12'. https://rkvy.nic.in/static/SAP/JH.pdf. Accessed on 24 October 2022.

National Skill Development Corporation (NSDC). n.d. 'District-Wise Skill Gap Study for the State of Jharkhand 2012–2017 and 2017–2022'. https://www.nsdcindia.org/sites/default/files/files/jharkhand-sg-report.pdf. Accessed on 16 September 2022.

Nelson, J. A. 2016. 'Husbandry: A (Feminist) Reclamation of Masculine Responsibility for Care'. *Cambridge Journal of Economics* 40: 1–15.

Prabhat Khabar. 2022. 'Kednra Sarkar ki Swamitva Yojana Jharkhand mein Nahin Hoga Lagu, Bhumi ke Digital Survey aur Drone Mapping par Rok'. 12 March. https://www.prabhatkhabar.com/state/jharkhand/ranchi/swamitva-yojana-jharkhand-central-govt-ownership-scheme-to-be-not-implemented-digital-survey-of-land-and-drone-mapping-will-be-banned-srn. Accessed on 26 October 2022.

Press Trust of India (PTI). 2017. 'Nitish Kumar Pulls Up Jharkhand Government for Tenancy Act Amendment'. *Economic Times*, 11 June. https://economictimes.indiatimes.com/news/politics-and-nation/nitish-kumar-pulls-up-jharkhand-government-for-tenancy-act-amendment/articleshow/59099020.cms. Accessed on 26 October 2022.

———. 2021a. 'Over One Lakh Youths in Jharkhand Employed in Private Companies'. *Business Line*, 6 December. https://www.thehindubusinessline.com/news/national/over-one-lakh-youths-in-jharkhand-employed-in-private-companies/article25961152.ece. Accessed on 16 September 2022.

———. 2021b. 'Six-Fold Rise in Registered Unemployed People in J'khand in Last 2 Years: Govt'. *Hindustan Times*, 22 December. https://www.hindustantimes.com/cities/ranchi-news/sixfold-rise-in-registered-unemployed-people-in-j-khand-in-last-2-years-govt-101640196102416.html. Accessed on 16 September 2022.

Raman, S. 2021. 'Women's Groups That Helped Rural India through the Pandemic Are Themselves Struggling to Survive'. *Scroll.in*, 1 August 2021. https://scroll.in/article/1001522/womens-groups-who-helped-rural-india-through-the-pandemic-are-themselves-struggling-to-survive. Accessed on 24 October 2022.

Ranjan, M. 2021a. 'Products Made by Jharkhand Women Go Global under 'Palash' Brand'. *New Indian Express*, 23 November. https://www.newindianexpress.com/nation/2021/nov/23/products-made-by-jharkhand-women-go-globalunder-palash-brand-2386969.html. Accessed on 24 October 2022.

———. 2021b. '4K Kitchens to Provide Free Food in Jharkhand'. *New Indian Express*, 30 May. https://www.newindianexpress.com/thesundaystandard/2021/may/30/4k-kitchens-to-provide-free-food-in-jharkhand-2309277.html. Accessed on 24 October 2022.

———. 2021c. 'Jharkhand Self-Help Groups Help 'Witchcraft' Victims to Lead a Dignified Life'. *New Indian Express*, 14 February. https://www.newindianexpress.com/good-news/2021/feb/14/jharkhand-self-help-groups-help-witchcraft-victims-to-lead-a-dignified-life-2263673.html. Accessed on 24 October 2022.

Rao, N. 2008. *'Good Women Do Not Inherit Land': Politics of Land and Gender in India*. New Delhi: Social Science Press.

―――. 2017. 'Assets, Agency and Legitimacy: Towards a Relational Understanding of Gender Equality Policy and Practice'. *World Development* 95: 43–54.

Rao, N., N. Narain and G. Sabir. 2022. 'Cameras in the Hands of Indigenous Youth: Participation, Films, and Nutrition in India'. *Current Developments in Nutrition* 6(8). DOI: 10.1093/cdn/nzac114.

Ray, D. 2019. 'Jharkhand Rolls Out Action Plan to Tackle Anaemia'. 26 February. https://timesofindia.indiatimes.com/city/ranchi/state-rolls-out-action-plan-to-tackle-anaemia/articleshow/68159368.cms. Accessed on 26 October 2022.

Sharan, R. 2005. 'Alienation and Restoration of Tribal Land in Jharkhand: Current Issues and Possible Strategies'. *Economic and Political Weekly* 40(41): 4443–46.

―――. 2009. 'Alienation and Restoration of Tribal Land in Jharkhand'. In *Legal Grounds: Natural Resources, Identity and the Law in Jharkhand*, edited by N. Sundar, 82–112. New Delhi: Oxford University Press.

Singh, A. 2019. 'Many Faces of the Pathalgadi Movement in Jharkhand'. *Economic and Political Weekly* 54(11): 28–33.

Sushmita. 2022. 'In Jharkhand, Villagers Are Being Dispossessed through Subversion of Land Laws'. *Scroll.in*, 26 July. https://scroll.in/article/1029011/in-jharkhand-villagers-are-being-dispossessed-through-subversion-of-land-laws. Accessed on 26 October 2022.

Swaniti. 2017. 'Jharkhand: The Road Ahead: An Analysis of Socio-Economic Indicators'. https://www.swaniti.com/wp-content/uploads/2022/10/Brief-Note-on-Jharkhands-Development.pdf. Accessed on 24 October 2022.

Tankha, R. 2021. 'Women's Leadership in COVID-19 Response: Self-Help Groups of the National Rural Livelihoods Mission Show the Way'. *EPW Engage*, 8 May.

The Telegraph. 2021. 'Jharkhand Sees Drop in Anaemia among Children, but Concerns Remain'. 25 November. https://www.telegraphindia.com/jharkhand/jharkhand-sees-drop-in-anaemia-among-children-but-concerns-remain/cid/1840563. Accessed on 26 October 2022.

Times of India. 2020. 'Jharkhand: SHG Women Lead Supply Line in Coronavirus Battle'. 28 March. https://timesofindia.indiatimes.com/city/ranchi/jharkhand-shg-women-lead-supply-line-in-coronavirus-battle/articleshow/74857585.cms. Accessed on 24 October 2022.

Totapally, S., P. Sonderegger, P. Rao, J. Gosselt and G. Gupta. 2019. *State of Aadhaar Report 2019*. https://stateofaadhaar.in/assets/download/SoA_2019_Report_web.pdf. Accessed on 24 October 2022.

Upadhyay, C. 2009. 'Law, Custom and Adivasi Identity: Politics of Land Rights in Chhotanagpur'. In Legal Grounds: Natural Resources, Identity, and the Law in Jharkhand, edited by N. Sundar, 30–55. New Delhi: Oxford University Press.

World Bank. 2001. *World Development Report 2000/2001: Attacking Poverty*. New York: Oxford University Press.

Xaxa, V. 2019. 'Is the Pathalgadi Movement in Tribal Areas Anti-Constitutional?'. *Economic and Political Weekly* 54(1): 10–12.

Index